CRITICAL THEORY AND EUROPEAN UNION LAW

This collection examines what 'critical theory' as a distinct intellectual tradition in social, political, and legal thought contributes to the study of EU law and to the future of the European project. Covering a broad range of substantive fields of EU law and the history of legal integration, including constitutional law, the design of monetary union and economic law, fiscal integration and taxation, labour law, fundamental rights and anti-discrimination law, gender equality, migration law and policy, data protection, and the Common Foreign and Security Policy (CFSP), the volume illustrates how a more rigorous engagement with critical theory helps to navigate the post-crisis European legal landscape. The contributors bring fresh, thoughtful, and innovative perspectives to EU law and theory, diagnosing the deep-seated challenges facing contemporary EU law and reimagining the emancipatory possibilities still available for it.

Critical Theory and European Union Law

The Question of Postnational Emancipation

Edited by
Päivi Johanna Neuvonen and
Paul Linden-Retek

•HART•
OXFORD • LONDON • NEW YORK • NEW DELHI • SYDNEY

HART PUBLISHING
Bloomsbury Publishing Plc
Kemp House, Chawley Park, Cumnor Hill, Oxford, OX2 9PH, UK
1385 Broadway, New York, NY 10018, USA
Bloomsbury Publishing Ireland Limited, 29 Earlsfort Terrace, Dublin 2, D02 AY28, Ireland

First published in Great Britain 2026

1

A catalogue record for this book is available from the British Library.

A catalogue record for this book is available from the Library of Congress.

ISBN: HB: 978-1-50998-202-8
ePDF: 978-1-50998-204-2
ePub: 978-1-50998-203-5

Typeset by Amnet

For product safety related questions contact productsafety@bloomsbury.com

To find out more about our authors and books visit www.hartpublishing.co.uk. Here you will find extracts, author information, details of forthcoming events and the option to sign up for our newsletters.

CONTENTS

LIST OF CONTRIBUTORS

Sarah Glaser is a Max Weber Fellow at the European University Institute (EUI), Italy. Her doctoral thesis develops a theory of justice in the field of bio-innovation. Prior to her legal studies at Sciences Po Paris, Sarah was enrolled as a civil servant at École Normale Supérieure de Lyon, where she studied German Literature and History.

Marco Goldoni is Professor of Philosophy of Law at the University of Glasgow, UK. He is co-editor of the journal *Jurisprudence* and of the new book series *Law and Political Economy* (Cambridge University Press).

Barbara Havelková is an Associate Professor of Law at the Faculty of Law and a Tutorial Fellow in Law at St Hilda's College, University of Oxford, UK.

Jussi Jaakkola is a Postdoctoral Researcher at the Turku Institute for Advanced Studies (TIAS) and at the Faculty of Law, University of Turku, Finland. Besides other positions, he has worked as a senior research fellow in public law at the University of Tampere. Jaakkola's research has been published eg in *European Law Open*, *New Political Economy*, *European Constitutional Law Review* and *German Law Journal*. His research addresses EU law, public law and political economy of taxation.

Paul Linden-Retek is Associate Professor of Law and Co-director of the Buffalo Human Rights Center at the University at Buffalo School of Law, USA. He writes and teaches in the areas of constitutional law, international human rights, and critical legal theory, with an emphasis on comparative constitutional law, constitutional theory, European Union law, and refugee and asylum law. He is the author of *Postnational Constitutionalism: Europe and the Time of Law* (Oxford University Press, 2023).

Susanna Lindroos-Hovinheimo is Professor of Public Law at the University of Helsinki, Finland. Her fields of expertise lie in EU law, constitutional law and legal theory. Her book *Private Selves - Legal Personhood in European Privacy Protection* (Cambridge University Press, 2021) analyses the ways in which personhood is constructed in privacy law.

Luigi Lonardo is Associate Professor of European Law at the Luxembourg Centre for European law, University of Luxembourg and adjunct faculty at Sciences Po Paris. His areas of expertise and research are the law and politics of EU foreign policy, as well as EU constitutional law more broadly. He is the author of two monographs, *EU Common Foreign and Security Policy after Lisbon: Between Law and Geopolitics* (Springer, 2022) and *Russia's 2022 War against Ukraine and the Foreign Policy Reaction of the EU: Context, Diplomacy, Law* (Palgrave, 2023).

Alezini Loxa is an Emile Noël Fellow at New York University School of Law (NYU) and a Post-Doctoral Research Fellow in EU law at Lund University, Sweden. She has published widely in the field of EU migration law and social rights. She is the author of the monograph *Sustainability and EU Migration Law: Tracing the History of a Contemporary Concept* (Cambridge University Press, 2025) and the editor of *The Reasoning of the Court of Justice of the EU: A Normative Assessment* (Oxford University Press, 2026) together with Luigi Lonardo.

Meemi Matero is a Research Associate at University College Dublin's Sutherland School of Law, Ireland. She holds a PhD in Law from the University of Strathclyde, UK. Her thesis, entitled 'Rethinking Parenting Leave, Sexual Division of Labour, and Substantive Equality: A Transformative EU Parenting Leave Model', offered a feminist critique and reconstruction of the EU's parenting leave framework with a view to facilitating substantive equality between parents.

Päivi Johanna Neuvonen is Associate Professor in European Law and Co-Director of the Durham Center for Law and Philosophy at Durham University in the UK. She is also affiliated with the University of Helsinki, Finland as Docent in European Law. Her main research interests lie at the intersection of European law and legal theory broadly understood.

Luca Tenreira is a PhD researcher in Law at the EUI, Italy. His dissertation, 'The Law of Global Value Chains Investigated: Frictions after the Turn to Due Diligence', critically examines and deconstructs how multinational corporations mobilise knowledge forms – such as impact assessments and sustainability metrics – to shape the meaning of accountability in global production networks. Through legal and ethnographic inquiry, he engages with a broad range of transdisciplinary experts, activists and local communities to advance more situated forms of EU and transnational governance in the field.

Kaius Tuori is Professor of European Intellectual History at the University of Helsinki, Finland. He is a legal historian who has worked on legal heritage and the uses of the past. His latest book *Empire of Law* (Cambridge University Press, 2020) explores the role of refugee scholars in the formation of European narratives of law.

Jacob van de Beeten is an Emile Noël Fellow at the NYU Jean Monnet Center, US. He has published in the fields of EU constitutional law, legal philosophy and administrative law. He is currently working on a book that identifies and critiques the systemic logic in the case law of the Court of Justice. This book is based on his PhD thesis which received the 2024 European Law Faculties Association (ELFA) award.

Michael A Wilkinson is Professor of Law at London School of Economics (LSE) in the UK. He researches in the areas of constitutional theory, European integration, and political, legal, and social theory. He has held visiting professorships at Cornell, Paris II, the National University of Singapore, and Keio University, Tokyo, and his work has been translated into Portuguese, Italian, Spanish, and Turkish. He is the author of *Authoritarian Liberalism and the Transformation of Modern Europe* (Oxford University Press, 2021).

Raphaële Xenidis is Assistant Professor of European Law at Sciences Po Law School in France. Her research focuses on European discrimination and equality law. Her current work explores issues of data-driven inequalities, intersectional discrimination, and critical approaches to European equality law. Raphaële is a Senior Expert of the European Network of Legal Experts in Gender Equality and Non-Discrimination Law and a Global Research Fellow at iCourts at the University of Copenhagen.

Rebecca Zahn is Professor of Law at the University of Strathclyde, Glasgow, UK. Her research examines labour law from European, comparative and interdisciplinary perspectives. She held a Leverhulme Research Fellowship from 2022–2024 for a project entitled 'Revealing the Importance of Ideas: The Intellectual History of Labour Law'.

PREFACE
Critical Theory and European Union Law

PÄIVI JOHANNA NEUVONEN AND PAUL LINDEN-RETEK

The central rationale of this edited volume is to show how a more deliberate engagement with critical theory as a distinct intellectual tradition in social, political, and legal theory can transform the study of European Union (EU) law. The book will both (1) present critical theory as a relevant analytical framework for understanding EU law and (2) elaborate the potential of critical theory to address the challenges of post-crisis EU law in a political environment in which the traditional forms of legal integration are increasingly under strain. This inquiry is particularly timely because it connects the distributive and macroeconomic challenges facing the EU legal order to the EU's deeper value crisis. In parallel with these intra-EU objectives, the book offers an in-depth case study of the application of critical theory to transnational law. Contemporary critical theorists have demonstrated significant interest in the project of European integration. But they rarely engage in detailed legal analyses, which are essential for understanding how critical theory can advance the critical project in EU law.

I. Why Does EU Law Need (More) Critical Theory?

There is currently no lack of critical engagement in EU legal studies, but the critique of EU law still remains under-theorised in important ways. This situation arguably reflects a more common pattern to disparage theoretical questions in EU law scholarship. Yet, the tendency to under-value theory is particularly problematic in critical studies of EU law because the concept of critique itself becomes easily inflated. Therefore, this book seeks to explore what a more developed critical theory of EU law would look like. The need to retheorise the critical project in EU law is closely linked to the EU's recent and ongoing crises. Post-crisis EU law scholarship seeks guidance from political theory, history, sociology and, to a lesser extent, from social theory. But the rich tradition of critical social theory is still strikingly under-explored in EU law, setting the field apart, for instance, from the study of international law.[1] For the purposes of this book, critical theory should thus not be confused with the Critical Legal Studies (CLS) movement.[2]

[1] For this point, see also PJ Neuvonen, 'A Way of Critique: What Can EU Law Scholars Learn from Critical Theory?' (2022) 1 *European Law Open* 60, 63.

[2] For a CLS-based study of EU law, see, eg, T Perišin and S Rodin (eds), *The Transformation or Reconstitution of Europe The Critical Legal Studies Perspective on the Role of the Courts in the European Union* (Hart/Bloomsbury, 2018).

As the first book-length study of critical theory in EU law, this volume expands and strengthens the theoretical foundations of EU legal studies.

At present, EU law scholars' engagement with critical theory remains partial and fragmented. Much of recent critical research attempts to address systematically the surge of crisis and emergency laws during the sovereign debt crisis.[3] This branch of scholarship shares common ground with critical theory when it highlights the importance of political economy analyses of EU law. A related analytical lens is provided by the theory of material constitutionalism,[4] but its relation to critical theory currently remains unclear. Recent research has also more directly addressed the role of Marxist and neo-Marxist thought in EU legal studies.[5] While all of these themes are relevant to critical theory, an important difference is that critical theorists seek to integrate the critique of political economy into a broader social and cultural critique of capitalist societies.[6] Some EU law scholars already draw on critical theory in their individual research projects.[7] But a broader synthesis of how critical theory can inform research across the EU legal order is still missing, and the present book seeks to fill this gap. In doing so, the book contributes to the 'methodological turn'[8] that EU law scholarship is currently undergoing.

In this book, critical theory invites us to rethink what it means to pose the 'question of emancipation' in EU legal studies. However, the value of critical theory is misunderstood if our focus only lies in what immediate practical applications critical theory could have in EU law. This instrumentalist mindset, of course, is not unique to EU law scholars. For instance, Cordero notes that 'in a world where the worth of things primarily depends on utility and potential use, critique is repeatedly urged to offer positive answers and constructive alternatives'.[9] The idea of critical praxis is important to critical theory.[10] But critical theorists usually reject the view that theory can or should be 'translated directly into practice'.[11] This does not mean that critical theory claims no societal relevance. On the contrary, it can be argued that critical theorists 'view theoretical

[3] eg E Nanopoulos and F Vergis (eds), *The Crisis Behind the Eurocrisis: The Eurocrisis as a Multi-dimensional Systemic Crisis of the EU* (Cambridge University Press, 2019); C Joerges and C Glinski (eds), *The European Crisis and the Transformation of Transnational Governance: Authoritarian Managerialism versus Democratic Governance* (Hart/Bloomsbury, 2017) and the different contributions in the special issue 'Austerity and Law in Europe' in (2017) 44 *Journal of Law and Society* 1 (edited by M Bartl and M Karavias). For a broader crisis focus, see also, eg, PF Kjaer and N Olsen (eds), *Critical Theories of Crisis in Europe: From Weimar to the Euro* (Rowman & Littlefield, 2016).

[4] M Goldoni and MA Wilkinson, 'The Material Constitution' (2018) 81 *MLR* 567–97 and different contributions in M Goldoni and MA Wilkinson (eds), *The Cambridge Handbook on the Material Constitution* (Cambridge University Press, 2023).

[5] See, eg, the different contributions to the 'Symposium on Marxist Approaches to EU Law' (2025) 4 *European Law Open* 286 (edited by R Knox, E Nanopoulos and A Woodhouse).

[6] For more on this, see chapter 1 by Päivi Neuvonen in this book.

[7] eg P Linden-Retek, *Postnational Constitutionalism: Europe and the Time of Law* (Oxford University Press, 2023).

[8] Neuvonen (n 1) 61 (and 69 and 77).

[9] R Cordero, *Crisis and Critique: On the Fragile Foundations of Social Life* (Routledge, 2017) 40.

[10] eg E Christodoulidis, 'Critical Theory and the Law: Reflections on Origins, Trajectories and Conjunctures' in E Christodoulidis et al (eds), *Research Handbook on Critical Legal Theory* (Elgar, 2019) 9 posits that 'the responsibility that befalls theory . . . is to lend praxis expression in terms that are *adequate to it*'.

[11] S Chambers, 'The Politics of Critical Theory' in F Rush (ed), *The Cambridge Companion to Critical Theory* (Cambridge University Press, 2006) 226 and 227.

activity as a moment in the general life of society'.[12] But generating a lasting intellectual, societal, and political change may be a project more subtle and incremental than what a simple argument for the immediate realisation of theory suggests. Similarly, developing a critical theory of EU law does not mean promising easy or quick solutions to difficult and enduring problems.

First, it is important to recognise that theory, including critical theory, primarily offers 'approaches to solving problems and developing explanations rather than the solutions and explanations themselves'.[13] As such, it can provide 'an aid in thinking through changed circumstances and new possibilities'.[14] But theoretical research can also play an important role in revealing how 'the status quo' is internally contradictory.[15] Second, it goes without saying that a single theoretical approach can hardly ever 'ask all the interesting questions about any really significant phenomenon'.[16] Similarly, this book does not argue that critical theory offers the only relevant theoretical approach in EU law or that all EU law scholars should view themselves as critical theorists. What it nevertheless aims to show is that something important about EU law goes missing as long as critical theory remains an under-represented field of inquiry in EU legal studies. Finally, insofar as the anti-theoretical mindset is presented as an attack against opaqueness, it should be noted that a rigid search for clarity and conciseness can also amount to 'an intellectual withdrawal from the analysis of complex, confusing, and seemingly nontransparent situations'.[17] This explains why insights from critical theory may help us to notice things about EU law that would otherwise remain concealed.

II. What Does 'Critical Theory' Mean in This Book?

The term 'critical theory' can be used both in a narrow and a broad sense, and individual chapters of this book vary in their approaches to critical theory. The narrow definition of critical theory usually refers to the work of the different generations of the Frankfurt School critical theory,[18] whereas the broader definition covers its multiple offspring in the field of social, political, and legal theory, as well as critical theorists who distance themselves from Frankfurt-style critical theory. Although the Frankfurt School critical theory plays an important role in several chapters (including our own chapters), we agree with Calhoun that 'it is not helpful to restrict the idea of critical theory to the Frankfurt School'.[19] In legal scholarship, the broad legacy of critical theory becomes visible, for example, in feminist theory, critical race theory, postcolonial theory, American

[12] S Benhabib, *Critique, Norm, and Utopia: A Study of the Foundations of Critical Theory* (Columbia University Press, 1986) 4.

[13] C Calhoun, *Critical Social Theory: Culture, History, and the Challenge of Difference* (Wiley-Blackwell, 1995) 6.

[14] ibid 9.

[15] F Rush, 'Conceptual Foundations of Early Critical Theory' in Rush (n 11) 31.

[16] Calhoun (n 13) 8.

[17] S Lettow, 'Emancipation: Rethinking Subjectivity, Power, and Change' (2015) 30 *Hypatia* 501, 510.

[18] For a short introduction, see R Celikates and J Flynn, 'Critical Theory (Frankfurt School)' in EN Zalta and U Nodelman (eds), *The Stanford Encyclopedia of Philosophy* (Winter 2023 Edition), available at https://plato.stanford.edu/archives/win2023/entries/critical-theory/.

[19] Calhoun (n 13) 34–35.

critical legal studies, postmodern jurisprudence, and law and literature.[20] The term 'critical legal theory' seeks to do justice to this diversity of critical perspectives. At the same time, we argue that it is important not to conflate 'critical theory' with 'critical legal theory' or the CLS movement, as the former delves into questions of social theory and critique in ways that the latter too often overlook or remain oblivious to.[21]

Even when more narrowly understood as referring to the work of the Frankfurt School critical theorists, critical theory can be described as 'rather fluid, even by design'.[22] There is no author whose work alone could be said to comprise the 'major principles, methodology, and findings' of critical theory.[23] But critical theorists were united by their shared 'theoretical interests'.[24] Their version of the critical theory of society rejected both Hegel's idealism and orthodox Marxism.[25] Moreover, the interplay between the philosophical and the empirical is a central theme in the Frankfurt School critical theory.[26] On the one hand, 'adequate empirical grounding' was viewed as necessary for social critique.[27] On the other hand, critical theorists highlighted that 'to generalize from existing social conditions is to miss their location in history'.[28] Historical and genealogical analyses therefore play an important role in critical theory. But critical theory also differs from empirical history because it searches for 'contradictions and conditions that contain emancipatory possibilities'.[29] For instance, Benhabib formulates this tension that is central to the identity of critical theory as follows:

> Without an explanatory dimension, critical theory dissolves into mere normative philosophy; if it excludes the dimension of anticipatory-utopian critique, however, it cannot be distinguished from other mainstream social theories that attempt to gain value-free knowledge of the social world.[30]

The approach of critical theory, as articulated by Benhabib, combines 'explanatory-diagnostic' social analysis with 'anticipatory-utopian' normative inquiry, in which the theorist diagnoses social and political pathologies behind crisis or social struggle and then, on that basis, considers emancipatory paths available to society moving forward.[31] In contemporary critical theory, this normative ambition resurfaced with the publication

[20] eg N Lacey, 'Normative Reconstruction in Socio-Legal Theory' (1996) 5 *Social & Legal Studies* 131, 131-132.

[21] For more on this point, see also chapter 1 by Päivi Neuvonen in this book.

[22] Rush (n 15) 7.

[23] RA Gorman, 'Critical Conundrums – Logic and Politics in Frankfurt Critical Theory Prior to the Linguistic Turn' in HF Dahms (ed), *No Social Science Without Critical Theory* (Emerald Publishing, 2008) 56.

[24] RJ Antonio, 'The Origin, Development, and Contemporary Status of Critical Theory' (1983) 24 *The Sociological Quarterly* 325, 330.

[25] However, it should be noted that both Hegel's dialectical method and its materialist reappropriation by Marx influenced the work of early Frankfurt School critical theorists in important ways. ibid 343.

[26] See, eg, M Horkheimer, 'The State of Contemporary Social Philosophy and the Tasks of an Institute for Social Research' in SE Bronner and D MacKay Kellner (eds), *Critical Theory and Society: A Reader* (Routledge, 1989 [1931, in German]) 33 (concerning 'the coexistence of philosophical construction and empirical research in the theory of society').

[27] Antonio (n 24) 348.

[28] C Calhoun, 'The Critical Dimension in Sociological Theory' in JH Turner (ed), *Handbook of Sociological Theory* (Springer, 2001) 89.

[29] Antonio (n 24) 344.

[30] Benhabib (n 12) 142.

[31] See ibid. For an insightful overview of this method and its purchase in the context of European integration, see P Verovšek, *Memory and the Future of Europe: Rupture and Integration in the Wake of Total War* (Manchester University Press, 2020) 10ff.

of Jürgen Habermas's *Between Facts and Norms: Contributions to a Discourse Theory of Law and Democracy*, which notably cast law as mediating 'the tension . . . between facticity and validity' and 'guarantee[ing] that the socially integrating network of communication stretched across society as a whole holds together'.[32] Habermas's work has been informed by the hope of European integration, motivated by its troubles, and also compromised by its crises.[33] The soundness of Habermas's elevation of law into the primary source of social integration in post-metaphysical society remains open to challenge.[34] But the debates Habermas conducted with Dieter Grimm and Wolfgang Streeck about constitutionalising the EU reflect the ability of critical theory to comprehend and respond to the crisis of democratic capitalism.[35] In this regard, Habermas's warnings concerning the 'lure of technocracy' tempting European politics portend the exhaustion of contemporary critical theory as much as its necessity.[36] They suggest, specifically, the need to clearly pose the question, as this volume does, of the relation between EU law and the critical theory of society.

Law also had an explicit role in the original research agenda of the Frankfurt School critical theory, which Max Horkheimer formulated when he became the director of the Institute for Social Research in 1930. In his inaugural lecture, Horkheimer mentioned law as one of 'those phenomena that can be interpreted only in the context of the social existence of humans', thus identifying it as a focus of social philosophy and critical theory.[37] Horkheimer also outlined in this context that critical theory should focus on exploring

> the question of the connection between the economic life of society, the psychological development of its individuals and the changes within specific areas of culture to which belong not only the intellectual legacy of the sciences, art and religion, but also law . . .[38]

For Horkheimer, a crucial part of critical theory was to challenge 'the autonomy of thought' itself.[39] As Calhoun notes, critical theory therefore requires 'a continual reflexive inquiry into the historical, intellectual, and institutional conditions of the critical theorists' own work'.[40] It is arguable that critical EU law scholars should follow critical theorists' methodological commitment to self-reflexivity.[41]

[32] J Habermas, *Between Facts and Norms: Contributions to a Discourse Theory of Law and Democracy* (MIT Press, 1996 [1992]) 444, 56; see T Hedrick, *Reconciliation and Reification: Freedom's Semblance and Actuality from Hegel to Contemporary Critical Theory* (Oxford University Press, 2019) 218.

[33] It is worth remembering the extent to which Habermas's work – the foundations of his critical theory of law and democracy – are interwoven with his engagement with European politics. For discussion, see, eg, P Verovšek, *Jürgen Habermas: Public Intellectual and Engaged Critical Theorist* (Columbia University Press, 2026).

[34] For a recent appraisal, see J Abromeit, M Dimick and P Linden-Retek (eds), *Critical Encounters with Habermas's Political and Legal Theory* (Brill Publishers, 2025).

[35] Consider eg C Bickerton, *European Integration: From Nation- States to Member States* (Oxford University Press, 2012); J Komárek (ed), *European Constitutional Imaginaries: Between Ideology and Utopia* (Oxford University Press, 2023).

[36] J Habermas, *The Lure of Technocracy* (Polity, 2015).

[37] Horkheimer (n 26) 25.

[38] ibid 33.

[39] M Horkheimer, 'Materialism and Metaphysics' in M Horkheimer, *Critical Theory: Selected Essays* (Continuum 1975, translated by M O'Connell and others) 32.

[40] Calhoun (n 28) 89.

[41] For this point, see Neuvonen (n 1).

A more difficult question is whether critical theory can also steer the critique of EU law from a more substantive perspective. Some commentators postulate that 'the theoretical challenges from which the members of the school had won their insights threaten to fall into oblivion'.[42] A related concern is that the early Frankfurt School theorists seemingly failed to implement their original programme to combine theoretical and empirical research in a genuinely new way.[43] In particular, Horkheimer and Adorno's pessimistic analysis of 'instrumental reason' and 'culture industry' in late capitalist societies has sometimes been described as 'a critical failure'.[44] However, it should be noted that the Frankfurt School critical theorists never formed a unified group. The first-generation critical theorists were already divided in their views, but a particularly important dividing line runs between pre- and post-Habermasian critical theory.[45] For some, this diversity of positions may come across as a profound weakness. But the fact that critical theorists disagree on 'what kind of enterprise critical theory should be'[46] in our view makes it a more fruitful basis for rethinking the critical project in EU law. Instead of proposing a simple formula that should be applied to EU law, a closer look at the issues that divide critical theorists can help us to better understand what questions the critique of EU law should be asking.

A different, more powerful, attack against critical theory is presented by the so-called post-humanist and new materialist theories, which depict the focus of classic critical theory as too narrow and anthropocentric. Their main concern is that critical theory is unable to properly respond to today's larger ecological crisis.[47] But 'strong' posthumanism comes with its own problems.[48] For instance, Lettow has noted that the refusal to distinguish between different 'forms of material agency' undermines the critical project insofar as 'relations of domination, power and difference within and among human societies are ignored'.[49] Therefore, a proper understanding of both 'human-nature relations' and 'socio-technological regimes' will require a more nuanced understanding of agency and subjectivity than what is currently presented by many non-humanist and new materialist theories.[50] All of these questions about the theoretical basis of the critical project are also relevant to the critique of EU law. Moreover, although the idea of

[42] A Honneth, 'A Social Pathology of Reason: On the Intellectual Legacy of Critical Theory' in A Honneth, *Pathologies of Reason: On the Legacy of Critical Theory* (Columbia University Press, 2009, translated by J Ingram) 19.

[43] Antonio (n 24) 348.

[44] N Kompridis, *Critique and Disclosure: Critical Theory between Past and Future* (MIT Press, 2006) 257 (although it could arguably also be viewed as 'an authentic critical response to the times in which they lived'). See also M Horkheimer and TW Adorno, *Dialectic of Enlightenment* (Stanford University Press, 2002 [1947], edited by G Schmid Noerr, translated by E Jephcott).

[45] ibid 256. This is also why it is problematic to reduce the Frankfurt School critical theory to Habermas although his intersubjective discourse-theoretic paradigm informs the work of many contemporary critical theorists.

[46] ibid 258.

[47] For an overview, see, eg, H Rosa et al, 'Critical Theory and New Materialisms: Fit, Strain, or Contradiction?' in H Rosa et al (eds), *Critical Theory and New Materialisms* (Routledge, 2021) 5.

[48] S Lettow, 'Turning the Turn: New Materialism, Historical Materialism and Critical Theory' (2017) 140 *Thesis Eleven* 106, 107.

[49] ibid 107. Moreover, Lettow argues that 'the "nonhuman" world, too, is inadequately addressed through a terminology that does not make any distinction other than that of human/nonhuman'. ibid 112.

[50] ibid 111. For a similar point, see also Rosa et al (n 47) 7.

critical theory as 'a single comprehensive social theory'[51] may no longer be sustainable, this book suggests that we should take seriously the interdisciplinary critical project that the early Frankfurt School critical theory outlined.[52]

However, we do not argue that EU law scholars should uncritically endorse views held by critical theorists. Such a mindset would undermine the very idea of critique and it would also be practically impossible. After all, there is no single point of view that would capture the tradition of critical theory as a whole. Instead, this book maintains that a better understanding of critical theory is an important step towards a more rounded and versatile critique of EU law. One point in which most critical theorists converge, their many disagreements notwithstanding, is that the law is a social phenomenon that cannot be meaningfully studied in isolation of the surrounding social reality. This insight guides our analyses of EU law in this book. But it is possible to also learn from the different blind spots evinced by critical theorists.[53] From the perspective of EU law, what is missing from both classic and contemporary critical theory may be just as interesting and informative as what is included in it. And while it might be tempting to delegate the task of elaborating the critical theory of EU law to historians, philosophers, or social theorists, EU law scholars also need to consider what theoretical commitments inform the critique(s) of EU law.

III. How Can We Do Critical Theory in EU Law?

The different ways in which critical theory can be conceived imply that no single-authored research project could easily capture the multiple intersections between critical theory and EU law. Similarly, as the editors of this book, it was clear to us that a more collective intellectual effort was needed to illustrate what critical theory can add to EU legal studies. This book accordingly brings together a group of established and early-career scholars from Continental Europe, Scandinavia, the United Kingdom, and the United States. The composition of this group ensures that the book engages with both the Continental and the American strands of critical theory. At the same time, the subject-matter expertise of contributors spans broadly across the EU legal order. While one book project alone cannot exhaust this topic area, gathering the emerging group of critical EU law scholars makes a significant contribution to the elaboration of critical EU legal studies as a distinct field of inquiry in EU legal studies by thus paving the way for further discussion and debate.[54]

The book includes both thematic and subject-specific chapters. One set of chapters focuses on mapping key questions and controversies that a more deliberate engagement

[51] Kompridis (n 44) 258. See also Cordero (n 9) 44 about 'skepticism toward holistic and universalistic theorizations of society'.

[52] In the age of Artificial Intelligence, it may even be healthy to at least momentarily pause to reflect on whether critical theorists were just ahead of their time with their concern about totalising 'instrumental rationality'.

[53] For discussion, see, eg, A Allen, *The End of Progress: Decolonizing the Normative Foundations of Critical Theory* (Columbia University Press, 2016).

[54] For another recent attempt to map the field, see the special issue, 'Critical Legal Approaches in EU Law' (2024) 15 *Transnational Legal Theory* 493 (edited by I Isailović).

with critical theory will raise in EU law scholarship. Several chapters also apply these insights to substantive EU law. The authors' engagement with different branches of classic and contemporary critical theory reveals distinct problems and proposed solutions within diverse fields of EU law. Chapters converse both methodologically and substantively. But ultimately each chapter also forms a world, or a critical project, of its own. In the spirit of methodological pluralism, the book does not advocate a single framework of analysis within the rich tradition of critical theory. Several chapters also adopt a more questioning approach to critical theory, raising questions and issues that critical theory may not alone be able to answer in EU legal studies. In this respect, the book emphasises that a critical theoretical inquiry into EU law ought to be seen as much an inquiry into the meaning of contemporary critical theory as an application of it to the European legal order. If the reader considers the volume as a whole, its motivating questions become dual: 'What is critical theory to EU law, and EU law to critical theory?'

This engagement with critical theory covers a broad range of substantive fields of EU law and the history of legal integration, including constitutional law, the design of monetary union and economic law, fiscal integration and taxation, anti-discrimination law, gender equality, labour law, data protection, migration law and policy, and the Common Foreign and Security Policy (CFSP). The selection of topic areas was guided by the fact that all authors are experts of both their respective fields of EU law and critical theory. While some areas of substantive EU law therefore remain undiscussed, we are confident that this book is able to offer a representative overview of how critical theory challenges the practice of EU law and what alternative paths it presents for the EU and EU law. However, it should be noted that the Anthropocene forms an important theme in contemporary critical theory. As editors of this book, we regret that our attempts to find a suitable author to cover this area of critical theory and EU law remained unsuccessful. This gap, however, is instructive insofar as it highlights that a critical mass of EU law scholars who are both able and willing to engage with critical theory is still only emerging in many fields of EU law.

Chapter one by Päivi Neuvonen revisits the critical project that is currently unfolding in EU legal studies. For Neuvonen, critical legal theory alone cannot sustain the critical project in EU law because it tends to overlook the importance of social theory for the critique of law and, thus, the deeper crisis of normative critique that underlies the critical project. Instead, she turns to the critical theory of society to develop a critical theory of EU law. This inquiry reopens both the social and the political question in critical EU legal studies. First, a closer look at the Frankfurt School critical theory suggests that the crisis of capitalist society is not adequately captured in the traditional Marxist critique of political economy. This analysis challenges the narrow view of emancipation as mere decommodification in the critique of EU law. Second, Neuvonen's chapter considers whether critical theorists can resolve the crisis of normative critique either through the method of immanent critique or by framing critique as a form of political practice. This discussion shows how critical theory also problematises the essentialist (statist) concept of the political and invites us to reconsider the meaning of the political question in the depoliticisation critiques of EU law.

Chapter two by Kaius Tuori submits the histories and historiography of EU law to critical evaluation. His analysis builds on the genealogical tradition in critical theory. As a legal historian, Tuori explores how writing a critical history of EU law would differ from the more traditional historiography of the EU and its law. For Tuori, the central task of critical history is to unsettle the way in which history often operates as a legitimating tool for the present and the future. From this starting point, his chapter shows how the ideas of the common past and tradition are used to legitimate European integration in a highly selective manner. Tuori also applies critical historiography to identify and deconstruct three historical metanarratives that have played an important role in the integration project. While a closer look at the institutional, human rights, and anti-totalitarian narratives reveals the contested nature of some of the EU's 'founding myths', Tuori's critical historiographical analysis also shows how 'historical teleology', which presents individual events as steps towards the EU's unquestioned purpose, often goes hand in hand with legal teleology in EU law.

Chapter three by Michael Wilkinson explores why critical interventions based on the Frankfurt School critical theory are prone to overlook the ways in which European integration generates depoliticisation and de-democratisation. In his chapter, Wilkinson follows Wolfgang Streeck in maintaining that a critique of the EU and EU law requires a more developed understanding of the political economy and the fundamental contradictions of democratic capitalism. For Wilkinson, this also means that an effective critique of EU law cannot remain siloed into different substantive fields of EU law but must focus on the EU's 'constitutional function'. Wilkinson's chapter shows that the tension between democracy and capitalism became subdued in the work of many first- and second-generation Frankfurt School critical theorists due to the influence of Friedrich Pollock's theory of state capitalism. But he also illustrates how a more autonomous concept of the political was preserved by Franz Neumann and Otto Kirchheimer, neither of whom belonged to the 'inner circle' of the Frankfurt School. For Wilkinson, it is their understanding of political freedom and popular sovereignty that can offer a more robust basis not just for the critique of the EU and EU law but also for the renewal of critical theory itself.

Chapter four by Marco Goldoni engages in a more detailed political economy analysis of EU law by zooming into the single currency. For Goldoni, the critique of political economy forms the core of critical theory. His chapter thus sets out to examine the particular governing function that the single currency fulfils for the EU's political economy. A closer look at the fundamental objectives and institutional design of this governing function demonstrates how the process of valorisation within the Euro monetary constitution operates to insulate the Euro monetary system from the national political processes, while simultaneously making it increasingly dependent on global financial markets. The normative dimension of Goldoni's analysis highlights that these processes of valorisation generate distinct forms of domination in relation to the labour force. Moreover, his critique of the post-pandemic emergency and recovery measures, such as the PEPP (Pandemic Emergency Purchase Programme) and the NGEU (NextGenerationEU), suggests that these more innovative and unconventional interventions have also failed to genuinely transform the processes of valorisation that currently shape the political economy of the Euro monetary constitution.

Chapter five by Jussi Jaakkola examines how European income tax integration remodels the power to tax in post-war democratic capitalism. Jaakkola's chapter draws on the different branches of critical state theory to illustrate that the structural tension between fiscal democracy and market capitalism remains unresolved in democratic capitalism because the emancipatory capacities of the democratic tax state depend on resources that the capitalist market generates. A careful analysis of the historical evolution of European income tax integration offers a concrete example of how EU law reshapes the relationship between democracy and capitalism at the national level. At the same time, Jaakkola argues that these findings about the 'in-built' contradiction of the emancipatory function of taxation are relevant to the current debates on the EU's 'fiscal constitution' because this same contradiction will resurface at the European level if the EU gains a more independent power to tax in the future. While theorising EU law from a distinctively fiscal perspective, Jaakkola's analysis of how the EU has transformed the power to tax also illuminates the changing relationship between the state and the economy from a perspective that has remained largely undiscussed in contemporary critical theory.

Chapter six by Rebecca Zahn and Meemi Matero shows how European labour law embodies the deep-seated asymmetry between economic and social integration in the EU. But their chapter also highlights that the recent politicisation of the EU and EU law has resulted in the renewed interest in EU-level labour law measures. From this starting point, Zahn and Matero engage in a genealogical critique of European labour law to rethink both its normative foundations and future directions. More specifically, they use the critical lens of 'minor comparativism' to consider what the normative commitment to solidarity means in European labour law. In Zahn and Matero's analysis, this critical method works to recover a specific minority perspective on the labour question and solidarity that was formulated by Albert Thomas's 1931 International Labour Organization Memorandum. In their chapter, this revised account of solidarity, which emphasises the importance of collective representation, also paves the way for a discussion on the European Instrument for Temporary Support to Mitigate Unemployment Risks in an Emergency (SURE) and the 2022 Minimum Wage Directive as two recent examples of how the value of solidarity has been activated in European labour law.

Chapter seven by Raphaële Xenidis sets EU anti-discrimination law against the type of society that it helps to generate. Through this analysis, she illustrates how and why EU anti-discrimination law has failed to live up to its emancipatory promises. Xenidis's chapter draws on the materialist, post-structuralist, and feminist strands of critical theory to show how legal rules that promise equality operate to distribute 'social goods' and create 'social hierarchies'. She unfolds this argument through three distinct, but interconnected, critical moves, which first 'reembody' the subject of EU anti-discrimination law, then 'trouble' the way in which its categories manipulate social relations, and finally 'disenchant' the forms of socialisation that 'integration through anti-discrimination law' cultivates within the EU. Xenidis's chapter also offers a powerful critique of the reasoning of the Court of Justice of the EU (CJEU) in a series of recent cases assessing the legality of workplace rules and practices that prohibit the wearing of religious clothing. This case study serves to expose the deeper 'epistemological commitments' of EU anti-discrimination law. For Xenidis, rethinking EU anti-discrimination law only becomes possible after the false assumption of its neutrality is first demolished.

Chapter eight by Barbara Havelková asks what feminists should think of EU law. Feminist critique presents an important corrective voice within the tradition of critical theory. Similarly, Havelková's attempt to bring together the feminist and critical analyses of EU law adds a valuable perspective to the critique of EU law in this book. Havelková identifies the following four objectives for the feminist study of EU law: 'women as EU lawmakers'; 'gender equality acquis'; 'gender in other EU substantive law'; and 'gender in the EU legal order'. However, in the spirit of feminist writing, Havelková's chapter replaces the 'view from nowhere' with a personal account of a feminist scholar with a post-state-socialist Central European perspective. In doing so, Havelková acknowledges that a 'definitive definition' of feminist critique of EU law would be an oxymoron because feminism, and even critical legal feminism, is not a singular or monolithic project. Havelková's own feminism is based on inclusiveness, structuralism, and pragmatism. From this starting point, she posits that the EU's existing competences can be harnessed to improve the situation of women. Yet, her chapter also highlights that the EU legal order 'as a system' still lacks a 'comprehensive feminist critique'.

Chapter nine by Susanna Lindroos-Hovinheimo illustrates how the 'individualistic logic' of EU data protection law falls short of addressing challenges that define life in digital societies. Her chapter draws on French critical thinking informed by structuralism and Marxism, with a particular focus on the work of Jean-Luc Nancy, Jacques Rancière, and Henri Lefebvre. Throughout the chapter, Lindroos-Hovinheimo also converses with the relevant case law of the CJEU. First, a closer look at how the General Data Protection Regulation is interpreted shows that the singular focus on the privacy rights of individuals currently prevails over other more 'communal' values, which maintain the democratic legitimacy of the political and legal system. Second, Lindroos-Hovinheimo's chapter demonstrates that the individualistic legal framework is unable to effectively resist the exploitation of data in digital capitalism. From this perspective, the law's individualism manifests the capitalist political economy of contemporary digital societies. Finally, a careful analysis of the nature of data highlights that data only exists 'in between people' and, thus, 'defines us in our social being'. This is why Lindroos-Hovinheimo also concludes that the current individualistic legal framework cannot effectively regulate data itself.

Chapter ten by Luigi Lonardo considers how critical theory can help to clarify the purpose of the EU's foreign policy. Lonardo's critique has both a diagnostic and a transformative dimension. Through a contextual and historical analysis, Lonardo first identifies security as the 'overarching purpose' of the EU's foreign policy. Drawing on the Welsh School of Critical Security Studies, he then outlines what it would mean to view security as a precondition for emancipation. For Lonardo, this critical reinterpretation of security has direct relevance for EU law because it can guide how the different foreign policy objectives under Article 21 of the Treaty on European Union are prioritised. But it also operates to expose the 'structural and cultural forces' that shape the EU's foreign policy. The EU's colonial legacies and seemingly inconsistent approach to the principle of self-determination offer two concrete examples of why correcting structural injustices needs to be prioritised in the EU's foreign policy. But Lonardo's analysis also examines the EU itself both as an 'object' and an 'agent' of cultural and ideological hegemony and domination. These findings highlight that the EU's foreign policy is currently in need of 'reimagination' and that a purely state-centric model of security is insufficient in this context.

Chapter eleven by Alezini Loxa maps the value of critical theory for EU migration and asylum law. Her chapter shows that, unlike many other fields of EU law, EU migration and asylum law already displays a strong tradition of critical engagement. From this starting point, Loxa sets out to thematically systematise the existing critical approaches to show, first, how they expose 'different types of domination' that the categories of EU migration law generate and, second, where their potential gaps lie. Loxa's analysis highlights that critical studies of EU law can learn from the diverse ways in which critique is conducted in EU migration and asylum law, including post-colonial approaches, critiques of governmentality, and feminist and queer critiques. But she also argues that it is important to more explicitly integrate questions of political economy into the critique of EU migration and asylum law. For Loxa, 'racial capitalism' provides a critical lens that connects racial and capitalist forms of exclusion in EU migration and asylum law, thus offering 'a more complete picture of the variable inclusions and exclusions constituted by EU law'. As such, Loxa's chapter also illustrates what a broader understanding of law and political economy could look like in EU legal studies.

Chapter twelve by Paul Linden-Retek develops a critique of the constitutional theory of the EU and argues, in turn, that a theory of European constitutionalism should orient itself around the ambitions of critique. While postnationalism aspires to overcome a conception of political life rooted in the desire for sovereign control, existing theories of EU law merely transpose this desire across various levels of governance without questioning its flawed premises. Linden-Retek's chapter argues that the issue lies, at its root, in *legal form*, which refers to the kinds of relations instantiated and legitimated by law. Drawing on a range of post-Marxist critical theorists, the chapter shows how the legal form endorsed, often tacitly, by EU constitutionalism partakes in 'reification': systematically misattributing social and historical relationships as timeless relations among things. It considers how this reification of political life becomes a constitutional problem, distorting the material and symbolic foundations of political legitimacy, the boundaries of civic membership, and the function of adjudication. For Linden-Retek, better criticising these distortions reveals itself to be the task of European constitutional law properly understood – and thus recommends rival legal forms (principles and practices) that might yet realise Europe's postnational aspirations.

The book concludes with an Epilogue by Sarah Glaser, Luca Tenreira, and Jacob van de Beeten. The conversation that unfolds in the Epilogue between the three protagonists – the Genealogist, the Anthropologist, and the Deconstructionist – offers a gripping picture of the challenges and possibilities that face the critique of EU law. The question that captivates the attention and imagination of each individual interlocutor is whether immanent critique can 'reconnect' EU law with social reality in ways that break free from EU law's 'self-referential vocabulary' without altogether rejecting the transformative potential of 'legal normativity'. These reflections are enlivened by examples from the authors' ongoing research projects in the field of EU law. Yet, Glaser, Tenreira and van de Beeten move beyond 'a single authoritative point of view' in ways that exquisitely capture the editorial vision of more collective intellectual work that we had in mind when we started this project on 'Critical Theory and European Union Law'. At the same time, their dialogic writing combines playfulness and intellectual rigour in ways that reflect the spirit of critical theory at its best.

1

Emancipation, Immanence, Utopia

The Critical Project in EU Law

PÄIVI JOHANNA NEUVONEN

I. Introduction

This chapter revisits the critical project that is currently unfolding in European Union (EU) law. First, it problematises the view that a simple causal relation exists between the EU's various crises and critical studies of EU law. Instead, a closer look at the dialectical relationship between crisis and critique in the first main section suggests that critique is an active historical force in EU legal studies and that the critique of EU law is not immune to the broader crisis of normative critique, which engulfs contemporary social and critical theory. From this starting point, the chapter will move to examine the limited capacity of critical legal theory alone to sustain the critical project in EU law. The central claim in the second main section is that critical interventions that are rooted in the Critical Legal Studies (CLS) movement tend to remain too superficial in their engagement with social theory and, thus, with the crisis of normative critique that underlies the critical project in EU law. Moreover, a simple distinction between internal and external critique in the CLS-inspired critiques overlooks the methodological importance of immanent critique in EU legal studies. Against this background, the final section of this chapter argues that a more solid theoretical basis for developing a critical theory of EU law can be found in the Frankfurt School critical theory of society.

In this chapter, this inquiry into the critical theory of society reopens both the social and the political question in the critique of EU law.[1] It will first explain why the traditional Marxist critique of political economy should be replaced with a more comprehensive critique of capitalist society in EU law. This discussion challenges the narrow view of emancipation as mere decommodification. But it also points to the more problematic intellectual legacy of emancipation in the critical project. This controversy over critique's emancipatory goals offers a concrete example of the deeper crisis of normative critique that impedes the critical project in EU law. In critical theory, the method of immanent critique and the quest for critical praxis attempt to address this

[1] From a distinctively more methodological perspective, see also PJ Neuvonen, 'A Way of Critique: What Can EU Law Scholars Learn from Critical Theory?' (2022) 1 *European Law Open* 60.

crisis. Immanent critique provides an important alternative to the internal and external critiques of EU law, as it maintains that critical emancipatory potential can arise even from deeply flawed and contradictory social reality. In depicting critique as a form of political praxis, critical theory also subjects the concept of the political to critical scrutiny. From this perspective, the so-called depoliticisation critiques of EU law miss the crux of the political question if they leave the concept of the political unproblematised. But it will also be seen that the critical project may need at least a dash of critical utopian thinking to reconsider the political question.

II. Crises, Critique, and the Crisis of Normative Critique in EU Law

The EU's past and ongoing crises provide a common explanation for the growing interest in critique in EU legal studies. This does not mean that there was no critical project in EU law before the EU's more recent crises, which include at least the Euro-zone crisis, the Brexit crisis, the COVID-19 pandemic, as well as the broader geopolitical and climate crises. The first critical introduction to EU law was published already in 1996.[2] Critical scholars set out to undo the seemingly innate link between EU law and 'a largely unarticulated but immanent and symbolically pervasive concept of integration'.[3] Classic critical texts have also questioned the prominent role of the Court of Justice of the EU (CJEU) in the integration project from the 1980s onwards.[4] A parallel strand of critical research has focused on uncovering the neoliberal tendencies of EU law.[5] Both of these discourses are closely linked to the EU's democratic deficit and the potentially de-politicising effects of legal integration.[6] A related concern is that EU law is likely to produce alienation if it disregards the importance of 'daily life experiences' and 'co-presence' for human attachments.[7] These earlier critical developments notwithstanding, it has been suggested that the present 'multifacetous crisis'[8] of European integration might explain

[2] See I Ward, *A Critical Introduction to European Law* (Butterworths, 1996). The third edition of this book was published by Cambridge University Press in 2009.

[3] J Shaw, 'European Union Legal Studies in Crisis? Towards a New Dynamic' (1996) 16 *OJLS* 231, 237.

[4] See, eg, E Stein, 'Lawyers, Judges, and the Making of a Transnational Constitution' (1981) 75 *American Journal of International Law* 1; H Rasmussen, *On Law and Policy in the European Court of Justice A Comparative Study in Judicial Policymaking* (Martinus Nijhoff Publishers, 1986); JHH Weiler, 'The Transformation of Europe' (1991) 100 *Yale Law Journal* 2403; K Alter, *Establishing the Supremacy of European Law: The Making of an International Rule of Law in Europe* (Oxford University Press, 2001); AS Sweet, *The Judicial Construction of Europe* (Oxford University Press, 2004).

[5] See, eg, FW Scharpf, 'The Asymmetry of European Integration, or Why the EU Cannot be a "Social Market Economy"' (2010) 8 *Socio-Economic Review* 211 and W Streeck, 'The Crises of Democratic Capitalism' (2011) 71 *New Left Review* 5, 7 and 26. For more discussion, see also chapter 3 by Michael Wilkinson and chapter 5 by Jussi Jaakkola in this book.

[6] From different perspectives, see, eg, A Somek, *The Cosmopolitan Constitution* (Oxford University Press, 2014); D Grimm, *The Constitution of European Democracy* (Oxford University Press, 2017); MA Wilkinson, *Authoritarian Liberalism and the Transformation of Modern Europe* (Oxford University Press, 2021).

[7] eg D Chalmers, 'The Unconfined Power of European Union Law' (2016) 1 *European Papers* 405, 415–17 and 437.

[8] A Vauchez, 'The Map and the Territory: Re-Assessing EU Law's Embeddedness in European Societies' (2020) 27 *Maastricht Journal of European and Comparative Law* 133, 134.

why critique has gained a more prominent role in EU law scholarship in recent years. The link between crisis and critique arguably reflects a larger trend in which 'EU studies follow ... the "ups" and "downs" of their very object of study'.[9]

While the trajectory linking crisis and critique is plausible, it would be a mistake to view the critique of EU law as a straightforward counter-reaction to the EU's different crises. The problem with this narrative is that it too readily presumes a shared understanding (or phenomenology) of crises within the EU. The term 'crisis' can operate as both a 'descriptive' and 'diagnostic' tool in the critical project.[10] From a normative perspective, it usually signals the lack of political or social legitimacy.[11] A 'temporal' understanding of crisis entails that it is possible to ultimately move beyond it.[12] Yet, crisis can also gain a degree of 'permanence'.[13] This malleability may explain the appeal of the concept of crisis in human and social sciences.[14] But the crisis-critique nexus is attenuated by the fact that no obvious consensus exists on the meaning of crisis. At the same time, the normalisation of 'crisis jargon' weakens the explanatory and critical potential of crisis phenomena.[15] What is particularly problematic in this context is how the generic discourse on crises overlooks more specific 'social-historical struggles' that underlie and generate crises experiences.[16] Therefore, it is important to consider how the concept of crisis is deployed in the critique of EU law.

The normalisation of crisis-mode resonates with the argument that crisis can be understood as a permanent, and even necessary, feature of European integration.[17] But it also aggravates the challenges that the critical project encounters in EU law. To better understand the nature of these challenges, critical EU law scholarship may need to look beyond its own boundaries to the post-Hegelian tradition of critical social theory. Crises, or 'objective situations of disturbance',[18] are often depicted as a necessary 'basis' for social critique in critical theory.[19] This is understandable insofar as the critical project focuses on identifying 'the deficiencies or even contradictions lying in the social formation'.[20] But the deconstruction of a simple crisis-critique nexus highlights that there is no singular experience of crisis within the EU and that the critical project is shaped by the choice over whose voices are heard when the relevant crises of European integration are identified. Moreover, even one and the same crisis is experienced differently by different

[9] ibid 134. See also L Azoulai, 'Solitude, Community, and Critique. Motives for a Reshaping of EU legal Studies' (2015) 50 *Politique Européenne* 82.

[10] R Koselleck and M Richter, 'Crisis' (2006) *67 Journal of the History of Ideas* 357, 369.

[11] B Isenberg, 'Critique and Crisis. Reinhart Koselleck's Thesis of the Genesis of Modernity' (2012) *Eurozine – Network of European cultural journals* 5, available at www.eurozine.com/critique-and-crisis/.

[12] Koselleck and Richter (n 10) 361, 371–72.

[13] ibid 358.

[14] ibid 374.

[15] W Schinkel, 'The Image of Crisis: Walter Benjamin and the Interpretation of "Crisis" in Modernity' (2015) 127 *Thesis Eleven* 36, 48 and 39.

[16] R Cordero, *Crisis and Critique On the Fragile Foundations of Social Life* (Routledge, 2017) 25. From this perspective, a pressing question to any critical project is whether crisis can be reinstated as a genuinely critical concept. ibid 32.

[17] From a historical perspective, see, eg, K Patel, *Project Europe: A History* (Cambridge University Press, 2020) 47–48, 226 and 272–80.

[18] Cordero (n 16) 2.

[19] R Jaeggi, *Critique of Forms of Life* (Harvard University Press, 2018, translated by C Cronin) 213.

[20] ibid 192.

groups and stakeholders. The obvious, and much-discussed, example is the Euro-zone crisis.[21] But this is also true with the EU's other crises.

The call for a more reflexive understanding of crisis[22] is closely linked to another key insight that the post-Hegelian critical theory adds to the critique of EU law; namely, that the relationship between crisis and critique is hardly ever one-directional. On the contrary, it is arguable that the dialectical relation between crisis and critique shapes the critical project in ways that require more attention in EU legal studies. For instance, Jaeggi formulates this point by noting that 'criticism is at the same time a component of the crisis'.[23] Critique generates the crisis 'by making it explicit in language'.[24] This, however, means that critique may also enable us to reconsider what constitutes a crisis and why.[25] This insight about the dialectical relationship between crisis and critique debilitates any simple claim about critique as an unequivocally progressive historical force.[26] Moreover, it problematises the idea of unengaged critique. The term 'crisis of critique'[27] highlights that a purely unmasking critique is not possible and that critique is simultaneously both shaping and shaped by the crises that form its object.[28]

The crisis of normative critique is reinforced by how critique often promises to offer 'a meta-standpoint' without acknowledging that it, too, adopts a particular perspective within society.[29] This problematic is captured in Judith Butler's observation that 'power pervades the very conceptual apparatus that seeks to negotiate its terms, including the subject position of the critic'.[30] Butler, however, posits that 'this implication of the terms of criticism in the field of power is . . . the very precondition of a politically engaged critique'.[31] In a similar vein, many critical theorists from Marx onwards have assigned critique the task of generating political and social change.[32] But the idea of critical praxis in critical theory differs from a simple argument for the political realisation of critique.[33] As a 'praxis- and action-oriented philosophy', critical theory is preconditioned on the search for 'freedom, the absence of which is the object of its critique'.[34] This means that the critical project must carefully investigate the conditions for social

[21] eg AJ Menéndez, 'Not Seven, but Eleven? European Crises or "New Normal"?' (2018) 24 *European Law Journal* 2, 4. On the links between the EU's financial, fiscal, and political crises, see also AJ Menéndez, 'The Existential Crisis of the European Union' (2013) 14 *German Law Journal* 453.

[22] Cordero (n 16) 32.

[23] Jaeggi (n 19) 173.

[24] Cordero (n 16) 53.

[25] ibid 4.

[26] For a notably pessimistic interpretation of the dialectic relationship between crisis and critique, see R Koselleck, *Critique and Crisis: Enlightenment and the Pathogenesis of Modern Society* (MIT Press, reprint 2000 [1959, in German]) 171–72 and 183.

[27] Isenberg (n 11) 5. See also PJ Neuvonen, 'The "Crisis of Critique" in EU Law' (*VerfBlog*, 7 May 2025), available at https://verfassungsblog.de/the-crisis-of-critique-in-eu-law/.

[28] On the impossibility of unmasking critique, see, eg, E Laclau, 'The Death and Resurrection of the Theory of Ideology' (1997) 112 *Modern Language Notes* 297, 299 and 319–20. In the context of EU legal studies, see also Neuvonen (n 1) 67–69 and 76.

[29] Cordero (n 16) 49 (and 53).

[30] J Butler, 'Contingent Foundations: Feminism and the Question of "Postmodernism"' in J Butler and J Scott (eds), *Feminists Theorize the Political* (Routledge, 1992) 6.

[31] ibid 6–7. But see also J Butler, 'Performative Agency' (2010) 3 *Journal of Cultural Economy* 147, 159.

[32] See Marx's 11th thesis on Feuerbach. K Marx, 'Theses on Feuerbach' in R Tucker (ed), *The Marx-Engels Reader*, 2nd edn (W. W. Norton & Company, 1978).

[33] For more discussion, see also section IV.B of this chapter.

[34] Koselleck and Richter (n 10) 384.

and political freedom, that is, emancipation.[35] Similarly, a meaningful critical praxis in EU law is preconditioned on the concept of freedom or emancipation that steers the critical project in EU law.[36]

In short, critique is often depicted as a logical consequence of the EU's various crises. But it is important to consider whether our concept of crisis presumes a problematic vision of 'a unitary, autonomous and coherent social order'[37] in the EU. This question points to the challenges that the critical project in EU law faces as soon as the simple causality between crisis and critique is dismantled. Critique can be viewed as 'a historical force . . . that still determines our lives, regardless whether we consider ourselves to be post- or late- modern'.[38] It can also be viewed as a form of praxis insofar as it fuels some crises, while trivialising others. In practice, the critique of EU law may need to both identify 'social pathologies' and imagine 'more just and fulfilling forms of collective life'.[39] But its capacity to do so is weakened by the crisis of normative critique, as discussed in this section. This also explains why a meaningful critical project will require a careful critique of concepts, which recognises the conceptual realm as a potential site for struggles against 'domination and exclusion'.[40] Below in this chapter, this is illustrated in relation to the concepts of emancipation and the political – both of which play an important role in the critique of EU law.

III. On the Limits of Critical Legal Theory in the Critique of EU Law

Critical legal theory offers one account of how EU law scholars could embark on the critical project. Two main branches of critical legal theory are the offspring of the American CLS movement and of the British Critical Legal Conference (CLC or 'Brit Crit').[41] The differences between these two critical movements have been described as 'quite pronounced, although not always acknowledged'.[42] For Douzinas and Gearey, the main difference is that the CLS was more focused on critiquing 'judicial institutions and reasoning', whereas the CLC engaged with the theme of 'law's injustice' from a broader social and political perspective.[43] It is arguable that 'critical theories' have become 'an important voice in the canon of integration theory'.[44] Similarly, there is a

[35] A genuinely 'emancipatory transformatio[n]' would provide an 'adequate' and 'non-regressive' solution to the crises that inflict a particular social formation. N Fraser and R Jaeggi, *Capitalism A Conversation in Critical Theory* (Polity Press, 2018) 164.

[36] For more on this point, see section IV.A. of this chapter.

[37] Cordero (n 16) 27.

[38] Isenberg (n 11) 2.

[39] MP Lara, 'The Conceptual Semantic Field of "Crisis" and "Critique"' in A Siegetsleitner et al (eds), *Crisis and Critique: Philosophical Analysis and Current Events* (De Gruyter, 2021) 20.

[40] Cordero (n 16) 89–90 and 92.

[41] But critical legal theory can also more broadly refer to 'normative legal theory which is specifically concerned . . . to interrogate the deeper political, historical and philosophical logics which underpin the power of law'. N Lacey, 'Normative Reconstruction of Socio-Legal Theory' (1996) 5 *Social & Legal Studies* 131, 131.

[42] C Douzinas and A Gearey, *Critical Jurisprudence The Political Philosophy of Justice* (Hart, 2005) 240.

[43] ibid 240 and 241.

[44] T Diez, 'Towards a Critical Theorising of European Integration' in D Bigo et al (eds), *The Routledge Handbook of Critical European Studies* (Routledge, 2020) 16.

growing interest in 'critical legal approaches' in EU law.[45] The risk with a broad usage of critical 'theories' or 'approaches' is that the concept of critique becomes inflated. But it will be seen in this section that the endorsement of a more niche CLS-based critique is equally problematic. While the internal critiques of EU law assume the normativity and autonomy of EU law, the CLS-inspired external critiques are prone to overlooking the deeper crisis of normative critique. This is arguably due to their insufficient engagement with social-theoretic questions that underlie the critical project EU law.

It has been noted that '[t]he critical thinking of the 1970s did not find its way into European legal scholarship'.[46] This lack of critical engagement at the early stages of the integration project is normally explained by the close affinities between academic and institutional actors, as documented by the recent critical histories of EU law.[47] These affinities may also explain why critique has so often come across as 'sympathetic' rather than 'radical'.[48] For example, Everson and Joerges postulate that '[i]f legal critique is argued to encompass bodies of thought that challenge legal orthodoxies or fictions, the study of European law is full of critical legal thinkers'.[49] Their concern, however, is that the functionalism of EU law scholarship renders the call for critique 'hollow'.[50] This picture has recently become more complex, as we have witnessed a new surge of critical interventions in EU law. And if we accept the explanatory power of the crisis-critique nexus, this is not surprising since the intellectual coming of age for the current generation of EU law scholars took place in parallel with the EU's various, and seemingly formidable, crises.

In EU legal studies, a CLS perspective has been defended, for instance, by Perišin and Rodin as the editors of *The Transformation or Reconstitution of Europe: The Critical Legal Studies Perspective on the Role of the Courts in the European Union*. Rodin and Perišin invoke critical legal theory 'as a benchmark for an external critique of national legal rules, principles and concepts'.[51] For them, the value of the CLS critique lies in showing that a change of perspective can take place 'within the existing referential framework'.[52] But this vision of external critique resembles an internal critique of EU law insofar as it takes the CJEU's autonomy thesis as its starting point.[53] A different

[45] eg I Isailović, 'Introduction: Critical Legal Approaches in EU Law—Reflections on New Research Directions' (2024) 15 *Transnational Legal Theory* 493 and the other contributions in the same special issue.

[46] HW Micklitz, 'A European Advantage in Legal Scholarship' in R van Gestel et al (eds), *Rethinking Legal Scholarship A Transatlantic Dialogue* (Cambridge University Page, 2017) 275. For a similar observation, see also Shaw (n 3) 236.

[47] eg M Rasmussen, 'Revolutionizing European Law: A History of the Van Gend en Loos Judgment' (2014) 12 *International Journal of Constitutional Law* 136; P Lindseth, 'The Critical Promise of the New History of European Law' (2012) 21 *Contemporary European History* 457; and M Rasmussen, 'Towards a Legal History of European Law' (2021) 6 *European Papers* 923. For a methodological perspective, see also chapter 2 by Kaius Tuori in this book.

[48] Diez (n 44) 16.

[49] M Everson and C Joerges, 'Facticity as Validity: The Misplaced Revolutionary Praxis of European Law' in E Christodoulidis et al (eds), *Research Handbook on Critical Legal Theory* (Elgar, 2019) 423.

[50] ibid 423.

[51] S Rodin and T Perišin, 'Transformation or Reconstitution of Europe: The European Critical Legal Studies Perspective' in T Perišin and S Rodin (eds), *The Transformation or Reconstitution of Europe: The Critical Legal Studies Perspective on the Role of the Courts in the European Union* (Hart, 2018) 11.

[52] ibid 6 (and 10).

[53] Although Rodin and Perišin note that 'in terms of the CLS social agenda, EU law can be both a desired outcome and the object of severe criticism', their account of 'European critical legal thinking' is primarily used to uphold the autonomy of EU law vis-à-vis national legal systems. ibid 11.

view of the CLS-inspired external critique is offered by Caruso and Nicola, who argue that EU law is in need of 'critical rethinking'.[54] By external critique, they refer to 'the scholarly activity of highlighting the distributive stakes – and therefore the political and ideological dimensions – of legal disputes adjudicated by the CJEU'.[55] Caruso and Nicola accordingly posit that

> [p]rogressive scholars are best positioned to voice the inner limits of legal argumentation, to aid the Court in identifying gaps, conflicts and ambiguities in the law, and hopefully to promote distributive justice and inclusion as paramount goals of the EU legal system.[56]

But an unencumbered external critique of EU law reinforces the crisis of normative critique insofar as it fails to acknowledge the critic's own social embeddedness. Moreover, the elevation of progressive legal scholarship points to a set of deeper problems within the CLS-style critical legal theory. The idea of a 'fundamental contradiction' between formal law and social reality is central to the CLS critiques of liberal legalism.[57] From this starting point, law appears as a major force in the reproduction of 'human subordination and domination'.[58] But CLS scholars often have difficulties in formulating a theoretical framework that can account for this contradiction in social reality and law, and part of the problem is arguably 'a tendency to cite the theoretical origins of their positions in a very loose way'.[59] Examples include Kennedy's synthesis of structuralist, phenomenological, and neo-Marxist perspectives and Tushnet's fusion of semiology, phenomenology and Marxism.[60] However, from the perspective of this chapter, the issue is not so much the eclectic character of some CLS analyses. A more significant problem is the CLS's seemingly ambivalent relation to social theory.

For instance, Somek has noted that many CLS scholars 'take great pride in the fact that they have unremittingly abdicated any and all types of social theory'.[61] Douzinas and Gearey similarly observe that 'a general mistrust of the models of classical social and critical thought came to mark critical legal writing'.[62] A different version of this story is presented by Tushnet, who argues that the CLS movement can be viewed as a critique of social theory.[63] But Tushnet, too, admits that the lack of interest in social theory makes CLS 'ahistorical'.[64] By this, he means that '[i]nstead of having political positions flow from social theory, the dominant CLS project simply takes political positions'.[65] However, CLS scholars do not form a unified group in their approaches to social

[54] D Caruso and F Nicola, 'Legal Scholarship and External Critique in EU Law' in Perišin and Rodin (n 51) 224.

[55] ibid 226.

[56] ibid 239.

[57] eg D Kennedy, 'The Structure of Blackstone's Commentaries' (1979) 28 *Buffalo Law Review* 205, 211–12 and 213 about the 'fundamental contradiction' of law and of our social existence.

[58] A Hunt, 'The Theory of Critical Legal Studies' (1986) 6 *OJLS* 1, 43.

[59] ibid 23. See also, eg J Přibáň, 'Sharing the Paradigms? Critical Legal Studies and the Sociology of Law' in R Banakar and M Travers (eds), *An Introduction to Law and Social Theory* (Hart, 2002) 119.

[60] Hunt (n 58) 23. See also M Tushnet, 'Post-Realist Legal Scholarship' (1980) 15 *The Journal of the Society of Public Teachers of Law* 20, 31–32.

[61] A Somek, 'From Kennedy to Balkin: Introducing Critical Legal Studies from a Continental Perspective' (1994) 42 *University of Kansas Law Review* 759, 767.

[62] Douzinas and Gearey (n 42) 242.

[63] M Tushnet, 'Critical Legal Studies: An Introduction to Its Origins and Underpinnings' (1986) 36 *Journal of Legal Education* 505, 509.

[64] ibid 512.

[65] ibid 515. For a similar point, see also eg Přibáň (n 59) 129–30.

theory. While Kennedy's direct followers tend to be more wary of social theory, the CLS movement engaged with the phenomenological and existential reappropriations of Marxism.[66] Moreover, the British CLC has generally expressed more interest in 'wider social theory' than its American counterpart.[67]

Some argue that the CLS's 'legacy' could provide us with 'the parameters of a radical social theory of law'.[68] But it has been seen in this section that the CLS movement's engagement with social theory is ambiguous, to say the least. What is also concerning is that the idea of external critique remains largely unproblematised in the CLS-inspired studies of EU law. This does not mean that critical legal theory could not be fruitfully deployed by EU law scholars. The CLS insights about law's intertwinement with structural power can make a significant contribution to the development of, for example, a critical theory of EU anti-discrimination and equality law, feminist critiques of EU law, as well as to the emerging field of decolonisation in EU legal studies.[69] But it is important to recognise that critical legal theory tends to overlook the deeper crisis of normative critique in ways that reduce its capacity to support the critical project in EU law. As will be seen in the next section, the Frankfurt-style critical theory of society provides a stronger basis for developing a critical theory of EU law because it forces us to more clearly articulate and defend social-theoretic choices that inform the critique of EU law.

IV. Now's the Time: Developing a Critical Theory of EU Law in the Post-Crisis Legal Landscape

Critical legal theory cannot alone sustain the critical project in EU law insofar as it disregards the importance of social theory for the critique of law. Law is a central category in social theory, where it can be viewed as a source of both social integration and conflict. But social theory also forms 'the indispensable setting for any credible legal theory'.[70] In EU law, the social is often depicted as a self-explanatory counter-force for the economic. As the political economy critiques of EU law show, the danger is that both the social and the economic thereby become instruments for depoliticisation. At the same time, the renewed interest in the social in EU legal studies highlights 'EU law's embeddedness in European societies'[71] and its 'disconnect with social reality'.[72] But there is no consensus on 'what society really is, how it

[66] On these diverging tendencies, see, eg, F Munger and C Seron, 'Critical Legal Studies versus Critical Legal Theory: A Comment on Method' (1984) 6 *Law & Policy* 257, 264-65.

[67] Douzinas and Gearey (n 42) 241. However, instead of the Frankfurt School critical theory, the CLC primarily drew inspiration from French social theory (eg Foucault, Derrida, and Lacan). ibid 242.

[68] S Moyn, 'Reconstructing Critical Legal Studies' (2024) 134 *Yale Law Journal* 77, 90 and 77.

[69] On how to bridge the gap between critical legal and social theory, see also chapter 6 by Rebecca Zahn and Meemi Matero, chapter 7 by Raphaële Xenidis, chapter 8 by Barbara Havelková, chapter 9 by Susanna Lindroos-Hovinheimo, chapter 10 by Luigi Lonardo, and chapter 11 by Alezini Loxa in this book.

[70] Moyn (n 68) 84.

[71] Vauchez (n 8) 135.

[72] L Azoulai, 'Reconnecting EU Legal Studies to European Societies' (*Verfassungsblog*, 19 March 2024), available at https://verfassungsblog.de/reconnecting-eu-legal-studies-to-european-societies/. See also L Azoulai, 'The Turn to European Society and its Problems: Connecting EU Law and Social Theory' (EUI LAW Working Paper 2025/09).

ought to be and whether it actually exists at all'.[73] This is why critical theorists warn against 'the naturalization of the category of the social'.[74] The discussion on the social reality of EU law must similarly avoid uncritical reliance on the concept of the social. The critical theory of society illuminates both society's 'structural conditions' and its 'particular way of being contingent'.[75] As such, it helps to illustrate what a more developed critical theory of EU law would look like.

First, this section will draw on the Frankfurt School critical theory of society to explain why the Marxist critique of political economy should be replaced with a more holistic critique of capitalist society in EU law. This analysis, which invites us to reconsider the meaning and role of emancipation in the critical project, contests the way in which the social question is often framed in critical EU law scholarship (section IV.A.). Second, the Frankfurt School critical theory is relevant to EU legal studies because it seems to offer a much-needed alternative to the internal and external critiques of EU law. In critical theory, recourse to immanent critique enables the critical project when no source of normativity is fully shielded from the logic of capitalism. But a closer look at the historical faultlines of the Frankfurt School shows that immanent social critique often reaps either negation or universalism, both of which wither the critical project. While critical theorists therefore fail to fully resolve the crisis of normative critique, reframing critique as a form of political practice helps them to navigate this crisis. This, however, means that critical theory also summons us to reconsider the political question in the critique of EU law (section IV.B).

A. Reconsidering the Social Question: From the Critique of Political Economy Towards a Critique of Capitalist Society in EU Law

The EU constitutes without doubt 'a political economy phenomenon'.[76] Therefore, it is logical that the political economy analyses of law have gained more space in EU legal studies in the aftermath of the Euro-zone crisis.[77] Both the traditional critique of political economy and the more recent Law and Political Economy (LPE) scholarship call into question rigid boundaries between the economic, the political, and the social. As such, they contribute to the emerging critical theory of EU law. But the current debates on the political economy of EU law leave many important questions unexplored. It is relatively uncontroversial that political economy analyses view 'the practices of social production

[73] Cordero (n 16) 155.

[74] ibid 47. See also TW Adorno, 'Society' in SE Bronner and D MacKay Kellner (eds), *Critical Theory and Society A Reader* (Routledge, 1989) 269 (and 267) [1966, in German].

[75] S Müller-Doohm, 'The Critical Theory of Society as Reflexive Sociology' in T Huhn (ed), *The Cambridge Companion to Adorno* (Cambridge University Press, 2006) 281–82.

[76] eg B Rosamond, 'Critical Political Economy and European Integration' in Bigo et al (n 44) 155.

[77] See, eg, I Kampourakis, 'Bound by the Economic Constitution: Notes for "Law and Political Economy" in Europe' (2021) 1 *Journal of Law and Political Economy* 301 and the 'Transformative Law of Political Economy in Europe' special issue in (2022) 1 *European Law Open* 749. See also chapter 4 by Marco Goldoni in this book.

and reproduction' as the primary context in which law is studied.[78] However, the role they assign to law varies significantly. While many contemporary LPE scholars rely on the transformative potential of law, the more orthodox Marxist critiques of political economy maintain that the law takes a 'commodity form' in capitalist societies, thus lacking any autonomous transformative potential.[79] This same ambivalence over the role of law resurfaces in the political economy analyses of EU law.

While one branch of LPE scholarship in EU legal studies invokes the concept of political economy without properly addressing its relationship to the Marxist critique of political economy, the other branch endorses the Marxist position seemingly uncritically. If we agreed with Marxist EU law scholars that '[a] Marxist approach . . . presupposes a break with capitalism and imperialism and, hence, with EU law as a social form',[80] the question about the adequacy of the Marxist or neo-Marxist alternative becomes pressing. But this question does not seem to trouble scholars who posit that 'the tools of Marxist analysis are . . . essential for understanding EU law and, ultimately, for assessing and transforming the "European Project" in an emancipatory direction that would truly work to the benefit of all'.[81] As this section will next demonstrate, this optimism can be contrasted with how the early Frankfurt School critical theorists sought to reappropriate the Marxist critique of political economy in late capitalist societies.

Marxist EU law scholars want to show how '[the] existing critical approaches to EU law . . . could be developed in a materialist direction'.[82] But they fail to critically interrogate the concept of materialism. Materialism does not automatically generate 'an emancipatory kind of thinking'.[83] This more prudent approach to the question of emancipation distinguishes the Frankfurt School critical theory from orthodox Marxism.[84] Critical theorists also warn that Marxist historical materialism often has a flavour of 'quasi-metaphysical determinism' in it.[85] Max Horkheimer, the founder of the Frankfurt School critical theory, explicitly rejected 'badly understood Marx', by which he refers to the view that 'the economy, material being, is the only true reality; the human psyche as well as law, art, and philosophy are purely derivative and mere reflections of it'.[86]

[78] E Christodoulidis, 'Critical Theory and the Law: Reflections on Origins, Trajectories and Conjunctures' in Christodoulidis et al (n 49) 22.

[79] eg E Pashukanis, *The General Theory of Law and Marxism* (Routledge, 2001 [1924, in Russian]). However, Marx's own analysis of law and legal theory remained unfinished. Moreover, within the tradition of historical materialism, eg Antonio Gramsci's argument of law as a historical force that helps to maintain the cultural hegemony of the dominant classes refuses to view law as a mere derivative of the economic base. For discussion, see, eg, AC Cutler, 'Gramsci, Law, and the Culture of Global Capitalism' (2005) 8 *Critical Review of International Social and Political Philosophy* 527, 530.

[80] R Knox et al, 'Capitalism, Imperialism and European Union Law: Towards a Marxist Approach' (2025) 4 *European Law Open* 290, 326. This conclusion is rooted in their endorsement of Pashukanis's understanding of the relationship between law and commodity form. ibid 325 and 317.

[81] Knox et al, 'Introduction: Symposium on Marxist Approaches to EU Law' (2025) 4 *European Law Open* 286, 287. For a Marxist perspective on the historical development of EU law, see also E Nanopoulos, 'From Class-Based Project to Imperial Formation: European Union Law and the Reconstruction of Europe' in P O'Connell and U Özsu (eds), *Research Handbook on Law and Marxism* (Elgar, 2021).

[82] Knox et al (n 80) 315.

[83] S Jarvis, 'Adorno, Marx, Materialism' in Huhn (n 75) 81.

[84] RJ Antonio, 'Immanent Critique as the Core of Critical Theory: Its Origins and Developments in Hegel, Marx and Contemporary Thought' (1981) 32 *The British Journal of Sociology* 330, 337.

[85] ibid 337.

[86] M Horkheimer, 'The State of Contemporary Social Philosophy and the Tasks of an Institute for Social Research' in Bronner and MacKay Kellner (n 74) ([1931, in German]) 34.

Horkheimer accordingly distinguished 'simple' and 'reductive' materialism from 'critical' materialism.[87] The core of Horkheimer's critical materialism is that it 'always understands thinking to be the thinking of particular men within a particular period of time'.[88] Against this background, Horkheimer argued that many seemingly materialist approaches include idealist 'traits', which undermine the materialist claim.[89] These same tensions between materialism and idealism and between different forms of materialism resurface in the critique of EU law.

Thus, it needs to be clarified what kind of materialism informs the critical project in EU law. How we answer this question has implications for what can be said about agency, subjectivity, society, and, also, the law. In contrast to 'metaphysical' or 'ontological' materialism, critical materialism holds that 'lived social realities' can simultaneously have both material and ideal dimensions.[90] It is also useful to bear in mind that the quest for materialism exists outside the strictly Marxist discourse. In EU law, a broader account of materialism has recently been adopted, for instance, by Floris de Witte, who (with reference to Bruno Latour) uses the term 'materiality' to refer to 'the material world', understood as 'the biophysical, spatial, infrastructural, or cultural reality'.[91] The materialist starting point is arguably important because it recognises '*both* law's normative expectations of reality *and* the actual reality'.[92] De Witte observes that 'this focus on the socio-material contingency in EU law presupposes a methodological shift towards . . . work that understands EU law and governance at an experiential level: empirical work, ethnographic studies, cultural or sociological studies'.[93] However, while being critical of the transformative potential of EU law, De Witte's materialism does not reduce the law to the logic of capitalism alone.

The choice between metaphysical and critical materialism is important to the emerging critical theory of EU law because the critical project under critical materialism is not reducible to a mere critique of political economy. Instead, political economy, cultural analysis, and social psychology were all central to Horkheimer's vision of critical interdisciplinary materialism.[94] As Postone notes, a distributive analysis alone cannot grasp 'the contradictory character of the social totality'.[95] It is arguable that Marx himself never reduced the problem of capitalism to 'any single positive sphere of society'.[96] Many

[87] F Rush, 'The Conceptual Foundations of Early Critical Theory' in F Rush (ed), *The Cambridge Companion to Critical Theory* (Cambridge University Press, 2006) 11.

[88] M Horkheimer, 'Materialism and Metaphysics' in M Horkheimer, *Critical Theory: Selected Essays* (Continuum, 1975, translated by M O'Connell and others [1933, in German]) 32. As Horkheimer also notes, critical materialism 'challenges every claim to the autonomy of thought'. ibid 32.

[89] ibid 33.

[90] S Lettow, 'Turning the Turn: New Materialism, Historical Materialism and Critical Theory' (2017) 140 *Thesis Eleven* 106, 114–15.

[91] F de Witte, 'Is this Europe? EU Law's Rendering of European Society' (2025) 4 *European Law Open* 674, 680.

[92] ibid 680. For a similar argument in relation to the concept of EU law, see PJ Neuvonen, 'The Concept of EU Law: A Realist Reappraisal' (2026) 27 *German Law Journal* (advance online publication doi: 10.1017/glj.2026.10218).

[93] De Witte (n 91) 681.

[94] Horkheimer (n 86) 33–34. For discussion, see, eg, D Strecker, 'The Architecture of Social Critique: Three Models of Ideology Critique and the Legacy of the Frankfurt School' in HF Dahms (ed), *No Social Science Without Critical Theory* (Emerald Publishing, 2008) 91.

[95] M Postone, 'Critique, State, and Economy' in Rush (n 87) 188 (and 167–69 and 176–77).

[96] A Chari, *A Political Economy of the Senses Neoliberalism, Reification, Critique* (Columbia University Press, 2015) 106.

contemporary political economy critiques of law therefore emphasise that the commodity exchange also produces 'abstract forms of social domination'.[97] From this perspective, it can be argued that the political economy analysis of law does not need to rank the economic over the social.[98] In EU law, for example, Isailović's analysis of the political economy of gender and Ashiagbor's emphasis on 'the larger political economy' in social and employment law reflect this broader understanding of political economy.[99]

But it is important to notice that the political economy critiques of law need critical social theory to substantiate this broad 'social' account of political economy. The relationship between 'political economy', 'social life' and 'subjectivity' is a central theme in the Frankfurt School critical theory.[100] Moreover, the Frankfurt School's wrestle with 'Marxist categories'[101] reveals challenges that also face the political economy critiques of EU law. While they did not succeed in achieving all the goals that critical interdisciplinary materialism set for the critical project,[102] the early Frankfurt School critical theorists can be credited for their attempt 'to reformulate Marxian theory in view of the changed relations between politics, economics, and culture in our societies'.[103] The traditional Marxist critique of political economy presumes 'the existence (actual or potential) of a class with a general interest in emancipation', whereas the Frankfurt School critical theory 'transforms this *a priori* into the most important empirical/historical issue within Marxism'.[104] Their problematisation of both the social totality and the purely distributive focus of orthodox Marxism should also be of interest to the critical theory of EU law. Here the important point is that critical theorists are able to identify forms of domination that the more traditional critique of political economy misses. This can be illustrated by taking a closer look at the critique of emancipation in EU legal studies.

It is well established that emancipation provides 'an interesting lens through which to look at projects of regional integration'.[105] Moreover, it is arguable that emancipation as 'the genus of which democracy, solidarity and social justice are species' underlies the EU's various 'deficits'.[106] As has been seen above in this chapter, emancipation is also the goal of critical praxis in the critical theory of society. It can even be argued that a central aim of the Frankfurt School critical theory was 'to preserve Marxism's founding emancipatory cognitive interest . . . by rethinking the project of emancipation within

[97] eg N Tzouvala, 'International Law and (the Critique of) Political Economy' (2022) 121 *The South Atlantic Quarterly* 297, 310 and 311.

[98] eg C Blalock, 'Introduction: Law and the Critique of Capitalism' (2022) 121 *The South Atlantic Quarterly* 223, 229.

[99] I Isailović, 'Gender in Political Economy and EU Law' (2024) 15 *Transnational Legal Theory* 525, 527 and D Ashiagbor, 'Decentring Europe in EU Social Law Scholarship' (2023) 2 *European Law Open* 479, 481.

[100] Chari (n 96) 63 (and 95).

[101] RJ Antonio, 'The Origin, Development, and Contemporary Status of Critical Theory' (1983) 24 *The Sociological Quarterly* 325, 330 (with reference to Leo Lowenthal in 'The Origins of Critical Theory: An Interview with Leo Lowenthal' (1981) *Telos* 141, 147).

[102] For discussion, see, eg, Antonio (n 101) 348 and Postone (n 95) 188–89 and Strecker (n 94) 93–94.

[103] S Benhabib, *Critique, Norm and Utopia A Study of the Foundations of Critical Theory* (Columbia University Press, 1986) 347.

[104] Antonio (n 101) 342.

[105] F de Witte, 'Integrating the Subject: Narratives of Emancipation in Regionalism' (2019) *30 European Journal of International Law* 257, 257.

[106] A Somek, 'The Individualisation of Liberty: Europe's Move from Emancipation to Empowerment' (2013) 4 *Transnational Legal Theory* 258, 265.

the historical contexts where it must be achieved'.[107] From this perspective, emancipation came to be seen above all as decommodification.[108] But Georg (György) Lukács's critique of reification also played an important role in the early Frankfurt School critical theory.[109] The reification critique shifted the focus of the critical project to how 'subjects in capitalist society naturalize their social world'.[110] As such, it opened the door for a more complex understanding of both domination and emancipation in capitalist societies. This is relevant to the critique of EU law because the idea of emancipation as decommodification often dominates the discussion on the social question in critical EU law scholarship.

In EU legal studies, Somek, in particular, has linked the social question to emancipation by arguing that an 'ambitious' answer to the 'social question' aims at 'emancipation'.[111] Somek defines emancipation as 'a mode of rising above markets that involves establishing collective control'.[112] Against this background, he warns that the project of European integration favours 'empowerment', understood as 'an individualised and entrepreneurial form of liberation', over emancipation.[113] For Somek, the EU's focus on empowerment essentially 'reverses' the Marxist view of human emancipation.[114] This contrast between emancipation and empowerment depicts 'discrete and context-specific efforts at leveling power asymmetries' as an insufficient substitute for a more radical 'redistribution of power'.[115] While Somek's critique of transnational economic liberalism is convincing, his analysis of the social question leaves the idea a of social totality largely unproblematised. Somek briefly refers to '[e]mancipation from traditional social powers',[116] but this point is not properly developed in his analysis.

A different account of 'the emancipatory potential of EU law' is presented by De Witte, who defines emancipation as 'the release from domination in the individual's private process of discovering her authentic and innermost hopes, fears, and aspirations; and the release from domination in the individual's (public) realisation of those hopes, fears or aspirations'.[117] De Witte does note in this context that '[h]istorically . . . emancipation can be understood to resist the domination of *economic* (market) institutions' and that 'economic emancipation attempts to protect the individual from

[107] Antonio (n 101) 342.

[108] C Calhoun, *Critical Social Theory – Culture, History, and the Challenge of Difference* (Blackwell, 1995) 15. On Marx's defetishising critique, see K Marx, *Capital, Volume 1* (Penguin Books, 2004 [1867, in German], translated by B Fowkes) ch 1.

[109] G Lukács, *History and Class Consciousness: Studies in Marxist Dialectics* (MIT Press, 1971 [1923, in German]).

[110] Chari (n 96) 122 and 123. For an insightful application of the reification critique to EU law, see P Linden-Retek, *Postnational Constitutionalism Europe and the Time of Law* (Oxford University Press, 2023) ch 3.

[111] A Somek, 'The Social Question in a Transnational Context' (LEQS Working Paper No 39/2011 4 and 22). Somek distinguishes between 'the merely modest ("taking care of the needy")' and the more 'ambitious ("extricating life from the market")' approaches to the social question. ibid 6. Somek also distinguishes 'decommodification' from 'full liberation'. ibid 19. But this latter distinction is not properly developed.

[112] Somek (n 106) 258.

[113] ibid 258.

[114] ibid 277 and 281. Somek explains that his discussion on emancipation 'reflect[s] a certain, albeit uncertain, Marxist sensibility'. ibid 262.

[115] ibid 277.

[116] ibid 272.

[117] F de Witte, 'Emancipation through Law?' in L Azoulai et al (eds), *Constructing the Person in EU Law: Rights, Roles, Identities* (Hart, 2016).

commodification'.[118] But his analysis is more focused on the individual's self-realisation – a choice that may be understandable since it tries to determine whether EU law can claim emancipatory potential.[119] Moreover, although De Witte's 2019 article links emancipation to subject-formation, it does not properly address the question about the constitution of the emancipatory subject.[120] The idea of emancipation as the capacity to self-realisation effaces the relational dimension of subject-formation,[121] thus making it vulnerable to the charge that 'the Union . . . has put the individual at the centre'.[122]

A more nuanced understanding of social domination in critical theory calls into question the simple account of emancipation as mere decommodification as well as the more individualistic view of emancipation as self-realisation. This means that critical theory also challenges the explanatory power of a simple economy-society dualism.[123] Nancy Fraser, a prominent contemporary Frankfurt School theorist, emphasises that 'what commodification erodes is not always worth defending'.[124] Instead, she argues for an emancipatory project that would tackle 'domination rooted in both economy and society'.[125] This approach presents the crisis of capitalism as 'a multifaceted historical process, as much social, political, and ecological as economic'.[126] As an alternative to Polanyi's famous 'double movement',[127] Fraser's 'triple movement' reveals the 'normative ambivalence' of both social protection and marketisation.[128] Fraser's concern is that Polanyi overlooks a wide range of 'social struggles' and 'emancipatory movements' that rightly challenge the 'hierarchical, exclusionary, [and] communitarian understandings of social protection'.[129] But the 'triple movement' also seeks to 'complicate the project of emancipation' by resisting its 'marketizing tendencies'.[130] A similar 'triangulation'[131]

[118] ibid. For a more recent discussion on commodification in EU legal studies, see, eg, T Fia and IJ Murray, 'Commodification and EU Law: A Genealogy' (2023) 2 *European Law Open* 372 and the other contributions in the same special issue.

[119] In brief, De Witte doubts that the EU could be viewed as 'an emancipatory project', but he does not altogether reject the possibility that EU law could be conceived as 'an instrument for emancipation'. ibid.

[120] De Witte (n 105).

[121] On the process of subject-formation in EU law, see, eg, PJ Neuvonen, 'Retrieving the "Subject" of European Integration' (2019) 25 *European Law Journal* 6.

[122] Somek (n 106) 272.

[123] For discussion, see, eg, Fraser and Jaeggi (n 35) 138, 143–44 and 148–49.

[124] N Fraser, 'Can Society be Commodities all the Way Down? Post-Polanyian Reflections on Capitalist Crisis' (2014) 43 *Economy and Society* 541, 548.

[125] N Fraser, 'Marketization, Social Protection, Emancipation: Toward a Neo-Polanyian Conception of Capitalist Crisis' in C Calhoun and G Derluguian (eds), *Business as Usual: The Roots of the Global Financial Meltdown* (NYU Press, 2011) 140 (and 145).

[126] ibid 143. See also Fraser and Jaeggi (n 35) 144 for a reference to 'a single critical theory of capitalism, viewed as an institutionalized social order'.

[127] The tension between marketisation and social protection is a central theme in K Polanyi, *The Great Transformation: The Political and Economic Origins of Our Time* (Penguin Books, 2024 [1944]). In EU law, see, eg, C Joerges, 'Why European legal scholarship should become aware of Karl Polanyi: *The Great Transformation* and the integration project' (2022) 1 *European Law Open* 1067.

[128] N Fraser, 'A Triple Movement? Parsing the Politics of Crisis after Polanyi' (2013) *New Left Review* 119, 129. For discussion on the 'normative ambivalence', see also, Chari (n 96) 68.

[129] Fraser (n 128) 127 and 131. Examples that Fraser offers include 'anti-racism, anti-imperialism, anti-war, the New Left, second-wave feminism, LGBT liberation, [and] multiculturalism'. ibid 127. Fraser's concept of 'emancipation' overlaps with Somek's usage of 'empowerment', whereas Somek's concept of 'emancipation' is mainly confined to what Fraser means by traditional 'social protection'.

[130] ibid 130-31. Fraser expresses the concern that 'emancipation's ambivalence has been resolved in recent years in favour of marketization'. ibid 130.

[131] Chari (n 96) 86.

of emancipation is arguably needed when the social question is discussed in EU law. It would provide us with a richer account of emancipation as the basis of critique.

From the perspective of disadvantaged social groups and minorities, it is clear that genuine struggles for emancipation can be fought against 'traditional social powers'. The failure to recognise this would mean that the critique of EU law oversimplifies the social-historical struggles for emancipation. But contemporary critical theorists also problematise emancipation at a more foundational level. The concept of emancipation is closely linked to the nineteenth century philosophy of history, in general, and to the 'ideas of progress', in particular.[132] As Allen notes, this means that it may easily become 'entangled with insufficiently problematized assumptions about the developmental superiority of European or Western modernity, hence, with informally imperialist structures of domination'.[133] From this perspective, the crucial question facing the critical project is 'What questions, debates, and perspectives are associated with the concept [of emancipation], and what aspects of critique and social change does it help to articulate – or, indeed, foreclose?'.[134] Similarly, critical EU law scholars must more directly confront the intellectual history of emancipation and other concepts that inform the critique of EU law.

B. Reconsidering the Political Question: Which Way Forward for the Depoliticisation Critiques of EU Law?

The controversy over the meaning and role of emancipation in the critical project manifests the deeper crisis of normative critique that underlies the critique of EU law. It has been seen above in this chapter that neither internal nor external critiques of EU law offer a sufficient solution to this crisis. The internal critiques of EU law uncritically assume the normativity of EU law, including the CJEU's autonomy thesis. The external critiques of EU law offer a radical critique of EU law without properly addressing their own social embeddedness. In the critical theory of society, immanent critique is presented as a 'mediating position' between internal and external forms of critique.[135] Therefore, this section will next consider whether immanent critique could resolve the crisis of critique in EU law.[136] This inquiry shows that critical theorists often circumvent the limits of immanent critique with recourse to either 'pure negation'[137] or universalism, and each solution comes with its own problems. But it will also be seen that critical theory can try to navigate these issues by reframing critique as a form of political practice. A closer look at how critical theorists

[132] S Lettow, 'Emancipation: Rethinking Subjectivity, Power, and Change' (2015) 30 *Hypatia* 501, 503 and 504.

[133] A Allen, 'Emancipation without Utopia: Subjection, Modernity, and the Normative Claims of Feminist Critical Theory' (2015) 30 *Hypatia* 513, 520 (and 521).

[134] Lettow (n 132) 503.

[135] Jaeggi (n 19) 210.

[136] On the *need* of immanent critique in EU legal studies, see PJ Neuvonen, 'A Revised Democratic Critique of EU (Citizenship) Law: From Relative Homogeneity to Political Judgment' (2020) 21 *German Law Journal* 867, 882 and Neuvonen (n 1) 73–74. On the *possibility* of immanent critique in EU law, see also the Epilogue by Sarah Glaser, Luca Tenreira, and Jacob van de Beeten in this book.

[137] RA Gorman, 'Critical Conundrums – Logic and Politics in Frankfurt Critical Theory Prior to the Linguistic Turn' in Dahms (n 94) 72.

understand the political question in this context problematises the essentialist concept of the political in the depoliticisation critiques of EU law.

Immanent critique can be broadly defined as 'the evaluation of society according to criteria that are in some sense contained within it, rather that imposed from without'.[138] In critical theory, critique's immanence is meant to explain, first, how the emancipatory critical potential can develop and survive under deeply flawed social conditions and, second, how such critique can avoid making universalist validity claims.[139] The quest for immanent critique forms part of the larger 'transformation' of critique that was initiated in social theory by Hegel.[140] As Benhabib notes, the post-Marxist understanding of immanent critique agrees with Hegel that 'the given is not a mere fact, that to understand it to be actuality is also to criticize it by showing what it could be but is not' and that this is based on 'criteria . . . by which the object or phenomenon judges itself'.[141] Immanent critique seeks to uncover the 'unrecognized possibilities' that are embedded in the social reality.[142] Therefore, immanence must not be confused with immediacy (ie direct or unmediated access to the object). Beyond this starting point, however, opinions diverge on what immanent social critique actually entails.

Weak forms of immanent critique only criticise social reality from a historical or genealogical perspective.[143] As such, they are not easily distinguishable from internal social critique, which seeks to evaluate 'how well a society measures up to its own standards'.[144] In contrast to this, stronger versions of immanent critique maintain that norms themselves can be both internally and implicitly contradictory. This point is captured, for instance, in Jaeggi's statement that 'immanent criticism does not only take aim at a contradiction between norm and reality – namely, the fact that norms are not realized in reality; rather, it is directed at the *internal contradictoriness* of reality and its constitutive norms'.[145] This means that a strong immanent critique of EU law cannot just focus on the perceived conflict between social reality and the norms of EU law (eg the values expressed in Article 2 of the Treaty on European Union). Instead, it will also need to explore the internal contradictions within these norms and values to better understand where the immanent critical potential might lie in EU law.

Immanent critique normally proceeds from a 'moment of crisis' that is internal to a particular social formation.[146] But a strong version of immanent critique can also criticise social formations and forms of life for failing 'to perceive the crisis experiences to which they are exposed in appropriate ways'.[147] The immanent critical potential of

[138] S Diehl, 'Why Immanent Critique?' (2022) 30 *European Journal of Philosophy* 676, 677.

[139] A close link often emerges between universalism and essentialism when the object's essential identity or characteristics are depicted as the source of a universalist validity claim.

[140] Jaeggi (n 19) 191.

[141] Benhabib (n 103) 35 and 33. However, it remains controversial whether Marx's historical materialism constitutes a genuinely immanent critique of society. See, eg, ibid 34 and 42 and A Buchwalter, 'Hegel, Marx, and the Concept of Immanent Critique' (1991) 29 *Journal of the History of Philosophy* 253, 269–70.

[142] Calhoun (n 108) 23.

[143] Antonio (n 84) 338.

[144] Diehl (n 138) 678. See, eg, M Walzer, *Interpretation and Social Criticism, The Tanner Lectures on Human Values* (Harvard University Press, 1987/1993) 53–56 on the idea of internal social criticism.

[145] Jaeggi (n 19) 201. For Jaeggi, this means that immanent critique is by nature 'transformative' rather than 'reconstructive'. ibid 203.

[146] ibid 202 (and 201).

[147] ibid 315.

crisis is therefore more 'structural' than 'substantive'.[148] That is, it focuses on how crises unsettle the 'conditions of possibility' for a particular social formation,[149] such as the EU. Moreover, a relevant crisis can also be 'latent'.[150] A project of strong immanent critique would therefore need to consider which crisis experiences remain currently unrecognised in EU law. This, however, brings us back to my earlier point that crises and crises experiences are hardly ever objective facts, and this is also true in the EU.[151] As Jaeggi notes, 'the normative point of reference' in immanent critique remains ambivalent because there is no consensus over what amounts to a relevant 'practical contradiction or crisis'.[152] This same challenge is captured in Diehl's observation that 'whether social criticism meets the immanence constraint depends on who receives it'.[153]

Because the standards of critique must ultimately be accepted by the subjects of criticised social practices,[154] the project of immanent critique can only exist in plural in EU legal studies. After all, even the same material conditions and contradictions are experienced differently by different social groups within the EU. This, however, does not mean that the project of immanent critique should renounce theory. On the contrary, critical theory is needed if we agree with Jaeggi that 'the crisis . . . as a problem lying in the social relations . . . must always be analyzed and uncovered in the first place at the theoretical level'.[155] The idea of immanent critique promises to discover 'higher-order problems'[156] that require more attention in EU legal studies. But an immanent critique of EU law is always also 'a self-grounding process' where the critical standards are found through critical engagement.[157] This dynamism means that the critical project is needed in EU legal studies to determine the standards against which EU law is evaluated, and not just to apply some pre-existing normative standard.

Although immanent critique provides an important alternative to the internal and external forms of critique, it has also been called into question from within the critical theory of society. In practice, many critical theorists lost their faith in immanent critique when they first had lost faith in the Hegelian idea of 'historically effective reason'.[158] While TW Adorno reframed immanent critique as 'negative dialectics',[159] Jürgen Habermas as the leading second-generation Frankfurt theorist distanced himself from the idea of immanent critique by replacing the Marxist paradigm with a theory of communicative action.[160] Habermas's intersubjective paradigm ultimately locates

[148] Fraser and Jaeggi (n 35) 154.
[149] ibid 155.
[150] ibid 160 and 161.
[151] Section II of this chapter.
[152] Jaeggi (n 19) 211.
[153] Diehl (n 138) 688.
[154] ibid 685. See also, eg, A Procyshyn, 'The Conditions of Immanent Critique' (2022) 23 *Critical Horizons* 22, 33 and 38.
[155] Jaeggi (n 19) 192.
[156] ibid 209.
[157] ibid 193 (and 212).
[158] See, eg, A Honneth, 'A Social Pathology of Reason: On the Intellectual Legacy of Critical Theory' in A Honneth, *Pathologies of Reason On the Legacy of Critical Theory* (Columbia University Press, 2009, translated by J Ingram) 20 (and 31–33).
[159] TW Adorno, *Negative Dialectics* (Continuum 1973 [1966, in German], translated by EB Ashton). Although Adorno's negative dialectics could disturb identity thinking in philosophy and art, it could not do so in the social and political field. For discussion, see, eg, Chari (n 96) 154 and Benhabib (n 103) 220–22.
[160] J Habermas, 'The Tasks of a Critical Theory of Society' in Bronner and MacKay Kellner (n 74) 305.

the critical potential in how communicative practices are justified discursively.[161] This, however, had dramatic implications for the critical project. First, Habermas's version of critical theory 'proceeds reconstructively, that is, unhistorically'.[162] Second, he explicitly states that 'theory developed in this way can no longer start by examining concrete ideals immanent in traditional forms of life'.[163] Habermas wanted to rescue the critical project from excessive pessimism.[164] But he did so by endorsing a universalist position that critical theorists generally find problematic.[165]

These historical faultlines of the Frankfurt School critical theory are important for this chapter because they illustrate that the project of immanent social critique is often prone to either negation or universalism. In both cases, the crisis of normative critique remains unresolved because critique's immanent basis is effectively dismantled.[166] But critical theorists can try to navigate this crisis by framing critique as a form of political practice. The Frankfurt School critical theory has sometimes been criticised for diluting Marx's vision of critical praxis.[167] But the meaning of critical praxis can be understood in more than one way in critical theory.[168] For instance, Chambers highlights that 'the relationship between early Critical Theory and politics is complicated by its own attempt to forge a new relationship between theory and practice'.[169] From this starting point, it can be argued that 'theory *does* something in the world – that it is political in and of itself'.[170] However, as Chambers also notes, this may call for a revised understanding of the political.[171] Critical theorists do not view the 'political' as a mere synonym for 'politicised'.[172] Instead, the argument of critique as a form of political practice usually goes hand in hand with a detailed analysis of the concept of the political. In result, the focus of the critical project shifts from the justification of normative 'validity claims' to what the conditions for meaningful political action are.[173] I will therefore conclude this section by showing how critical theory can also reopen the political question in the critique of EU law.

[161] J Habermas, *Between Facts and Norms Contributions to a Discourse Theory of Law and Democracy* (MIT Press, 1996, translated by W Rehg). For discussion, see, eg, C Browne, *Critical Social Theory* (Sage, 2017) 6.

[162] Habermas (n 160) 296.

[163] ibid 296.

[164] For discussion, see, eg, Cordero (n 16) 67 and Antonio (n 101) 335 and 336 (with reference to J Habermas, *Communication and the Evolution of Society* (Beacon Press, 1979, translated by T McCarthy).

[165] For instance, Kompridis argues that Habermas's universalism 'produced a split between new and old critical theory so deep that the identity and the future of critical theory are at risk'. N Kompridis, *Critique and Disclosure: Critical Theory between Past and Future* (MIT Press, 2006) 17. A related concern is that Habermas's recourse to 'independent normative criteria', accompanied with his 'procedural' understanding of democracy, reduces critical theory to a liberal theory of justice. See, eg, S Chambers, 'The Politics of Critical Theory' in Rush (n 87) 231 and 237 and Browne (n 161) 18.

[166] However, in contemporary critical theory, eg Rahel Jaeggi's critique of 'forms of life' offers an alternative account of immanent social critique. Jaeggi (n 19).

[167] eg G Therborn, 'The Frankfurt School' (1970) *New Left Review* 67, 69–82. For more discussion, see also, eg, Antonio (n 101) 342.

[168] See also section II of this chapter.

[169] Chambers (n 165) 220.

[170] ibid 222.

[171] ibid 220.

[172] eg L Zerilli, 'Critique as a Political Practice of Freedom' in D Fassin and BE Harcourt (eds), *A Time for Critique* (Columbia University Press, 2019) 48.

[173] eg L Zerilli, 'Truth and Politics' (2006) 9 *Theory & Event*, section 10.

The so-called depoliticisation critiques of EU law hold that legal integration has detrimental effects on democratic politics in the Member States.[174] The strength of depoliticisation critiques ultimately depends on their concept of democracy and the political.[175] Therefore, it is surprising how little these critiques often say in support of their preferred concept of the political. Leaving the concept of the political unproblematised, adds an essentialist and ahistorical tint to the depoliticisation critiques.[176] A well-known example of an essentialist concept of the political is Carl Schmitt's argument that '[t]he specific political distinction to which political actions and motives can be reduced is that between friend and enemy'.[177] A Schmittian 'political entity' is 'sovereign', 'authoritative' and 'unified' because it must hold the capacity to decide over the friend-enemy distinction and, in extreme cases, 'to fight' the enemy.[178] Therefore, it is logical that Schmitt views the state as 'the decisive political entity'.[179] While direct references to Schmitt are not common in EU legal studies, the depoliticisation critiques often depict the state as something inherently more political than any form of transnational cooperation. This is understandable insofar as the focus lies in the EU's current democratic deficit. But a Schmittian view of the state as the 'decisive political entity' would explain why some depoliticisation critiques show so little interest in resolving the EU's democratic deficit.

Critical theory can help us to see, first, that endorsing an essentialist (statist) concept of the political is not the only way to develop the depoliticisation critique of EU law and, second, that the focus and outcomes of critique look different if the underlying concept of the political changes. Both critical feminist and radical democratic theories have tried to rescue Schmitt's antagonistic view of the political from its essentialist traits. While these theories share Schmitt's animosity towards political liberalism, they call into question his ideas of 'the sovereign' and a 'unified' people as preconditions for meaningful political action. Instead, the political question is redefined as the question of how our political practices can resist 'the ensemblistic-identitary logic which denies the contingency of human action and thus freedom'.[180] Democratic politics can then be viewed as 'an ongoing attempt to live with and among strangers, that is, in the context of plurality'.[181] For instance, Zerilli emphasises in this context that '[p]lurality is not [just] a demographic or existential fact, but a political relation to social differences'.[182]

[174] See, eg, the literature cited above in n 6. For a different perspective, see also, eg, G Romeo, 'What's Wrong with Depoliticisation?' (2022) 1 *European Law Open* 168.

[175] See also Neuvonen (n 136) 868 and 877–82.

[176] The basic problem with essentialist and ahistorical thinking is that it obscures the existing differences and diversity. But note also, eg, JR Martin, 'Methodological Essentialism, False Difference, and Other Dangerous Traps' (1994) 19 *Signs* 630, 643 warning against 'methodological essentialism' ('when the historical approach is deemed essential, other equally important ones are all too likely to be sacrificed').

[177] C Schmitt, *The Concept of the Political* (The University of Chicago Press, 2007 [1932, in German], translated by G Schwab) 26.

[178] ibid 38, 39, 44 and 45.

[179] ibid 46. In fact, Schmitt develops a concept of the political that the concept of the state presupposes. The first sentence of *The Concept of the Political* states that '[t]he concept of the state presupposes the concept of the political'. ibid 19. Therefore, it would seem tautological to use Schmitt's concept of the political to explain why we should also accept his theory of state.

[180] L Zerilli. 'Castoriadis, Arendt, and the Problem of the New' (2002) 9 *Constellations* 540, 541.

[181] L Zerilli, 'Politics' in L Disch and M Hawkesworth (eds), *The Oxford Handbook of Feminist Theory* (Oxford University Press, 2016) 646.

[182] L Zerilli, 'Refiguring Rights through the Political Practice of Sexual Difference' (2004) 15 *Differences A Journal of Feminist Cultural Studies* 54, 68.

This position finds support from Hannah Arendt's argument that plurality and 'the presence of others' are preconditions for meaningful political action and the validity of political judgment.[183]

For radical democratic theories, the 'moment of the political' seeks to capture 'the contingency of being'.[184] This means that democracy cannot be reduced to 'a set of formal institutions' or to 'a particular form of government'.[185] Instead, democractic politics is focused on enabling 'new institutions', 'new ways of living' and 'new forms of political association'.[186] Moreover, the idea of 'prefigurative politics' suggests that it is possible to 'create microcosms supported by alternative legitimation stories, irrespective of whether similar structures are feasible at the level of the whole society'.[187] But it is important to notice that many critical theorists simultaneously caution against the 'reification of the political' by radical democratic theories.[188] A related concern is that radical democratic theories often operate with an overly 'abstract' understanding of power.[189] These warnings reflect the interdisciplinary methodological commitment of critical theory, as discussed in this chapter. This mindset is visible, for instance, in Lois McNay's observation that '[c]ritical theorists have long insisted on the interdisciplinary nature of critique, that it is, by its very nature, . . . situated somewhere between political and social theory'.[190] By locating the critical project in the intersection of social and political theory, critical theorists see the social and the political question as closely intertwined.

If political action is always socially embedded, the depoliticisation critiques of EU law must more clearly articulate what their understanding of *democratic society* looks like. This would arguably require a more developed negative critique of social power relations in the study of EU law. But it also raises the question of the role of utopian thinking in the critical project in EU law. The concept of 'utopia' is often used as a pejorative term, and this is also true to the critical theory of society.[191] But it is arguable that political action, just like critique, requires 'some conception of a different ordering of society'.[192] In EU legal studies, Somek has depicted transnationalism as a problematic 'post-utopian' replacement for more genuinely utopian hopes for political and social change.[193] His concern is that it replaces 'our fantasy with regard to what life might be like within a bounded unit', with a

[183] H Arendt, *Lectures on Kant's Political Philosophy* (edited by R Beiner) (University of Chicago Press, 1982) 64. See also L Zerilli, '"We Feel Our Freedom": Imagination and Judgment in the Thought of Hannah Arendt' (2005) 33 *Political Theory* 158, 165. On why Arendt should not be interpreted in a communitarian manner, see also the discussion and cited literature in Neuvonen (n 136) 877–80.

[184] For discussion, see, eg, L McNay, *The Misguided Search for the Political* (Polity, 2014) 95.

[185] Zerilli (n 180) 544.

[186] ibid 544 and Zerilli (n 182) 60.

[187] E Rossi, 'Being Realistic and Demanding the Impossible' (2019) 26 *Constellations* 638, 647 and 648.

[188] McNay (n 184) 95.

[189] ibid 8.

[190] ibid 215–16.

[191] eg C Calhoun, 'The Critical Dimension in Sociological Theory' in JH Turner (ed), *Handbook of Sociological Theory* (Springer, 2002) 87 about how 'critical theory was disciplined by Marx's rejection of abstract utopianism'. See also, eg, N Rismal, *The Ends of Utopian Thinking in Critical Theory* (Brill, 2023) chs 1 and 2. For Marx's position, see, eg, K Marx and F Engels, 'Manifesto of the Communist Party' in Tucker (n 32) 498–99.

[192] LT Sargent, 'The Three Faces of Utopianism Revisited' (1994) 5 *Utopian Studies* 1, 27. See also B Macdonald, 'Utopias, Radical Imaginaries, and Political Action' (2025) 47 *New Political Science* 152, 159. On the role of hope in the critique of EU law, see also chapter 12 by Paul Linden-Retek in this book.

[193] Somek (n 111) 48. Somek uses the terms 'cosmopolitanism' and 'transnationalism' interchangeably in this context. ibid 48 and 49.

political vision that is 'essentially formal and linked not to forms of human association'.[194] Somek's affirmation of utopian thinking is important, but the way in which he confines the political space to a bounded (primarily national) unit seems problematic. It has been noted that 'nostalgia for the nation-state provides a poor model for orienting us effectively to whatever liberatory political possibilities there may be now'.[195] Moreover, as Knox et al highlight in their overture of Marxist EU law scholarship, Marxist scholars might also want to problematise 'the capitalist nation-state'.[196]

Instead of just rejecting the transnational space as 'an infinite [cosmopolitan and apolitical] space',[197] it seems important to critically revisit the transnational space that we have created in the EU. The concept of *utopia* can also contribute to that discourse as a spatial descriptor that differs from *topia* ('the here and now').[198] A common mistake is to assume that 'perfection' is a necessary component of utopian thinking.[199] Utopia, however, can simply be defined as a currently 'non-existent' place or society.[200] Critical 'non-perfectionist' utopian thinking is arguably needed to 'defamiliarize us from entrenched ways of being and living'.[201] Therefore, a 'utopian standpoint' becomes particularly important if the aim of critique is to find alternatives to 'the already-same of existing political and social practices'.[202] But it is important to recognise that critical utopian thinking about the EU is also always 'ideologically imbricated, conditioned, and moulded by social conflicts here and now'.[203] That is, the critical project cannot overcome the crisis of normative critique by recourse to utopian thinking. Moreover, it is entirely possible that the critical value of utopian thinking 'lies not in helping us to imagine a better future but rather in demonstrating our utter incapacity to imagine such a future'.[204] The EU can thus also have utopian value that is not linked to the 'longevity'[205] of the current integration project but to how and why the EU fails as a utopian political project.

V. Conclusion

This chapter argued that the critique of EU law can no longer overlook the crisis of normative critique that lies at the heart of the critical project. Critical legal theory has left this crisis unaddressed in ways that reduce its usefulness for the critical project in EU

[194] ibid 48.

[195] B McKean, 'What Makes a Utopia Inconvenient? On the Advantages and Disadvantages of a Realist Orientation to Politics' (2016) 110 *The American Political Science Review* 876, 886.

[196] Knox et al (n 81) 288.

[197] Somek (n 111) 48.

[198] eg M Thaler, 'Hope Abjuring Hope: On the Place of Utopia in Realist Political Theory' (2018) 46 *Political Theory* 671, 680; Macdonald (n 192) 154–55.

[199] Sargent (n 192) 6. Similarly, McKean (n 195) 876.

[200] Sargent (n 192) 9. For Sargent, 'eutopia' refers to 'positive utopia' and 'dystopia' to 'negative utopia'. ibid 9.

[201] eg M Thaler, 'Utopia, Breakdown, Repair: Failure and Success in Social Dreaming' (2023) 45 *New Political Science* 431, 433 and 435. See also Thaler (n 198) 690.

[202] Macdonald (n 192) 154.

[203] Thaler (n 198) 688. For a similar point, see also F Jameson, 'The Politics of Utopia' (2004) 25 *New Left Review* 35, 47.

[204] Jameson (n 203) 46. See also R Levitas, 'Looking for the Blue: The Necessity of Utopia' (2007) 12 *Journal of Political Ideologies* 289, 303.

[205] Sargent (n 192) 16 ('After the end point, it is possible to speak of influence.')

law. Therefore, this chapter turned to the critical theory of society to develop a critical theory of EU law. This inquiry into critical social theory reopened both the social and the political question in the critique of EU law. First, it showed how a more comprehensive critique of capitalist society calls into question a narrow definition of emancipation as mere decommodification in critical studies of EU law. Second, a closer look at the internal faultlines of the Frankfurt School critical theory clarified the potential and limits of immanent critique as an alternative to the internal and external critiques of EU law. In the strong form of immanent critique, the critical potential emerges from contradictions that are internal to the values that the EU proclaims. But whether the social reality of EU law can generate such immanent critical potential ultimately also depends on how open the critical project is to the diverging crises experiences and whether the adopted critical standard is acceptable to the subjects of those crises. Therefore, this chapter also considered how critical theorists can navigate the unresolved crisis of normative critique by framing critique as a form of political practice.

In critical theory, the argument of critique as a form of political practice is normally accompanied by a detailed analysis of the concept of the political. For many critical theorists, plurality is not so much a moral or ethical commitment but a condition for meaningful political action. Moreover, critical theory emphasises that the political question cannot be separated from the social question because the conditions for political action are always shaped by asymmetrical power relations. As such, critical theory challenges the essentialist (statist) concept of the political and adds more depth to the basic tension between democracy and capitalism in the critique of EU law. That this choice between different concepts of the political often remains unpronounced in the depoliticisation critiques of EU law should not obscure the fact that our preferred concept of the political determines the direction that the critical project takes in EU law. This engagement with critical theory also highlighted that the intellectual history of concepts that inform the critique of EU law deserves more attention and that conceptual choices can become sites of power struggles that shape the future of the critical project in EU law. In this sense, the critique of EU law is indistinguishable from our 'theory of history, society, and human action'[206], and to pretend otherwise would be highly problematic.

[206] Fraser and Jaeggi (n 35) 156.

2

Critical Histories and the Uses of the Past in European Law

KAIUS TUORI[1]

I. Introduction

Historical writing has played, or perhaps still plays, a vital role in the making of nation-states. By writing about the past – about a nation's great heroes and moments of adversity and glory – historians have contributed to national projects by formulating a shared past for the imaginary entity that is the nation. Drawing on these narratives, children were, for decades or even centuries, taught fittingly inspiring and heroic stories as part of the national school curriculum. As a result, people learned about medieval battles like Agincourt (1415) or Kosovo Polje (1389) and came to think of them as meaningful to their existence in the here and now, many centuries later. After nationalist mythical histories and their notions of friends and enemies had been an integral part legitimating the worst bloodshed and violence of the twentieth century – not only during the two world wars but also in smaller conflicts – historians began to critically evaluate and dismantle the historical writing that could be said to have contributed to these horrors. Particularly since the 1990s, critical historiography has been used with devastating effect to deconstruct historical narratives of nation-states and population groups, where history has served as a tool for legitimating the nation and its politics.[2] Critical historical inquiries not only in Europe but equally in North America or Australia demonstrated not just how nationalist myths relating to culture, race, belonging, or property rights – such as promised lands, golden age, white marble theory, manifest destiny, indigenous title, and many others – were historically inaccurate, but also how they were upheld

[1] The author wishes to thank Visa Tuomela, Vera Lampila and Edit Ahtiainen for their assistance in the preparation of the text. He would also like to express his gratitude to Tuuli Talvinko, Paolo Amorosa and Ville Erkkilä for their patience in discussing the themes of text and reading some of the early drafts. The present work has received funding from Academy of Finland funded Centre of Excellence in Law, Identity and the European Narratives (EuroStorie.org), funding decision number 312154.

[2] This refers to the discussion initiated by B Anderson, *Imagined Communities: Reflections on the Origin and Spread of Nationalism* (London, Verso, 1991). On the connection between history, memory and the nation-state, see, eg, A Rigney, 'Remembrance as Remaking: Memories of the Nation Revisited' (2018) 24 *Nations and Nationalism* 240.

because they were useful in maintaining the legitimacy of social, cultural and political domination over minorities and marginalised groups.[3]

I argue that the histories of European integration and law are long overdue for a similar critical evaluation.[4] This chapter examines the writing of the history of EU law and European legal history by investigating the historical narratives they present, and the use of the historical past to legitimate legal integration. It seeks to demonstrate how the ideas of tradition and heritage were used as legitimating tropes within integration, and the way in which critical historiography may be used to deconstruct such historical narratives. The chapter connects this analysis with a critical exploration of the concept of teleology in EU law, arguing that the historical framing of the European project as a legal enterprise rests on a historiographical foundation that seeks to weave together the past, present, and future into an air of inevitability, thereby constraining political choices. Much like the teleological interpretation developed in EU law, the history of integration is often written as a teleological narrative, a historical teleology to complement the legal one. Similar to the critique of nationalist historiography, the task of a critical history of EU law is to examine the invented traditions and imagined communities that are created through historical writing, to untangle and expose the implicit biases and meanings within the historical tradition.

The notion of critical history requires some explanation. If all historical writing is inherently critical, what makes critical history different? The notion of critical history emerged in the wake of critical theory, incorporating its motifs into historical writing – for example, by uncovering the forgotten histories of marginalised groups, a theme where they had a strong connection of Marxist historiography.[5] Although generalisations are problematic, it is apparent that much of the early critical historiography relied on the visible/hidden dichotomy, sometimes referred to as dietrology: the idea that the things that actually matter are concealed behind a screen or façade designed to obstruct and to prevent people from seeing the truth.[6] This means that the historian's task is to expose and reveal things that are hidden or unseen, to shift perspectives, and perhaps even to influence the present. There is a need for conceptual clarity even within the historiographical toolbox.

[3] See, eg, J Coakley, 'Mobilizing the Past: Nationalist Images of History' (2004) 10 *Nationalism and Ethnic Politics* 531. In recent years, this debate has been reformulated and expanded to the field of memory studies, see, eg, U Belavusau and A Gliszczyńska-Grabias (eds), *Law and Memory: Towards Legal Governance of History* (Cambridge University Press, 2017).

[4] However, see F Nicola, 'Introduction: Critical Legal Histories in EU Law' (2013) 28 *American University International Law Review* 1173. There are a number of interesting new projects that seek to bring about a more comprehensive and holistic approach to European law and its history; see, eg, SR Larsen, 'European Public Law After Empires' (2022) 1 *European Law Open* 6. On the European project and its history in general, see the review article by F Krawatzek and F Pestel, 'New Histories of and for Europe: Narrating the European Project' (2023) *Contemporary European History* 1.

[5] How to define critical history as a field is contentious, but M Goswami, M Postone, A Sartori, and WH Sewell Jr, 'Introducing Critical Historical Studies' (2014) 1 *Critical Historical Studies* 1 highlight both links with the critical theory of Marx and the Frankfurt School, as well as a general emancipatory agenda, with intersectional, contextual and theoretical emphasis.

[6] Here, I refer to work that in Britain was published in journals such as the *History Workshop Journal* and authors such as Stuart Hall, and to a lesser degree to more mainstream scholars such as EP Thompson or Eric Hobsbawm. Parallel movements gained recognition in Italy, France and elsewhere in Europe and the Americas.

In the present inquiry, the word history is primarily used in the meaning of historical narratives, while the writing of history refers to the creation of such narratives. And when we talk about the process of narrative formation, it is a reference to historiography, which generally signifies a metalevel investigation. These distinctions are fairly complicated, and they themselves are a source of contention, as is the whole idea of critical inquiry in history. For instance, at its most basic format, historical writing is about recounting events in the past, about what happened. For many, even for professional historians, the only worthwhile exercise is to gather more sources about the past and publish more detailed accounts of it, engaging in debates about the facts of history, the who did what and when, even why. However, in critical histories, the question is often not what and when, but what it meant. This search for meaning and the discussion of what it means that historical writing gives a certain significance to past acts are the fundamental points of critical historical writing. It does this by reversing viewpoints, asking questions about agency and seeking to disentangle the various voices within historical narratives.[7] In the following I use the concept of historical teleology to refer to the style of historiography which sees events and actors only as bit players in the inevitable progression towards a predetermined endpoint, which is never seriously questioned. Legal teleology, in turn, is understood as the view that law has a certain purpose which it must fulfil, a view which naturally precludes interpretations of the text itself that would be contrary to this purpose.

By critical theory, I refer in this context to the genealogical tradition that has its foundations in Foucault, the seeking of unacknowledged or hidden origins. This approach seeks to trace alternative lineages and ways of reading, situating historical narratives within their specific contexts.[8] While traditional critical research has relied on what has often been described as the drama of exposure – the moment of revealing unstated origins and hidden motivations beneath the surface – this process aligns with what was termed the hermeneutics of suspicion, raising the question of whether history has a particular relationship with critical social theory. Historians, by default, are adept at taking a step back, questioning assumptions and offering alternative readings.[9] Does this mean that critical history is a tautology, a way of restating the obvious? Perhaps, but not necessarily. The term critical history has often been linked with the notion of deconstruction, but in historiography, it is often associated with the idea of tracing the genealogy of concepts and ideas.[10] In the history of EU law, the notions of seeking genealogies, hermeneutical inquiries to untangle interpretation or even to deconstruct narratives and legitimating constructions, offers a toolbox to see more clearly, to adopt a critical viewpoint towards hegemonic narratives such as those offered by the powers that be.

[7] For example, a typical 19th and early 20th century convention was to situate the nation as the actor of history, seeking its place and historical fulfilment. See the literature in n 2 for further references.

[8] M Foucault, 'Nietzsche, Genealogy, History' in D Bouchard (ed), *Language, Counter-Memory, Practice: Selected Essays and Interviews* (Cornell University Press, 1977) 139–64.

[9] R Felski, *The Limits of Critique* (The University of Chicago Press, 2015) 1–10, does an excellent job of rethinking the role of critique.

[10] On this, see E Kleinberg, 'Haunting History: Deconstruction and the Spirit of Revision' (2007) 46 *History and Theory* 113.

What would a critical history of EU law and integration therefore entail? The typical critics of the EU naturally focus on its undemocratic nature and the way that it promotes a neoliberal agenda.[11] From a historical perspective, this is uncontroversial and thus not particularly interesting. Instead, in the following, I discuss two strands of research: the instrumental and the historiographical. In the first, I will explore the uses of the past in European discourse, not only as legitimising factors but also as tools for influencing policy choices. Here, I seek to apply critical theory to discuss the uses of the past – the ways in which historical narratives have been used, not only in political discussions but also in EU law scholarship. In short, how the past has been utilised to legitimate and guide integration. Through this, I will discuss the potential of critical historiography to explore the historical narratives of integration and law. In the second, historiographical strand, I will discuss three main themes, storylines, or metanarratives: the integration narrative, the European human rights narrative and the totalitarian past narrative. I call these metanarratives as a historiographical descriptor, as they are groupings of numerous specific narratives about the development of European integration and law, for instance the integration metanarrative consisting of various themes about the role of institutions and legal actors. The aim of this narrative separation is to enable discussion of the metanarratives of the histories of European integration and law as well as of the possibilities offered by critical historiography. I maintain that metanarratives about the historical origins of European integration, its links with Nazi and Fascist policies and theorists, offer openings for critical historiography. In both strands, the crucial focus is on approaching the changing contexts and motivations of historical writing and how they are reflected in the works themselves. Nowhere is this more obvious than in the concept of teleology, both legal and historical, which symbolises not only the distinctive way that the EU judicial branch operates but also the instrumentalist approach that the EU and its predecessors have taken towards history.

II. Uses of the Past: Which Path for the Future of the European Past?

One of the most cherished founding myths of European law and integration is that of the community as a project grounded in law. Although scholars such as Patel have maintained that, in its early days, the European Economic Community (EEC) was just one of many different interstate organisations aimed at promoting European unity,[12] the community's own historiography presents a different narrative. In this account, Walter Hallstein's words from a 1962 speech at the University of Padua appear prophetic:

> This Community was not created by military power or political pressure, but owes its existence to a constitutive legal act. It also lives in accordance with fixed rules of law and its

[11] The 'democratic deficit' of the EU lies at the heart of the problem, despite the much-touted attempts to rectify it. For a concise analysis, see J-W Müller, 'The EU's Democratic Deficit and the Public Sphere' (2016) 115:779 *Current History* 83.

[12] KK Patel, 'Provincialising European Union: Co-Operation and Integration in Europe in a Historical Perspective' (2013) 22 *Contemporary European History* 649.

> institutions are subject to judicial review. In place of power and its manipulation, the balance of powers, the striving for hegemony and the play of alliances, we have for the first time the rule of law. The European Economic Community is a community of law . . . because it serves to realize the idea of law.[13]

One of the most crucial and, at the same time, controversial features of European legal integration has been the concept of teleological interpretation of law. Succinctly put, this means that the Court of Justice of the European Union (CJEU), when interpreting EU law, pays particular attention to the aim and purpose of the law. As such, teleological interpretation is not based on any particular ruling, rule, or principle, but has instead emerged as an interpretation of what the Court has been doing. Although teleological, or purposive, interpretation has been accepted as a standard approach since the 1950s – with authorities such as Pescatore asserting that this has always been the Community's intention – the core issue has rarely been addressed: namely, since 1945, purposive interpretation of law has been regarded as anathema to any kind of legal system claiming to adhere to the rule of law principle.[14] Instead, purposive interpretation has been a favourite tool for authoritarian and totalitarian regimes from Nazi Germany to the Soviet Union. The teleological interpretation of law adopted by the lawyers drafting European legal integration was thus in direct contradiction with the ideas of legalism and rule of law that Hallstein praised. What appears evident is that the EU would thus aim to combine both legal and historical teleology.

In a recent article, Gilbert has argued that one of the main tasks of the historian is to complicate these triumphalist views and see the nuances behind them. He revisits the idea of Whig history, of presenting history as the onward march of progress, the constant improvement of humankind and its institutions.[15] Instead, historians should attempt to look beyond the simplistic tenor of marketing statements such as Hallstein's. This presents an interesting and problematic version of the classic dilemma between normative and contemplative interpretation. The normative approach seeks to produce a solution, a rationale to be applied as a rule in the future. The contemplative interpretation seeks to appreciate the past in its context, placing the actions that were taken and the people involved within their historical, social and ideological frameworks, without considering further lessons of history or the applicability of the ruling in the present. I would contend that the problem with the history of European integration is that much of it is written in an attempt to justify what it is writing about, a normative interpretation of the past to legitimate further integration.

A central part of the use of the past to justify contemporary policy has been the judicialisation of the values of the EU in the interpretation of Article 2 of the Treaty on European Union (TEU). The values thus enshrined are historically constituted, as something already shared and therefore in themselves contain an argument for unity. Their utilisation as membership criteria as well as enforcement criteria for infringement

[13] Quoted in R Manko, 'The EU As a Community of Law: Overview of the Role of Law in the Union' (March 2017) *European Parliament Briefing* 2.

[14] S Brittain, 'Justifying The Teleological Methodology of the European Court of Justice: A Rebuttal' (2016) 55 *Irish Jurist* 134; M Rasmussen, 'Revolutionizing European Law: A History of the Van Gend en Loos Judgment' (2014) 12 *International Journal of Constitutional Law* 136.

[15] M Gilbert, 'Historicising European Integration History' (2021) 8 *European Review of International Studies* 221, 223.

actions has led to a strange quasi-codification of values.[16] The problem is naturally that the historical foundation of legally binding values demands a clear and selective historical interpretation of what particularly constitutes acceptable behaviour.[17] Thus, when someone makes an assertion of shared values, traditions or history, it is actually a normative statement, not a value-free historical claim.

The importance of adopting a critical historical approach is that it reveals alternative ways of reading the past and episodes that do not reflect well on the European project, such as the long-standing neo-colonial origins of the whole integration idea. As is well known, the EEC emerged at a time when the European overseas empires were slowly collapsing, with protracted colonial wars demonstrating how empty the promises of respect for legal guarantees or the rule of law were outside the European mainland. Even the visionaries of the history of European integration were tied to the colonial mindset, as is evident in the less discussed works of, among others, Coudenhove-Kalergi on the integration of Europe and its African colonies. It has even been claimed that parity in colonialism and using the economic opportunities offered by colonies was one of the first arenas of European collaboration and integration.[18] Critics of both the EU's Africa policy and its human rights regime have rightly pointed out that instead of a benevolent partnership in development, much of the normative framework imposed by the EU on African countries, from migration control to economic policies and human rights initiatives, has echoes of the colonial past. Even now, in the debate on immigration, the question of whether non-Europeans are entitled to the protections of the European human rights system is, incredibly, being raised again by populists and the far right.

The significance of the past for the future of the European project depends on which parts of the historical past are highlighted and which are forgotten. The type of past presented – whether in historical writing, speeches, or policy papers – is no coincidence, as these narratives often serve as blueprints for the future that the speaker envisions. What is remembered of the past and what is considered as exemplary and worthy of emulation are considered to be the 'tradition' or 'heritage', even if it is based on a faulty or selective reading of past events. To claim that something is part of a tradition consists of a number of normative statements, beginning from the supposed community to which this tradition would belong to or be shared by, to the content of the tradition.

This kind of selective remembering of the past is a recurring theme even in European political debates, as well as at the policy and resolution level. The traditions referenced continue to depend on the speaker and the topic at hand. For example, improvements in workplace health and safety would be described as being 'conditions in accordance with the European tradition of social progress'.[19] In stark contrast to contemporary debates,

[16] K Lane Scheppele, D V Kochenov and B Grabowska-Moroz, 'EU Values Are Law, after All: Enforcing EU Values through Systemic Infringement Actions by the European Commission and the Member States of the European Union' (2020) 39 *Yearbook of European Law* 3; A Jakab and D Kochenov (eds), *The Enforcement of EU Law and Values: Ensuring Member States' Compliance* (Oxford University Press, 2017).

[17] On the problematic nature of shared values, see P Akaliyski, C Welzel and J Hien, 'A Community of Shared Values? Dimensions and Dynamics of Cultural Integration in the European Union' (2021) 44 *Journal of European Integration* 569.

[18] BJ Thorpe, 'Eurafrica: A Pan-European Vehicle for Central European Colonialism (1923–1939)' (2018) 26 *European Review* 503.

[19] Resolution on the Commission's action program relating to the implementation of the Community Charter of fundamental social rights for workers - priorities for 1991-1992 (A3-175/90), [1990] OJ C260/124, 169.

in 1994, the Commission discussed the 'European tradition of openness, the historical successes of Europe in integrating immigrants and the contribution this has made to economic success and demographic and societal vitality'.[20]

In a similar vein, issues such as diversity[21] and solidarity[22] were also regarded as European traditions that needed to be preserved in the discussions of the 1990s. In the context of enlargement, the connection between the past and the future was instrumental:

> EU enlargement is essential for Europe's future. A common European tradition, cultural diversity and the peace process which began after the Second World War are the determinants of a united Europe. From a historical perspective we are now returning to a normal state of affairs in Europe, in which some of the artificial boundaries of the past have been removed.[23]

This statement contains a whole range of questionable historical justifications. The future unity of Europe is a return to the past, which is somehow more natural and normal than the present. The shared common tradition is a sign of unity, but at the same time it is a requirement of unity. It is all very complicated and tautological.

The use of tradition as argument continued to expand, including ever more themes. By the early 2000s, the rule of law and the safeguarding of human rights also came to be regarded as European traditions,[24] in ways that soon began to have a life of its own. However, as with the discussion on values, the notion of rule of law is problematic, especially if it is instrumentalised. While the concept of rule of law would appear as simple legalism, within the practice of the Commission, especially in relation to the expansion and the inclusion of the former Communist countries, it has become shorthand for abiding to the EU requirements and regulations.[25] As Toni Marzal has recently suggested, the historical teleology that he dubs as 'lawful messianism' bends not just concepts but even legal culture itself.[26]

What is evident is that tradition functions in these discussions as a legitimating instrument. It is not a reference to an existing thing or a description of one, but a normative statement that has a future orientation. The problem of the normativity of history

[20] European Social Policy, *A Way Forward for the Union* (White Paper, COM/94/333FINAL, 27 July 1994) 29.

[21] Report from the Commission, *Employment in Europe 1994* (COM/94/381FINAL, 14 September 1994) 158; Opinion of the Committee of the Regions on the Communication from the European Commission on Cohesion policy and culture - a contribution to employment [1997] OJ C379/21, 23.

[22] Opinion of the Committee of the Regions on the White Paper on growth, competitiveness, employment: The challenges and ways forward into the 21st Century [1995] OJ C210/1, 7.

[23] Opinion of the Committee of the Regions on the 2000 Intergovernmental Conference [2000] OJ C156/6, 7.

[24] Proposal for a Council Directive on the conditions of entry and residence of third-country nationals for the purpose of paid employment and self-employed economic activities [2001] OJ C332E/248; Opinion of the Economic and Social Committee on the Proposal for a Council Directive on minimum standards on procedures in Member States for granting and withdrawing refugee status [2001] OJ C193/77, 83.

[25] There is a vast amount of literature on the rule of law in the European context, see, eg, C Closa and D Kochenov, *Reinforcing Rule of Law Oversight in the European Union* (Cambridge University Press, 2016), but very little of it has a seriously critical angle. Much of the earlier literature appears to suggest that rule of law would be brought about by expanding the jurisdiction of the CJEU. See, eg, L Pech, '"A Union Founded on the Rule of Law": Meaning and Reality of the Rule of Law as a Constitutional Principle of EU Law' (2010) 6 *European Constitutional Law Review* 359 on the suggested rule of law deficit.

[26] T Marzal, 'Between Integration and the Rule of Law: EU Law's Culture of Lawful Messianism' (2023) 24 *German Law Journal* 718.

is naturally that there is a strong need to sanitise the past, to forget episodes such as colonial oppression and its neocolonial continuation. Only what supports the narrative is remembered, selectively. Following the logic of conservatism, if something has been around for an extended period of time, it is assumed to be good and worthy of preservation. However, what is the remembered past and who decides what of the past is considered worthy is another, very important discussion that critical scholarship is particularly well positioned to engage in.

III. Metanarratives: A Suitable Legal Past for Europe

The idea of a metanarrative is to focus on the meaning given to a historical narrative, namely its perceived role in the wider historical development. In the following, I will examine three contrasting metanarratives of EU and European legal history – the institutional narrative, the human rights narrative and the totalitarian roots narrative – to explore how they relate to critical approaches to EU legal history. Each is subject to conflicting interpretations when presented by self-described critical historians, in contrast to more traditional practitioners of event history.

The first metanarrative, the institutional narrative of European integration as a legal process, is a mainstay of EU history, where the stage-by-stage exploration of meetings and treaty preparations, as told by those who were present and by the documents made available through archives, answers a fundamental question of history: What (actually) happened?[27] In this context, the Rankean addition of 'actually' is the crux of the matter, opening the field for self-described critical history. Would the actually meaningful developments be those taking place in the meetings themselves, making it worthwhile to go through the recurring drama of endless meetings where sometimes very little of consequence appears to take place? Or would it be the framing of a shared understanding of the future aims of the administration of the Commission? Or the nation-states, their political decision-makers and judiciaries, acquiescing to the gradual expansion of the European jurisdiction?

This means that there are many ways of writing history, eg, the legal history of European integration, but at the same time the larger issue is which parts of that history are truly significant. Because it is possible to write histories of institutions that did not ultimately lead to anything consequential, of the proverbial rearranging of the deck chairs of the Titanic or having meetings on palace protocol when the revolutionary crowd is coming to burn the whole place down. However, at the same time it is very hard to have two historians to actually agree on what would have been consequential.

The history of the EU and its law has long remained the domain of teleological narratives focused on institution-building and the people involved. In the European legal history written by the institutions themselves, there is a strong emphasis on the idea of

[27] A selection of the more notable histories: L van Middelaar, *The Passage to Europe: How a Continent Became a Union* (Yale University Press, 2013); KK Patel, *Project Europe: A History* (Cambridge University Press, 2020); M Gilbert, *European Integration: A Political History*, 2nd edn (Rowman & Littlefield, 2020). For critical histories, see H Schulz-Forberg and B Stråth, *The Political History of European Integration: The Hypocrisy of Democracy-through-Market* (Routledge, 2010).

an ever-closer union, where the legal developments themselves are presented as milestones but never as integral parts of the past. Their value and meaning are thus reduced to contributing to something that came afterwards.[28] The concept of teleological narrative refers to a process of seeking the origins of the present form of a historical phenomenon in the past, often excluding the complexities of development along the way, such as studying the history of human rights as a process of them coming into being as we now know them, studied as a process of becoming. Treaties, treaty negotiations, and figures such as Jean Monnet, who drove integration, provide content for a history shaped by the present. In standard works on EU law, this narrative typically appears in the introductory chapters.[29] It is an event-based history of what happened and who was involved, without much context on why and how events unfolded. This event history is presented as a coming-of-being of the present, without any analysis or discussion of underlying motivations. In contrast, the burgeoning histories of EU law that have emerged over the past decade or so follow two interlinked approaches: that of examining individuals and that of examining institutions, both of which offer an internal history of the making of the EU legal apparatus.[30] In addition, a new set of inquiries has arisen, focusing on the relationship between EU law and national law in legal development, and approaching matters from a dogmatic perspective.[31] What these newer inquiries offer is an emerging view of historical contestations instead of historical teleology.

What kind of historical narratives of the EU, EU law or European integration do these studies offer?

The answer is difficult to determine with any confidence, mainly because the narratives they present focus on institutions and the people working within them. This is due to research relying on sources provided by those people themselves, with the EU archives largely unavailable and unhelpful due to various kinds of restrictions to access, either due to time limits or the apparently missing material especially from the early years. It remains to be seen what kind of scholarship will be produced in the future, but the first generation of studies has not been encouraging. In these works, the shift from the historiography of European visionaries such as Count Coudenhove-Kalergi or Altiero Spinelli to the nuts and bolts of functionalist integration has proven challenging, not least because the idealism of the visionaries was excluded from the early integration process and its technocratic nature.[32]

[28] There is, for instance, the tripartite history of the European Commission: M Dumoulin et al (eds), *The European Commission: 1958–72 : History and Memories* (Office for Official Publications of the European Communities, 2007); M Dumoulin (ed), *The European Commission: 1973–1986 History and Memories of an Institution* (Luxembourg, Office for Official Publications of the European Communities, 2014); É Bussière et al (eds), *The European Commission 1986–2000: History and Memories of an Institution* (Publications Office of the European Union, 2019).

[29] See, eg, P Craig and G De Búrca (eds), *The Evolution of EU Law*, 3rd edn (Oxford University Press, 2021).

[30] M Rasmussen and B Davies, 'Towards a New History of European Law' (2012) 21 *Contemporary European History* 305; F Nicola and B Davies (eds), *EU Law Stories: Contextual and Critical Histories of European Jurisprudence* (Cambridge University Press, 2017).

[31] eg A Küsters, *The Making and Unmaking of Ordoliberal Language. A Digital Conceptual History of European Competition Law* (Klostermann, 2023). Many recent studies on private law also have a deep theoretical focus, eg, H-W Micklitz, *The Politics of Justice in European Private Law: Social Justice, Access Justice, Societal Justice, Cambridge Studies in European Law and Policy* (Cambridge University Press, 2018).

[32] Another idea that fell by the wayside was the notion of social Europe; see AD Andry, *Social Europe, the Road not Taken: The Left and European Integration in the Long 1970s* (Oxford University Press, 2022).

However, recent critical historical writing, or critical historiography, has sought to circumvent this by embracing methods that are not explicitly critical – quite the opposite, in fact. The biographical method is literally the oldest tool of historiography and has little or nothing to do with social criticism. Despite this, emerging scholars such as Vera Fritz have managed to overcome the limitations imposed by the lack of sources – in her case, those related to the CJEU – by seeking material around and beyond the limited official sources, searching for individual judges and their records. This has allowed her (and others using similar methods) to trace the history of the judicial revolution undertaken by the Court in the 1960s and 1970s, and the emergence of a whole cadre of judges who were intent on establishing a supranational European legal order in the federalist vein.[33] Another relatively recent study is that by Julie Bailleux, who criticises the notion of a clear linear development, in which one or more heroic actors set the European legal system on a predetermined path – a teleology of the teleology. Instead, she argues that the emergence of the whole notion of community law was a convoluted, contingent and haphazard process, in which the notion of creating a new field was shared only at a much later stage.[34] The critical perspective of these studies focuses on individuals and their motivations, highlighting their influence in guiding EU law and integration at key moments, relies on the dynamics of revelation and a suspicion of whether the stated motives are the whole truth. Much like Tommaso Pavone's recent book, these works argue that a whole generation of pro-integration lawyers were driving integration behind the scenes. Pavone claims that their work contributed to selecting landmark cases that were perceived to have constitutional implications, and promoting them within national courts and through referrals to the European Court of Justice (ECJ).[35] A similar hidden-actor narrative is evident in some of the studies on academics behind the EU law doctrine, such as the *Integration Through Law* (ITL) project.[36] In much of this literature, there is a desire to bring to the fore contrasts between the official, stated agenda and the unstated motivations and driving forces within the development.

In recent years, the opening of the archives of the CJEU in 2015 has led to a flood of histories of the Court. Scholars such as Morten Rasmussen have been vocal in calling for a new critical history of EU law based on sound archival research. This call has been followed by a group of historians who have utilised both the newly opened EU archives but also the wealth of private archives that enable scholars to circumvent the restrictions of central archives. Rasmussen argues that because of the relative poverty of the tradition of legal history of EU law, the field began to be filled by historians with little

[33] On the method, see V Fritz, 'Judge Biographies as a Methodology to Grasp the Dynamics inside the CJEU and Its Relationship with EU Member States' in MR Madsen, F Nicola, and A Vauchez (eds), *Researching the European Court of Justice: Methodological Shifts and Law's Embeddedness* (Cambridge University Press, 2022) 209; V Fritz, *Juges et avocats generaux de la Cour de Justice de l'Union européenne (1952–1972): une approche biographique de l'histoire d'une revolution juridique* (Vittorio Klostermann, 2018).

[34] J Bailleux, 'L'Europe et ses légistes: Le Service juridique des Exécutifs européens et la promotion d'un droit communautaire autonome (1957–1964)' (2013) 41 *Politique européenne* 88, 92; J Bailleux, *Penser l'Europe par le droit: L'invention du droit communautaire en France* (Dalloz, 2014).

[35] T Pavone, *The Ghostwriters: Lawyers and the Politics Behind the Judicial Construction of Europe* (Cambridge University Press, 2022).

[36] R Byberg, 'The History of the Integration Through Law Project: Creating the Academic Expression of a Constitutional Legal Vision for Europe' (2017) 18 *German Law Journal* 1531.

or no legal training, who started to study the archives using the methods of contextual history.[37] The danger of these first histories is naturally that of reliance on description instead of analysis, of following the logic of the archive instead of critical thought. For the historian to be able to read against the grain, to question the logic and justification of the institutions and individuals producing the archival material, requires a deep and analytical understanding of not just the institutions, the law and the history behind them, but also the competing visions of the future that informed them.

In the last few years, the debate over EU constitutionalism has become a central arena in which historical facts and interpretations have been used to undermine the grand narrative of ever-closer union. For instance, Davies and Rasmussen have maintained that the constitutionalisation narrative should be seen as a legitimating strategy of the ECJ, not a proven historical fact.[38]

In this context, it is interesting to note the contrast between the historical narratives of EU law and those of European human rights law. The history of EU law, its early role conceived in technical functionalist collaboration, does not lend itself as readily to grand narratives as the history of the Council of Europe (CoE) and the European human rights system. However, the burgeoning historiography of human rights has developed with a critically informed notion of human rights themselves, enabling a critical detachment of the subject matter and the grand narratives involved, while that of EU law is only beginning to embark on a similar critical process.

This takes us to the second metanarrative, which concerns the role of human rights in the European integration. The narrative of subjective rights and their spread is one of the most common Whig histories in modern historiography, as has been pointed out.[39] The concept of Whig history refers to the understanding of history as the continuous march of progress, where the individual's position – whether materially, economically, culturally, legally, or socially – is seen to improve over time. Coined by British historian Herbert Butterfield (1900–1979), known for coining catchphrases (he also came up with the notion of 'scientific revolution'), 'Whig history' has since become a pejorative term, describing a naïve and uncritical view of the complexities of historical development.[40] In human rights history, the Whig interpretation is presented as a simplistic view of the development of human rights as a victory march from the French Revolution to the Universal Declaration of Human Rights after World War II. This view has been

[37] M Rasmussen, 'Towards a Legal History of European Law' in M Cremona, C Kilpatrick and J Scott (eds), Special Section: *Using the Historical Archives of the EU to Study Cases of CJEU* (2021) 6 *European Papers*.

[38] B Davies and M Rasmussen, 'Towards a New History of European Law' (2012) 21 *Contemporary European History*. See also F Bignami, 'Rethinking the Legal Foundations of the European Constitutional Order: The Lessons of the New Historical Research' (2013) 28 *American University International Law Review* 1311; M Rasmussen and D Sindbjerg Martinsen, 'EU Constitutionalization Revisited: Redressing a Central Assumption in European Studies' (2019) 25 *European Law Journal* 251; P Leino-Sandberg, 'Enchantment and Critical Distance in EU Legal Scholarship: What Role for Institutional Lawyers?' (2022) 1 *European Law Open* 231. On the implications of the narrative disjunction, see N Scicluna and S Auer, 'Europe's Constitutional Unsettlement: Testing the Political Limits of Legal Integration' (2023) 99 *International Affairs* 769.

[39] L Hunt, *Inventing Human Rights: A History* (W.W. Norton, 2007); S Moyn, *The Last Utopia: Human Rights in History* (Belknap Press of Harvard University Press, 2010); P Slotte and M Halme-Tuomisaari, 'Revisiting the Origins of Human Rights: Introduction' in P Slotte and M Halme-Tuomisaari (eds), *Revisiting the Origins of Human Rights* (Cambridge University Press, 2015); S Moyn, *Human Rights and the Uses of History* (Verso, 2017).

[40] H Butterfield, *The Whig Interpretation of History* (G. Bell and Sons, 1931).

superseded by robust criticism of the various failings of human rights and the different human rights regimes in addressing issues such as extreme poverty.[41]

The European human rights narrative can easily be presented as an unparalleled success story, in which the war-torn countries of Europe come together to formulate not just a treaty or convention, but also a court. Their aim is clear: to ensure that the horrors of the Holocaust and totalitarianism are never repeated, even if it means limiting the sovereignty of the states themselves. This is an inspiring narrative, and even the critical historical observations – such as the rejection of economic and social rights from the European Convention on Human Rights (ECHR) – are not fundamental, but rather illustrate the evolving nature of the system.[42] However, this is a story where the EU and its predecessors are notably absent, during the emergence of the European human rights regime until the 1990s. There is a clear duality in the narrative of human rights, where the rights discourse rested on the CoE, while the European integration had little to do with it, which lasted until the Lisbon Treaty negotiations.

Even the critical historical work on the European human rights system, primarily centered around the CoE, the ECHR and the European Court of Human rights, such as that of Duranti, offers a rich narrative in which political development, legal change and geopolitics are intertwined in ways that provide a powerful introduction to the creation and internal dynamics of the system. There is also substantial critical work on the limitations of the early European human rights regime, which has noted that pioneers of the system were not prepared to recognise persons of non-white or non-European backgrounds as full holders of human rights, nor to extend the European system of human rights to its colonies. In a similar vein, they were adamant about rejecting the inclusion of economic, social, or cultural rights in the Convention, initially limiting it to purely classical liberty rights.[43] This is parallel to the early developments of European integration, where race and ethnic nationhood were central determinants of belonging and exclusion, where colonial subjects were not included among those who would benefit from the new rights.

The duality of integration relating to rights, where the CoE was tasked with the enforcement of a human rights system, changed dramatically with first the Maastricht and then the Lisbon Treaty. The nebulous yet curiously precise formulation of Article 2 of the TEU established that the EU is founded on the 'values of respect for human dignity, freedom, democracy, equality, the rule of law and respect for human rights, including the rights of persons belonging to minorities'. Even in the early comments, there was a clear scepticism of the uniformity and the shared nature of the values so

[41] R Dickinson et al, *Examining Critical Perspectives on Human Rights* (Cambridge University Press, 2012); J Lacroix and J-Y Pranchère, *Le Procès des droits de l'homme. Généalogie du scepticisme démocratique* (Seuil, 2016); D Lochak, 'Critiques des droits de l'homme' in *Les droits de l'homme* (La Découverte, 2009); Z Manfredi, 'Recent Histories and Uncertain Futures: Contemporary Critiques of International Human Rights and Humanitarianism' (2013) 22 *Qui Parle: Critical Humanities and Social Sciences* 3; J Slaughter, 'Hijacking Human Rights: Neoliberalism, the New Historiography, and the End of the Third World' (2018) 40 *Human Rights Quarterly* 735.

[42] This reflects a broader reluctance; see CO Lichuma, 'In International Law We (Do Not) Trust: The Persistent Rejection of Economic and Social Rights as a Manifestation of Cynicism' (2019) 4 *Völkerrechtsblog.*

[43] M Duranti, *The Conservative Human Rights Revolution: European Identity, Transnational Politics, and the Origins of the European Convention* (Oxford University Press, 2017); A Saunders, 'Animated by the European Spirit' in Saunders et al (eds), *Revolutions in International Law: The Legacies of 1917* (Cambridge University Press, 2021) 367-400.

enshrined, as well as their use as parts of an enforcement mechanism.[44] What the discussions demonstrated was the close linkage between the new human rights narrative and the anti-totalitarian narrative which we will turn to next. In the Maastricht Treaty (Article F, Article 6.1), the values were still principles and the list was shorter: 'The Union is founded on the principles of liberty, democracy, respect for human rights and fundamental freedoms, and the rule of law, principles which are common to the Member States.' What this essentialising statement already demonstrated was the willingness of the EU to attach itself to the human rights narrative, recognising its significance also as a source of legitimation.

The European human rights system, despite its detractors, can be seen as an unquestioned success story of the CoE, offering to the Western European alliance a way to demonstrate its moral and legal rebirth after the years of war and totalitarian rule. The EU and its predecessors were for a very long time content on leaving human rights to the CoE, and their inclusion as principles in the Maastricht and as values in the Lisbon Treaty may appear as opportunistic. Nevertheless, the timing coincides with the period of great enthusiasm for human rights and a certain kind of value universalism beginning in the early 1990s.

The third metanarrative is that of democracy and anti-totalitarianism. This is an oddly bifurcated narrative as opposing sides of it have been utilised both by the supporters of the EU and its opponents. The supporters claim that the EU was inspired by the anti-totalitarian movements after World War II, while critics have pointed to the fact that authoritarian and totalitarian regimes such as Nazi Germany supported European integration on their own terms and could thus be called the precursors of the EU in proposing economic integration. The traditional justification for not just the EU but also its enlargement is rooted in opposition to authoritarianism and support for democracy and the rule of law. While the CoE could set standards and provide a degree of enforcement, only the EU was able to institutionalise the demands of democracy and prevent the return of authoritarianism after the fall of the Soviet Union. In the histories of integration, the inclusion of former dictatorships Portugal, Spain, and Greece, followed by the ex-Soviet satellites of East Germany, Poland, Hungary, the Czech Republic, Slovakia, Romania, Bulgaria, Slovenia, and Croatia, ensured that their nascent democracies became stable and viable.

This kind of historical writing is most pervasive in popular accounts of EU expansion or in the EU's own self-presentation. According to this interpretation, the Union was conceived as a peace project, designed to bind the different states together with ties of prosperity, from which practices such as democracy and the rule of law would ensue.[45] Of course, the fact that authoritarian practices and different forms of democratic backsliding are widely present in Member States does somewhat undermine the narrative.

In contrast, an important strand of the critical history of EU integration has sought to trace its origins to Europe's totalitarian past, both in politics and law. One of the

[44] See, eg, M Claes, 'Editorial Note: How Common are the Values of the European Union?' (2019) 15 *Croatian Yearbook of European Law and Policy* VII.

[45] On this notion and its limits, see discussions in A Pagden, *The Pursuit of Europe: A History* (Oxford University Press, 2022) 228–314; and S Ghervas, *Conquering Peace: From the Enlightenment to the European Union* (Harvard University Press, 2021).

most enduring preoccupations of the critical histories of European integration has been the role of totalitarian states as its supporters, suggesting that the roots of the idea of European integration lie not in the quest for a democratic future, but in the opposite, such as the Nazi idea of the New Europe. While Europe had earlier served as a convenient common denominator for strongmen seeking to give their ambitions of power a more palatable moniker, nowhere was this more widely used than in Nazi Germany and among its allies. Among its predecessors in this regard, Napoleon famously presented a vision for shared European law and institutions, but this did not really find any practical application beyond a singular statement.[46] The vision of Europe formulated by Nazi Germany and adopted by enthusiastic followers, such as in Vichy France, was not driven by grand plans for the future, but rather by a conservative, backward-looking hostility towards progressive movements of various kinds both within and without, ranging from liberalism to socialism.[47]

This episode became a crucial talking point especially in the British media, where scholars like Laughlan argued that the European project was rotten from the start. This long-lived narrative of the authoritarian nature of European integration and the threat that it posed to Britain was used with great effect to argue in favour of Brexit.[48]

In addition to the politically programmatic works that sought to expose the Fascist roots of European integration – mainly to argue against pursuing integration at all – a range of more serious works has sought to engage with the intellectual roots of economic integration in particular, and its origins in the Nazi and Fascist thinkers of the 1930s and 1940s. One of the first studies in this vein was the volume *Darker Legacies of Law in Europe* (2003), which offers a representative sample of the early critical legal histories of European law.[49]

There are two main aspects of the Nazi project that make it difficult to trace a Nazi lineage for the European project as a whole. The first is that the Nazi Europeanism was primarily culturally conservative, aimed at attracting Christian conservatives with talk about the dangers of communism and liberalism. These ideas were largely propagated by the SS side of Nazi propaganda, where garnering support from the occupied territories was a central preoccupation. In this context, Europe was portrayed as a Christian bastion under attack from external forces: on the one hand, the barbarian communists from the East, and on the other, the depraved Anglo-Saxons from the West.[50] There is an interesting continuity of this narrative in the contemporary tradition of illiberalism and value conservatism among the European far right and certain authoritarian regimes in Europe.

[46] T Yepremyan, 'Napoleonic Paradigm of European Integration: Theory and History' (2021) 39 *Napoleonica. La Revue* 35, 47.

[47] Recently, numerous excellent studies on the Nazi New Europe have appeared; see O Heilbronner, 'Großraum Europa: The Nazi Concept of "Greater European Space"' (2021) 136:583 *The English Historical Review* 1574.

[48] J Laughlan, *Tainted Source: The Undemocratic Origins of the European Idea* (Sphere, 1998). On the convoluted narratives underpinning British voting behaviour, including imperial nostalgia and opposition to European domination, see, eg, R Saunders, 'Brexit and Empire: "Global Britain" and the Myth of Imperial Nostalgia' (2020) 48 *The Journal of Imperial and Commonwealth History* 1140.

[49] C Joerges and N Singh Ghaleigh (eds), *Darker Legacies of Law in Europe* (Hart Publishing, 2003).

[50] On Nazi New Europe, see J Dafinger, 'Show Solidarity, Live Solitarily: The Nazi "New Europe" as a "Family of Peoples"' (2017) 24 *European Review of History* 905; J Dafinger and D Pohl (eds), *A New Nationalist Europe under Hitler: Concepts of Europe and Transnational Networks in the National Socialist Sphere of Influence, 1933–1945* (Routledge, 2019).

The second aspect was the Nazi legal programme, which was not at all conservative, but rather revolutionary. One of the primary ways in which the Nazi party programme related to socialism was through its emphasis on social justice. For both Nazi and Fascist party legal policies, the enemy was the rule of law and formal jurisprudence, which could obstruct the reforms that the party sought to implement. This revolutionary nature of the law, and the primacy of the will of the movement over the text of the law, led to both the legal system and the courts being used as tools of repression rather than functioning as independent entities.[51]

This revolutionary idea of the law as a tool at best and an obstacle at worst also led to a remarkable transformation after the war, when European legal tradition and heritage became catchwords not only for the reconstitution of the legal system after totalitarianism, but also for the foundation of European legal unity. Tradition and history, even the Roman law tradition that was vilified by Nazis, provided a source of stability and continuity, a legitimating presence in the face of demands for change and reform. The European legal tradition, especially the idea of a shared legal heritage, could show how there was a fundamental unity that could serve as a model for future integration.[52] The crux of this was the idea of law as something beyond the politics of the nation-state and the authoritarian leaders eager to utilise it as a tool. The historical constitution of the foundations of law to elements such as Roman law served a similar purpose as the technocratic functionalism of the early integration, claiming that the rules and regulations embedded in the law were somehow neutral and beyond politics. This was of course not true, but it served as an aspiration for the future.

The unifying thread between the three metanarratives is that they illustrate the contested nature of some of the most cherished founding myths of the European project and, by extension, of European law. While traditional histories of the European legal tradition and that of EU law rely on the idea that law was a tool for making Europe a better place – improving societies, acting as a bulwark to safeguard individual rights, ensuring successful cooperation between former enemies, and promoting economic prosperity – critical historiography often emerges as a spoiler, killing enthusiasm and idealism with uncomfortable truths. This is, of course, often the assumed role of critics and reflects the typical position of critical scholarship in general, as people who do not necessarily make a positive contribution, but point out problems and inconsistencies instead. In the metanarratives, critical historiography has engaged all three with a modicum of success. Inquiries into the institutional narrative have uncovered the presence of a whole group of lawyers who sought to use law as a tool for deepening integration and the construction of a supranational legal order, but the work has been painstaking due to the limitations of source materials. Within the human rights narrative, critical studies have analysed how the EU not only sought to support human rights, but strove for

[51] On Nazi law and its nature, see M Stolleis, *The Law under the Swastika: Studies on Legal History in Nazi Germany* (University of Chicago Press, 1998); L Gruchmann, *Justiz im Dritten Reich* (Oldenburg, De Gruyter 2002); C Benson and J Fink, 'New Perspectives on Nazi Law' (2012) 3 *Jurisprudence* 341.

[52] K Tuori, *Empire of Law: Nazi Germany, Exile Scholars and the Battle for the Future of Europe*, Cambridge Studies in European Law and Policy (Cambridge University Press, 2020). On the role of history as a future path to law by some central actors, see W Hallstein, *Der unvollendete Bundesstaat. Europäische Erfahrungen und Erkenntnisse* (Econ, 1969) 33; R Zimmermann, 'Roman and Comparative Law: The European Perspective (Some Remarks Apropos a Recent Controversy)' (1995) 16 *The Journal of Legal History* 28.

greater legitimacy with association in human rights. In the anti-totalitarian narrative, the discussion on the anti-totalitarian roots of the European integration has subsided, leading to a new appreciation of the role of tradition in legal discourse. In all of these, critical inquiries into the past have oscillated between the deconstructive urge to illustrate the troubling associations behind many of the characteristics of European legal integration and the more careful discussions over the genealogies of ideas and practices. This has been the narrative arc of the historical criticism itself, from the negation of the simplistic marketing spiels used to justify integration to the observation of nuances and shades of grey.

IV. Conclusions

The idea of a critical history of European law is attractive, but the obstacles to producing a truly groundbreaking study are formidable. The future of the European past is so closely tied to the ways in which the EU draws on its past that breaking away from it would require access to sources that are not linked to the aims of the institutions in the present.

Within the traditional historiography of the EU and its law, there is a deep vein of inspirational history – historical writing that presents a suitable past for an envisioned future, highlighting founding heroes and key moments of triumph. In this sense, the EU may be seen to emulate nation-states, which have grounded their meaning and sense of belonging in historical narratives.

Famed historian Reinhard Koselleck pointed out that history – writing about the past – is always primarily a question about the future. While it may be written to answer the questions of today, its focus lies in the future. A student of Carl Schmitt, Koselleck himself was a former soldier in the Nazi German army, surviving both the Eastern Front and the camps, but with a deeply pessimistic worldview.[53] Thus, it is unlikely that he meant history to be seen as inspiring or as presenting a conventional path to the future; rather, his view suggests that the past, present, and future are all intertwined in historiography.

If traditional historical writing focuses on the events of the past, the actors, and their thoughts and deeds, which were then used to legitimate political processes such as that of integration, what is the role of a critical history of EU law? What is the drama of exposure that critical historians aim for in this context? In the EU archives, particularly concerning the early years, that drama has been muted, as the record has been curated in such a way that few of the early controversies remain. It appears that, in the early days, archiving practices had not yet developed to the level customary in national archives.

However, the role of legal history is significant in the scholarship on EU law, as law has been a key factor in shaping the EU. Particularly in discussions about the role of teleology, critical scholarship has sought to determine whether the law was seen as a tool – a means to an end – or whether the rule of law was genuinely a preoccupation and a value for the early integration lawyers. Thus, the critical examination of the concept of

[53] S Haselby, 'Repetition and Rupture' (*Aeon*, 1 September 2020), available at https://aeon.co/essays/reinhart-kosellecks-theory-of-history-for-a-world-in-crisis.

teleology and teleological interpretation cannot avoid the uncomfortable comparisons with authoritarian traditions such as Nazi, Fascist, or Soviet law, where the law was simply a tool for achieving political ends.

If history serves as a tool for legitimating the present and the future, the role of critical history is to point out the problems within the legitimating narrative. The past is a foreign country, and although there is a long tradition of nationalistic historical writing that conjures imagined communities, is this something on which the EU or its law should build its legitimacy? Compared with the histories of human rights, which have flourished in recent years, the historiography of EU law has remained tediously technical. This stems in part from the subject matter – economic developments rarely evoke the same drama as the struggle for justice and fundamental rights – but an even deeper reason lies in the sterile nature of the available sources. Much remains inaccessible, and what is available often appears suspiciously clear. For the new critical history to achieve its aims of deeper analysis and unfettered access, much work has been done to circumvent such window-dressing with the use of private archives.

As seen in the brief overview of the uses of the past in EU institutions, the distinction between the contemplative and instrumental uses is clear. In instrumental terms, what is understood to be the heritage of Europe is viewed as beneficial for the future, meaning that evaluations of the past, present, and future are interlinked. The possibility of a critical history is inexorably tied to the rejection of the exemplary nature of the past, to its use as an argument in the present. What is evident is that for the actors and institutions in the EU, the value of history is instrumental, and the content of what is considered to be exemplary and traditional, a part of heritage, is conditioned by the present.

This is relevant because, for the past decade or so, there has been an uninterrupted discussion of crisis. As has become apparent, crises are not moments when new solutions are being thought out, but rather times when old solutions become more palatable due to a lack of alternatives. Rodgers, in his classic *Atlantic Crossings*, describes crises as eruptions of the past into the present.[54] Within European history, there is a recurring narrative of crisis and renewal, which has seeped into the history of EU law. This is not the kind of fundamental crisis that Husserl referred to when discussing the crisis of rationality, nor the crisis of democracy examined by Popper. Instead, these crises have allowed past mistakes and bad practices to resurface in the present, most vividly during the Eurozone crisis. In terms of the future of critical historiography of EU law and integration, it is evident that there will be a fruitful field of inquiry ahead as the archival restrictions are lifted. Already now, the writing of critical history of EU law has produced promising results, demolishing the polished image or the Whig history of European legal integration.

[54] DT Rodgers, *Atlantic Crossings: Social Politics in a Progressive Age* (Belknap Press of Harvard University Press, 1998) 414.

3

Down on Politics

How the Tension between Democracy and Capitalism Went Missing in Frankfurt and How It Might Be Recovered

MICHAEL A WILKINSON

I. Introduction

One of the key messages conveyed from critical reflections on European integration throughout the euro-crisis was the centrality to its unfolding dynamic of the tension between democracy and capitalism. The work of Wolfgang Streeck was central to the return of this heuristic and its renewed explanatory power. His articles published at the height of the crisis were incendiary, sparking life into a new generation of critical theorists of the European Union (EU), all the more so because they came from a figure from within or close to the mainstream of the academy.[1]

Streeck's achievement was to have brought the agency of 'capital' back into view, surpassing democratic theories that modelled only the relation between the state and its people and any intermediary representative institutions. In place of the normative abstractions associated with theories of deliberative democracy, he offered a sociologically-grounded analysis which highlighted that the functioning of the economy is itself a political and not only a technical matter.

An upshot of this renewed attention to political economy was the realisation that legitimation crises could result from the pressure placed by investors and financial markets as much as by citizens and their withdrawal of support. But it also meant that the relationship between states and markets, citizens and investors, must be understood as a reflection of how the state is politically and legally organised, rather than determined by any 'natural order'. Streeck's work thus drew attention to the processes, institutions and ideologies of economic and social ordering that framed and reframed the relationship between democracy and capitalism, for which the EU – and EU law – had become central.

[1] See W Streeck, 'The Crises of Democratic Capitalism' (2011) 71 *New Left Review* 5–29; W Streeck, 'Markets and Peoples: Democratic Capitalism and European Integration' (2012) 73 *New Left Review* 63; W Streeck, *Buying Time: The Delayed Crisis of Democratic Capitalism* (Verso, 2014).

Recovery of this dynamic of state transformation is essential for understanding EU law's role in a system of governance which systematically privileges capitalism over democracy and markets over peoples. Detailed critiques or reforms of particular areas of EU law cannot remedy this; it requires an analysis of the constitutional function of the EU and of the role it plays in the de-politicisation of social conflict and occlusion of political freedom. In examining critical theory's approach to these aspects of the state, we can also reveal the blind-spots in certain strands of critical theory itself and suggest how they might be overcome.

We will begin by outlining the idea of a tension between democracy and capitalism as renewed in Streeck's work and in his criticism of the second-generation Frankfurt School's turn away from political economy under the influence of Jürgen Habermas (section II). We then consider how this heuristic was already lost in key thinkers of the first-generation Frankfurt School, specifically due to Friedrich Pollock's theory of 'state capitalism', which instrumentalises the concept of the political (section III). If instead we reach back to Franz Neumann and Otto Kirchheimer, two theorists on Frankfurt's outer fringes, we can recover the perspective of a tension between democracy and capitalism, the ambivalence of juridification in managing it, and the importance of political sovereignty in staging it (section IV). Neumann and Kirchheimer's focus on the concept of the political transcends their reflections on the collapse of Weimar and the rise of National Socialism and is a core part of their critiques of the political alienation in postwar Europe (section V). Recovering this perspective thus enables us to reconnect critical theory with a full-bodied critique of the project of European integration, which hollows out democracy in both normal and emergency modes of governing and yet is stubbornly affirmed in Habermasian theory and practice (section VI).

II. The Tension between Democracy and Capitalism

Stated briefly, the response to the financial crisis of 2008 revealed a deep-seated tension, or dynamic disequilibrium, between the imperatives of capital, which subject politics to the pressures of the financial markets, and those of democracy, which subject politics to the demands of the people. In the EU, this tension was characterised by an acute and increasing antagonism, structurally favouring the interests of capital over those of democracy and of markets over peoples. Aided by that heuristic, I argued in 2013 that the EU's constitutional trajectory presaged a new constellation of 'authoritarian liberalism', a form of governing that combined political authoritarianism and economic liberalism, restricting democracy in order to maintain systems of capital accumulation, notably through the imposition of austerity.[2]

The lineages of authoritarian liberalism could be traced back at least to the interwar era and the writings of German constitutional theorist Hermann Heller, who saw the

[2] MA Wilkinson, 'The Spectre of Authoritarian Liberalism: Reflections on the Constitutional Crisis of the European Union' (2013) 14 *German Law Journal* 527. This formed the basis for a long durée analysis in MA Wilkinson, *Authoritarian Liberalism and the Transformation of Modern Europe* (Oxford University Press, 2021).

rollback of democracy towards the end of Weimar as an attempt to protect the capitalist economy.[3] In an important sense, Streeck's reconstruction was thus not an original insight but revived a theme which, as well as present in the work of Heller, had coursed through Karl Polanyi's seminal text *The Great Transformation*,[4] and had punctuated Karl Marx's political writings, notably on the class struggles in France emerging around the failed 1848 revolution.[5] The notion of a conflict between democracy and capitalism had in fact been adopted even by some classical liberals in the nineteenth century, who expressly justified the need to devise methods to protect private property from the newly enfranchised masses.[6] In a different register, the overarching tension could be traced back to themes from Rousseau and Hegel on the unsustainability of a legitimate state and social contract in the face of stark inequalities in civil society.[7]

The dynamic nature of democracy and capitalism meant that the nature of their social and political relation would evolve as their institutional forms evolved. And Streeck complemented his conjunctural analysis of the global financial crisis with a more abstract conceptual framework underscoring a fundamental tension in their underlying logics.[8] These logics, while not transhistorical as such, pick out more basic and long-run differences in their operation, which means that their tension transcends crisis periods, representing more general features of the modern political condition. The crisis of democratic capitalism thus signalled a deeper tension in their respective ethical demands: if the market reflects a marginal ethics, by advancing the prospect and expectation of rational egoism and competitive accumulation, democratic society reflects a maximal ethics, by holding out the prospect of and need for solidarity, collaboration and concern for human well-being.

What prevents disequilibrium from turning into outright collapse is the state itself, understood as a totality, combining the market ethos of a capitalist political economy with the moral restraints imposed by social and democratic norms. But although perceiving these forces to be managed through the unified political authority of the modern state, Streeck also cautioned against a functionalist worldview in which the success of efforts at taming capitalist excesses are guaranteed. Democracy is a fragile achievement and one that the process of European integration was in danger of annulling.

The separation of the economy from democracy, a process of 'de-democratisation' of capitalism, which accelerated after the crisis of 2008, of course reflected global and not only European currents. But the key to understanding the significance of the EU was to see it as effecting this separation in a constitutional manner, creating an external constraint, or *vincolo esterno*. As Hayek foresaw in his work on the interstate federation, supranational integration could be a means to insulate the state from the democratic pressure of the people and render it subject to the pressures of the market. It would

[3] H Heller, 'Autoritärer Liberalismus' (1933) 44 *Die Neue Rundschau* 289-298, H Heller (translated by S Paulson), 'Authoritarian Liberalism?' (2015) 21 *European Law Journal* 295-301.

[4] K Polanyi, *The Great Transformation: The Political and Economic Origins of Our Time* (Beacon Press, 2001 [1944]).

[5] See, eg, K Marx, 'The Class Struggle in France' in *Political Writings* (Verso, 2019 [1850]).

[6] See Polanyi (n 4) 234.

[7] J-J Rousseau, *A Discourse on Inequality* (translated by M Cranston, Penguin, 1984); F Ruda, *Hegel's Rabble: An Investigation into Hegel's Philosophy of Right* (Bloomsbury, 2011).

[8] See W Streeck, 'Taking Capitalism Seriously: Towards an Intuitionalist Approach to Contemporary Political Economy' (2011) 9 *Socio Economic Review* 137.

be several decades for Hayek's vision to come to fruition, as postwar Europe initially saw the building of a transnational mixed economy. But from the mid-1970s onward, 'European integration grew out of its Keynesian illusions and its enthusiasm for planning, and the more integration progressed and advanced into the centre of the European political economy, the more it followed Hayek's intuitions of 1939'.[9]

In reviewing the neoliberal era since the 1970s, Streeck also took to task the second-generation Frankfurt School in general and Jürgen Habermas in particular for avoiding issues of political economy and thus being unprepared for capital's revolt. In the early 1970s, Habermas's reading of the postwar period was that the crisis tendencies of capitalism had potentially been overcome or at least deferred through the enhanced technical capacities of the state in managing the economy. The result would not necessarily be a renewed era of stability, but the displacement of systemic economic crises into legitimation crises of the political order.[10] In the subsequent decade, Habermas would turn away from political economy altogether, developing his theory of communicative action which later became the basis for a fully normative turn towards liberal constitutionalism, culminating in his discourse theory of law and democracy.[11] Thus by the late 1970s his youthful scepticism of the postwar bourgeois *Rechtsstaat* had been substituted for a 'constitutional patriotism' around which rational consensus could be forged.[12]

Habermas's early ambivalence about the colonising effects of juridification on the lifeworld would be replaced by a faith in the civilising mission of law, one which would then be effortlessly upscaled into a 'postnational' project in the 1990s.[13] The transition from state theory to constitutionalism which characterised postwar West Germany in particular, and over time, European constitutional culture in general, had Habermas as its symbolic reference point.

In substituting theories of liberal democracy for political economy, Streeck argues, the second-generation Frankfurt School 'paid the penalty of forgoing a key part of Marx's legacy'.[14] In Streeck's recounting, it was the turn away from political economy that created a blind-spot, leaving the Frankfurt School unprepared for the return of 'capital' as agent as it pushed for the 'rollback of state intervention and the return to the market as the prime mechanism of resource allocation' in the era of neoliberalism.[15] Whereas Habermas had envisaged legitimation crises in which people would rebel against the intrusions into the lifeworld of an overly bureaucratised administrative system, it would, on the contrary, be capital that would lead the revolt against the postwar consensus. Habermasian theory was thus blindsided by key aspects of the reorganisation of political economy: the revival of accumulation through privatisation, marketisation and deregulation; expansion of the consumer society 'beyond all expectations'; and the economic implications of rising public and

[9] Streeck 2014 (n 1) 102.

[10] J Habermas, *Legitimation Crisis* (translated by T McCarthy, Beacon Press, 1975).

[11] J Habermas, *Between Facts and Norms: Contributions to a Discourse Theory of Law and Democracy* (MIT Press, 1996).

[12] For a detailed overview, see M Specter, *Habermas: An Intellectual Biography* (Cambridge University Press, 2010).

[13] J Habermas, *The Postnational Constellation: Political Essays* (MIT Press, 2001).

[14] Streeck 2014 (n 1) 2

[15] ibid 28.

private debt. Crucially, even as it later diagnosed the democratic deficits accrued through the building of the EU, Habermasian theory urged their settlement in a postnational future.[16]

Just as Habermas was embracing a vision of democracy that was proceduralised, formalised and juridified, the state's interventionist powers were increasingly deployed or delegated in the service of the market and the interests of capital. Through the decades of neoliberalism, commitment to market integration would be upscaled through a supranational economic constitution, which exacerbated the tension in the pairing of democracy and capitalism that grew out of the neoliberal rupture with the postwar settlement and consolidated the power of capital. Although critical in some of its particulars, this was a commitment that Habermas not only generally supported but saw as a 'stepping stone to the constitution of a world society'.

The 'postnational' constitutional narrative, which became so popular with 'the end of history', was not arrested by the failure of the Constitutional Treaty in 2005 nor even with the advent of the global financial crisis shortly after. On the contrary, the failure of the Constitutional Treaty and its symbolic difference with the Lisbon Treaty often barely registered, Habermas opening his *Crisis of the European Union* book with the observation that Europe 'is now *more than ever* a constitutional project' (emphasis added).[17] In reflecting on the EU after the onset of crisis, Habermas continued to present both the sociological and political dynamics of globalisation in highly naturalistic and functionalist terms. They were unstoppable social-evolutionary forces bound up with a capitalist dynamic of 'functionally-driven opening' followed by 'socially integrative closure'. Even with the initial failures of the EU in the euro-crisis laid bare, European integration still represented 'an important stage' – not to European unification, but along the route to a 'politically constituted world society'.[18] The political fragmentation precipitated by the euro-crisis was merely a stumbling block to be overcome by the natural-evolutionary force of constitutional law.[19]

III. The Eclipse of the Political in Frankfurt: Pollock's Theory of State Capitalism

What undergirded Habermas's evasion of political economy, and the assumption that the contradictions of democratic capitalism had been resolved? Streeck attributes this to the influence of Friedrich Pollock, founding member of the Institute for Social Research and close collaborator of Horkheimer and Adorno. For the first-generation Frankfurt School, Streeck notes, modern capitalism was already a system of 'technocratic economic administration', a diagnosis largely attributable to Pollock, who considered capitalism to have become thoroughly state-planned in the course of its development,

[16] See, eg, J Neyer, *The Justification of Europe: A Political Theory of Supranational Integration* (Oxford University Press, 2012), building on R Forst, *The Right to Justification: Elements of a Constructivist Theory of Justice* (Columbia University Press, 2011).

[17] J Habermas, *The Crisis of the European Union: A Response* (Polity Press, 2012) 1.

[18] ibid 2.

[19] ibid 1–12.

'so that nothing essential was left to the laws of the market'.[20] In Pollock's view, the development of increasingly sophisticated instruments of state planning in the interwar era had 'meant that the age of laissez-faire was well and truly over', and that 'advanced capitalism' had mutated into an 'essentially crisis-free economic machinery'.[21] For Pollock, 'the primacy of politics had succeeded the old primacy of economics and had thereby overcome the crisis tendencies in the original, chaotically disorganised, competitive form of capitalism'.[22] But what kind of politics had triumphed in this account?

This question points to a teleology of political and economic progress adopted by Pollock and in fact suggests a distinct blind-spot, which is unremarked by Streeck and raises a different concern: not only that the concept of 'state capitalism' discounted a return to laissez-faire economics or to rampant capitalism, but that its functionalism occluded the autonomy of the political realm and the phenomenon of political freedom. It was not a triumph of politics that this model depicted, but of technocracy, a method of governing that would later be consummated through the project of European integration. In other words, *it was not only the agency of capital that went missing in Frankfurt, but the agency of the people themselves.*

Sketched out in exile in 1941 and drawing on analyses of the USSR and Roosevelt's New Deal as well as German Fascism, 'state capitalism' was, for Pollock, the general form capitalism would take after the demise of its nineteenth century 'free market' liberal variant. 'State capitalism' designated a political form in which technical rationality had come to dominate society, political administration replaced free economic exchange, and the market mechanism was subordinated to centralised command and control.[23] With the abandonment of the market as an independent regulator of production and distribution, liberal capitalism, or what Pollock termed 'private capitalism' had been superseded by a new 'bureaucratised' form, a 'postliberal capitalism'.[24] State capitalism offered a new set of rules: the profit motive is subordinated to the power motive, individual interests are replaced by the interest of the ruling group as a whole, spontaneous organisation gives way to scientific management and private initiative and personal responsibility are integrated within the framework of 'the general plan' adopted by a new ruling class.[25]

Monopoly capitalism had functioned as an intermediary phase in the evolution from private to state capitalism, paving the way for state control of the economy through increasing concentrations of power, as monopolistic organisations harnessed immense technical capacity and developed the ability to allocate resources and labour in defiance of market pressure. Monopolisation had generated the technical means of total control of society, including methods of accounting, planning and training, as well as the rationalisation of administrative processes. Organisations that had been developed by business interests (trade associations, cartels, chambers of commerce) were

[20] Streeck 2014 (n 1) 12.
[21] ibid 13.
[22] ibid 14.
[23] F Pollock, 'State Capitalism: Its Possibilities and Limitations' in A Arato (ed) *The Frankfurt School Reader* (Continuum Publishing, 1982 [1941]) 71–95.
[24] For discussion, see M Gangl, 'The Controversy over Friedrich Pollock's State Capitalism' (2016) *History of the Human Sciences* 23–41.
[25] Pollock (n 23) 77.

transformed into government agencies for the control of production. Complemented by the control of money through the acquisition of private banks, state capitalism effected a fundamental transformation in the quality of private property, through 'regulation of prices, limitation of distributed profits, compulsory investment of surplus profits. . . and drastic taxation'.[26] All these measures converged to transform the capitalist entrepreneur into a mere rentier whose income was no longer subject to the vagaries of the market and whose profit motive became subordinated to the greater interest of the ruling group.

Pollock's key claim was that state capitalism had abolished the 'autonomy of economic laws' of supply and demand, with the command economy replacing the price mechanism in determining production and distribution. With all the technical means for efficient planning available, the only task was to find a stimulus for new investment and technical progress; hence the drive towards war and 'competitive rearmament', which could remain a hegemonic project as long as external threats could be identified.[27] The only limitations to state capitalism were those that derived from the natural conditions of mankind and even then, the 'drive for power over men might combine with the will to power over nature'.[28]

This was not only a new phase of capitalism; it appeared to Pollock to have ended any dialectical materialism. 'Economic problems in the old sense no longer exist' Pollock argued, 'when the coordination of all economic activities is effected by conscious plan instead of by the natural laws of the market'.[29] As Horkheimer declared in his introduction, Pollock drew 'a picture of an authoritarian society that might embrace the earth'. Such a society, Horkheimer noted, 'can endure for a long and terrifying period', there being no economic limitations to its expansion.[30]

Pollock's summary assessment was that 'state capitalism', by de-differentiating between state and market, had changed 'the character of the whole historic period, signifying no less than 'the transition from a predominantly economic to an essentially political era'.[31] The 'primacy of politics over economics, so much disputed under democracy, is clearly established'.[32]

In replacing the formal equality of market exchange and commodity production with a political hierarchy, state capitalism partially resembled a return to a feudal-type order. 'Under state capitalism', Pollock argued,

> men meet each other as commander and commanded; the extent to which one can command or has to obey depends in the first place upon one's position in the political set-up and only in a secondary way upon the extent of one's property.[33]

Although the state had taken over the steering and direct control of labour, production, and distribution, it had led to a formation that was in significant respects less emancipatory than its liberal predecessor.

[26] ibid 79.
[27] ibid 86.
[28] ibid 88.
[29] ibid 87.
[30] M Horkheimer, 'Preface' (1941) *Studies in Philosophy and Social Science* IX(2): 195–99, 198.
[31] Pollock (n 23) 78.
[32] Pollock, 'Is National Socialism a New Order?' (1942) *Studies in Philosophy and Social Science* IX(3): 440–55, 453.
[33] Pollock (n 23) 78.

This conclusion appeared to leave classical Marxism at a dead-end: labour, which had been considered the source of potential emancipation by Marx, was now a source of pure domination in a command economy. Markets and private property seemed to have been overcome and the profit motive subordinated to a political programme, but without any prospect of freedom. Pollock's theory of the primacy of the political suggested a non-contradictory and one-dimensional society 'possessing no intrinsic dynamic that could point toward the immanent possibility of its historical negation'.[34]

Not only were the immanent contradictions of capitalism apparently overcome; there was no meaning given to democracy, or what distinguishes it from authoritarianism or totalitarianism. Political questions appear only in technical form, to attain 'effective organisation of resources, yet at the same time retain the maximum freedom of individual action'.[35] Other than the end of laissez-faire economics, the triumph of politics is devoid of meaning; the political character of state capitalism is entirely hollow. Politics reaches its apogee and is simultaneously reduced to a functionalist, technical, administrative phenomenon.[36]

Despite some privately shared doubts, Pollock's theory eventually found favour with Adorno and Horkheimer, Adorno reproducing Pollock's functionalism in a different register, moving to decipher 'the psychological mechanisms that undergird the "totally" administered state–capitalist order',[37] and Horkheimer coming to view the state merely as a tool of domination, which 'became a kind of pervasive condition in the society as a whole'.[38] Pollock's pessimistic worldview would then be reinforced with Adorno and Horkheimer's *Dialectic of Enlightenment*, which presents society's domination of nature and advance in the development of the productive forces and technical rationality as totally dehumanising. Echoing Pollock's interpretation, they argue that centralised planning had eliminated 'the objective laws of the market', replacing it with 'the conscious decision of the managing directors' of political capitalism, and reimposing the 'old law of value and hence the destiny of capitalism' itself.[39] Solace would be found in psychology, culture and philosophy.

Although the core members of the Frankfurt school converged around Pollock's thought that state capitalism 'clearly established' the 'primacy of politics over economics', the concept of the political appears to be reduced to a crude assertion of organisational capacity, brute force, terror or violent coercion. And if the victory of 'democratic state capitalism' is only due to its material superiority, the political form of democracy is similarly reduced to technical competence and instrumental rationality, not to mention the ideological and repressive apparatus of United States (US) imperialism. What of the

[34] M Postone, 'Critical Theory and the Historical Transformations of Capitalist Modernity' in MJ Thompson (ed), *Palgrave Handbook of Critical Theory* (Palgrave, 2016) 146.

[35] Pollock (n 23) 93.

[36] See W Scheuerman, 'Critical Theory and the Present Crisis' (2019) 26 *Constellations* 451, 454. Pollock's account, Scheuerman notes, 'entailed a strongly functionalist social theory: the state-capitalist social totality's component parts function more or less hand-in-hand to uphold the overall system of social domination'.

[37] ibid.

[38] M Jay, *The Dialectical Imagination: A History of the Frankfurt School and the Institute of Social Research 1923 - 1950* (University of California Press, 1996) 165–66.

[39] TW Adorno and M Horkheimer, *Dialectic of Enlightenment* (Verso, 1997) 38. Although the theory of state capitalism 'implied a new theory of rule', it was one that Horkheimer and Adorno 'did not always make explicit'. Gangl (n 24).

'actually existing' democratic – or undemocratic – aspects of the US model of 'democratic state capitalism'?[40] In both cases, whether democratic or totalitarian, the so-called primacy of the political state over the economic is nominal, reducing politics to an instrument of pure domination.

IV. Recovering the Political: Neumann and Kirchheimer's Assessment of National Socialism

Paradoxically, adoption of Pollock's theory of state capitalism led the inner circle of the Frankfurt School away from Marxism and from political economy more generally. They 'no longer considered the economic substructure the crucial locus of the social totality' and instead paid increased attention to 'technological rationalization as an institutional force', 'instrumental rationality as a cultural imperative' and the 'psychosocial mechanisms of obedience and sources of violence'.[41]

Although the inner group of the Frankfurt School around Horkheimer spoke of a primacy of politics with respect to 'state capitalism', they ignored what would today be considered 'essential topics in political science'.[42] As Buchstein puts it, despite making important advances in cultural theory and social psychology, the Frankfurt School 'did not achieve comparable results in the field of politics and its institutions; at no point in theory production did this circle have an elaborated theory of the political or of political institutions at its disposal'.[43] Simply put, this was 'critical theory without politics'.

It was also critical theory without political theory. Far from expressing the primacy of politics, state capitalism, on the contrary, appears to be a wholly *de-politicised* state and one in which political life has been subsumed in a totally administered world. This hollowness in Pollock's analysis is revealed by a brief contrast with the work of Hannah Arendt. To borrow Hannah Arendt's conceptual framing, state capitalism appears as a paradigmatically unpolitical form, in both its totalitarian and 'democratic' versions.

Arendt's distinction between power and violence suggests that the joint action in concert connoted by the idea of 'power' essential to the phenomenon of politics is replaced in totalitarianism, with a singular and instrumental rationality of ideology and violence. Violence itself is an *anti-political* concept, closely bound up with bureaucracy, 'rule by nobody', a regime where no one takes political responsibility.[44] Totalitarianism, in Arendt's reconstruction, is the death of politics because it erodes the public sphere and the human condition of plurality, ultimately destroying the one right to membership of a political community, 'the right to have rights', on which all others depend.[45]

'Democratic state capitalism' appears similarly unpolitical from an Arendtian perspective, and democratic in name only; its rule is based on technical superiority

[40] Herbert Marcuse's critique of liberal capitalism in the West would require separate analysis.
[41] Jay (n 38) 166.
[42] H Buchstein, 'Otto Kirchheimer and the Frankfurt School: Failed Collaborations in the Searchfor a Critical Theory of Politics' (2020) 47 *New German Critique* 81, 101.
[43] ibid 82.
[44] The conceptual distinction between power and violence is outlined in H Arendt, *On Violence* (Allen Lane, 1970).
[45] H Arendt, *The Origins of Totalitarianism* (Harcourt, 1966) 292.

and the managerial competence of a new ruling class. As Arendt argued in *The Human Condition*, the rise of the social over the long nineteenth century, which reduces humans to statistical aggregates in line with preoccupations of liberal political economy erases the public realm of politics where we appear to one another as equals with the capacity to act together.[46]

In Arendt's own words,

> the greater the bureaucratization of public life, the greater will be the attraction of violence. In a fully developed bureaucracy, there is nobody left with whom one could argue, to whom one could present grievances, on whom the pressures of power could be exerted. Bureaucracy is the form of government in which everybody is deprived of political freedom, of the power to act; for the rule by Nobody is not no-rule, and where all are equally powerless we have a tyranny without a tyrant.[47]

The relationship between Arendt and the Frankfurt School was difficult, and further complicated by her strained relationship with Marxism, and there is no space here to consider it in detail.[48] In any case, Pollock's thesis, although adopted by Horkheimer and Adorno, was far from uncontroversial even within the Frankfurt School itself as it was strongly contested by Franz Neumann and Otto Kirchheimer, two theorists on the outer fringes of the first generation.[49]

Neumann, in private correspondence with Horkheimer, criticised Pollock's theory not only for having departed from dialectical materialism but because the absence of antagonism, contradiction, and class conflict imparted 'a sense of complete powerlessness'.[50] Kirchheimer also viewed Fascism as far more fragile than Pollock's account suggested, 'not as a stable political order in Germany but as a system of constant rivalries between power groups' and one that would struggle because of its dependence on military expansion and imperialism.[51] Neumann and Kirchheimer's differences with Pollock went deeper than concern over his worldly pessimism, going right to the conceptual underpinning of his theory. Their concept of the political is particularly relevant to draw out here because it problematises the very idea of a 'totalitarian state capitalism' *and* it offers a critique of the political trajectory of so-called 'democratic state capitalism'.

[46] H Arendt, *The Human Condition* (University of Chicago Press, 1958) ch 2.

[47] Arendt (n 44) 81.

[48] On the similarities and differences between Arendt's theory of totalitarianism and those of interwar Marxism, see N Devlin, 'Hannah Arendt and Marxist Theories of Totalitarianism' (2023) 20 *Modern Intellectual History* 247–69. On the difficult relationship between Arendt and the Frankfurt School, see S Benhabib and C Picker, 'Arendt and the Frankfurt School' in P Gordon, E Hammer and A Honneth (eds), *The Routledge Companion to the Frankfurt School* (Routledge, 2019) 295. It has been suggested more specifically that Neumann's work had a profound influence on Arendt's *Origins of Totalitarianism*, see V Iakovu, 'Totalitarianism as a Non-State: Hannah Arendt's Debt to Franz Neumann' (2009) 8 *European Journal of Political Theory* 429.

[49] C Thornhill, *Political Theory in Modern Germany: An Introduction* (Blackwell, 2000) 92, notes they have both been described as 'left-wing Schmittians' owing to the clear influence of Schmitt on their work. In his compendious overview, Wiggerhaus notes how Kirchheimer and Neumann were treated 'strangely' by the institute's directors (R Wiggerhaus, *The Frankfurt School* (Polity Press, 1995) 223-36. As a biographical matter, it is notable that both were more closely engaged in legal and political practice during the Weimar Republic and had been members of the Social Democratic Party of Germany, retaining a proximity to political action that eluded figures such as Horkheimer and Adorno.

[50] See Gangl (n 24) 29.

[51] Buchstein (n 42) 94.

In the importance they place on the relative autonomy of the political realm and the significance of political freedom, Neumann and Kirchheimer share a great deal with Arendt. But in contrast to Arendt, they are consistently clear about the countervailing logic not only of bureaucracy and violence but of capitalism and – a neglected point – of legalism and juridification. Their work thus enables us to resume focus on the dynamic tension between democracy and capitalism and the role of institutional and constitutional factors in shaping it.

Key to Neumann and Kirchheimer's understanding of societal development was consideration of the relationship, interplay and conflict between politics and economics, and particularly the role of institutions in framing the relationship. Both theorists saw how governing institutions could be de-politicised in a way that would function to undermine democratic decision-making on the economy. Kircheimer's experience in interwar France, for example, showed how rendering central banks free from political oversight and potential socialist majorities in parliament 'was itself a political decision made in the interest of financial capital' since independent banks could use their power to undermine left-leaning governments.[52]

Political and legal institutions mattered for Neumann and Kirchheimer not only because some may prove more successful than others in terms of maintaining a system of domination but also due to the centrality of democracy as a phenomenon and its fragility in conditions of capitalism. As Scheuerman puts it,

> Neumann's revalorization of democracy and, more generally, the political sphere—a core strength of his version of critical theory, particularly when compared to its rivals—stems in part from his rejection of the problematic Frankfurt School notion of a seamlessly integrated social order.

Once that picture of society is rejected, 'along with all of its reductionist and functionalist connotations', we can begin 'to take politics—as a sphere of struggle and contestation, between and among competing social groups—seriously'.[53]

Neumann contested the notion that Fascism signalled a fundamentally new form of capitalism rather than a continuation of its monopoly phase. This difference with Pollock drew on a different historical account of nineteenth century capitalism In marked contrast, Neumann had long argued against the linear narrative of a binary of laissez-faire *or* state planning, liberal *or* managed capitalism, noting that the so-called 'Nightwatchman' state of the liberal imagination was *always* a myth. The liberal state of the long nineteenth century was always

> as strong as the political and social situation. . . demanded. It has conducted warfare and crushed strikes; with the help of strong navies it has protected its investments, with the help of strong armies it has defended and extended its boundaries, with the help of the police it has restored 'peace and order'.[54]

[52] ibid 94.

[53] Scheuerman (n 36) 456.

[54] F Neumann, *Der Funktionswandel des Gezetzes im Recht der bürgerlicken Gesellschaft* [*The Change in the Function of Law in Modern Society*] (1937) 6 *Zeitschrift für Sozialforschung* 542 (German), translated and reprinted in F Neumann, *The Democratic and Authoritarian State: Essays in Political and Legal Theory* (Herbert Marcuse ed, Free Press of Glencoe, 1957) 22.

Neumann's account of the nineteenth century 'liberal state' closely resonates with the work of Karl Polanyi and his pithy summary: 'laissez faire was planned, planning was not'. There was, for Neumann, no strong dichotomy of planning *or* laissez-faire, public coercion *or* private freedom. In parallel with early work by theorists associated with American legal realism, such as Robert Hale, Neumann conceptualised the variety of forms of power that could be exercised over others, both in public and in private, and problematised the drawing of any clear boundaries between the two domains.[55]

Although sometimes presented as a defender of the rule of law, Neumann's account of the virtues of legality was highly nuanced.[56] Even as a youthful optimist in the capacity of Weimar's labour constitution to effect a transition towards democratic socialism he criticised the judicial empowerment of the *Reichsgericht*, which, occurring through a revival of natural law, was in danger of fulfilling 'counterrevolutionary' functions. This position emerged against several conservative jurists (including his teacher Carl Schmitt) arguing for law to be used against the expropriation of private property following the hyperinflations of the 1920s. Neumann notes that the use of 'general principles of law' characteristic of the 'free law school', a 'kind of secret natural law', transformed the legal system by 'giving an immense amount of discretionary power to the judge'.[57] In particular, Article 153 of the Weimar Constitution which protected private property was utilised by liberals and conservatives in an attempt to frustrate the goals of legislative socialism. Through the juridical application of principles of economic freedom, Franz Neumann eventually lamented, the meaning of the Weimar Constitution, if initially conducive to a labour constitution, was 'transformed into its exact opposite'.[58]

By 1933, following the Nazi seizure of power, Neumann argued that social democracy failed in Germany because, in the mistaken belief that social democracy was possible without political democracy, it had restricted the working class to economistic strategies, failing to create a 'democratic consciousness'.[59] Instead of extending political freedom, the left had surrendered the political state to the bourgeoisie and sought reconciliation and compromise within the economic system. In other words, just when the dominant conservative political and economic classes were *politicising* their struggle in the early 1930s, the left and the unions were reduced to economism, retaining reformist strategies, and flatly opposing political strikes.[60] As Neumann would later come to realise, in pursuing this approach, and explicitly or tacitly accepting the organised and increasingly monopolised rule of capital, the left allowed the ruling class to effectively destroy the 'constitutional platform for the emancipation of labour', namely Weimar's parliamentary democracy.[61]

In other words, it was not only monopoly capitalism that prepared the ground for Fascism, but the erosion of parliamentary sovereignty and the left's own complicity in

[55] See C Offe, 'The Problem of Social Power in Franz L. Neumann's Thought' (2003) 10 *Constellations* 211.

[56] *cf* W Scheuerman, 'Critical Theory and the Law' in PE Gordon et al (eds), *The Routledge Companion to the Frankfurt School* (Routledge, 2019) 486–500.

[57] Neumann (n 54) 53–55.

[58] F Neumann, 'On the Preconditions and Legal Concept of an Economic Constitution' in K Tribe (ed), *Social Democracy and the Rule of Law: Otto Kirchheimer and Franz Neumann* (Allen & Unwin, 1987) 55–56.

[59] ibid 29.

[60] FL Neumann, *Behemoth: The Structure and Practice of National Socialism, 1933 – 1944* (Ivan R Dee, 2009 [1942]) 17.

[61] ibid 34–37.

de-politicisation. In his monumental study of the Nazi regime, *Behemoth*, Neumann focused not only on the political economy of National Socialism, but on its distinct political form. Like Pollock, he highlighted that the Nazi governing apparatus was supported by a broad hegemonic bloc combining four distinct groups: 'big industry, the party, the bureaucracy and the armed forces'.[62] But in contrast to Pollock, Neumann rejected the label 'state' for this combination and even argued that state capitalism was a contradiction in terms. For Neumann, the monopolisation of industry and the cartelisation of power politics combined into a form of 'totalitarian monopoly capitalism'. The point of this phrase was to stress its 'politically totalitarian but economically monopolistic' nature.[63]

In legal scholarship, the focus is often on how Nazi ideology transformed the essence of the rule of law, from a principle regulating the relationship between rulers and ruled to a hierarchical model based on the Führer's command. For Neumann and Kirchheimer, this subordination to command did not abolish private law but instrumentalised it, privatisation coming 'to serve the aims of authoritarian coercion of the Third Reich'.[64] This emerged in conjunction with the partial privatisation of state violence, through 'an (il)legitimate use of force by ideological groups in society', enforced by 'racketeering gangs' that occupied a space in between the family and civil society, organised around informal affiliation and personal loyalty.[65] Replacement of the generality of the rule of law by direct hierarchical command and the state by a cartel of interest groups was directed to the predominant goal of pursuing capital accumulation in an aggressive, imperialistic and expansionary manner, with fewer fetters on capital than in liberal democratic form. Although continuous with the Weimar era in further concentrating economic and political power, the Nazi regime was transformative in combining monopoly capital control with a full command economy. In other words, it retained features of a private capitalistic economy but with a highly concentrated and cartelised political form.

Aside from this insistence on continuity in the development of the capitalist economy, Neumann's characterisation of National Socialism as a form of 'totalitarian monopoly capitalism' directly contradicted Pollock's thesis of 'state capitalism' on another crucial point. As a constitutional matter, totalitarian monopoly capitalism marked a rupture, in Neumann's view, not only from liberal capitalism but from the state as a representation of political sovereignty. This is missed in the literature which focuses only on Neumann's claim that the rule of law ceased to exist in the Nazi dictatorship, in contrast to Ernst Fraenkel's account of the 'dual state', combining a normative system of private law with unfettered prerogative power of the Party. Although Neumann viewed National Socialism as 'a decisionistic, situation-specific, deformalized' system in which the rule of general laws had been eradicated and law became merely a technical means,[66] he also saw in the Nazi order the destruction of the state as such. The system of National

[62] ibid 361.

[63] Devlin (n 48) 259.

[64] C Corradetti, 'Coercion or Privatisation? Crisis and Planned Economies in the Debates of the Early Frankfurt School' (2024) *Jus Cogens* 7, 14.

[65] ibid.

[66] D Kelly, *The State of the Political: Conceptions of Politics and the State in the Thought of Max Weber, Carl Schmitt, and Franz Neumann* (Oxford University Press, 2003) 296.

Socialism was a 'form of society in which the ruling groups control the rest of the population *directly*, without the mediation of the state' (emphasis added).[67] Neumann also thought that the kind of economic programme pushed by the Nazis, which favoured intense monopolisation of capital, would be impossible to pursue on a democratic basis: 'The complete subjugation of the state by the industrial rulers could only be carried out in a political organisation in which there was no control from below, which lacked autonomous mass organisations and freedom of criticism'.[68]

In the Weimar era, Kirchheimer was even more insistent than Neumann that capitalism and democracy were formally incompatible. He cautioned against the economistic and legalistic strategies of the social democrats and trade unions, and instead favoured 'mass participation' in political will-formation, and for the state to be 'genuinely superseded by a worker's democracy'.[69] Coining the term 'juridification' in 1928, Kirchheimer 'expresses concern that the reduction of political conflicts to legal questions will rob the working class of radical forms of action'. Where the class dispute is 'given a legal form, the class struggle is formalized and therefore neutralized'.[70] Kirchheimer, whose position has been described as a 'theoretical fusion of Marx and Schmitt', was one of the few left-wing thinkers connected to the German Social Democrats to have actively resisted the 'toleration policy' adopted by the Party towards the Presidential cabinets ruling by emergency dictates and decrees in the period prior to the Nazi seizure of power.[71]

Kirchheimer, like Neumann, argued that National Socialism was not a fundamental departure economically, but rather 'the last, logical position in the accelerated concentration of capital and cartelization which characterised the Weimar period'.[72] In accordance with Neumann, Kirchheimer rejected the label of 'state' for the Nazi regime and focused on its fragmentation of power among competing groups. What held the regime together was 'the unfolding program of [military] expansion', which had 'given the various groups the possibility ... of satisfying their desires without too much need of getting in each other's way'.[73] And, like Neumann, Kirchheimer's emphasis was on the Nazi destruction of the political and legal structures and institutions of democracy rather than its supersession of the economic laws of liberal capitalism.

For Kirchheimer, the concentration of political and economic power under National Socialism tended to conserve private property even as it abolished the freedom to contract. In place of contract, 'the administrative sanction now has become the alter ego of property itself'. Through imperialist expansion, the yearning of the discontented middle class to share in the prosperity of powerful industry 'could be fulfilled to the benefit of both the government and big business'.[74] In contrast to Pollock, both Kirchheimer and Neumann maintained that the profit motive remained an operational

[67] Neumann (n 60) 470.

[68] ibid 261.

[69] Thornhill (n 49) 119–21.

[70] D Loick, 'Juridification' in A Allen and E Mendieta (eds), *The Cambridge Habermas Lexicon* (Cambridge University Press, 2019) 208.

[71] Thornhill (n 49) 120. This was the formation belatedly described by Heller as 'authoritarian liberalism', even after he himself had initially supported the policy of toleration, along with Franz Neumann.

[72] ibid 124.

[73] O Kirchheimer, 'Changes in the Structure of Political Compromise' (1941) 9 *Studies in Philosophy and Social Sciences* 264, 287.

[74] Jay (n 38) 161.

logic of the system. The distinctive feature of the Nazi regime was thus the combination of monopoly capital and totalitarian political power.[75]

Far from an intense politicisation, National Socialism pursued a deliberate atomisation of the masses and a strengthening of the prevailing class culture of Germany's society, albeit introducing a new hierarchy between lower and lower-middle class.[76] Domination in National Socialism was not merely technical; class elements remained, and Neumann and Kirchheimer both thought that there would still be tension between technological rationalisation and profit-maximisation, as well as between capital and labour.

The differences with Pollock on the economy of National Socialism mirrored their differences on its political form. In Neumann and Kirchheimer's analysis, National Socialism, rather than bringing forth the truly political state, in fact undermined the real source of legal and political power, namely the principle of 'sovereignty'. The principle of sovereignty was 'specific to the political sphere' and made little sense in terms of sheer 'command' or 'control'.[77] The system of National Socialism triumphed, in other words, not, or at least not primarily, through transcending the contradictions of market liberalism, but through the destruction of the institutions of the political realm. The moment of 'genuine politics' was completely attenuated in National Socialism 'by technical and pluralist (private-legal) modes of coercion'.[78]

With this in mind, we can make sense of Schmitt's claim that in January 1933, with the appointment of Hitler as Chancellor, 'Hegel died'.[79] This was nothing to be celebrated. Unlike some of the orthodox Marxists of the era, Neumann and Kirchheimer saw the 'premature realization of "statelessness" in contemporary capitalism' as being 'likely to generate… unmediated control by those possessing de facto power'. For both Neumann and Kirchheimer, political sovereignty remained an essential characteristic of the state: 'only the modern state could effectively rein in privileged power blocs: its dismantlement under present-day conditions portended not utopia but instead dystopia'.[80]

If we follow this line of reconstruction, Neumann's account in *Behemoth* can be read as an account of the end of politics and of the institutions of the political state that had been born with the Weimar Republic. The unified constituent and sovereign will of the people, 'which stood at the root of the democratic state' would be forgotten in National Socialism. In effect, 'the people', in the Nazi regime, 'existed simply to be ruled'.[81] It was, in other words, a further, and decisive erosion of the concept of popular sovereignty, in continuation with its decline in liberal political and juridical thought, that signalled the end of the Weimar Republic, just as Hermann Heller had foreseen.[82]

[75] ibid 164. In maintaining variations on this thesis, Neumann and Kirchheimer were joined with Arcadius Gurland, a Russian-born German political scientist who was associated with the institute between 1940 and 1945.

[76] ibid 164.

[77] Kelly (n 66) 291.

[78] Thornhill (n 49) 127.

[79] C Schmitt, *Staat, Bewegung, Volk* (Hanseatischer Verlaganstalt, 1933) 32

[80] Scheuerman (n 56) 489.

[81] Kelly (n 66) 293.

[82] MA Wilkinson, 'Hermann Heller's Critique of Liberalism' (2024) *Jurisprudence.*

V. Political Alienation in Postwar Europe

Perhaps due to their work during the war with the US Office of Strategic Services, their involvement in postwar reconstruction in Germany and association with Columbia University, Neumann and Kirchheimer are sometimes characterised as having moved to a more mainstream, even if somewhat 'uneasy liberal' position after World War II.[83] Such a characterisation, however, not only underestimates their critique of postwar liberal democracy; it also neglects the continuities in their thinking. Neumann and Kirchheimer's emphasis on the political dimension of the state and popular sovereignty transcended debates around Weimar and National Socialism. Significantly, they not only identified the key and enduring conflict between democracy and capitalism but also the necessity of political sovereignty in staging it. This emphasis in fact becomes even clearer in their postwar writings, when their discussion turns to the erosion of political freedom and the decline of parliamentary authority in notionally liberal democratic states in Western Europe.

This continuity in their thought is significant because it shows that critical theory does have the tools to offer a robust critique of the postwar projects of European integration and the building of supranational law but only if it looks beyond Frankfurt's inner circle. To reconstruct this, we will begin by returning to Neumann's account of the concept of political freedom, outlined in the 1950s before his premature death. Neumann offers a theoretical account of freedom which demonstrates the importance of its political aspect and the continuing valence of the principle of sovereignty, which second-generation critical theory so often attempts to transcend.

Political freedom for Neumann comprises three elements: juridical freedom, or what is usually understood by negative liberty; cognitive freedom, which is knowledge of nature, society and human psychology; and volitional freedom, namely active participation in politics in a system of representative government. Juridical, or liberal freedom, the basis of which is philosophical individualism, is on its own wholly inadequate and implies an acceptance of political alienation. Indeed, historically, Neumann notes, German liberalism was content 'to trade political freedom for economic advance and security'.[84] Although it carries a non-negligible moral value of formal equality, the political role of its conception of freedom 'is to hide the locus of power'.[85]

If political freedom were reduced to mere juridical freedom, democracy would have little value in itself; constitutional monarchy, Neumann notes, would do 'just as well'. But political freedom is a more concrete and capacious notion. It requires insight into natural necessity as well as human potentiality to control its own environment; it requires cognition of the current stage of social development, its potential as well as its limits. So to understand the operation of liberty concretely, it must be understood that private power 'can be as dangerous to liberty as public power'.[86] Applying this conception of political freedom to two key concepts of the contemporary world, Neumann sees private property to have only a relative contingent value but sovereignty to be a key component.

[83] Jay (n 38) 166.
[84] F Neumann, 'The Concept of Political Freedom' (1953) 53 *Columbia Law Review* 901, 911.
[85] ibid 912.
[86] ibid 919.

Although a concept 'fashionable to defame', Neumann presents sovereignty as essential to the democratic political system and its reconciliation of freedom and coercion. It is not only an antidote to the impoverished conception of juridical freedom in the liberal imagination, but also an antidote to imperialism, and to any notion of the superiority of a particular class or race. Its equalising and limiting functions appear most strikingly when contrasted with the National Socialists' notion of racial imperialism (which rejected state sovereignty for racial supremacy) and with the doctrine of the sovereignty of the international proletariat, represented by the Third International. The notion of state sovereignty, he notes, is 'anti-imperialist' precisely because internationally it functions as a principle of formal equality among states. Strikingly, this idea of an anti-imperialist inter-nationalism is echoed only a year later in the principles of postcolonial sovereignty expounded by the Bandung conference and then in the constitution of the Non-Aligned Movement.[87]

Political freedom, finally, requires a volitional element, as 'some kind of identification through action is necessary to prevent the total political alienation of the citizen'.[88] The volitional element means that freedom cannot be 'given' to man by a ruler but must be realised by his own action. Only in a democracy can this be pursued, and the three elements of freedom be combined:

> the democratic political system is the only one which institutionalizes the activist element of political freedom; it institutionalizes man's opportunity to realize his freedom and overcome the alienation of political power. All three elements of the notion of political freedom are given a chance in the democratic system. The rule of law (expressed in civil rights) prevents the destruction of minorities and the oppression of dissenting opinion; the mechanism of change (inherent in the democratic system) allows the political system to keep pace with the historical process; the need for self-reliance of the citizen gives the best insurance against his domination by anxiety.[89]

Taking stock of the situation in Europe, and, if to a lesser extent, in the US, Neumann observes that 'citizens' alienation from democratic political power was increasing at a 'tremendous speed'.[90] Identifying this phenomenon with three types of apathy – literal apathy as an attitude of political indifference, the Epicurean approach, and a total rejection of the possibility of political alternatives – Neumann suggested it would likely lead to a return of demagoguery and various forms of 'Caesarism', the term used for an authoritarian populist or dictatorial solutions. Various symptoms and causes of political alienation are offered, including the 'growing complexity of government', the 'growth of bureaucracies in public and private life', the 'concentration of private social power' and 'the hardening of political parties into machines'.[91]

In Neumann's analysis, it is fear of politics which ultimately makes and sustains Caesarism, a type of authoritarianism combining populist appeals and direct acclamation. Fear and the associated political anxiety lead to dictatorship and transform a

[87] See, eg, A Anghie, 'Bandung and the Origins of Third World Sovereignty' in E Fakhri and N Bandung (eds), *Bandung, Global History, and International Law* (Cambridge University Press, 2017) 535–52.
[88] Neumann (n 84) 927.
[89] ibid 928.
[90] ibid 932.
[91] ibid 932.

people into a mob. But he cautions against descending into the kind of psychological reductionism invited by Adorno's study of the authoritarian personality; for Neumann political and legal institutions matter, as do the material implications of governing policy.[92] This is not a crude institutionalism, but one which has to contend with the social relations underlying institutions: if 'divorced from the context of power relationships', institutionalism is unintelligible, or worse, it descends into decisionism.[93]

The antidote to political alienation offered by Neumann is as moderate as it now appears radical; not mass participation in political decisions, but a functioning representative democracy: 'the free election of representatives and the preservation of spontaneous responsiveness to the decisions of the representatives'.[94] This requires an institutional set-up that is capable of responding to majoritarian pressure, as well as intermediary institutions that are capable of harnessing social demands. With specific regard to West Germany, he warns against 'constitutional fetishism' in the obsession centring on the Bonn Basic Law, foreshadowing the turn to constitutionalisation and constitutional patriotism later taken by Habermas and others.

Neumann's analysis of political retreat and parliamentary decline in the postwar era is echoed by Kirchheimer, in several concrete analyses of the political scene in Europe, where he notes that political power was shifting away from Parliament and structurally towards the judiciary, the executive, and the administration. In an analysis that extended far beyond the West German political scene, he theorised a process leading to the hegemony of a 'catch-all party' and then a 'state-party cartel', which was rational, pragmatic, and based on an ideological de-mobilisation of the masses.[95] Observing the birth of the French Fifth Republic, for example, Kirchheimer noted the 'conversion of the participant citizens into bewildered, bemused, or embittered spectators'.[96] As its parliamentary democracy was increasingly side-lined by De Gaulle, Kirchheimer eventually described the state of the Fifth Republic in the late 1960s as 'a ravaged parliament with an executive power in the hands of a technocratic leadership'.[97]

Just as for Neumann, Kirchheimer's focus on popular sovereignty and representative politics showed a continuity with his Weimar writings. His evaluation of Weimar's collapse had suggested the need for a socialist version of popular sovereignty in conjunction with a representative parliament. Without this, constitutional government would displace power 'to the executive, the administration of the state, and the courts, opening the way to dictatorship'.[98] In his view it was the failure of the left to claim political sovereignty and oppose the Weimar Constitution, which 'allowed the dictatorial moment of sovereignty within liberal democracy to turn into outright dictatorship'.[99] In condi-

[92] See Scheuerman (n 36).

[93] Jay (n 38) 146.

[94] Neumann (n 84) 934.

[95] FS Burin and KL Shells (eds), *Politics, Law and Social Change. Selected Essays of Otto Kirchheimer* (Columbia University Press, 1969).

[96] O Kirchheimer, 'France From the Fourth to the Fifth Republic' in FS Burin and KL Shells (eds), *Politics, Law and Social Change: Selected Essays of Otto Kirchheimer* (Columbia University Press, 1969) 215.

[97] ibid 241.

[98] P Breiner, 'The Paradigmatic Example of Weimar and Postwar Political Science: The Case of Otto Kirchheimer' in R Lebow and L Norman (eds), *Weimar's Long Shadow* (Cambridge University Press, 2024) 84–119, 85.

[99] ibid 93.

tions of social inequality and universal suffrage, liberal democracy is entwined with the logic of dictatorship: just as Heller and Polanyi had argued, liberals, in order to prevent socialist claims, specifically to prevent parliament intervening with the interests of capital, would defect from democracy and support authoritarianism.

This affinity between liberalism and authoritarianism was not unique to Weimar. The famous Article 48 of the Weimar Constitution granting emergency presidential powers was not a peculiarity; it was 'a necessary feature of all capitalist democracies that guarantee only universal suffrage' but not the equalisation of social power necessary for 'true democracy'.[100] Although in the postwar period, Kircheimer's socialism may have been subdued, his commitment to political democracy was not. He 'used the lesson he drew from the Weimar exemplar to criticise the forms of de-ideologised party politics and loss of contentious mass mobilisation typical of postwar liberal democratic regimes'.[101] He also continued to insist on the significance of social class; specifically on the significance of the new middle class, a 'service class' essential to stabilising and moderating postwar politics with its position of relative privilege. It was the growth of these middle strata, forming the base of bourgeois parties, that was largely responsible for the decline of political ideology and political mobilisation.

In a recent reassessment, Kirchheimer's work has been said to capture the erosion of parliamentary democracy as a result of 'vanishing political antagonism and principled opposition', as parties became increasingly disconnected from their social bases. The professionalisation of party organisation and appeal to personal politics accompanied an 'extensive depoliticisation, political apathy of the mass population and the waning of the classic separation of legislative, executive and judicial powers'.[102] In conjunction with the deradicalisation of the left and right and emergence of powerful non-partisan interest groups, party politics across the spectrum became more centrist in the attempt to transgress social cleavages. As it did so, it would also turn to the personal political appeal of individualities.

Kirchheimer was not only describing this new formation; he warned that it would make 'politics devoid of substance, conflict and choice'.[103] He was, in other words, warning of 'new political vacuums that could be created through the dissipation of political-ideological parties and political-ideological conflict', the upshot of which was a politically demobilised and alienated citizenry.[104] In Peter Breiner's view, this warning can only be understood against the background of the 'long shadow' cast by Weimar.

Arguing against the passivity of a consensus-oriented politics, Kirchheimer saw in its apparent stability a serious flaw, 'a fundamental reduction of active citizens to consumers', the rise of an 'executant class' in a new and specialised division of labour, and the predominance of a sphere of management and de-politicised group participation.[105] 'Privatisation', the 'turning inward of interests and a concentration upon private affairs', was for Kirchheimer 'one of the decisive characteristics of German postwar

[100] ibid 95.
[101] ibid 88.
[102] A Krouwel, 'Otto Kirchheimer and the Catch-All Party' (2003) 26 *West European Politics* 23, 31.
[103] ibid 24. For a contemporaneous description of the 'depoliticization' of the 1950s, see various articles in G Vedel (ed), *La Depolitisation, mythe ou realite?* (Armand Colin, 1962).
[104] Breiner (n 98) 104.
[105] ibid 109.

life'.[106] When Kirchheimer speaks of the decline of principled political opposition and the transformation of the mass class-based party into the catch-all party, he is critiquing the complacency of postwar social democracy, and thinking back to 'a left that failed to unify against the dictatorial tendencies in the formally pluralist constitution of Weimar' by failing to present a case for a socialist principle of popular sovereignty above the Constitution.[107] He was, in other words, drawing the opposite lesson of mainstream liberal democracy, which deemed excessive politicisation and polarisation to have led to the collapse of Weimar.

These reflections on the shallowness of postwar democracy are shared even by scholars who have little or no attachment to critical theory but have documented the remarkably controlled, circumscribed and limited form of democracy adopted in Europe. As historian Martin Conway recounts, in a recent retrospective of the postwar Western European age, the re-founding of Europe after 1945 while bringing 'unprecedented stability and uniformity' to the politics of the western half of the continent, inaugurated a democracy that 'was always circumscribed by the stability it would achieve and the interests it was constructed to serve'. In 'creating a top-down democratic order', he notes 'the architects of post-1945 European democracy limited opportunities for popular control of rulers and for expressions of dissent at the same time as they enhanced the freedom of action of state officials'. The consequence, in his view, was a '"formal democracy", founded on the regular rituals of parliamentary elections and negotiation with a range of interest groups, but from which the people, and something of the noise and vibrancy inherent to a pluralist democratic culture, was at times strangely absent'.[108]

VI. The Hollowing Out of Western Democracy: From Integration through Law to Integration through Fear

Neumann and Kirchheimer's postwar analyses offer an early taste of Peter Mair's later, more celebrated account of the 'hollowing out' of western democracy and the emergence of a 'void' between rulers and ruled.[109] Joining their critiques with the work of Mair enables us to see the significance played by the project of European integration in consolidating and exacerbating the process of de-politicisation and de-democratisation they outlined in the 1950s and 1960s.

To the extent that all EU economies had become 'semi-sovereign' by the mid-1990s, with the demos subject 'to a set of constraints and persuasions that lie outside [its] own direct control', the scope of partisan politics had been severely limited by integration, affecting the capacity of parties to act as representative agents of popular or class interests.[110] As Mair argued, the accelerated decline of traditional partisan politics, and the

[106] O Kirchheimer, 'Notes on the Political Scene in Western Germany' in Burin and Shells (n 96).
[107] Breiner (n 98) 104.
[108] M Conway, *Western Europe's Democratic Age: 1945 – 1968* (Princeton University Press, 2020) 8.
[109] P Mair, *Ruling the Void: The Hollowing Out of Western Democracy* (Verso, 2013). Mair acknowledges the debt to Kirchheimer.
[110] P Mair, 'Political Parties, Popular Legitimacy and Public Privilege' in J Hayward (ed), *The Crisis of Representation in Europe* (Routledge, 1996) 46.

move away from representative agencies and towards 'public office holders', was intimately connected with a process of integration that was emptying politics of content. If parties could no longer make a substantial difference, it 'would then hardly be surprising to find that ordinary voters might also have despaired of a partisan intent'.[111]

Integration through law had seen the creation of rules, institutions and ideas that insulated market logic from democratic pressures and removed decision-making from fora of democratic accountability, structuring a tightly constrained democracy through various counter-majoritarian means. Although this began inconspicuously in the 1960s, through various legal pressure groups in conjunction with an activist European Court of Justice (ECJ), it accelerated in the 1980s and 1990s.[112] As has been recently documented in meticulous detail, the key tenets of neoliberal constitutionalism infuse all the three layers of the European Economic Constitution: fundamental freedoms of movement, competition, and budgetary discipline.[113]

European law had played a crucial role in this recalibration. The Court's 'fundamentalist' approach to economic freedom had overturned the original 'de-coupling' of national social spheres and supranational market law, with any distortion of competition or obstacle to market access presumed to be caught by the Treaty prohibitions and subject to proportionality testing. Fritz Scharpf, Streeck's predecessor as director of the Max Planck institute, had long emphasised EU law's structural asymmetry and its neo-liberalising effects on domestic political economy. Favouring 'non-political actors' over political actors and negative integration over positive integration, Scharpf identified integration through law and the case law of the ECJ as central in constructing an imbalance between law and politics.[114] Scharpf focused on the period since the early 1980s, when 'economic integration has accelerated and intensified, and the liberal transformation, which Hayek had expected, has, indeed, been taking place in the multilevel European polity'.[115] With later cases such as *Viking* and *Laval*, economic freedoms would then trample on sensitive national arrangements and structures of autonomous bargaining, and in areas where the EU itself had no legislative competence and therefore no means to close any regulatory gap.[116]

These constraints had a substantial impact on domestic politics, both constitutional and ordinary. By 'removing more and more policy areas from the national political arena', Vivien Schmidt noted, long before the euro-crisis, the EU was further 'narrowing the policy repertoire and space for political deliberation' leading to an increase in domestic 'politics without policy'. In this arrangement of political power, national electorates were

[111] ibid 47.

[112] On the initial push, see M Rasmussen, 'Agents of Constitutionalism: The Quest for a Constitutional Breakthrough in European Law, 1945–1964' in MM Payk and KC Priemel (eds), *Crafting the International Order: Practitioners and Practices of International Law since c.1800* (Oxford University Press, 2021).

[113] G Grégoire, 'The EU's Neoliberal Constitutionalism(s)' (2024) *European Law Open* 705; A Menéndez, 'The Terrible Functional Constitution of the European Union: Sound Money, Economic Freedoms and Free Competition' in M Goldoni and MA Wilkinson (eds), *The Cambridge Handbook on the Material Constitution* (Cambridge University Press, 2023).

[114] F Scharpf, 'The Double Asymmetry of European Integration: Or Why the EU Cannot Be a Social Market Economy' (2010) 8 *Socio-Economic Review* 211.

[115] ibid 212.

[116] Case C- 341/ 05 *Laval v Svenska Byggnadsarbetareförbundet* [2007] ECR I- 11767; Case C- 438/05 *International Transport Workers' Federation and Finnish Seamen's Union v Viking Line* [2007] ECR I-10779.

'frustrated by the inability of elected leaders to deal directly with the questions which are of greatest concern to them, such as globalization and immigration'.[117]

A significant aspect of this narrowing of political possibilities was the more general decline of traditional identities within civil society, leading to the 'erosion of traditional boundaries based on class and religion', 'changing patterns of social stratification', and 'a greater emphasis on individualistic or particularistic identities'.[118] As an economic consumer rather than a political citizen, the individual had little need for political representation; existential meaning conveyed by lifestyle choices required only an enhanced personal freedom, which could be guaranteed by technical and juridical means. This would be increasingly regulated through provisions on non-discrimination across various domains, where EU law and policy would play a particularly prominent role. Unlike traditional social policy, anti-discrimination law was not about creating solidarity among the members of a collective but focused on eliminating arbitrary factors that might affect individual life choices.[119]

The erosion of traditional class identities and political representation would be reinforced by a turn of the liberal left towards a politics of multiculturalism and cultural pluralism. With critical theory embracing a moralistic discourse of inclusion, social solidarity and political mobilisation was abandoned, with the principle of 'recognition' substituted for issues of power and redistribution.[120] The new millennium would see a growth in these trends, amounting to a qualitative state–society transformation, signalling not only a dis-embedding of political parties from class but also their re-embedding in the state, as they moved away from civil society and became part of the state apparatus and a new establishment culture. From that position, established parties could derive income, office, and access to state-regulated media – a combined strategy to increase their public profile and privileges.[121] This even gave rise to a new ideal type: a form of representative government where the electorate appears, 'above all, as an *audience* which responds to the terms that have been presented on the political stage', heralding rule by media expert.[122]

Tracing this trajectory back to the 1970s and changes to the global economy associated with the era commonly described as 'neoliberal', Mair noted that the project of European integration functioned only as an accelerant of this decline, with the opacity of European law-making and the Europeanisation of policy-making further narrowing the scope for class politics. In Mair's own words, European integration would blur the differences among parties within the mainstream to 'almost non-existence'. As it contributed to severing the link between the working class and social democracy, the EU would also be a mechanism for social democratic parties, which had become more firmly pro-European, to connect 'with the salaried and educated middle strata of the

[117] VA Schmidt, *Democracy in Europe: The EU and National Polities* (Oxford University Press, 2006) ch 4.

[118] ibid 50.

[119] A Somek, *Engineering Equality: An Essay on European Anti-Discrimination Law* (Oxford University Press, 2011).

[120] A Somek, 'From Workers to Migrants, from Distributive Justice to Inclusion: Exploring the Changing Social Democratic Imagination' (2012) 18 *European Law Journal* 711. See more generally N Fraser, 'From Redistribution to Recognition? Dilemmas of Justice in a "Post-Socialist" Age' (1995) *New Left Review* 68.

[121] Mair (n 110) 53–54.

[122] B Manin, *The Principles of Representative Government* (Cambridge University Press, 1997) 220.

population'.[123] European integration would thus reinforce the left's turn towards cultural liberalism, transnationalism and new forms of identity politics.

If de-politicisation was initially pursued in the mode of 'integration through law', in the later euro-crisis period following the global financial crisis, this was complemented by a different method, 'integration through fear', as the threat of catastrophe precipitated by the potential collapse of the euro was used to push through political and economic reforms in ways that bypassed normal legal and constitutional routes. Etienne Balibar identified in this a potential 'revolution from above', a transformation of Europe 'which the leaders of dominant nations and the Brussels and Frankfurt technostructure' were attempting under 'the whip of necessity'.[124]

As the imbalance between democracy and capitalism became increasingly acute it required more conspicuous intervention from executive powers acting in legal grey areas, recalling the Caesarism or Bonapartism of an earlier era.[125] The unorthodox measures would also be challenged in domestic legal settings, notably by the German Constitutional Court. But the shift from integration through law to integration through fear, backed by executive power at the national and supranational levels, was generally rubber-stamped by the ECJ.

To adopt a different terminology, there was a shift from a passive authoritarianism – the era of 'permissive consensus' on European integration – to more active forms of governing outside or in the margins of the law, pursued both by formal institutions such as the European Central Bank, institutions such as the Eurogroup, which was appositely characterised as 'formally an informal group' and hard dictates from Berlin and Brussels that transcended any institutional configuration, such as Merkel's insistence that 'if the euro fails, Europe fails'. The democratic deficit of the EU became a democratic default, with debtor states facing a condition akin to 'occupation' by the Troika.[126]

With the series of crisis responses taking place in a way that violated normal principles of legality, the challenges to them exposed counter-majoritarian institutions to greater scrutiny than before, but they were frequently justified as exceptional measures for exceptional situations. This discourse of 'emergency politics' would be adopted by many of the key players in the euro-crisis saga, both in terms of justifying departure from the plain Treaty text and conventional understanding (eg of the meaning of a no-bailout clause or prohibition of central bank financing), and in terms of their prospective limited duration: their purpose was only to restore the normal liberal logic of capital accumulation and the project of European integration.[127]

The way the euro-crisis was managed provoked strong popular reaction in Greece and elsewhere, as left populist parties contested the austerity that came as a *quid pro quo* of financial assistance. This represented not only an opposition to the policy of austerity, but, at least in some formations, the return of an 'opposition of principle', directed at

[123] Mair (n 110) 47.

[124] É Balibar, 'Europe's Revolution from Above' *The Guardian* (London, 23 November 2011), available atwww.theguardian.com/commentisfree/2011/nov/23/europe-revolution-from-above.

[125] See C Durand and R Keucheyan, 'Bureaucratic Caesarism: A Gramscian Outlook on the Crisis of Europe' (2015) 23 *Historical Materialism* 23.

[126] G Majone, *Rethinking the Union of Europe Post-Crisis: Has Integration Gone too Far?* (Cambridge University Press, 2014) 196–207.

[127] See J White, *Politics of Last Resort: Governing By Emergency in the European Union* (Oxford University Press, 2019).

the undemocratic mode of governing associated with the Troika. There were even the hints of a *counter-hegemonic* and pro-democratic project, as social movements sought 'not only to contest specific austerity policies but to rupture the (post-political) consensus around the neoliberal order'.[128] But this opposition of principle frequently came up against the difficulty of thinking outside of the constitutional imaginary of European integration, which undoubtedly constrained the potential of Syriza in Greece.

Just as Neumann and Kirchheimer foresaw, liberal democracy in conditions of harsh social inequality had an inbuilt switch towards forms of dictatorship, to protect the material interests of capital as well as projects in which ruling elites had invested their own political capital.[129] This would be complicated in a regional setting that had its own unique constitutional configurations; but in essence it was replicating a geopolitical version of the tension between democracy and capitalism, as Streeck outlined. The conflicts that played out, although new in their particulars, were symptomatic of longstanding tensions and the asymmetric manner of their resolution. As projects of left populism were repressed, as well as pursuing their own mistaken strategies by failing to reclaim popular sovereignty and to mobilise for a rupture from the system, the terrain was open for the right to capitalise on. The remnants of Frankfurt clung to an ideological faith in emancipation through Europeanism or postnationalism, which had become the empty signifiers to save all.

VII. Conclusion

In Göran Therborn's withering retrospective on the first-generation Frankfurt School, critical theory lacked any 'specific political anchorage', an evasion caused in part by its interpretation of the victory of National Socialism in Germany, which jettisoned any 'conjunctural analysis of the nature of the Fascist State' and replaced it with a purely 'philosophical critique of capitalism'.[130] In retreating from politics and a state theory which gives the political realm its due, the approach becomes merely to 'denounce' from the outside. Even if it still associated itself with the struggle of the oppressed against capitalist class rule, critical theory was 'unable to situate this association in the political arena'. Marxism more generally was rejected as a guide to political action, with the revolutionary agent confined to philosophy,[131] providing 'legitimation for a purely ideological radicalism smugly installed in the cosy academic institution' and without even an indirect relationship to politics as experienced by the masses.[132]

Instead of analysing fascism as the expression of a political moment in the unfolding of liberal capitalism itself, fascism comes to reflect only the material and technological development of the productive forces. In place of concrete constitutional, political and

[128] C Fominaya, 'European Anti-Austerity and Pro-Democracy Protests in the Wake of the Global Financial Crisis' (2017) 16 *Social Movement Studies* 1, 2.

[129] This tendency for liberal democracy to turn to authoritarianism was also outlined by Greek Marxist, Nicos Poulantzas, see *State, Power, Socialism* (Verso, 2000), first published in 1978 as *L'etat, le pouvoir, le socialism*.

[130] G Therborn, 'The Frankfurt School' (1970) *New Left Review* 94.

[131] ibid 84, 94.

[132] ibid 86.

social analysis, the phenomenon of authoritarianism is psychologised by Horkheimer and Adorno in an individualistic and transhistorical manner, which owed more to Freud than to Marx. This form of historicism, the making of fascism on the one hand a function of individual psychological repression and on the other an inevitability of capitalist modernisation – of the transition to monopoly capitalism and the logic of enlightenment science –, was lacking 'the concrete analysis of a concrete situation'.[133] Ironically, it is liberalism that is then taken to be the antidote to authoritarianism and the liberal person taken as the paradigmatic anti-authoritarian personality type. Crucially missing is any account of the authoritarian turn of liberalism itself, prior to the Nazi seizure of power, as closely documented by Hermann Heller, and noted by Neumann and Kirchheimer, who extend their critique of liberalism into the postwar era.

Although Pollock's worldview originated in the interwar period, its legacy endured in key Frankfurt School diagnoses after the destruction of the Nazi war economy and the end of World War II. Variations on the theme of state capitalism dominated critical thinking in the postwar era under labels such as 'late capitalism', 'organised capitalism', or the term adopted by Habermas, 'advanced capitalism'. In these political forms, the dialectics of political and social change based on the fundamental tension between democracy and capitalism was essentially lost.

The notion that Marx's theories of capitalist contradictions may have been valid for liberal capitalism but had become anachronistic as a result of successful state intervention in the economy appeared plausible in the postwar decades, during the so-called *trentes glorieuses* or 'golden age'. However, this was not a golden age of democracy; as Neumann and Kirchheimer argued, it was a period of political and democratic retreat. This was exacerbated and consolidated by European integration, a technocratic-juridical process, supported by ideologies of 'post-sovereignty' and 'post-politics', which became more overtly authoritarian throughout the euro-crisis period. Streeck's work drew attention to the processes, institutions and ideologies of economic and social ordering that had framed and reframed the relationship between democracy and capitalism, for which the EU – and EU law – had become central.

Even as Jürgen Habermas, the standard bearer of the second-generation Frankfurt School critical theory, rendered increasingly apologetic academic texts on the EU, he was forced to acknowledge the strength of Streeck's diagnosis.[134] But Habermas had evaded the long-run development of democratic capitalism and the constitutional changes that had accompanied the transformation of the 'nation-state' into a 'Member State' in the process of European integration.[135] Having pinned his flag to the mast of the EU, he stubbornly clung to it even as he was occasionally critical of its iwayward course. His early ambivalence about the colonising effects of juridification on the lifeworld had been replaced by a faith in the civilising mission of law, one which would be effortlessly upscaled into a 'postnational' project in the 1990s, signalling an effective convergence

[133] ibid 84.

[134] See J Habermas, *The Lure of Technocracy* (Polity Press, 2015). For an overview and 'application' of the Streeck-Habermas debate in the context of Syriza's fate in Greece, see M Sumonja, 'The Habermas-Streeck Debate Revisited: Syriza and the Illusions of the Left-Europeanism' (2019) 43 *Capital & Class* 427.

[135] See C Bickerton, *European Integration: From Nation-State to Member-State* (Oxford University Press, 2012).

between critical theory and liberal political theory in terms of their reaction to and fear of mass democratic politics.

The break with the unity of theory and practice heralded by the Frankfurt School, and the retreat from politics it entails, has been said to be characteristic of 'Western Marxism more generally'.[136] But if Therborn's assessment, although harsh, appears accurate in respect of the inner circle of the first-generation of the Frankfurt School, and is reaffirmed after the fact by Habermas's turn to a normative theory of law and democracy in the second-generation, it is far from the mark if we enlarge the circle to incorporate the work of Neumann and Kirchheimer. By recovering their critiques of juridification and political alienation, and their analyses of sovereignty and political freedom, we can resume the task of critical reflection on the EU and its law. Detailed analyses of areas of EU law can be part of this, but critique must also go to the very existence of the EU, to the de-politicising effects of European integration, and to the way Europe 'buys time' for capitalism and sells democracy short. All this remains critical to the revival of critical theory today.

[136] See P Anderson, *Considerations on Western Marxism* (Verso, 1976).

4

Critique of the Political Economy of the Euro Monetary Constitution

MARCO GOLDONI

I. Critical Theory and the Critique of the Political Economy of EU Law

This chapter applies the critique of the political economy of European Union (EU) law to a specific and concrete aspect of the EU legal order. The *object* of the analysis is the function and role of the supranational single currency (more specifically, of its institutional design) within the current EU legal order. The *goal* of the analysis is to show that the euro monetary constitution is part and parcel of a specific constitutional regime and that the legal design of the currency can be understood as one of the means not just for regulating, but for *governing* the political economy of the Union. In brief, the critique of the political economy of the euro monetary constitution intends to show that the European monetary regime is a project of government in its own right, with its own fundamental aims, and of constitutional magnitude.[1] Under this aspect, the critique of the law and political economy of the euro retains a classic feature of critical theory: in the analysis of the building blocks of that monetary constitution, the chapter aims at unveiling the objectives of that legal design and highlighting in which sense the entrenchment of the rules that make up the single currency intensifies a form of domination, especially on labour, as exploitation.[2] This is where a critical approach to the political economy can wield some interesting insights with its ability to identify conditions under which money and its legal organisation can generate a specific form of

[1] As known, an alternative reading sees the Economic and Monetary Union (EMU) as an unfinished or incomplete project. See, for an historical reconstruction, E Mourlon-Druol, 'History of an Incomplete EMU' in F Amtenbrink and C Hermann (eds), *EU Law of Economic and Monetary Union* (Oxford University Press, 2020) 12–36.

[2] Recently, there has been a resurgence of materialist political theory attentive to the domination brought about by a capitalist political economy. See, *ex multis*, R Clare Williams, *Marx' Inferno: The Political Theory of Capital* (Princeton University Press, 2016); N Vroussalis, *Exploitation as Domination* (Oxford University Press, 2022) (Vroussalis sums up this view in a very effective way: capital is 'monetary title to control over the labour capacity of others'); L Cicerchia, 'Structural Domination in the Labor Market' (2022) 21 *European Journal of Political Theory* 4–24; less recently, M Postone, *Time, Labour, and Social Domination* (Cambridge University Press, 1983). *Contra*: C Cordelli, 'What is the Wrong of Capitalism?' (2025) *American Journal of Political Science* (First View) (whose analysis favours alienation as the distinctive wrong brought about by a capitalist political economy).

domination by coercing or forcing institutions and people into decisions that appear to be taken 'freely' but are actually necessitated.[3]

In essence, the main objective or fundamental goal to be pursued through the exercise of this governing function is the preservation of economic and financial value. This entails that the euro monetary constitution must not only protect the value of the currency (by controlling inflation) but also strengthen the position of creditors and the valorisation of financial assets. There is a second important aim that comes attached to the particular design of the euro: the weakening of labour power with the consequent containment of its costs as a backing for financial valorisation and monetary stability, and the concomitant abandonment of the objective of full employment.[4] Pursuing valorisation within the constitutional design of the euro monetary constitution indeed entails an increased pressure for the exploitation of labour.[5] But before focusing on the pillars that constitute this governing activity as it was set up during the first years of the single currency, a detour on what it means for a monetary arrangement to be part of a constitutional project is in order (see section II). Ultimately, what is truly original and almost unique about the euro monetary constitution is not its main objective (which can be found in other monetary orders) of price (and financial) stability, but its peculiar constitutional organisation (ie, the organisation that pursues that objective). In section III, the practice through which the fundamental objective of price stability is pursued is identified in an activity of valorisation articulated around four pillars. Sections IV and V analyse the principles that animate the governing organ of the euro monetary constitution (namely, the European Central Bank), while section VI clarifies how external factors also participate in (and constrain) the exercise of the governing function. Section VII addresses the question of whether recent events have brought about a fundamental change in the objectives of the euro monetary constitution. Section VIII concludes with a sceptical assessment of this potential transformation and a reminder of why the euro monetary constitution exercises a dominating pull.

II. A Supranational Currency as a Governing Monetary Union

That a currency can be understood in constitutional terms is certainly not a novel argument, though for several decades money was not thematised as such by constitutional lawyers. Christine Desan's work on the constitutional history of money[6] has provided

[3] I follow the argument made by W Bonefeld, *Critical Theory and the Critique of Political Economy* (Bloomsbury, 2014) ch 8.

[4] The degree of intensity with which full employment has been expelled or marginalised in monetary policies varies according to the jurisdiction (and to the economic phase) but, at least formally, it is rather peculiar to the euro monetary constitution. For a recent constitutional analysis, see P Piluso, *L'obbiettivo della piena occupazione nelle trasformazioni della costituzione economica* (Editoriale Scientifica, 2025).

[5] This is the case because labour is the factor of production which, in this context, is easier to deal with. Part of the following argument is inspired by C Lapavitsas, *Marxist Monetary Theory* (Haymarket, 2017) chs 11 and 12.

[6] C Desan, *Making Money* (Oxford University Press, 2014); *cf* J Moudod, 'Analyzing the Constitutional Theory of Money' (2018) 31 *Leiden Journal of International Law* 289–313.

an essential historical and methodological point of reference for the understanding of the constitutional relevance of monetary design. By adopting an historical analysis of how money came to be identified as credit, Desan has convincingly demonstrated that the framing of a national currency (ie, a currency designed and adopted by a political community) is not the outcome of a spontaneous aggregation of different preferences or, as it is often portrayed in the specialistic literature, the emergence of a social convention which establishes social convergence over a token simply because every actor expects that others will do the same.[7] Rather, a currency is a politically designed institution with certain properties (the type of token that instantiates it, for example, coins of gold or silver) and selected purposes. In this constitutional approach to money, a currency is a token of value (and a measure of that value) that can ultimately be withdrawn from circulation by accepting it as a means of payment for taxes. It is therefore intimately connected to the fiscal competence (and capacity) of a political community. Accordingly, it is not surprising that a national currency has often been indicated as one of the attributes of the principle of sovereignty.[8]

The last point is emphatically not the case for the euro as a single currency. The supranational currency is not a sovereign currency in the sense that it is not backed by a classic form of political sovereignty and, most importantly, it is created out of the alleged decoupling between monetary and fiscal (and economic) policies.[9] This is an essential aspect of the design of the supranational currency because it is functional to pursuing one of the fundamental objectives of the EU. Clearly, if the EU were to acquire important fiscal powers, then this statement ought to be qualified. Be that as it may, the separation remains inscribed in the Treaties (namely, in Title VIII of the Treaty on the Functioning of the European Union (TFEU)) in an unmistakable way. Fiscal and economic policies are left to the competences of the Member States and to their coordination (Art 119 TFEU),[10] while monetary policies are an exclusive competence of a dedicated institution, the European System of Central Banks (ESCB), comprised of the European Central Bank (ECB) and the national central banks.[11]

[7] This is usually how the commodity conception of money explains the emergence of a currency within a community or a social group: see G Ingham, *The Nature of Money* (Routledge, 2004) ch 2.

[8] This is most visible, in recent times, in Modern Monetary Theory: R Wray, *Modern Monetary Theory* (Palgrave, 2015); S Kelton, *The Deficit Myth: Modern Monetary Theory and the Birth of People's Economy* (PublicAffairs, 2020).

[9] For the sake of clarity, economic and fiscal policies designate the power to define the sources and the level of fiscal revenues, how these revenues are distributed as public expenditures and to whom. Monetary policies, on the other hand, include the power of issuing currency with legal tender, controlling (as far as possible) the monetary basis, setting interest rates, and intervening in financial transactions through so-called open market operations.

[10] Note that these acts of coordination do not produce hard law, but only suggestions (Arts 5, 120, 121, and 136 TFEU) usually in the form of the Economic and Financial Affairs Council's (ECOFIN) recommendations. As we shall see, the coordination power introduced for the correction of excessive macroeconomic imbalances is more stringent.

[11] On the position and role of national central banks within the monetary and economic union, see M van der Sluis, 'National Central Banks in EMU: Time for Revision' (2022) *Journal of Banking Regulation* 23, 19ff. It should be added that the governing function is exercised by the ECB while national central banks are charged with the task of implementing the directives coming from the Directive Council. National central banks have retained their autonomy for all the functions that are not directly related to monetary policies. But even in that case, the Directive Council can decide that these functions interfere with the objectives of monetary policy (Art 14, para 4 Statute of the ECB).

The separation in question comes with two important features. First, an important *asymmetry* is introduced between supranational currency governance and national levels of political representation and fiscal governance. It is indeed this asymmetry which enables the primacy of monetary-driven objectives over other ones by forcing or pressuring national institutions into pursuing objectives dictated by the currency's needs.[12] It should be added that the idea supporting this asymmetry was precisely to nudge many of the Member States toward a partially voluntary convergence on important aspects of their political economy. These aspects include, crucially, not only things like international commerce and trade, but also the organisation of factors of production at the national level such as labour and other necessary commodities for production and distribution. In other words, uploading the monetary constitution at the supranational level accompanies and consolidates the already ongoing transformation of the processes of production within European societies.[13] The central piece of this new productive configuration is the abandonment of the fundamental aim of full employment for major institutions such as Finance and Labour ministries and, equally important, central banks; a corollary of this change in fundamental aims is the weakening of political labour power (especially trade union) through politics and law (for example, containment of the right to strike). Furthermore, the pressure that the constitutional design of the single currency exercises on states' public finances reduces the capacity to invest for industrial policies and, at the same time, reduces the resources available for social policies (including those in support of the labour market).

Evidence of the impact due to the rise of this asymmetry can be found in the transformation of the relation between monetary governance and ordinary politics within many of the Member States that participated in the launch of the single currency.[14] Before the entry into force of the euro, in many Member States the national central bank was acting as an agent for the national government and monetary policies were not constitutionalised, making them contestable at the level of ordinary politics.[15] The creation of the monetary union subtracted monetary policies from the circuit of political decision-making and adopted a different model of central banking as trustee of the government (ie, in favour of a more independent model of central banking).[16]

Second, the insulation of monetary policies from ordinary representative politics has also been enhanced, at least during the first decade of the single currency, by a rule-based type of governing style which not only settled the question of the kind of monetary philosophy European institutions ought to adopt, but also entrenched the core of that philosophy into the Treaties. Governing by rules was supposed to support the a-political functioning of the institutions entrusted as guardians of the monetary constitution in virtue of the limitation of the space for arbitrary political decision-making. Furthermore, given how

[12] Part of the reason for the way the asymmetry has been shaped has to do with national fiscal cultures of some of the wealthiest Member States, with Germany playing a crucial role.

[13] This transformation of the Member States' political economy has been brilliantly captured by C Bickerton, *European Integration* (Oxford University Press, 2012).

[14] Paul De Grauwe has identified this paradigm as the Anglo-French one, in contrast with the German model: P De Grauwe, 'Independence and Accountability of Central Banks' in J Stiglitz (ed), *Governance, Equity, and Global Markets* (Oxford University Press, 2001) 138–40.

[15] Paul Tucker observes that this was the *modus operandi* of the Bank of England until 1997: P Tucker, *Unelected Power* (Princeton University Press, 2018) 94–95.

[16] See, on this model, M Dani, *La banca centrale nel diritto pubblico europeo* (Franco Angeli, 2024) 32–38.

notoriously difficult it is to amend the Treaties (see Art 48 TEU), one can easily understand how tight these monetary objectives were entrenched into the EU legal order.

Desan's important work serves, within the context of a critique of political economy, to dig up the non-neutral dimension of the monetary design. In particular, it allows the thematisation of how the generation of economic value is concocted via legal engineering.[17] Accordingly, a monetary constitution instantiates a particular and specific form of valorisation (that is, of the process through which value organises modes of production)[18] through the institutional organisation of the currency. Among those effects, the most noteworthy is the management of states' public debts according to criteria that are mostly market-based (ie, criteria whose satisfaction signals market approval of the public debt's financial sustainability). The aim was to nudge Member States' public finances toward a virtuous convergence for limited deficits and public spending.[19] It also participates in the directing aspect of the political economy by creating mechanisms of compulsion, command, pressure, and incentive over the organisation and division of labour. As already noted, the kind of valorisation intrinsic to the euro constitution produces, among its effects, a containment of the cost of labour and an effective pressure in the reduction in labour political autonomy.[20] The first effect is dictated by competitive pressure within the internal market and in external trade, especially for those economies that produce commodities with low added value (and low technological innovation). The best way to compete domestically and externally is by containing the non-fixed variable of the labour cost. In other words, the asymmetry and the separation between monetary and economic/fiscal constitutions indicated above serve the purpose of setting up a monetary regime with distinctive targets and aims.

III. The Law of Valorisation in the Eurozone: The Principle of Sound Money

Seen as a legal institution, and even with its asymmetries and separations, the euro monetary constitution is constitutively comprised of some fundamental objectives and functions. When it comes to the latter, the single currency clearly performs all the standard functions of money: unit of account, means of payment, and store of value. But more importantly, the euro has been designed with a specific political economy in mind and for this reason, as a legal institution, it pursues prominently the purpose of realising the principle of 'sound money'.[21] If this is correct, perhaps

[17] C Desan, 'The Key to Value' in I Feichtner and G Gordon (eds), *Constitutions of Value* (Routledge, 2023) ch 7.

[18] D Harvie and K Milburn, 'How Organizations Value and How Value Organizes' (2010) 17 *Organization* 631–36.

[19] On the impact of the euro, I follow the analysis of P de Grauwe, *Economics of Monetary Union*, 13th edn (Oxford University Press, 2020) and K Dyson, *States, Debt, and Power* (Oxford University Press, 2014). See, also, for some important insights, W Streeck, *Buying Time* (Verso, 2013).

[20] B Braun, D di Carlo, and S Diessner, 'Planning Laissez-faire: Supranational Central Banking and Structural Reforms' (2022) 32 *Zeitschrift für Politikwissenschaft* 716.

[21] For an enlightening analysis which inspires part of this section, see A Menéndez, 'The Terrible Functional Constitution of the European Union' in M Goldoni and M Wilkinson (eds), *The Cambridge Handbook on the Material Constitution* (Cambridge University Press, 2023) ch 25.

the third function (store of value) enjoys the status of *primus inter pares* among the classic monetary functions, as it entails the stability of the value of the currency. To support this relative hierarchy of functions (relative because it does not make the other two marginal or redundant) a particular legal design is necessary as a tool to stabilise the expectations related to sound money. Accordingly, the stabilisation of expectations around the currency requires an effective governing mechanism. This point introduces us to the core features of the euro monetary constitution, which will be broached in the following subsections.

A. The Entrenched Primacy of Price Stability

The fundamental goal of the monetary constitution of the euro is price stability. It is not possible to equivocate or misunderstand the central importance of this goal as the language of the Treaties is extremely clear. In several articles (Art 119, para 2, Art 137 para 1, Art 282, para 2 TFEU, and Art 2 of the ECB statute), price stability is identified unequivocally as the primary objective. It should be added that price stability is measured by the ECB itself in terms of inflation (consumption prices) rather than financial assets' prices, a detail – as it has been noted[22] – that is rather significant for determining the content of the euro monetary constitution. Furthermore, the other objectives are defined as secondary and they can be pursued only as long as they do not impinge disproportionately on the primary objective.[23]

The rationale behind this clear and strict hierarchy is evident: maintaining the currency's value and pursuing an anti-inflationary policy are non-negotiable principles. This is the case even for those economic phases where anticyclical monetary policies (ie, those monetary decisions that go against the economic cycle: eg, raising interest rates when economic growth is increasing rapidly) might help in supporting the general economic policies of the Union, employment levels or, more generally, citizens' welfare. In an early commentary to the law of the ECB, it is indeed noted that price stability is the *Grundnorm* of the monetary union.[24] The traction of this fundamental norm has been confirmed after the financial and economic crisis of 2008/9, where policies necessary to overcome the crises which might have caused higher inflation (such as an increase in funding for social rights or more pro-wages policies) were immediately rejected. Behind the anti-inflation narrative lies the protection of the full value of public debt and private assets (sovereign debt being in fact key to the preservation of cumulated capital). The primacy of price stability entails that the monetary constitution inclines toward the valorisation of various assets and, accordingly, to the protection of creditors.[25] The latter point has been juridified by the ratification of norms that protect creditors like the

[22] ibid at 352.

[23] For an analysis of the secondary objectives and how to interpret them in a less formalistic way, see J Van'T Klooster, and N De Boer, 'What to Do with the ECB's Secondary Mandate' (2023) 61 *Journal of Common Market Studies* 730ff.

[24] C Zilioli and M Selmayr, *The Law of the European Central Bank* (Hart Publishing, 2001) 80.

[25] This is a point that is not exclusive to the euro monetary constitution, but a more general dynamic that affects contemporary finance: P Mehrling, *The New Lombard Street* (Princeton University Press, 2011); K Pistor, *Code of Capital* (Princeton University Press, 2019) ch 1.

priority of the repayment of principal and interest of public debt over any other public expenditure.

B. Austerity

Coupled with price stability is the other fundamental principle intrinsic to the monetary constitution of the euro: austerity (or sound budgetary policies). Given the separation between monetary and fiscal policies, the valorisation of the currency is in an important sense (though not exclusively) grounded on the assessment of the solidity of Member States' budgets. It is rather difficult to imagine an alternative way for supporting a supranational currency that is not backed by fiscal power. For this reason, the institutionalisation of 'sound' budgetary policy within the EU is not merely a matter of normative aspiration but is concretely operationalised through a sophisticated apparatus of fiscal surveillance and enforcement. Central to this apparatus is the European Semester, a procedural framework introduced to coordinate national fiscal policies in alignment with overarching EU economic objectives. Initially conceived as a mechanism for soft coordination, the European Semester has evolved into a key instrument of macroeconomic governance, significantly enhancing the European Commission's capacity to steer national policy agendas and to shape the national budgetary culture.[26]

At the heart of this transformation lies the growing normative and coercive authority of the Commission's 'recommendations'. Although formally non-binding, these recommendations carry considerable weight due to their institutional embeddedness within a broader sanctioning regime. According to Art 126(11) TFEU, failure to comply with the EU's fiscal rules may trigger punitive measures, a process further elaborated in Arts 11 to 16 of Regulation 1467/97.[27] The subsequent ratification of the Fiscal Compact has further enhanced the Commission's enforcement powers.

More significantly, the legal framework of the organisation of budgetary policies has begun to blur the lines between soft coordination and binding regulation. Article 17(3) of Regulation 241/2021,[28] which established the Recovery and Resilience Facility, exemplifies this shift. It affirms that recommendations issued by the Commission within the European Semester framework have, in practice, acquired quasi-obligatory status.[29] This regulatory transformation signals a broader juridification of economic governance, whereby Member States' economic choices are increasingly constrained by supranational oversight.

This process of fiscal discipline, however, is not maintained solely through formal legal channels. The infrastructural power of private financial actors plays an equally

[26] For an overview, though pre-pandemic, see J Zeitlin and A Verdun (eds), *EU Socio-Economic Governance since the Crisis: The European Semester in Theory and Practice* (Routledge, 2019). For a case study on Italy and Belgium, see D Bokhorst, 'The Influence of the European Semester: Case Study Analysis and Lessons for Its Post-Pandemic Transformation' (2021) 59 *Journal of Common Market Studies* 101–17.

[27] Council Regulation (EC) No 1467/97 of 7 July 1997 on speeding up and clarifying the implementation of the excessive deficit procedure [1997] OJ L209/6.

[28] Regulation (EU) 2021/241 of the European Parliament and of the Council of 12 February 2021 establishing the Recovery and Resilience Facility [2021] OJ L57/17.

[29] B Braun, 'Central Banking and the Infrastructural Power of Finance' (2020) 18 *Socio-Economic Review* 395.

pivotal role. Two Treaty provisions are especially salient in this regard. First, Art 123(1) TFEU prohibits the monetary financing of public deficits by the ECB, compelling states to seek financing through financial markets. Second, Art 63(1) TFEU enshrines the free movement of capital, both within the Union and globally, allowing investors unrestricted discretion in the allocation of their funds.[30]

The convergence of these legal constraints creates a structural asymmetry: while Member States must rely on financial markets to fund public spending, investors retain the liberty to select sovereign bonds based on perceived fiscal prudence. This asymmetry renders Member States structurally dependent on the preferences and expectations of global financial actors. The resulting disciplinary dynamic has been aptly characterised as a form of market-based fiscal governance, wherein investment decisions function as a de facto political vote on national economic policies (meaning: it is difficult for political institutions to adopt certain decisions when they envisage a negative reaction from markets), especially for those concerning capital taxation.[31] In brief, in order to attract investments, national governments need to maintain a low intensity level of taxation. The European Court of Justice has explicitly acknowledged this structural dependence, identifying it as a mechanism to ensure compliance with the Union's fiscal discipline framework.[32]

C. Freedom of Movement of Capital

A foundational component of the euro monetary constitution is the freedom of movement of capital. As known, the previous monetary compromise (based on the Bretton Woods agreements) did limit the freedom to move capital around as part of what can be defined as a form of embedded liberalism.[33] Within the European community, the status of the freedom of movement of capital was radically different when compared to the other basic freedoms. In a regime based on semi-fixed exchange rates between currencies, controlling the movements of capital was a quintessential feature of that type of embedded liberalism. It was widely recognised, already by the founding Member States, that it was not possible to have, at the same time, a fixed exchange rate system, an autonomous monetary policy and freedom of movement of capital. For this reason, in the Rome Treaty freedom of movement of capital was not given the same priority assigned to the other freedoms.[34]

The rapid ascendence, starting from the 1970s, of the financial sector and the rise of neoliberalism as a dominant intellectual approach,[35] paved the way for a relaxation of the controls over the movement of capital. In 1988, with the enactment of Directive 88/361,

[30] For the centrality of this measure see the following section.

[31] See also Jussi Jaakkola in chapter 5 in this book.

[32] *cf* E Christodoulidis, 'The ECJ and Total Market Thinking' (2013) 14 *German Law Journal* 2005–20.

[33] *cf* J Ruggie, 'International Regimes, Transactions and Change: Embedded liberalism in the Post-War Economic Order' (1982) 36 *International Organization* 379.

[34] *cf* E Mourlon-Droul, 'Accidental Neoliberalism: Democratic Accountability in the Making of the Euro, 1957-92' (2025) *Contemporary European History* (firstview).

[35] T Briebecher, *The Political Theory of Neoliberalism* (Stanford University Press, 2018).

restrictions to the movement of capital within the common market were abolished.[36] From that moment on, freedom of capital movement became an entrenched pillar of the common market and one that will never be contested again. To the contrary: the creation of an economic and monetary union required an even stronger freedom of capital movement. The Maastricht Treaty extended this freedom to the movements toward and from third countries as well (a provision that is also enshrined in Art 63 TFEU). Given this strong political support, the Court of Justice also shifted its position on the interpretation of this freedom, aligning its case law to that of the other fundamental freedoms.[37] The Court also limited the power of Member States to suspend or restrict freedom of capital movement, granting to the latter a growing autonomous profile.[38]

It is difficult to overestimate the impact (and the extent) of the liberalisation of capital movements within and outside the EU. The capacity of moving capital around with no real obstacles is constitutive of the disembedding of finance from national societies (especially in the absence of a fiscal mechanism of compensation) and, arguably, one of the centrepieces of the transformation of the political economy across the EU at the end of the previous century.[39] The disembedding has clear Polanyian echoes: freedom of movement of capital is a component of the commodification of money and of the submission of national societies to the imperatives of financial valorisation.[40] In other words, the economic motive takes over societal organisation and not the other way around.[41]

D. Impact of Euro Governance on Non-Eurozone Member States

A final remark concerns the impact of the governance of the euro on the other Member States. Although the disciplinary effects on non-Eurozone Member States is undoubtedly less intense, as these states still retain their national currency and a relatively autonomous national central bank, the effects of the principle of sound money radiate beyond the Eurozone.[42] For a start, Denmark (and Bulgaria as well before its adoption of the single currency) is voluntarily gravitating around the space of the Eurozone, as

[36] For example, Art 1 of the Directive stated that Member States could not restrict direct investments and operations in bonds and shares in capital markets. Directive 88/361/EEC of 24 June 1988 for the implementation of Article 67 of the Treaty [1988] OJ L178/5.

[37] See Joined cases C-163/94, C-165/94 and C-250/94 *Sanz de Lera and others* [1995] ECR I-04821.

[38] For an analysis of the changes around the regulation and case law on freedom of capital movement, see J Snell, 'Free Movement of Capital: Evolution as a non-linear Process' in P Craig and G De Búrca (eds), *The Evolution of EU Law* (Oxford University Press, 2011) 579–607.

[39] I follow here the reconstruction offered by R Abdelal, *Capital Rules: The Construction of Global Finance* (Harvard University Press, 2009) ch 4 (it should be noted that Abdelal puts a lot of emphasis on the role of European decision-makers in promoting freedom of capital not only for the EU, but as a constitutive feature of rule-based global finance).

[40] I thank Paivi Neuvonen and Paul Linden-Retek for having drawn my attention to this point about Polanyi's concept of embeddedness.

[41] K Polanyi, *The Great Transformation* (Beacon, 2001) ch 3.

[42] For an overview from the perspective of EU law see P Craig and M Markakis, 'The Euro-Area, Its Regulation, and Its Impact on Non-Euro Member States' in S Blockmans and P Koutrakos (eds), *Research Handbook on the EU's Common Foreign and Security Policy* (Edward Elgar, 2018) ch 14.

a member of the 'Exchange Rate Mechanism II', which pegs de facto its currency to the euro. Although this does not coerce these three Member States into accepting the exchange rate (after all, they can exit the mechanism), they are engaged in a conspicuous effort in keeping their national currencies as functional equivalents of the euro. The other five countries (Czech Republic, Sweden, Hungary, Poland, Romania) which remain outside of the Eurozone are in theory in a position of monetary autonomy. For example, they can pursue monetary policies that are less centred on the containment of inflation simply by choosing a different inflationary target. But with the exception of the derogations designed by Art 139 TFEU, all the other general norms of monetary governance apply to these Member States. Most importantly, Art 119.3 TFEU states that solid public finances, sound monetary conditions, and a sustainable balance of payments must be pursued by the economic policy of all Member States. One could say that these three principles that make up 'sound money' radiate their effects throughout the Union and its Member States.

IV. The Principle of the ECB's Independence

In the previous analysis, it has been taken for granted that the design and implementation of a monetary constitution is, under modern conditions, a necessary feature of the governing function. The latter concept ought to be understood as a set of practices and decisions that create and stabilise the unity of a specific legal order by pursuing fundamental aims.[43] In short, it is the teleological aspect of the function[44] that defines it. For this reason, how a monetary regime is designed and managed for the process of valorisation can be included within the scope of the governing function. It should be remembered that the process of valorisation shapes some central relations of the political economy (especially, as already noted, the organisation of labour, fiscal policies, and capital control).

What is not necessary is that the governing function of a constitutional order is taken up exclusively by what – following the tradition of continental constitutional scholarship – we could define as a single or unique constitutional 'organ'. It is often the case that the governing function is entrusted to a set of institutions, perhaps with different degrees of power and capacity, and under the condition that they are all committed to very similar aims or goals.[45] In the case of the monetary constitution, however, it is clearly the case that there is one organ that is practicing the governing function in the most effective way: The ESCB and, in terms of its capacity to steer monetary policies, the ECB. Indeed, the European Council and the ECB are allegedly the most important governing entities within the EU, the former because it is still representing the

[43] See, on the governing function in Anglosaxon public law scholarship, M Loughlin, *The Idea of Public Law* (Oxford University Press, 2003) ch 2.

[44] Given that it is controversial that functions can be identified with goals, the term is here loosely adopted (and mostly in adherence to a certain tradition of constitutional thought). The more correct term would probably be the governing activity.

[45] C Mortati, *Il governo nell'ordinamento italiano* (Giuffrè, 2001) ch 1.

assemblage of all the executives within the Union and it can dictate a (at times precarious) political direction to the whole of the Union.[46]

An essential feature that makes the ECB a governing institution is its independence. As documented by several studies, the principle of central bank independence was introduced, on a large scale, only during the last decades of the past century, and it can be associated with the rise of globalisation and financialisation of capitalism.[47] The entrenchment of a principle of independence comes with the creation of global value chains for the processes of production and the opening up of processes of valorisation to the assessment of global financial markets. Its rationale is clear: monetary policies are essential for the stabilisation of financial value and therefore they cannot be left to the ordinary political process. This applies both to the identification of the priorities of monetary policies and to the execution of these policies. Its institutional setting is equally clear: there must be some degree of separation between the political system and the central bank. If this were not the case, politics might be able to tinker with the formation of prices and this would disrupt market rationality. The justification for this arrangement has been stated in clear terms as well: an epistemic argument supports the independence of the central bank. Pursuing certain monetary objectives is presented as a technical activity which should be entrusted to experts so that market actors' expectations can be rationalised and stabilised without being disappointed by political interventions.[48]

Another asymmetry (in this case between financial ministers and central banks) was introduced at the inception of the euro. This was not common only to the Eurozone,[49] but in the case of the ECB this asymmetry was designed according to a level of dramatic separation from the political process that is especially unique to it. It is precisely this neat separation that allows the ECB to directly perform a governing function in the Eurozone because its institutional location allows it to operate as the bridge between financial markets and the political economy of national governments.

The Treaties are rather clear on this point. First, a set of detailed norms under Title VIII of the TFEU commands the ECB not to take instructions from any EU, national or local political authorities (see Arts 119 and 125). Second, unlike in those cases where the principle has been adopted via ordinary statutes, in the case of the ECB this strict principle of separation between politics and central banking is enshrined in the Treaties. As noted by Marco Dani, in the Eurozone the principle of independence represents a case of over-constitutionalisation (which strengthens the governing role of the ECB, as it protects it from ordinary politics) because to change the Treaties is politically and technically very expensive and time-consuming.[50] The complexities of amending the Treaties and the enormous and costly process that it entails are part of the guarantee

[46] See, on this point, U Puetter, *The European Council and the Council* (Oxford University Press, 2014).

[47] From different perspectives, see C Lapavitsas, *Profiting without Producing* (Verso, 2011); B Braun and D Gabor, 'Central Banking, Shadow Banking, and Infrastructural Power' in P Mader, D Mertens, and N van der Zwan (eds), *The Routledge Handbook of Financialization* (Routledge, 2020) 241–52.

[48] See, *ex multis*, R Dall'Orto Mas et al, 'The Case for Central Bank Independence' (2020) 248 *ECB Occasional Paper Series* 1–42.

[49] The classic reference goes to F Scharpf, 'The Asymmetry of European Integration, or Why the EU Cannot Be a Social Market Economy' (2010) 8 *Socio-Economic Review* 211–50.

[50] Dani (n 16) 294–95.

of the ECB's independence and one can imagine that this is also integral to the communication that the ECB sends to financial markets.

V. The Principle of the ECB's Dependence on Financial Markets

If the principle of central banking independence before the political system is undoubtedly inscribed in the Treaties and it has become ingrained in many legal orders as the cornerstone of central banking at least since the 1980s, during the last couple of decades the other side of the coin of central bank independence has become increasingly visible. While the ECB is relatively insulated from inputs coming from 'domestic' political systems, it is constantly alerted to the signals coming from other sources, starting from the activities of other major central banks (in the context of central banks' dialogue) and, more importantly for this section, global financial markets. The impact of the inputs coming from the latter can be hardly overestimated and, ultimately, it has constantly increased since the economic and financial crises of 2008/9 and the euro-crisis in 2011/12.[51]

For a start, as recently shown by Klaus Tuori,[52] during the last 15 years a new important objective has been added to the content of the ECB's primary mandate. The scope of the objective of price stability has been expanded to include the stability of the financial system as a whole (so-called financial stability). The justification for this widening of the scope of the ECB's objective is represented by the fact that without financial stability the so-called transmission mechanism of monetary policies[53] cannot work properly as its propagation would be disrupted by severe value fluctuation. But a clear consequence of widening the objective to include financial stability is that the ECB is openly taking under its guardianship the interests of the financial sector.

This guardianship institutionalises a third principle. The ECB is epistemically entangled with financial markets: its access to economic and financial knowledge is always mediated by exposure to market signals. Such entanglement entails an expansion of the ECB's sphere of intervention. It is interesting to note that this intervention has been described, at times, as an act of guardianship of both the Eurozone and of the financial solidity of its Member States. In certain cases, the praise for the intervention of the ECB during the financial crisis has brought commentators to see in it an exercise of solidarity in action or even a manifestation of constituent power by the 'Bank of the peoples'.[54] These views endow the ECB with the remarkable capacity to trigger a constitutional

[51] For an analysis of the transformation of the ECB, see D Fromage, G Monti (eds), *The New European Central Bank* (Oxford University Press, 2022).

[52] K Tuori, *The European Central Bank and the European Macroeconomic Constitution* (Cambridge University Press, 2022).

[53] The ECB defines the transmission mechanism as the process through which monetary policy decisions affect the economy in general and the price level in particular: see www.ecb.europa.eu/mopo/intro/transmission/html/index.en.html.

[54] V Borger, *The Currency of Solidarity* (Oxford University Press, 2020); H Lokdam, 'We Serve the People of Europe: Reimagining the ECB's Political Master in the Wake of its Emergency Politics' (2020) 58 *Journal of Common Market Studies* 978.

moment (supported and ratified by the political branches of the Union). With a closer look, a rather different picture emerges. Although (certain) Member States' finances benefitted from the intervention of the ECB through its unconventional monetary policies (and especially via the Public Sector Purchase Programme (PSPP)), the primary concern and objective of the ECB was to re-establish the viability of the monetary transmission mechanism by stabilising financial markets. Crucially, the criterion that establishes what counts as stabilisation is not decided autonomously – or at least, not at an autonomous epistemic level – by the Eurotower but by market actors' expectations. In other words, the threshold for meeting the objective was set by the ECB according to the expectations of market actors, that is, according to how prices would converge upon the preferences of market actors. But what about those cases of market failure where prices are considered to be 'irrational' and simply do not reflect the value of what is being priced? Given the dependence on market inputs, and in the case of market failure, the only option available to the ECB is to second-guess what would be the correct price as determined by market actors were they operating in the context of properly functioning competitive markets. In other words, the ECB intervenes to restore (and not to re-direct) the functioning of markets. This is the action logic behind the concept of the ECB as a 'market maker of last resort'.[55] The ECB (but in this case the concept can be applied to other major central banks) intervenes on financial markets with a view not only to redress market failures or to act as an ultimate lender for other banks, but to ensure that markets are supported and keep functioning according to a standard that is internal to market rationality.

It is at this stage that, already during the adoption of the strategy review of 2021, the ECB started to emphasise the importance of an efficient use of resources which should be restored in cases of market failure. More precisely, the Eurotower came to the realisation that at least some of the unconventional monetary policies (namely, the Corporate Sector Purchase Programme (CSPP), the programme for the buying of corporate bonds), inspired by the principle of market neutrality, were allegedly distorting markets and impinging upon the functioning of the price mechanism.[56] This has been especially important for the question of the environmental impact of unconventional monetary policies. The ECB came to the conclusion that markets were not pricing environmental risks adequately and felt that only a different standard could serve the purpose of introjecting that risk into price formation. But how to identify what counts as efficient use of resources in such a context? Which standard could be adopted for that purpose? Again, here we find the ECB going in circles around the functioning of markets and their inputs. If market actors are not pricing risks in the right (market-based) way, then the ECB has to redress this failure and restore an 'efficient allocation of resource' as stated by Art 127 TFEU.[57] It should be clear, at this point, that the standard

[55] *cf* B Braun, 'Central Banking and the Infrastructural Power of Finance' (2020) 18 *Socio-Economic Review* 395–418.

[56] *cf* C Fontan and J van 't Klooster, 'The Myth of Market Neutrality' (2020) 25 *New Political Economy* 865–79.

[57] For the analysis of the standard of market efficiency (as an alternative to market neutrality), especially in relation to environmental policies, see S Dietz, 'Green Monetary Policy between Market Neutrality and Market Efficiency' (2022) 59 *CML Rev* 395–432; J Solana and M Goldoni, 'The Legal Nature of Market Neutrality in the Euro Area's Monetary Policy' (2024) 3 *European Law Open* 7–49.

for market efficiency (which entails that resources are allocated rationally) requires an assessment by the ECB according to the principles of market rationality and not according to non-market-based principles (for example, solidarity or environmental protection). It is, once again, a case of coding objectives (in this case, secondary objectives like environmental protection) in terms of market rationality, even in the absence of properly functioning markets.

It is time to take stock. In constitutional terms, the entrenchment of the principle of the ECB's independence cannot be read as a successful moment of functional differentiation. It is rather the creation and consolidation of an asymmetry within the EU, whereby the monetary system is decoupled from the national economic order and upgraded to the supranational level without coupling with other supranational systems. Accordingly, this entrenchment cannot be read as the coupling between two different social sub-systems (in this case, the political and the economic, or the legal and the economic) as it is sometimes described, when it comes to central banking, in systems theory.[58] As noted, part of the growing literature on central banking tends to define central banks as the economic and financial equivalent of constitutional courts.[59] In light of the previous considerations, it should be evident that the role of the ECB is not one of self-limitation of the financial system nor that of the guarantor institution of a successful structural coupling. It is rather a constitutive part of the colonisation of the political and fiscal systems by the financial system. Its governing role instantiates not a differentiation between social subsystems, but rather an asymmetry that is brought about and sustained via the special constitutional position of the ECB. The main objective of this entrenchment is to support monetary policies for the protection of sound money and, on the other hand, the enhancement or consolidation of assets value. The two poles are not in contradiction: maintaining or increasing assets value entails a unit of account whose value is not diluted by inflation.

VI. The Euro and the International Political Economy: Hybrid Management

The euro is a currency whose existence is hardwired into a hard-power basis of central bank money, but – as most contemporary currencies – is not produced solely by the ECB, as noted above, but also by an array of private actors (eg, commercial banks, hedge funds) that operate by issuing credit instruments with liquid or quasi-liquid properties. Furthermore, these actors not only put money into circulation, but also regulate the terms of currency's international exchanges. The rise of this class of financial actors signals the re-emergence, alongside bank-made money, of market-made currencies. The euro is no exception to this phenomenon, and financial markets act as the institutions through which the euro can circulate according to a commodity logic rather

[58] For a classic reference, see G Teubner, *Constitutional Fragments* (Oxford University Press, 2011) 112.

[59] For more nuanced assessments, see R Ibrido, *L'Unione Bancaria Europea* (Giappichelli, 2021); A Conzutti, *Il governo della moneta nella prospettiva del diritto costituzionale* (Giappichelli, 2024).

than a credit-bearing instrument.[60] The commodification of the currency refers here to two analytically distinct but logically interconnected experiences. On the one hand, it refers to the fact that money becomes a value-producing asset through the creation of interest and, on the other hand, the generation of the currency is intimately related to the production and trade of commodities. In both cases, the process of valorisation is embedded not only in the domestic but also international political economy and its spheres of value chains as well. In this international context, valorisation of the currency is left to the assessment of forex markets, which treat the evaluation of currencies as those of financial assets.[61]

This points to a first significant limit to the capacity of the ECB of steering the amount and value of money in circulation through the setting of interest rates for high-powered money. The ECB, as many other central banks, is busy managing the value and the interest rate of the currency by transacting constantly in financial and forex markets. In this respect, it is confirmed that the agency of the ECB is not minimal, but it is conditional as it is dependent on the perception of the value of the currency by market actors.

The second limit to the capacity of managing the currency is represented by the growth of the creation of private money. Market-based finance is the main site for the generation of this kind of money, but not the exclusive one. So-called 'shadow banking', in the context of collateral-based finance, monetises credit and in this way circumvents the constraints of central and commercial banks by resorting to 'repo' contracts.[62] In a nutshell, the sale and purchase of securities can produce effects which endow those securities with properties very close to 'moneyness' in the absence of the direct backstop of a central bank or the support of the regulated banking sector, but in virtue of liquid collaterals whose credibility depends on the assessment by private financial institutions.[63] In this context, and in light of the constant demand for more liquidity, the backstopping by the ECB is somehow a necessity in order to preserve financial trust in the value of the currency. As highlighted by Benjamin Braun, the ECB is entangled within the infrastructural power of finance and for this reason is led to support repo and securitisation markets.[64] Even more importantly: if the value of the relevant collateral (which is often represented by sovereign bonds) is threatened by potential or actual falling prices, this fact pushes the ECB to intervene in order to maintain, within certain legal limits established by the Treaties, the value of the public debt of Member States. But in this way, the ECB also pursues its main objective of restoring or protecting financial stability.[65]

It is worth noting that these dynamics have paved the way for an unintended effect which has reduced the capacity of the single currency to achieve one of its intended

[60] See, on this, the brilliant analysis by A Chadwick, 'Rethinking the EU Monetary Constitution: Legal Theories of Money, the Euro, and Transnational Law' (2022) 3 *European Law Open* 468–509.

[61] The theoretical justification for this arrangement is the standard neo-classical value theory according to which the correct pricing of an asset is given by a set of information concerning its utility that drives demand and supply of said asset.

[62] D Gabor, 'Critical Macro-Finance: A Theoretical Lens' (2020) 6 *Finance and Society* 45, 51.

[63] ibid.

[64] B Braun, 'Central Banking and the Infrastructural Power of Finance: The Case of ECB Support for Repo and Securitization Markets' (2018) 18 *Socio-Economic Review* 395–418.

[65] C Sissoko, 'Repurchase Agreements and the (de) Construction of Financial Markets' (2019) 48 *Economy and Society* 316.

goals: insulate the value of national currencies and of sovereign debt from the powers of global finance and the domination that comes with the implicit hierarchy of the international monetary system. Instead of avoiding dependence on financialisation and market-based private money, the governance of the monetary union has fallen prey to these phenomena. This is not to deny that a significant amount of monetary power is concentrated in the hands of the ECB; however, it is the case that the creation and circulation of the euro cannot be explained only in terms of a credit-based theory of money. It is also a way to illustrate what was defined, in the previous section, as the principle of dependence on financial markets. It should be stressed that this is not a phenomenon unique to the euro, but it affects, by different degrees, all economies. Nonetheless, the point is relevant because part of the argument in support of the single currency (and, indeed, a plausible argument) is that scale is important, within global finance, for gaining a certain amount of political and economic autonomy.

VII. Post-Pandemic Phase: Yet Another Constitutional Moment?

According to the previous analysis, a critique of the political economy of the euro constitution shall put the accent on certain apparently neutral concepts that govern the single currency. The objective is to show how the law of the euro constitution is grounded on a fundamental norm of valorisation which is necessarily coupled with a specific political economy. In this context, it is very difficult to imagine a purely juridical countermovement (meaning: a legal operation that produces legal effects on the political economy) that de-commodifies the currency.

The COVID-19 pandemic, the invasion of Ukraine, the big wave of inflation that arose in 2022, and the second Trump presidency, have undoubtedly pushed the EU to act and adopt certain provisions that might be considered, once again, radically unconventional and potentially transformative in the sense of changing some of the fundamental objectives of the legal order. In this section, the focus is on the measures adopted during the first phase of the COVID-19 pandemic as they can be assessed by taking into account their medium-term impact.

It is possible to identify three main pillars constituting the core of the EU's reaction to another phase of economic and financial pressure. First, monetary and budgetary intervention intensified during the COVID-19 crisis, to the point of even suggesting the possibility of the beginning of a mutualisation of sovereign debt.[66] The core of these operations was represented by the PEPP (Pandemic Emergency Purchase Programme)[67] with which the ECB committed to buy further corporate and Member States' bonds. The aim pursued by the ECB (according to its own communication) was, once again, ensuring the correct functioning of the monetary policy transmission. On closer inspection, it is difficult not to see that there were other objectives. As noted by

[66] See the encompassing analysis by M Panascì, 'Unravelling Next Generation EU as a Transformative Moment: From Market Integration to Redistribution' (2024) 61 *CML Rev* 13–54.

[67] European Central Bank Decision 440/2020 (24 March 2020).

Tuori, 'the less clearly announced aim was to maintain cheap funding for the Member States'.[68] The entity of the programme was indeed remarkable[69] and, rather interestingly, it did not contain explicit conditionalities. Furthermore, in its communication the ECB stressed the higher degree of flexibility of the PEPP compared to the PSPP, as there was a clear instruction of adapting interventions according to the mutation of the financial context. In other words, this programme contained some indications that the ECB was willingly acting as the backstop for national sovereign debts.[70] It is indeed difficult to imagine that Member States had not realised that their national central banks would be instructed to buy national bonds 'to the extent deemed necessary and proportionate to counter the threats posed by the extraordinary economic and market conditions'.[71] One of the crucial criteria for the compatibility of unconventional monetary policies with the Treaties – ie, preventing Member States' moral hazard – was being clearly circumvented. Last but not least, the eligibility of the Member States' bonds, apart from a temporal limitation (minimum maturity of 70 days and maximum remaining maturity of 30 years), followed the existing framework established for the Asset Purchase Programmes (APP), with a level of flexibility on the basis of market conditions and the admission of previously excluded Hellenic bonds. Ultimately, the ESCB ended up buying around one fourth of sovereign bonds of each Member State during that period.[72]

The second pillar concerns the budgetary framework based on the Pact of Stability and Growth (PSG, which, as noted above, upheld the principle of financial austerity) which had also been suspended, initially because of the pandemic and then because of the war in Ukraine, allowing Member States to run higher annual deficits. This strengthened the impression of a major change in one of the fundamental objectives of the EU. In the meantime, a process of reform of the PSG was started and completed in 2024, when a new PSG was adopted by the European Parliament.[73]

Third, a 'recovery plan' (known as New Generation EU or NGEU) of euro 750 billion was adopted for supporting the recovery and the growth of Member States' economies.[74] The NGEU (whose central legal piece is Regulation 2021/241 establishing the Recovery and Resilience facility)[75] enables the Commission to transfer those resources, in the form of loans and grants, with the aim of ensuring the reprise of economic growth after

[68] Tuori (n 52) 247.

[69] *Cf* the data available at www.ecb.europa.eu/mopo/implement/pepp/html/index.en.html. PEPP amounted to 19% of euro area GDP (compared, for example, with 10% of the FED programme). Overall, the total envelope increased from 750 billion to 1860 billion.

[70] W Bateman, J van 't Klooster, 'The Dysfunctional Taboo: Monetary Financing at the Bank of England' (2024) 31 *New Political Economy* 426.

[71] Decision (EU) 2020/440 of the European Central Bank on a temporary pandemic emergency purchase programme (ECB/2020/17) [2020] OJ L91/1, Art 4.

[72] E Monnet, *Balance of Power. Central Bank and the Fate of Democracies* (Chicago University Press, 2024) 65.

[73] Regulation (EU) 2024/1263 of the European Parliament and of the Council on the effective coordination of economic policies and on multilateral budgetary surveillance and repealing Council Regulation (EC) No 1466/97 [2024] OJ L/1263.

[74] For a very positive assessment, see S Cafaro, 'The Evolving Economic Constitution of the European Union: Eulogy to Stability?' in G Grégoire and X Miny (eds), *The Idea of Economic Constitution in Europe* (Brill, 2022) 487–506.

[75] Regulation 2021/241 (n 28). The other two important pillars of the NGEU are Council Decision (EU, Euratom) 2020/2053 on the system of own resources of the European Union [2020] OJ L424/1 and Council Regulation (EU) 2020/2094 establishing a European Union Recovery Instrument to support the recovery in the aftermath of the COVID-19 crisis [2020] OJ L433I/23.

the pandemic.[76] Each Member State was invited to present national plans of recovery on a number of subjects, with a particular emphasis on digitalisation and the green transition. The legal basis for the recovery plan is identified in Art 175(3), that is, as a cohesion policy instrument.[77] Furthermore, with this instrument the Union's budget has been increased up to almost two per cent of the Union's Gross Domestic Product (GDP). In brief, in virtue of these elements, NGEU has been interpreted as the factual and symbolic end of austerity in the EU and the beginning of the emersion of a new economic policy paradigm that would inject important doses of solidarity across the Union.[78] According to this interpretation, the NGEU is not a one-off intervention, but: (1) it has broken the taboo of the European common debt; and (2) shown that even without formal Treaty change, important forms of redistribution and state intervention in the economy have become an integral part of the EU legal order.[79] In other words, the NGEU set in motion a different logic that is not compatible with the previous economic and financial paradigm as it has reversed two of its constitutive pillars: no redistribution among Member States and no mutualisation of the public debt.[80]

Against the background of this interpretation, as it often happens in EU law scholarship, the classic trope of the transformation of Europe ('the constitutional moment') has been once again mobilised and, allegedly, it would have transformed the euro monetary constitution as well. It is perhaps too early to pass a definitive judgment on the nature of the measures adopted to face those 'crises'.[81] But, *rebus sic stantibus*, the analysis of these exceptional interventions seems to confirm that there is not much that is truly transformative (and permanent) in the political economy of the European constitutional order. For a start, the process of valorisation is still largely organised around the same factors and relations of the last few decades.[82] The objectives of the monetary constitution are also largely the same: if anything has changed structurally, it is the fact that the primary objective of price stability has been expanded to include financial stability. Furthermore, any potential novelty does not have any permanent feature and, at the time of writing, does not seem that it will become permanent. The PEPP's last operations were performed on 17 December 2024, and were not renewed. At the time of writing,

[76] For a first assessment, see F Fabbrini, *EU Fiscal Capacity* (Oxford University Press, 2022).

[77] It is not possible here to develop this point, but the fact that one of the legal bases was identified in cohesion policy might say more about the concept of cohesion than the recovery plan. For an insightful analysis of the expansive concept of cohesion policy, see L Dìez Sànchez, 'Why Cohesion Policy Is not about Cohesion' (2025) 62 *CML Rev* 13–48; *cf*, also, P Lindseth and P Leino-Sandberg, 'Crisis, Reinterpretation, and the Rule of Law: Repurposing "Cohesion" as a General EU Spending Power' (2024) 16 *Hague Journal of the Rule of Law* 587–610.

[78] *cf* B de Witte, 'The European Union's Covid-19 Recovery Plan: the Legal Engineering of an Economic Policy Shift' (2021) 58 *CML Rev* 635–82.

[79] See, in support of this view, one of the most attentive analyses from a constitutional perspective: P Leino-Sandberg and M Ruffert, 'Next Generation EU and Its Constitutional Ramifications' (2022) 59 *CML Rev* 433–72.

[80] One could also add to this list, especially in virtue of the Green Deal, elements of planification that were previously excluded from the normality of EU law: *cf* I Kampourakis, 'A Post-Neoliberal European Order? Public Purpose and Private Accumulation in Green Industrial Policy' (2025) 88 *MLR* 769–803.

[81] For a nuanced but cautious assessment, see M Goldmann, *The Constitution of Capital* (Oxford University Press, forthcoming).

[82] Even the discourse remains largely the same. When inflation surged suddenly and dramatically in 2022, wage moderation was again at the centre of the concerns of EU institutions as one of the main pillars of the European strategy for containing inflation.

it seems that the PEPP was yet another exercise in emergency-based governance of the monetary constitution through unconventional monetary policies.[83] Although it should be noted that the PEPP was not *entirely* managed through a proportionate distribution of interventions according to capital key contributions, the mandate to national central banks was to buy mostly according to their capital key. As shown above, unconventional central banking has tried to correct markets' evaluations of Member States' bonds when they came across – from the perspective of market rationality – as irrational and inaccurate.

In the case of NGEU, the Regulation establishing the Recovery and Resilience Facility has provided a standard model for more recent interventions by the EU in other important sectors (for example, energy and social rights),[84] but it stipulates that national recovery plans must take into account the country-specific recommendations issued in the context of the European Semester.[85] In other words, although the NGEU contains some aspects of novelty and a degree of redistribution, it has not undermined the European Semester as an institutional framework for disciplining national budgets. This entails that NGEU has not overcome the logic of conditionality and has tied access to its loans and grants to economic and financial benchmarking. By introducing the possibility of suspending the payment to that Member State which would not comply with the fiscal rules set in the reformed PSG, NGEU might actually have created a more effective channel of control and nudging than the European Semester itself.[86] Accordingly, NGEU has not generated a different understanding of the PSG and, in many recovery plans, it has often distributed loans and grants according to a managerial logic rather than as a redistributive or corrective device.[87] Given that its effects are extended over a medium- to long-term perspective, one can also see how constraining for national governments' decisions on the political economy of a country (especially in the case of a change in political direction) this scheme can be.

In a recent article, Guillaume Grégoire assessed in an effective way the current status of the Economic and Monetary Union (EMU), when compared to its origins:

> its fundamentals have not changed: monetary policy is still, at least officially, entrusted to a central bank with a primary mandate of price stability; economic and budgetary policies remain decentralised, but are subject (and increasingly so) to controls designed to limit public spending and ensure compliance with balanced budget rules.[88]

All in all, while it would be wrong to describe some of the recent operations within the EMU as just cosmetic or superficial, the core content of the euro monetary constitution has not been transformed. Although there are cracks appearing here and there, for the

[83] See, for a general argument on the use of emergency politics in the EU, J White, *Politics of Last Resort* (Oxford University Press, 2018).

[84] See P Dermine, 'The Planning Method: An Inquiry into the Constitutional Ramifications of a New EU Governance Technique' (2024) 61 *CML Rev* 959–92.

[85] Art 17, para 3 and 18 para 4 of Regulation 2021/241 (n 28).

[86] This is the reading offered by T Biebricher, 'Covid-19, War and the End of Neoliberalism' in R Weber (ed), *The Financial Constitution of European Integration* (Bloomsbury, 2022) 105–06.

[87] On the problematic constitutional consequences of this method, see Dermine (n 84).

[88] G Grégoire, 'The EU Neoliberal Constitutionalism(s)' (2024) 4 *European Law Open* 705, 738. Given recent developments, it could also be added that the attempt at an energy transition has also been stifled.

moment there is enough political and economic consensus to form a block in support of this kind of economic and monetary 'equilibrium'.[89]

VIII. Conclusions

The critical angle adopted in this chapter (ie, critique of the political economy) to address the euro monetary constitution has made it possible to identify the fundamental objectives around which that monetary order is designed and how they are pursued. The chapter has identified under the principle of sound money, the organising pillar of the monetary constitution and the distinctive trait of the peculiar institutional organisation of the latter. From a monetary perspective, the critical analysis of the political economy of the euro monetary constitution sheds light on how the currency is managed as a pro-creditor institution and, at the same time, as a constraining factor for labour. It has done so by identifying the main institutional features of the euro constitution, especially by retrieving the role and function played by the central governing organ, the ECB, both in its relationship with other European institutions and financial markets. Finally, the previous section tested whether recent unconventional interventions have brought about a substantive transformation of this monetary constitution, concluding with some cautionary notes on their real impact. The assessment is roughly the same: despite some exceptional interventions, the fundamental objective of the monetary constitution remains not only the same, but rather it is expanded to include financial stability.

In this context, the normative relevance of a critical analysis of the monetary constitution can show how such an institutional design (pursuing such a fundamental objective) is prone to intensify the domination of its subjects. In this case, domination comes in two forms of arbitrary rule: one is the class-based exploitation (which can also be seen, according to some reconstructions, as an intersubjective form of domination) which is strengthened primarily by the primacy accorded to financial creditors; the other is the impersonal subjection to market forces,[90] which is aggravated by the epistemic subalternity of the monetary constitution (and its guardian) to market-based expectations. In this context, it is hard to imagine that a rebound against these forms of domination can materialise only through unconventional measures and without the involvement of labour.

[89] Lokdam and Wilkinson speak of a conservative transformation of the EMU, that is, a transformation of certain aspects of the economic governance framework without democratisation: see H Lokdam and M Wilkinson, 'The European Economic Constitution in Crisis: A Conservative Transformation?' in Grégoire and Miny (n 74) 461.

[90] This is part of what could be defined as structural domination; *cf* the view which extends this domination to the dominators as well in L Ypi, 'On Dominated Dominators' in V Mantouvalou and J Wolff (eds), *Structural Injustice and the Law* (UCL Press, 2024) 14–31.

5

Emancipation Entrapped?

The Social Model of Democratic Capitalism and the Europeanisation of the Power to Tax

JUSSI JAAKKOLA

I. Introduction

European integration figures among key transformative trajectories that have moulded the conditions of exercising the power to tax under the social model of democratic capitalism. Relying on intellectual resources emanating from critical theory, this chapter examines the evolving role of European Union (EU) law in shaping income taxation as a democratic institution for mitigating the disempowering effects of market capitalism. Focusing on income taxation, the chapter unearths how European law has fashioned the contradiction between democracy and capitalism. European integration displays this contradiction in a transnational form of liberal versus social Europe.[1] The chapter maintains that the structural dilemmas that have characterised the exercise of the power to tax in national contexts have increasingly made their appearance in EU law, although in more rudimentary or embryonic forms thus far. The dilemmas consist of efforts to maintain the self-directing market system while interfering with this system through taxation. Not only does European integration shape the conditions of asserting democratic capitalism by national states, but also reproduces the dilemmas of democratic capitalism within the corpus of European law.

In the post-war era, European political economies developed into systems of democratic capitalism. They embraced market capitalism but allowed it to operate within democratically established limits only. To a significant extent, politics was looked on as an endeavour by which people pursue emancipation from the distress resulting from the market.[2] The state was experienced as a political apparatus providing conditions for emancipation, authorised through collective democratic agency. In its social and democratic configuration, the state wielded public power that citizens could harness for liberating themselves from the unfettered market rule. For mastering the exigencies

[1] C Joerges, 'The Rechtsstaat and Social Europe: How a Classical Tension Resurfaces in the European Integration Process' in L Morlino and G Palombella (eds), *Rule of Law and Democracy: Inquiries into Internal and External Issues* (Brill, 2010) 163–83.

[2] In constitutional terms, see A Somek, *The Cosmopolitan Constitution* (Oxford University Press, 2014) 79–175.

produced by the market, a core state prerogative was the power to tax. It was used to decommodify goods vital for human existence, engender equality in economic resources and political power, manage macroeconomic conjunctures, and steer industrial production. The public purse was a key institution of giving life to what could be democratic in democratic capitalism.

Since its inception, democratic capitalism rested on contradictory rationalities of organising socio-economic reality: collective political choice in the sphere of democracy and contractual individual choice in the market sphere.[3] While the outright clash between the political and the economic, between democracy and markets, remained temporarily dormant during the post-war economic growth, these constitute an in-built contradiction within democratic capitalism.[4] The same structural contradiction underlies the coexistence of market economy and fiscal democracy. On the one hand, in reducing individuals' market dependence, the power to tax must interfere with the logic of the market. On the other hand, taxation must not frustrate the logic of the market, for which reason fiscal extraction remains constrained by an imperative of economic prudence, advising to insulate profit-making against political intervention. Hence, in democratic capitalism, the emancipatory promise of taxation is a real but fragile aspiration, susceptible to becoming undermined by various political and economic transformations that favour the market rule over the government through collective democratic agency. Beside technological development and globalisation of the economy, European integration figures as a key process transforming the political and economic reality of taxation.

For this chapter, a core contribution by critical theory is a focus on emancipatory processes capable of releasing individuals from constraints on human autonomy and self-actualisation. More specifically, building on the Marxist research tradition, critical theory studies emancipation from the exigencies of capitalist social formation.[5] Focusing on emancipation involves two aspects. First, as a form of intellectual activity, critical theory conceives itself as a practical undertaking.[6] With a commitment to emancipatory interest of knowledge,[7] it expedites the processes of emancipation. Second, while assuming an emancipatory function, critical theory analyses emancipatory tendencies underway in the existing social reality, albeit in a pre-theoretical or under-theorised form.[8] In this sense, critical theory engages in the immanent mode of critique and should not be seen as separate from the social praxis it studies. For critical theory, the contradiction between emancipatory tendencies and counterweights to these tendencies constitutes a pre-existing object of research. This chapter demonstrates how this

[3] A Przeworski and M Wallerstein, 'Structural Dependence of the State on Capital' (1988) 82 *American Political Science Review* 11, 11; W Merkel, 'Is Capitalism Compatible with Democracy?' (2014) 8 *Zeitschrift für Vergleichende Politikwissenschaft* 109, 113–14.

[4] C Offe, '"Ungovernability": The Renaissance of Conservative Theories of Crisis' in C Offe, *Contradictions of the Welfare State* (Hutchinson, 1984) 65–87, 83–84; W Streeck, 'The Crisis in Context' in W Streeck and A Schäfer (eds), *Politics in the Age of Austerity* (Polity, 2013) 262–86. For elaboration, see section II.

[5] A Honneth, 'A Social Pathology of Reason: On the Intellectual Legacy of Critical Theory' in A Honneth, *Pathologies of Reason: On the Legacy of Critical Theory* (Columbia University Press, 2009) 19–42.

[6] M Horkheimer, 'Postscript' in M Horkheimer, *Critical Theory. Selected Essays* (Continuum, 2002) 244–52, 246.

[7] J Habermas, *Knowledge and Human Interests* (Beacon Press, 1972) 301–17.

[8] A Honneth, 'The Social Dynamics of Disrespect: on the Location of Critical Theory Today' (1994) 1 *Constellations* 255, 256–58.

contradiction surfaces in European fiscal integration that provides for emancipation from market exigencies but remains constrained by the market.

The chapter examines the contradiction between fiscal democracy and market capitalism, which instantiates a broader conflict between the political and the economic.[9] In conceptualising this contradiction, the chapter borrows from critical theorists who have reflected on the capacity of the state to subordinate market forces to collective political will. It observes how this problematic was articulated by early representatives of the Frankfurt School (Frederick Pollock, Max Horkheimer), then by those taking part in the neo-Marxist state debate, and finally by Claus Offe and Wolfgang Streeck. The middle-group emphasised the determining force of capitalist economic laws, which the early generation of the Frankfurt School had set aside. The last-mentioned scholars viewed the political and the economic as mutually constitutive elements of the social order, which makes their contribution conceptually apt for analysing the dilemmas of democratic capitalism. Since critical theory provides a holistic view to the relationship between the political and the economic, it helps conceptualise the dilemmas of EU law that has grown to accommodate a great number of political aspirations.

While the interdependence between the state and economy has figured as a key research theme in critical theory, the power to tax, as a specific state prerogative, has not been analysed in any comprehensive sense, especially not in the context of EU law. This chapter fills the lacuna by examining how European integration transforms the emancipatory potential of taxation and how, in the social formation of democratic capitalism, the contradictions characterising the exercise of the power to tax resurface in the EU. Focusing on taxation, the chapter shows how efforts to tame the rule of the market by political means is contradicted by the dynamics of capitalist social formation, that is, by the object it aims to overcome.

The chapter proceeds in three steps. First, it elaborates how critical theory has conceptualised the role of the state in embedding market forces under democratic capitalism. The state theory is crucial for EU law scholars because it provides a conceptual apparatus that helps understand the dilemmas of political ordering that are present also in the EU but whose deeper theoretical and historical underpinnings are often neglected in strictly EU-focused approaches. Second, the chapter spells out the contradictions of income taxation as a democratic means of emancipation. Since taxes are strikingly absent from theoretically oriented EU studies, section II provides background for theorising the EU from a fiscal perspective. Third, the chapter analyses the implications of European income tax integration for the emancipatory exercise of the power to tax and how the contradictions of democratic capitalism resurface in EU tax policy. The chapter finds that the contemporary controversies over the appropriate fiscal constitution of the EU are iterations of more fundamental contradictions that taxation acquires over time in changing political contexts. These controversies essentially revolve around the twin-commitment of the EU: the EU must establish the market order and ensure that it may do its work but it must also intervene in the market in order to produce vital social goods.

[9] On the centrality of the notion of contradiction in critical theory, see RJ Antonio, 'Immanent Critique as the Core of Critical Theory: Its Origins and Developments in Hegel, Marx and Contemporary Thought' (1981) 32 *British Journal of Sociology* 330.

II. Critical Theory and the Contradictions of the Democratic Capitalist State

This section analyses how critical theory has conceptualised the role of the state *vis-à-vis* the economy. Remarkably, the early Frankfurt School of critical theory attributed to the state a certain primacy over the economy. At the turn of the 1970s, Marxist state theorists disputed the primacy, stressing the dependence of the state on the economy. Around the same time, Claus Offe, a representative of the second generation of the Frankfurt School, analysed the relationship between the state and the economy – or democracy and capitalism – without privileging one or the other. Wolfgang Streeck gave this approach a contemporary articulation that takes into account the EU and identifies also the most recent structural dilemmas of transnational capitalism. While critical theorists have never focused on taxation in any detail, their state theories help conceptualise the contradictions of taxation in democratic capitalism.[10] The state theoretical background is crucial also for understanding the EU.[11] The EU is not a *sui generis* entity detached from politico-legal concepts pertaining to the state. Hence, elements from state theory should be used to analyse the EU as a form of political government. More particularly, the problems of capitalism, democracy and government functions, as articulated in critical state theory, are not confined to state context but find a meaningful application in EU studies, too. The state has been the core political organisation operationalised to support emancipation. For this reason, the state theory helps to frame the analysis of the emancipatory effects of the EU and to situate the EU in a longer historical and political continuum of emancipation.

The Frankfurt School of critical theory emerged with an interest to analyse the internal contradictions of capitalism, of a system instigated by emancipatory aspirations but driving 'humanity into a new barbarism'.[12] Focusing on contradictions internal to capitalist production, critical theory followed a Marxist ethos. Yet, the focus soon shifted from internal contradictions of production to the relationship between the state and the economy.[13] In this shift, Frederick Pollock's notion of state capitalism was formative. Pollock observed how the state was assuming a key role in directing the economy. This process 'transform[ed] private capitalism into state capitalism'.[14] In state capitalism, private property is maintained but administered extensively by the state. Production and distribution are regulated by the state to an extent that 'nothing essential is left to the functioning of laws of the market or other economic "laws"'.[15] The state thus appeared as unconstrained by economic laws proper. Economic problems were turned into administrative and political problems, as a result of which 'economics as a social science . . . lost its object'.[16] Given that the

[10] On taxation in particular, see section III of this chapter.

[11] On the EU in particular, see section IV of this chapter.

[12] M Horkheimer, 'Traditional and Critical Theory' in Horkheimer (n 6) 188–243, 227.

[13] HF Dahms, *The Vitality of Critical Theory* (Emerald, 2011) 28–30.

[14] F Pollock, 'State Capitalism: Its Possibilities and Limitations' (1941) 9 *Zeitschrift für Sozialforschung* 200, 200.

[15] ibid 206–207; F Pollock, 'Is National Socialism a New Order?' (1941) 9 *Zeitschrift für Sozialforschung* 440, 453.

[16] Pollock (n 14) 217.

economy, as a roughly autonomous system, was vanishing, critical theorists' intellectual interest in the economy declined.

In Pollock's analysis, the state and state capitalism could exist in democratic or totalitarian form. While democratic state capitalism was not unimaginable as such, the ascendance of totalitarian regimes around the 1940s made it unlikely.[17] The totalitarian state of state capitalism exerted domination across the society and without democratic legitimation. Overcoming market capitalism happened at the cost of individuals becoming subservient to political domination. Even liberal capitalism entailed more emancipatory potential than the state-administered economy. The real-world totalitarian regimes gave Pollock a reason to portray the state rather as an instrument of oppression than as a means of emancipation.

The anti-utopian image of the state was taken up by Max Horkheimer, who cut an influential figure in shaping the early thought of the Frankfurt School. Like Pollock, he saw the state as gaining primacy over the economic. The state was, in principle, a potential emancipatory counterforce to liberal capitalism. In reality, the state had transformed into an authoritarian body, and ever 'more repression ha[d] developed in the administration of the [economic] plans'.[18] The state functioned as a planning authority that implemented its programme in an authoritarian mode. For early critical theory, this had two key consequences. First, since the state had subjugated the economy, the latter had lost much of its relevance as a topic of critique.[19] Second, since the state had proven bereft of emancipatory, democratic and utopian promises, it receded into the background in much of critical research. The state abode by instrumental mode of reason, whose operation critical theorists critiqued across the culture. In its entirety, the culture was emerging as an 'administered world'.[20] To a large extent, early critical theory turned into a theory of culture and its instrumentalist tendencies.

The Frankfurt School of critical theory ascribed to the state a certain primacy over the economy. This resembled the post-war social democratic thought in which the welfare state was believed to possess a capacity to act relatively independently from the economy and shape the functioning of the latter.[21] From the late 1960s onwards, the autonomy of the state was disputed by critical state theorists with Marxist roots. They rejected the 'politicist' belief in the omnipotence and primacy of the state.[22] Irrespective of whether ruled by the capitalist class or the more inclusive body of citizens, the state in a capitalist social formation is structurally determined by relations of production. As Wolfgang Müller and Christel Neusüss argued, the existence of the state apparatus consolidates the false 'illusion that the state is autonomous, that is, has an ability to "intervene" in "the economy"'.[23] The state remains constrained by the relations of

[17] ibid 221–25.

[18] M Horkheimer, 'The Authoritarian State' (1973) 15 *Telos* 3, 16.

[19] Frankfurt School was not exactly homogenous on the question of the economy. See MA Wilkinson in chapter 3 in this book.

[20] H-E Schiller, 'The Administered World' in B Best, W Bonefeld and C O'Kane (eds), *The SAGE Handbook of Frankfurt School Critical Theory. Volume 2: Themes* (SAGE, 2018) 834–51.

[21] For the social democratic primacy of the political and the state, see S Berman, *The Primacy of Politics. Social Democracy and the Making of Europe's Twentieth Century* (Cambridge University Press, 2006).

[22] S Clarke, 'The State Debate' in Simon Clarke (eds), *The State Debate* (Macmillan, 1991) 1–61, 1–5.

[23] W Müller and C Neusüss, 'Die Sozialstaatsillusion und der Widerspruch von Lohnarbeit und Kapital' (1971) 1 *PROKLA: Zeitschrift für Kritische Sozialwissenschaft* 7, 58.

capitalist production and private accumulation in a way that prevents it from overcoming them.[24]

If the autonomy of the state was overstated by the first-generation Frankfurt School and downplayed by later Marxist state theorists, Claus Offe, as a second-generation representative of the Frankfurt School, incorporated elements from both views. In the context of the EU, Offe's orientation paves the way to conceptualise the two-way tensions between the political and the economic and also the limits of the EU in shaping these tensions.

Offe has often been considered a politicist who unduly separates distribution (politics) from production (capitalism).[25] In a sense, this is correct, as Offe treated the contradictions of capitalism also as second-order contradictions of political legitimation. Yet, Offe did not disentangle political crises from economic crises, as the former 'are, of course, produced by the latter'.[26] Offe, for his part, blamed several state theorists for exaggerating the role of capitalist laws and for neglecting the specifically political logics of action. They had fallen prey to deterministic 'economism' simplistically reducing the state to a pre-determined reflex of the social relations of production. Offe called for a political crisis theory, which 'no longer traces the origins of crises exclusively to the dynamics of the sphere of production',[27] that is, to capitalist relations. In the system of post-war capitalism, economic contradictions were increasingly stabilised by state intervention, and more and more imperatives to act were addressed to the state. Yet, the state was structurally unable to fully respond to the demands, for which reason economic crises eventually turned into political crises within the state. Since an increasing number of functions had been assumed by the state, the need to legitimise the state had increased. The more interventionist the state became, the more it was faced by contradictory imperatives of action and popular expectations.

For Offe, the state, also as a welfare state, is a capitalist state. This twin-nature makes it a contradictory organisation. In its sharpest form, the contradiction appears between the two core state functions: accumulation and legitimation.[28] In its accumulation function as a capitalist state, the state must not interfere with capitalist production and, on the other hand, it must intervene in its processes so as to prevent the self-contradictory tendencies of capitalism from impelling the system to self-destruct. In its legitimation function as a democratic welfare state, the state must contain the disruptive externalities of the capitalist market on the society and do so by maintaining democratic legitimacy. The state has a twin-commitment to respect the autonomy of the market and intervene in its functioning. The 'precarious double function of the capitalist state continuously demands a combination of intervention and abstention from intervention,

[24] J Hirsch, 'Elemente einer materialistischen Staatstheorie' in C von Braunmühl, K Funken, M Cogoy and J Hirsch, *Probleme einer materialistischen Staatstheorie* (Suhrkamp, 1973) 199. See also J Holloway and S Picciotto, 'Introduction: Towards a Materialist Theory of the State' in ibid (eds), *State and Capital. A Marxist Debate* (Edward Arnold, 1978) 1–31.

[25] For instance, see Müller and Neusüss (n 23) 12–32.

[26] C Offe, '"Crises of Crisis Management": Elements of a Political Crisis Theory' in Offe (n 4) 35–64, 51. Therefore, economic crises are re-produced as crises of political reason without the latter being reducible to the former.

[27] ibid 61.

[28] C Offe, 'Legitimacy versus Efficiency' in Offe (n 4) 130–46.

of "planning" and "freedom".[29] The state simultaneously acts to maintain the capitalist market in operation and to emancipate people from the exigencies of the market society. It is entrapped in contradictory imperatives, neither of which it can ignore. What is more, capitalism cannot do without democracy and state intervention,[30] and the welfare state needs capitalism as a value-generating machine for its own existence.[31] Hence, the state must further the commodification and decommodification of vital resources. In the state that is both a capitalist state and a democratic welfare state, the contradiction between the political and the economic resurfaces as an unresolvable contradiction between democracy and capitalism. In democratic capitalism, the system integration between the emancipatory state and the market economy remains structurally incomplete. This holds true also for the EU, whose limits in furthering emancipation resemble those analysed by Offe in the state context.

Wolfgang Streeck shares Offe's diagnosis of democratic capitalism as a systemically contradictory social formation. The formation is 'ruled by an endemic conflict between capitalist markets and democratic politics, which forcefully reasserted itself when high economic growth came to an end in the 1970s'.[32] The contradiction boils down to the fact that under democratic capitalism, socio-economic reality is organised through fundamentally opposing institutions: market capitalism favours contractual private choice by individuals, democracy endorses majoritarian choices by citizens acting as a collective body.[33] The tragedy of democratic capitalism is a commitment to both institutional forms of organising social and economic life. Therefore, 'governments are theoretically required to honour both principles simultaneously, although substantively the two almost never align'.[34] The state remains entrapped in contradictions largely identified already by Offe. In the following sections, I will analyse the form these contradictions have acquired as regards the power to tax.

Streeck contends that crisis theories emerging in Frankfurt in the 1970s, such as that of Offe, focused excessively on legitimacy or at least on the wrong pillar of it. In the post-1970s era, the lack of legitimacy has not derived from the labour's or citizens' discontent with the state. Rather, crises of legitimacy have been triggered by capital's disappointment of being forced to live under democratic intervention in private accumulation. This transformed democratic capitalism and resulted in an increased insulation of capital against democratic intervention – something that has been identified as an aspect of democratic deficit in the EU. If the 1960s was still about taming capitalism by democracy, the post-1970s trajectories have been about domesticating democracy by

[29] Offe (n 26) 50.

[30] C Offe, 'Structural Problems of the Capitalist State: Class Rule and the Political System. On the Selectiveness of Political Institutions' in K von Beyme (eds), *German Political Studies. Vol. 1* (Sage, 1974) 31–54, 54; C Offe, 'Some Contradictions of the Modern Welfare State' in Offe (n 4) 147–61, 153. For a contemporary articulation of the problem that capitalism needs non-capitalist resources while constantly destroying these as its own conditions of possibility, see N Fraser, *Cannibal Capitalism: How our System is Devouring Democracy, Care, and the Planet – and What We Can Do About It* (Verso, 2023).

[31] Offe, Some Contradictions (n 30) 150. I will elaborate this further in section III of this chapter.

[32] W Streeck, 'The Crises of Democratic Capitalism' (2011) 71 *New Left Review* 6.

[33] W Streeck, 'Taking Capitalism Seriously: Towards an Institutionalist Approach to Contemporary Political Economy' (2011) 9 *Socio-Economic Review* 152. For further conceptualisations of the contradiction, see W Streeck, 'How to Study Contemporary Capitalism' (2012) 53 *European Journal of Sociology* 1, 13–16.

[34] Streeck (n 32), 7. See also W Streeck, 'Comment on Wolfgang Merkel, "Is Capitalism Compatible with Democracy?"' (2015) 9 *Zeitschrift für Vergleichende Politikwissenschaft* 49, 54–55.

capitalism, especially by capitalism in its transnationalised form. Rather than to legitimation processes within democratic institutions, focus must be shifted to capitalism as a force that conditions democratic authority.[35] Still, Streeck remains committed to political economy research. Rather than deriving political and legal institutions from the capitalist economy or *vice versa*, political economy examines them 'together as densely intertwined and closely interdependent'[36] instances shaping each other's functioning, also in their contradictory relations.

Streeck's political economy perspective is important in the context of European integration, under which capitalist economy and political institutions co-determine each other.[37] European political institutions and EU law play an absolutely essential role in determining the form that the contradiction between capitalism and democracy assumes, but their development also remains subject to this contradiction. The political economy perspective takes law seriously without falling prey to phantasies of law's omnipotence. The triangle of European political institutions, national states and (transnational) capitalist economy co-determine the extent to which the exercise of public power, as validated through democratic procedures, can be used for emancipation from market rule. In Streeck's analysis, the EU institutions have continuously undermined national democratic capacities to intervene in the market without having reconstituted any of these capacities at the European level.[38] This diagnosis complies not only with the views of other representatives of the Cologne School of political economy, such as Fritz W Scharpf and Armin Schäfer, but also with those put forward by Offe.[39] As will be shown in section IV, the power to tax has for long been among the powers undermined by European integration. Yet, more recent developments in the EU have displayed also an orientation to provide vital social goods and to rely on taxation in performing this task. Remaining alert to this twin-effect of the EU takes seriously the perception that views political organisations as performing both accumulation and legitimation functions.

This section has shown how the ideas on the relationship between the state and the economy have evolved within critical theory. Two conclusions emerge. First, in the social model of European post-war democratic capitalism, the state has been devised to intervene in capitalist markets so as to prevent their disruptive effects beyond the market sphere. The state has been instrumental in emancipating people from the most abrupt forms of market rule. Second, the state has continued to accommodate the reproduction of capitalism. In pursuing any policy goal, the state is embedded in capitalist constraints. The embeddedness of the state in the economic is nowhere as obvious as in the context of taxation. Hence, these conclusions pertain in particular to the power to tax, which is true in a national and in the EU context. In the following sections, I will show how these contradictions originally emerged in the nation-state context (section III) and were then gradually reproduced within EU law (section IV). Not only does EU law

[35] W Streeck, *Buying Time. The Delayed Crisis of Democratic Capitalism* (Verso, 2014) 1–46.

[36] Streeck, 'Taking Capitalism Seriously' (n 33) 138. See also Streeck, 'How to Study' (n 33) 21–26.

[37] See also MA Wilkinson in chapter 3 in this book.

[38] For a recent articulation, see W Streeck, *Taking Back Control? States and State Systems after Globalism* (Verso, 2024).

[39] C Offe, 'Demokratie und Wohlfahrtsstaat: eine europäische Regimeform unter dem Stress der europäischen Integration' (1998) 4 *Swiss Political Science Review* 35.

shape contradictions of fiscal democracy at the Member State level but also incorporates elements that reproduce these contradictions at the European level. As regards the EU as an emancipatory project, it stands in continuum with the nation-state, and the critical state theory provides significant intellectual resources to conceptualise this continuum.

III. Economic Constraints on the Emancipatory Use of the Power to Tax

Given its instrumental character, the power to tax can serve various social models and visions of emancipation. This section spells out the specific differences of the post-war emancipatory income taxation and the contradictions it has remained riddled with in democratic capitalism. The section provides intellectual resources to understand the forms in which these contradictions have been reproduced in EU law. In generalistic EU studies, taxation is a neglected issue. To make sense of the relationship between the power to tax and the EU, it is vital to familiarise oneself with the predicaments characterising state taxation.

In reaction to the nineteenth-century market society that produced a dehumanising class structure and made all spheres of existence dependent on the market, reformist factions emerged in the hope of precipitating the downfall of market capitalism, of what Horkheimer witnessed as having developed into 'a new barbarism'. Taxation was conceived as a political means of replacing market capitalism with a socialist and more humane order. In their most revolutionary design, taxes could permanently transfer private capital to public possession and eradicate the capitalist relations of production.[40] Taxation was experienced as a transitory power of overcoming the capitalist social formation. In such a role, it entailed a self-negation of a tax-financed state: since the market was to be abolished, also the tax state that lived off the market was to be replaced with an alternative political organisation. Whereas the self-directing market and the market-neutral tax system had supported the nineteenth-century bourgeois wish to emancipate from political rule, the call for market-interfering taxation displayed a political commitment to a rather complete emancipation from the market rule.

In Western Europe, abolishing market capitalism proved to be a mere aspiration. In actually existing post-war political economies, a compromise between capitalism and socialism was inaugurated. This happened in the form of democratic capitalism.[41] Also taxes were never programmed to squash market capitalism altogether. Yet, in comparison to the liberal social model, a radically new role was assigned to taxes. Taxes were to establish social spheres insulated against the unfettered market rule. In performing this task, post-war emancipatory taxation bore three key properties.

First, tax systems were internally redesigned. Tax rates rose to levels exceeding any peace-time norm. Beyond that, overreliance on regressive consumption taxes was relieved with wealth, inheritance and especially income taxes, which followed a progressive

[40] M Krätke, 'Sozialistische Steuerpolitik – gestern und morgen' (1986) 16 *Prokla* 34, 42–55. See also F Karl Mann, *Steuerpolitische Ideale* (Gustav Fischer, 1937) 275–324.

[41] See section II of this chapter.

pattern.[42] Second, new functions were attributed to taxation. In fact, while all the tax system properties mentioned above were invented before the post-war era, they turned to serve new political ends. The fiscal function of generating revenues remained but revenues were collected at higher levels and spent for new purposes, such as social entitlements. In their redistributive or social policy function, taxes corrected market-made distribution of resources so as to produce economic equality and factual conditions for political self-determination. In this social democratic sense, taxes enhanced individuals' democratic agency and fostered collective self-rule of the people beyond formal political rights.[43] In a sense of Keynesian fiscal policy, taxes were employed to steer macroeconomic trends and to prevent systemic crises. In all these functions, taxes operated as corrective means of reducing the authority of the market in governing individuals' socio-economic fate. In decommodifying key spheres of human life, taxes made individual choices less coerced by market imperatives.

Third, under general franchise and popular sovereignty, taxation could be experienced as a democratically legitimate form of imposition. The liberal order had made voting rights formally dependent on individual's economic standing.[44] By the ascent of democratic capitalism, political citizenship was decoupled from economic qualifications. Fiscal democracy was no more exhausted by the propertied individuals' consent to hand over their 'owned property' to the government, as still entailed by the old dictum 'no taxation without representation'. Rather, fiscal democracy came to refer to the power of the majority to make a polity correspond to collective political wishes.[45] Instead of being limited by formal property qualifications, fiscal democracy featured among institutions which defined private property in the first place. Taxes increasingly interfered with the society, but their legitimacy emanated from choices attributable to the collective self-government of the people. Therefore, in the post-liberal era, rehabilitation of the political should not be equated to oppressive minority rule representative of the pre-liberal era, and governing the economy democratically through the state was distinctly different from the totalitarian forms of state capitalism.

In post-war democratic capitalism, income taxation featured as a democratically validated political means by which people could pursue emancipation from the market dependence. In emanating from democratic self-rule of the people, taxation expressed political emancipation. In reshaping socio-economic conditions of individuals, it fostered social and human emancipation.[46] Taxes enabled democratic control over the economy, which amounted to a partial substitution of political laws for seemingly

[42] S Steinmo, *Taxation and Democracy. Swedish, British and American Approaches to Financing the Modern State* (Yale University Press, 1993); T Piketty, *Capital and Ideology* (The Belknap Press of Harvard University Press, 2020) 486–577.

[43] S Huhnholz, 'Refeudalisierung des Steuerstaates? Vorüberlegungen zu einer politischen Theorie der Steuerdemokratie' in S Boysen, A-B Kaiser and F Meinel (eds), *Verfassung und Verteilung. Beiträge zu einer Grundfrage des* Verfassungsverständnisses (Mohr Siebeck, 2015) 175–216, 205.

[44] JL Cardoso and P Lains (eds), *Paying for the Liberal State: The Rise of the Public Finance in Nineteenth-Century Europe* (Cambridge University Press, 2010).

[45] W Schön, 'Taxation and Democracy' (2018) 72 *Tax Law Review* 235, 242 and 266. For two political philosophies behind these differences, see M Goldoni, 'Rousseau's Radical Constitutionalism and Its Legacy' in MW Dowdle and MA Wilkinson (eds), *Constitutionalism Beyond Liberalism* (Cambridge University Press, 2017) 227–53.

[46] On political and social emancipation, see A Somek, 'Europe: From Emancipation to Empowerment'. LEQS Paper No 60/2013.

anonymous forces of the market. Yet, while the double commitment to emancipation increasingly embedded the economic in the political, the political also remained embedded in the economic. Indeed, despite the key modern ideal of the autonomous political sphere, the formation of the state and its system of public law remained mediated by economic imperatives.[47]

The embeddedness of the state in the economy is perhaps nowhere as obvious as in the context of taxation, and here Offe's analysis of the welfare state proves operational.[48] For Offe, the welfare state is a capitalist state. This means, first of all, that production is not taken over by the state but remains largely in private hands. The state has 'the *mandate* to create and sustain *conditions* of accumulation'[49] in the capitalist economy. Market economy is, in its own right, a core means of organising the society in democratic capitalism, and in exercising the power to tax, the government is urged to ensure the reproduction of the market. Secondly, a capitalist state is a tax state. It is not an economically self-standing entity but dependent on private accumulation. In the liberal era, the economic existence of the state was anchored on taxation and became dependent on the market that served as a source of revenue extraction.[50] In democratic capitalism, the market continued to function as the state's economic condition of possibility. As Offe notes, the state's economic dependence is most striking in its 'extensive reliance on resources created in the accumulation process and derived through taxation'.[51] In terms of feasibility, taxes may not exhaust the market dynamics that serve as an enabling condition for taxation. Hence, in redeeming emancipatory claims through taxation, the capitalist state is trapped in the contradiction of ensuring the functioning of the capitalist market and undoing the power of the market over individuals' socio-economic fate. Importantly, this applies to any political organisation relying extensively on monetary resources, including the EU.

The market can be protected against the power to tax by manifold constitutional rules. Yet, the state's economic dependence on private accumulation implies economic constraints on the power to tax. Should a tax burden imposed on the accumulation process be experienced as erosive of 'business confidence', acts of recoil, such as investment strikes and capital flight, could be initiated by economically powerful taxpayers.[52] In order not to compromise the functioning of the market, states must tailor tax policies to perceived economic necessities. This economistic episteme impels governments to reflect on what 'will happen if, at a given moment, we raise tax on a particular category of persons or a particular category of goods?'[53] The state interferes with the market but may not exhaust its dynamics. In this dual sense, Joseph Schumpeter pointed to the

[47] MA Wilkinson, 'Public Law and the Autonomy of the Political: *A Material Critique*' in MA Wilkinson and MW Dowdle (eds), *Questioning the Foundations of Public Law* (Hart, 2018) 181–205. For elaboration, see section II of this chapter.

[48] See section II of this chapter.

[49] C Offe, 'The Theory of the Capitalist State and the Problem of Policy Formation' in LN Lindberg and others (eds), *Stress and Contradiction in Modern Capitalism* (Lexington Books, 1975) 125–44, 126.

[50] R Goldscheid, 'Finanzwissenschaft und Soziologie' (1917) 9 *Weltwirtschaftliches Archiv* 253.

[51] Offe (n 49) 126.

[52] R Miliband, *The State in Capitalist Society* (Weidenfeld and Nicolson, 1969) 146–78; CE Lindblom, *Politics and Markets. The World's Political-Economic Systems* (Basic Books, 1977) 170–88; M Krätke, 'Steuergewalt, Versicherungszwang und ökonomisches Gesetz' (1991) 21 *Prokla* 112, 124.

[53] M Foucault, *The Birth of Biopolitics. Lectures at the Collège de France 1978–1979* (Picador, 2008) 15.

parasitic nature of the tax state: it feeds on its host but for the sake of its own reproduction, may not suck the host dry.[54] In such a contradictory role, taxation contributes to emancipation from the market while remaining constrained by economic imperatives arising from the market. Basing its existence on taxation, the state faces self-inflicted restrictions, and fiscal democracy is structurally 'imprisoned' by the market.[55] For instance, in the context of the EU internal market law, the capacity of mobile capital and corporations to move across borders in the pursuit of more relaxed tax obligations is a powerful obstacle to fiscal democracy.[56] As Max Weber already noted, even when the poorer strata are formally enfranchised, their democratic choice remains limited by the threat of mobile capital migrating to lower-tax territories.[57] Tax policy thus manifests the structures and power relations as shaped by market capitalist social formation, and taxation is systemically hamstrung in its effort to interfere with private accumulation.[58]

For critical theorists, the capitalist welfare state, as a tax state, displays the core contradiction between capitalism and democracy. In the 1970s, as the post-war economic growth was coming to an end, the contradiction turned from a dormant tension to recurrent (fiscal) crises. The capitalist welfare state is confronted with the predicament of ensuring the functioning of the market, enabling the emancipation from the market dependence, and performing these functions in a democratically legitimate way so as to retain mass loyalty.[59] The critical theorists shared a neoliberal diagnosis that capitalism and democracy contradict each other and result in constant boundary conflicts.[60] Hence, in post-war democratic capitalism, taxation displays the basic contradiction between capitalism and democracy. Income taxation has operated as a means by which to pursue, through collective democratic agency, emancipation from the unfettered market rule. The tendency has remained dampened by a simultaneous commitment to preserve private accumulation, which reflects the embeddedness of the political in the economic. The embeddedness of taxation has serious consequences for the state-mediated political self-rule in general because the 'levying of taxes concerns not just one principle but *the* principle underlying the authority of the national state'.[61] Since taxes are vital for implementing any public policy by which constituencies aspire to keep the disruptive tendencies of market capitalism in check, the capacity to tax, as an enabling nervous system, lies at the core of the entire political organisation. As will be shown in the next section, the EU has both undermined and aimed to reconstitute this

[54] J Schumpeter, 'Die Krise des Steuerstaats' in Rudolf Hickel (hrsg.), R Goldscheid/J Schumpeter. *Die Finanzkrise des Steuerstaats. Beiträge zur politischen Ökonomie der Staatsfinanzen* (Suhrkamp, 1976) 329–79, 341–52.

[55] CE Lindblom, 'The Market as Prison' (1982) 44 *Journal of Politics* 324. See also F Block, 'The Ruling Class does not Rule: Notes on the Marxist Theory of the State' (1977) 33 *Socialist Revolution* 6, 15–19.

[56] See section IV of this chapter.

[57] M Weber, *Economy and Society. An Outline of Interpretive Sociology* (University of California Press, 1978) 351–52.

[58] UK Preuß, 'Rechtsstaat – Steuerstaat – Sozialstaat. Eine Problemskizze' in W Abendroth et al (eds), *Ordnungsmacht? Über das Verhältnis von Legalität, Konsens und Herrschaft* (Europäische Verlagsanstalt, 1981) 46–68.

[59] For instance, see J Habermas, *Legitimation Crisis* (Beacon Press, 1975).

[60] This was a shared diagnosis among critical, Marxist and neoliberal theorists who, unlike much of the then-contemporary leftist political thought, did not shy away from articulating the fundamental role of the contradiction (G Esping-Andersen, 'The Incompatibilities of the Welfare State' (1983) 7 *Thesis Eleven* 42).

[61] U Beck, *What is Globalization?* (Polity, 2000) 4.

capacity, which reflects the recurring contradiction between capitalist and democratic rationalities. Importantly, these contradictions have gradually emerged in EU law itself, which displays a growing number of political aspirations that it must accommodate simultaneously. In the post-1960s period, the EU has played a significant role in reforming the compromise between capitalism and democracy.

IV. European Integration and the New Conditions for Exercising the Power to Tax

European integration has significantly shaped the relationship between the political and the economic in democratic capitalism. This section explains how it has altered the conditions of using income taxation as a political means by which to emancipate from the market rule. By looking at the history of European integration, the section identifies contradictions and limits that will likely afflict any future course of EU fiscal integration. The analysis demonstrates the relevance of critical theory for EU studies: it shows that the perception of capitalist social formation as a contradictory order helps make sense of European fiscal integration.

The years around World War II prompted contrasting intellectual visions for a European federation and for a social model it was to cherish. Some asserted that a transnational reorganisation of Europe must abide by a socialist blueprint[62] or envisioned a transnational federation endowed with market-correcting powers.[63] Neoliberals, such as Friedrich Hayek[64] and others,[65] called for a federation confined to upholding rules constitutive to a transnational market regime and averse to democratic intervention in the economy, not least through taxation. Involving variegated intellectual and political perceptions, the socio-economic mindset unleashing European integration was essentially polyphonic. This was demonstrated by the Treaty Establishing the European Economic Community (EEC), whose underlying social model, if there was such, remained open.[66] The EEC's dominant rationale was to establish a European market regime. Its implementation, however, unfolded under democratic capitalism, which stressed the need for national policies of decommodification and the viability of

[62] A Spinelli, 'The Ventotene Manifesto, 1941' in ibid, *From Ventotene to the European Constitution* (ARENA Report No 1/07) 11–28.

[63] O Rosenboim, 'Barbara Wootton, Friedrich Hayek and the Debate on Democratic Federalism in the 1940s' (2014) 36 *The International History Review* 894.

[64] FA Hayek, 'The Economic Conditions of Inter-State Federalism' (1939) 5 *New Commonwealth Quarterly* 131.

[65] Q Slobodian, *Globalists. The End of Empire and the Birth of Neoliberalism* (Harvard University Press, 2018).

[66] Some have viewed the EEC Treaty as essentially supportive of or complementary to the social and democratic state (JE Fossum and AJ Menéndez, *The Constitution's Gift. A Constitutional Theory for a Democratic European Union* (Rowman and Littlefield, 2011)). Others have stressed its market-oriented and democracy-inhibiting ethos (MA Wilkinson, *Authoritarian Liberalism and the Transformation of Modern Europe* (Oxford University Press, 2021)). The intermediate position suggests that the Treaty has been left deliberately pluralistic; rather than involving any specific socio-economic model, the model should only be fleshed out through post-Treaty political processes (C Kaupa, *The Pluralist Character of the European Economic Constitution* (Hart, 2016)).

these policies also under the new market regime.[67] The contradiction quintessential to democratic capitalism was thus in-built in the European project.

The contradictory tendencies were reflected in European income tax integration, the history of which consists of three phases. The first stretches from the founding of the EEC until the mid-1980s, the second from the late 1980s until the early 2010s, and the third from around the mid-2010s onwards.[68]

Over the first phase of income tax integration, European law acquired a structure routinely conceptualised as the asymmetry of European integration.[69] On the one hand, the European market regime was set up to a remarkable extent. On the other hand, no income tax harmonisation followed. The ensuing institutional framework fostered cross-border economic mobility while keeping income tax policy at national discretion. With such a design, European law incorporated a variant of a traditional duality of *imperium* as a territorially confined sphere of political sovereignty and *dominium* as a transnational sphere of market relations.[70] The asymmetry increased the interdependence of tax policies and the likelihood of spontaneous (competitive) tax integration. The market dynamics, spurred by European law, could constrain what national democracies make of their power to tax. Though not triggering legal effects on income taxation, European integration began to frame how Member States exercise the authority still formally at their disposal. Unleashing the market integration thus potentially contradicted national fiscal democracy without mitigating the loss through common European norms. Spontaneous tax integration is a key form in which European integration has come to shape the contradiction between democracy and capitalism. It is among the democracy-imprisoning forces to which critical scholars were alerted already at the turn of the 1970s when stressing the dependence of the state and taxation on the economic sphere.[71]

While the asymmetric structure of European law was visible as early as in the 1960s, it was entrenched only later and fleshed out in a gradual fashion. It remained rather embryonic until the 1980s, keeping also spontaneous income tax integration dormant. The rudimentary nature of the asymmetry resulted from a rough post-war consensus that economic integration must not dilute national market-embedding powers. Essentially, the European market took significant steps but proceeded still at a moderate level, especially as regards capital mobility.[72] Furthermore, Member States did not renounce their monetary powers. They could thus respond to pressures of competitiveness

[67] In international context, the settlement came to be known as 'embedded liberalism' (JG Ruggie, 'International Regimes, Transactions, and Change: Embedded Liberalism in the Postwar Economic Order' (1982) 36 *International Organization* 379).

[68] For a more extensive analysis, see J Jaakkola, 'Taming the Leviathan or Dismantling Democratic Government? Evolving Political Ideas on Spontaneous Income Tax Integration in the European Union' (2023) 2 *European Law Open* 575, 585–613.

[69] FW Scharpf, 'The European Social Model: Coping with the Challenges of Diversity' (2002) 40 *Journal of Common Market Studies* 645.

[70] S Picciotto, 'The Internationalisation of the State' (1991) 15 *Capital & Class* 63; R Palan, *The Offshore World. Sovereign Markets, Virtual Places, and Nomad Millionaires* (Cornell University Press, 2003).

[71] See sections II and III of this chapter.

[72] AJ Menéndez, 'Incompatible Constitutional Paths? Making (Constitutional) Sense of the Existential Crisis of the European Union' in M Dani and others (eds), *The Legitimacy of European Constitutional Orders. A Comparative Inquiry* (Edward Elgar, 2023) 282–303, 288–96.

by devaluating their currency.[73] Importantly, the asymmetric structure was not an aspiration deliberately executed. In fact, blueprints for income tax harmonisation were put forward.[74] Albeit introduced to ensure the rational functioning of the cross-border price mechanism, they involved harmonising norms not compatible with a purely asymmetric model. Therefore, while the core properties of the asymmetric order of competitive fiscal federalism were in the making, their emergence was embedded in the democratic and social aspects of democratic capitalism.

Over the second phase, income tax integration acquired a more variegated shape. Importantly, the asymmetric structure became sharper. On the one hand, the European market was significantly deepened and financial flows unleashed, which happened under a remarkable consensus among European policy-makers. On the other hand, the income tax harmonisation agenda was articulately abandoned.[75] This consolidated the conditions for spontaneous tax integration, which was even deliberately favoured over political regulation of taxation. This fostered tax competition among states and made visible what the dependence of taxation on the market, now also on transnational financial markets, involved. From a medium of decommodification, tax rules were turning into political commodities, as governments increasingly adapted taxes to the economic necessities produced by the market.

To address competitive income tax integration, European soft law[76] and State Aid law[77] were operationalised. Yet, both courses of action avoided harmonisation of tax systems and insisted only on the internal consistency of a national system. Member States were allowed to compete by taxes but only in a non-discriminatory fashion. In fact, as the work on tax competition proceeded (or dried up), spontaneous integration became portrayed as a healthy means of reining in excessive fiscal demands.[78] Market integration without tax harmonisation consolidated the disciplinary reins on fiscal democracy and subjected taxation to systemic necessities arising from the market. This was a dream-come-true of neoliberals who had put forward visions of European competitive fiscal federalism, a federal order constraining national majoritarian democracies without involving a European tax authority.[79] The European market regime came to function as a disciplinary constraint on emancipatory taxation and contributed to

[73] Jaakkola (n 68) 591.

[74] For instance, see Proposal for a Council Directive concerning harmonization of systems of company taxation and of withholding taxes on dividends [1975] OJ C253/2.

[75] Commission of the European Communities, Communication to Parliament and the Council: Guidelines on Company Taxation. SEC(90)601 final, of 20 April 1990, 11.

[76] Resolution of the Council and the Representatives of the Governments of the Member States, Meeting within the Council of 1 December 1997 on a code of conduct for business taxation [1998] OJ C2/2.

[77] W Schön, 'Taxation and State Aid Law in the European Union' (1999) 36 *CML Rev* 911.

[78] Commission of the European Communities, Towards tax co-ordination in the European Union. A package to tackle harmful tax competition. Communication from the Commission to the Council. COM(97) 495 final, of 1 October 1997.

[79] Hayek (n 64). Competitive fiscal federalism in the EU context was endorsed especially by constitutional political economists, such as James M Buchanan, Viktor Vanberg, Wolfgang Kerber and Michael Wohlgemuth. Yet, some constitutional political economists who supported the structure maintained that it had become compromised by the Treaty of Maastricht, which was seen as having introduced all types of social and industrial policy-making powers (ME Streit and W Mussler, 'The Economic Constitution of the European Community: From "Rome" to "Maastricht"' (1995) 1 *European Law Journal* 5). Those with more social democratic orientation deplored the competitive model of integration (J Habermas, 'The Postnational Constellation and the Future of Democracy' in idem, *The Postnational Constellation. Political Essays* (Polity, 2001) 58).

a Polanyian historical double movement, this time in the form of disembedding the market from the self-protecting measures of society.

Beyond entrenching conditions for spontaneous tax integration, European law began to impose legal limits on income taxation. These resulted from the market-making rationale. Importantly, they did not contradict the abandonment of the tax harmonisation agenda, as their logic differed from harmonisation. The normative requirements emanated from two different sources: from judicial and political modes of integration.

First, after the mid-1980s, the European Court of Justice (the Court) began to review whether national tax systems treated cross-border economic activities unfavourably in comparison to domestic situations. In conducting the review, the Court relied on the economic liberties inscribed in the Treaty. In striking down tax norms, the Court subordinated taxation to the rationality of market-making.[80] While this resulted in black-letter limits on how Member States may exercise the power to tax, governments could still decide how to reform national systems. Judicial review was thus an example of 'negative integration'. Second, in the political mode of integration, market-making directives on income taxation were issued. They identified situations in which states must refrain from taxing capital movements or intra-corporate transactions. Governments were obliged not to assert their power to tax. This form of integration displays an ethos of creating a transnational market by prohibiting the exercise of core public powers and doing so by formal command of law. Judicial and political modes of integration added another layer to the institutional fabric that not only fostered transnational market dynamics but also formally held back fiscal claims. They displayed the post-1980s neoliberal drift in integration that privileged market aspects of democratic capitalism and made the power to tax abide by the needs of transnational capital flows. Importantly, this displays the role of law in constituting the transnational system of capitalism and private accumulation, which has been emphasised by critical theorists and political economy research.

The third phase of income tax integration began amidst the European sovereign debt crisis. In response to the crisis, new forms of EU economic governance burgeoned and countries were pushed to adopt adjustments in core fields of decommodification, such as social policy[81] and taxation.[82] Rather than in democratic fashion, much of this took place in technocratic-authoritarian mode of governance. Yet, in any fiscal crisis, the role of taxation is ambivalent. On the one hand, scaling down taxes can enhance market dynamics. To some extent, this was the recipe endorsed in EU economic governance. On the other hand, in yielding revenues, taxation helps reduce deficits and mitigate fiscal crises. The latter choice was reflected in a series of Directive proposals put forward in a traditional mode of political integration. The proposals sought to address tax avoidance and tax competition. Rather than limiting the extent of public power, the proposals aimed to protect national power to tax. For instance, the Directive[83] on the minimum

[80] For an overview, see S Douma, O Marres, H Vermeulen and D Weber (eds), *Terra/Wattel. European Tax Law. Volume 1: General Topics and Direct Taxation* (Kluwer, 2022) chs 6–13.

[81] F de Witte, 'The Architecture of a "Social Market Economy"' in P Koutrakos and J Snell (eds), *Research handbook on the law of the EU's internal market* (Edward Elgar, 2017) 117.

[82] AJ Menéndez, 'Neumark vindicated: the three patterns of Europeanisation of national tax systems and the future of the social and democratic Rechtsstaat' in D Chalmers and others (eds), *The End of the Eurocrats' Dream. Adjusting to European Diversity* (Cambridge University Press, 2016) 78, 102–16.

[83] Council Directive (EU) 2022/2523 on ensuring a global minimum level of taxation for multinational enterprise groups and large-scale domestic groups in the Union [2022] OJ L328/1.

effective corporate tax rate harmonised corporate tax systems so that countries must impose a minimum tax on larger corporations. When new forms of macroeconomic governance and political harmonisation of taxes are viewed in combination, a contradiction between two economic rationales emerge. The former aims to make tax systems more competitive and more market-oriented, the latter imposes burden on the market. The EU may help Member States to assert their fiscal claims, but in doing so it remains committed to the market. This displays a contradiction between market-intervening and market-conforming state actions, resurfacing now at the EU level. This points to the fact that particular politico-economic contradictions, identified in critical theory in state context, are bound to reappear in political organisations with significantly different institutional properties, such as thin administrative capacities and national veto rights in legislating on taxation in the EU.

To an extent, European income tax law has become constitutive of public power. Unlike market-making directives that paraded since the 1990s, the new rules have introduced positive state obligations to make use of public authority. European law has turned reflexive and self-corrective, being geared towards recreating a core public power it undermined for decades. Yet, in such a task, the EU remains moderated at least by two constitutional constraints. First, Treaty provisions for harmonisation are market-making norms. Each tax initiative must be legitimised as promoting the European market or competition. Any political consensus may thus be confronted with substantive limits springing from the market rationale of the EU.[84] This may contradict any EU tax policy that involves serious redistributive and social aspirations but cannot be portrayed as market-minded, such as the wealth tax proposed by Thomas Piketty.[85] Second, tax integration requires unanimity among all Member States affected. The high consensus requirement is a two-edged sword.[86] On the one hand, unanimity ensures each government's democratic accountability to national constituencies for tax rules adopted by the EU. On the other hand, it hinders the adoption of EU income tax rules, even under a strong political demand from the public. The material constraint of market-making orientation and the procedural constraint of unanimity create a potential tension between political demand and the EU constitutional framework. This could result in a legitimation crisis in the sense analysed by Offe: people demand political response but European political institutions are over-constrained to provide it.[87] Because of the legal commitment to market rationale, the EU is constrained in interfering with the market and performing legitimation function.

Since the eruption of the European sovereign debt crisis, a political demand for the EU's own funds and taxes has increased. Rather than only regulating how Member States exercise the power to tax, the EU could raise revenues to perform its political functions.[88] In the Euro-zone crisis, new taxes were envisioned to constitute a new fiscal

[84] For this type of contestation, see G Brady, 'Tax Competition and Harmonisation under EU Law: Economic Realities and Legal Rules' (2014) 39 *EL Rev* 790.

[85] Thomas Piketty, *Capital in the Twenty-First Century* (Harvard University Press, 2014) 515–39.

[86] FW Scharpf, 'De-Constitutionalisation and Majority Rule: A Democratic Vision for Europe' (2017) 23 *European Law Journal* 315.

[87] See section II of this chapter.

[88] On the differentiation between tax-regulating and tax-collecting powers in the EU, see Jaakkola (n 68) 612–13.

capacity for the EU and enable financial assistance to indebted countries.[89] Since then, various tax-like payments for the EU have been mooted. Yet, instead of raising revenues by taxation, the EU has borrowed from financial markets, which has held true in the context of the COVID-19 crisis and of the aid to Ukraine.[90] Joint European debt has been proposed also to provide for the envisaged European sovereignty fund, which would be used for purposes of industrial policy.[91] In the absence of the EU's capacity to tax, the financial credibility of the EU depends on Member States' tax-collecting capacities. While the European effort to consolidate Member States' tax-collecting powers has remained thus far rather modest, it has nonetheless fortified national public purses and can therefore be seen as contributing indirectly to the EU's capacity to perform its governing functions. In essence, the EU spends but does not tax.

In the future, EU funds could be collected through EU taxes. Yet, the key question is the use of receipts. The history of EU financial arrangements has demonstrated that distribution of European funds to Member States abides by conditionality: in return for funds, countries must comply with terms imposed by the EU. In the sovereign debt crisis, countries were required to make structural adjustments to their socio-economic systems, and the logic of conditionality pertains also to the COVID-19 recovery facility. The history of the capitalist state, for its part, has shown that taxes may be collected to support private accumulation – rather than to keep its disruptive effects in check. Quite conceivably, then, the EU funds could be distributed to Member States for tasks unrelated to social purposes and in exchange for structural economic reforms, downward adjustment in social policy and reconfiguration of tax systems so as to enhance their competitiveness and incentive patterns. Essentially, the contradiction between market-intervening and market-conforming rationales of taxation would re-emerge in the relationship between the EU and Member States, as the latter would largely remain responsible for policies of decommodification and for protecting people from the market rule. Therefore, the problematique of EU taxation cannot be treated separately from EU spending.

European income tax integration has been a cumulative process. Each phase has introduced new mechanisms by which EU law frames the exercise of the power to tax. The first phase involved a rough symmetry between market integration and non-harmonisation of taxation, achieved by keeping market integration in check. The second phase deepened an asymmetry by abandoning the idea of income tax harmonisation while taking the European market to a new level and prohibiting certain forms of taxation. The third phase has witnessed elements of tax harmonisation and reflections on the genuinely European power to tax. In the process, more and more state-like functions have been assigned to the EU, which resembles, in a rudimentary form, the expansion of the state around the mid-twentieth century. This has been reflected in the EU's relationship to income taxation. To an extent, tax integration has been a constitutionally open process, whose outcomes have not been programmed in the EU treaties.

[89] President of the European Council, 'Towards a Genuine Economic and Monetary Union'. Interim Report (Brussels, 12 October 2012).

[90] For related documents, see https://commission.europa.eu/strategy-and-policy/eu-budget/eu-borrower-investor-relations/legal-documents-and-reports_en.

[91] European Commission statement/22/5543, 'A European Sovereignty Fund for an industry "Made in Europe"', Blog of Commissioner Thierry Breton' (Brussels, 15 September 2022).

Importantly, the actual process of European tax integration has displayed both accumulation and legitimation functions of the state. Therefore, it has been shaped by the structural tension between market-conforming and market-intervening commitments. This tension would remain even in the case of the EU transforming into a tax-collecting entity, as it must protect the dynamics of private value creation while extracting from it. The contradiction between capitalism and interventionist democracy, as analysed especially by Offe and Streeck, has thus resurfaced at the European level. This shows that critical theory provides meaningful intellectual resources to analyse the EU in continuum with other political organisations, especially the state, that display an emancipatory orientation.

V. Conclusion

Reflecting on institutions that foster emancipation has been key in critical theory. While bourgeois liberalism was initiated as an emancipatory undertaking, the early Frankfurt School of critical theory saw that market capitalism had turned averse to emancipation. They also observed how the state was developing into an authoritarian form of oppression, depriving people of genuine choice over their lives. Hence, liberal institutions favouring individual autonomy in the private sphere appeared as bankrupt as centralised institutions urging collective choices in the political sphere. Subsequent representatives of the Frankfurt School rendered this problematic useful for studying the contradictions of democratic capitalism and its institutions, both within national states and in the EU.

On long-term inspection, European integration has unfolded as a market-making enterprise, with an aspiration to disentangle the market economy from national rules and individuals from national borders. Yet, income tax integration has demonstrated that the EU has assumed market-intervening functions. In endorsing market-making and market-intervening commitments, the EU does not only shape the tension between market capitalism and interventionist democracy at the national level but also constantly reproduces this contradiction at the European level. In this development, the EU has assumed new state-like functions. In so doing, it has endorsed institutions that deviate from those supporting its original emancipatory course, that is, its aspiration to establish a transnational market regime with a broad freedom of choice for private economic actors.[92] This reorientation in politics of emancipation is a contextual phenomenon, to be studied in light of broader economic and political change. This is especially true in the case of constitutionally relatively open-ended forms of integration, whose socio-economic model remains vague or volatile.

Seeing European integration in light of the contradiction between capitalism and democracy stresses that analysing EU law should not be confined to the legal properties of the EU. Focusing on a mere formal relationship between decision-making procedures or between Member State law and European law neglects the fact that European

[92] On the original emancipatory model of European integration and other forms of regional integration, see F de Witte, 'Integrating the Subject: Narratives of Emancipation in Regionalism' (2019) 30 *European Journal of International Law* 257, 264–68.

integration is a struggle between different social, economic and political models, which rely more on democratic interventionist or market capitalist aspects of democratic capitalism. For analysing the role of EU law in this struggle, insights from critical theory provide important intellectual resources. First, European law should be seen as part of a broader capitalist social totality, consisting of complex relationships between the economic and the political. Second, the relationships between the economic and the political are mutually constitutive and contradictory relations, in which one member cannot be reduced to another. Third, under democratic capitalism, the tension between capitalism and democracy is a contradiction that acquires new shape in different political arrangements. The contradiction can thus be operationalised as an intellectual prism through which to analyse various political environments and institutions.

6

Critical Theory and European Labour Law

Insights from the Past

REBECCA ZAHN AND MEEMI MATERO

I. Introduction

The classic account of European social integration starts with the near exclusion of European social policy and labour law from the founding Treaty of the European Economic Community (EEC) (1957). The EEC's competence was limited to the free movement of workers, equal pay and co-operation in the area of social security. The final version of the Treaty reflected a consensus which relied on market forces for growth and wealth creation while social policy and labour law largely remained the preserve of the Member States. Although the EU's competence, and with that the number of European Union (EU)-derived social policy and labour law norms, has increased since 1957 there remains an asymmetry between European social and market integration. European labour law has a curious character. It is patchy in its coverage of rights and, at its heart, suffers from an equivocal purpose within the EU's framework. Underlying tensions between economic policy and social integration rose to the surface in the wake of the 2008 banking, and subsequent Euro-zone, crisis. In response, there has been an increase in the number of legislative initiatives launched by the European Commission,[1] as well as a proliferation of (largely unrealised) reform proposals from EU labour law scholars, social actors and governments which aim to reinvigorate social Europe.[2] There is general agreement on the long-term imperative to develop a social policy concept

[1] See, eg, European Parliament, Council and Commission, 'Interinstitutional Proclamation on the European Pillar of Social Rights' [2017] OJ C428/09; European Commission, 'Proposal for a Directive of the European Parliament and of the Council on work-life balance for parents and carers and repealing Council Directive 2010/18/EU' COM(2017) 253 final; European Commission, 'Proposal for a Directive of the European Parliament and of the Council on transparent and predictable working conditions in the European Union COM(2017) 797 final; European Commission, 'Proposal for a Directive of the European Parliament and of the Council on adequate minimum wages in the European Union' COM(2020) 682 final.

[2] See FW Scharpf, *Governing in Europe: Effective and Democratic?* (Oxford University Press, 1999). For a summary of recent labour law proposals and their evaluation, see M Weiss, 'The Need for More Comprehensive EU Social Minimum Standards' in R Singer and T Bazzani (eds), *European Employment Policies: Current Challenges* (Berliner Wissenschafts-Verlag, 2017) and F Vandenbroucke, C Barnard and G de Baere (eds), *A European Social Union after the Crisis* (Cambridge University Press, 2017). See also more recent writings by Schiek and others.

for the EU to mitigate the detrimental effects of economic integration on workers but different views on the role that the EU institutions should play to achieve that goal.[3]

This chapter observes that this prevalence of crises and the inadequacy of reform proposals at EU level calls for more critical, and more methodologically critical, EU labour law research.[4] It hence proposes to consider what critical theory could offer legal scholars and policy-makers thinking about the future of EU labour law and social Europe. The chapter conceives critical theory to be 'specifically concerned to dig beneath the surface of legal doctrines and practices; to go beyond a project of explication and rationalization and to interrogate the deeper political, historical and philosophical logics which underpin the power of law'.[5] To these ends, critical theory constitutes two defining actions: critique and reconstruction.[6] This chapter employs insights from critical theory to critique the current shape of European labour law and to generate insights into the different political, economic, and social factors which shaped its development. Cognisant of the need to engage in an adequately critical, socially embedded critique of EU labour law, the chapter examines the normative underpinnings of EU labour law and European labour law's relation to social and political conditions through a genealogical critique.[7] Genealogical critique 'explores how normative ideas change over time and how these "shifts of meaning" affect different social groups'.[8] For EU legal scholarship, such critique offers the opportunity to examine how the EU's foundational values such as democracy, equality and solidarity have developed during the process of European integration and to reveal, by highlighting the varied perspectives of different social groups, how the development of these values has impacted various social groups.[9] And by highlighting how these historical insights could inform a rethinking of the future of European labour law, the chapter engages with the transformative tenet of critical theory without which 'the critical project comes across as incomplete in EU law'.[10]

In order to undertake such a critique of European labour law, this chapter operationalises critical theory through minor literature and comparative law, or the concept of a 'minor comparativism'.[11] A 'minor comparativism' as a legal method aims to reveal something about the legal system that would not reveal itself but through the practice of adopting a 'foreign' or 'minority' perspective; focusing on those whose views have escaped the legal record. It enables scholars and policy-makers both to challenge conventional assumptions and to reimagine the development of the legal system by taking up the reflections of the minority. By adopting such a perspective, the critique of

[3] See, eg, C Barnard, 'EU Employment Law and the European Social Model: The Past, the Present and the Future' (2014) 67 *Current Legal Problems* 199.

[4] See PJ Neuvonen, 'A Way of Critique: What Can EU Law Scholars Learn from Critical Theory?' (2022) 1 *European Law Open* 60, 85; R Dukes, 'Critical Labour Law: Then and Now' in E Christodoulidis, R Dukes and M Goldoni (eds), *Research Handbook on Critical Legal Theory* (Edward Elgar, 2019) 345–62, 354, 359.

[5] N Lacey, 'Normative Reconstruction in Socio-Legal Theory' (1996) 5(2) *Social and Legal Studies* 131, 131.

[6] ibid 138.

[7] Neuvonen (n 4) 73. See further B O'Connor, *Adorno's Negative Dialectic: Philosophy and the Possibility of Critical Rationality* (MIT Press, 2004).

[8] Neuvonen (n 4) 74. See further E Christodoulidis, 'Critical Theory and the Law: Reflections on Origins, Trajectories and Conjunctures' in Christodoulidis, Dukes and Goldoni (n 4) 2–26, 15–16.

[9] Neuvonen (n 4) 74.

[10] ibid 84.

[11] See generally S Munshi, 'You Will See My Family Became so American: Toward a Minor Comparativism' (2015) *American Journal of Comparative Law* 655.

European labour law's historical development unearths the foundational value of solidarity which underpins European integration.[12]

Solidarity is often talked about in a European context, but its precise content is vague and this chapter cannot do justice to the growing literature which discusses the concept.[13] Solidarity is enshrined in several Treaty provisions;[14] it has been elevated to a core value of the EU (Article 2 Treaty on European Union (TEU)); and, along with the other foundational values of the EU, it has been recognised as a constitutional principle of EU law by the Court of Justice of the European Union (CJEU).[15] Critically, it is its characterisation as a 'force for good' that has legitimised and enabled its emergence as an all-pervasive 'founding and *existential* value of the Union' (emphasis added).[16] Though solidarity is integral to the very idea of EU integration and to its process, it is well established in the abundant literature on solidarity in the EU,[17] that the concept is difficult to grasp[18] and that its Europeanisation presents particular challenges.[19] In this regard, Hilpold observes that 'elements of a common European identity are still rather sparse while thinking in terms of national identity prevails'.[20] A further challenge arises from the fact that solidarity is particularly hard to fathom from a legal perspective. This is because solidarity is imbued with 'an element of moral, social or political engagement with the potential of facilitating the application of legal rules'.[21] For this reason, solidarity is often referred to as a principle in legal writing, 'which can serve as a doctrinal bridge between hard legal rules and theoretical considerations'.[22] It is thus not surprising that, at EU level, solidarity has emerged in multiple forms – as a principle,

[12] S Garben, 'The (Slow) Redress of the "Solidarity Deficit" in the EU and the Emerging Principle of Solidarity in EU Law' (2025) 31 *Maastricht Journal of European and Comparative Law* 748.

[13] See, eg, A Biondi, E Dagilytė and E Küçük (eds), *Solidarity in EU Law. Legal Principle in the Making* (Edward Elgar, 2018).

[14] In addition to Art 2 of the Consolidated version of the Treaty on the European Union [2012] OJ C326/13 (TEU), solidarity is mentioned in the Preamble to the TEU (6th indent) and Art 3(3) TEU, Art 21 TEU and Arts 24(2) and 24(3) TEU. In the Consolidated version of the Treaty on the Functioning of the European Union [2012] OJ C326/47 (TFEU), solidarity is mentioned in Art 80 TFEU, Art 122 TFEU, Art 194 TFEU and Art 222 TFEU. See further S da Lomba and R Zahn, 'A Historical Perspective on Solidarity and Integration: The Case of the Free Movement of Workers' (Society of Legal Scholars Annual Conference, 2021).

[15] Joined Cases C-402/05 P and C-415/05 P *Yassin Abdullah Kadi and Al Barakaat International Foundation v Council of the European Union and Commission of the European Communities* [2008] ECR 2008 I-06351, para 304.

[16] Joined Cases C-643/15 and C-647/15 *Slovak Republic and Hungary v Council of the European Union* ECLI:EU:C:2017:631, Opinion of Advocate-General Bot, para 18.

[17] See, eg, R Malcolm, 'Solidarity - A New Constitutional Paradigm for the EU?' in M Ross and Y Borgmann Prebil (eds), *Promoting Solidarity in the European Union* (Oxford University Press, 2010) 23–46; A Sangiovanni, 'Solidarity in the European Union' (2013) XXXIII *OJLS* 213; A Grimmel and SM Giang (eds), *Solidarity in the European Union: A Fundamental Value in Crisis* (Springer, 2017); V Moreno-Lax, 'Solidarity's Reach: Meaning, Dimensions and Implications for EU (External) Asylum Policy' (2017) 24 *Maastricht Journal of European and Comparative Law* 740; S Garben, 'Dignity- and Reciprocity-Based Solidarity as the Normative Framework of the EU's Constitutional Settlement' in A Hartzén, A Iossa and E Karageorgiou (eds), *Law, Solidarity and the Limits of Social Europe. Constitutional Tensions for EU Integration* (Edward Elgar, 2022) 158–81.

[18] M Kotzur, 'Solidarity as a Legal Concept' in A Grimmel and SM Giang (eds), *Solidarity in the European Union: A Fundamental Value in Crisis* (Springer, 2017).

[19] S Garben, 'The (Slow) Redress of the "Solidarity Deficit" in the EU and the Emerging Principle of Solidarity in EU Law' (2025) 31 *Maastricht Journal of European and Comparative Law* 748.

[20] P Hilpold, 'Understanding Solidarity within EU Law: An Analysis of the "Islands of Solidarity" with Particular Regard to Monetary Union' (2015) 34 *Yearbook of European Law* 257, 264.

[21] D Thym and E Tsourdi, 'Searching for Solidarity in the EU Asylum and Border Policies: Constitutional and Operational Dimensions' (2017) 24 *Maastricht Journal of European and Comparative Law* 605, 610.

[22] ibid 607.

value, and concept – with interrelated, and at times diverging,[23] meanings.[24] Another source of difficulty lies in the fact that solidarity is understood as both a precondition and objective of European integration. This ambiguity is not peculiar to *European* solidarity; at the national level, 'whether shared interests among groups marked by a feeling of solidarity are a result of, or rather a precondition for, unity'[25] remains disputed. It is also the case that solidarity 'is a concept that has to be practised and made explicit by the deed. [. . .] There is no such thing as solidarity unless it is practised, regardless of the underlying definition of what it means to act in solidarity'.[26]

Viewed against 'the unity of theory and praxis'[27] central to critical theory, the normative commitment to solidarity at EU level, including in European labour law, must translate into law and policy which builds solidarity between Member States and EU citizens. In order to discuss how that may occur, for the purposes of this chapter, the understanding of 'solidarity' developed by early attempts at European (social) integration in the framework of proposals for a European Federal Union will be adopted.[28] 'Solidarity' in this context was understood in terms of a moral community whereby Europeans recognise the innate inter-connectedness of their situation and are able to trust that one state will act in the interests of all states, to be able to speak with one voice in times of crisis and to reap the benefits of co-operation. The purpose of such a community was to make sure that economic integration would not negatively affect workers but that measures would be adopted which would ensure that living standards would rise to their highest possible levels across all states to ensure human well-being; this, in turn, would create trust and confidence between the peoples of Europe. Rediscovering such insights would enable scholars and policy-makers to reassess traditional narratives about European labour law and develop different starting points for European labour law's development which emphasise solidarity in the above sense.

This chapter is structured as follows. Section II provides an overview of European labour law's development. Section III introduces a minor comparativism. This is applied to European labour law in section IV. A final section concludes.

II. What Is European Labour Law?

The first complication which arises when writing about 'European labour law' is definitional.[29] The legal literature uses different umbrella terms, principally referring to either

[23] Hilpold (n 20) 259.

[24] G Butler, 'Solidarity and its Limits for Economic Integration in the European Union's Internal Market' (2018) 25 *Maastricht Journal of European and Comparative Law* 310, 311.

[25] F Greiner, 'Introduction: Writing the Contemporary History of European Solidarity' (2017) 24 *European Review of History: Revue européenne d'histoire* 837, 838.

[26] A Grimmel and SM Giang, 'Introduction' in A Grimmel and SM Giang (eds), *Solidarity in the European Union: A Fundamental Value in Crisis* (Springer, 2017) 3.

[27] Christodoulidis (n 8) 9.

[28] This is developed in more detail in R Zahn, 'What Future for the European Social Model? The Relevance of Early Intellectual Concepts of Social Integration' (2020) 7 *Journal of International and Comparative Law* 351.

[29] This section draws on summaries provided in R Zahn, *New Labour Law in Old Member States* (Cambridge University Press, 2017); Zahn (n 28) 351; D Schiek and R Zahn, *Europäisches Arbeitsrecht* (Nomos, 2025).

a broader European social policy/law or 'European labour law'. The latter encompasses narrow definitions of employment law within the EU's competence (and to an extent engages with the EU's rules on human rights, free movement of workers, social security co-ordination and equality laws where these relate to workers), while the former also encapsulates broader issues of social policy. If one focuses only on a narrow definition, then there is some scepticism in the literature as to the existence of a European labour law. Schmidt, for example, writes:

> In reality, there is not really such a thing as a set of 'European Labour Laws'. This is due to the absence, at a European level, of the usual division prevalent in . . . Member States between labour law as a form of private law and social security law as a form of public law. At a European level both categories fall under the umbrella of 'European social policy'.[30]

Such a categorisation of labour law as a form of private law and social security law as a form of public law neglects the many facets of the former in particular. It has long been recognised in a number of Member States that labour law at a national level is an autonomous discipline which comprises elements of contract, tort, criminal and commercial law as well as constitutional law.[31] In particular, the collective aspect of the discipline whereby trade unions and employers can set their own norms without state interference overlaps into the public law divide. However, it is correct to say that hitherto it has been impossible to imagine the recreation of a national understanding of labour law at the European level. There is a general acceptance that some European labour laws are necessary, yet the desired scope of a 'European labour law' is disputed, not (just) because of legal barriers but due to political difficulties. Collins describes this paradox of the impossible necessity of 'European labour law':

> European labour law is impossible because of the diversity of European labour systems, which embrace divergent national political settlements and rest upon different models of social regulation of capitalist markets. These differences provide the principal explanation for the absence of the formal competence of the EU in many aspects of labour law under the Treaties.[32]

European labour law can therefore only be seen as the 'counterweight to national labour law'.[33] It 'describes those labour law norms that originate at a European rather than a national level'.[34] This allows for a much broader interpretation of the term 'European labour law'. It permits the recognition of such a category of laws as long as one limits the ambit of the subject-matter to those social policy norms – defined broadly to include any measures which affect national labour law systems – emanating from a European level.

[30] G Haverkate, M Weiss, S Huster and M Schmidt (eds), *Casebook zum Arbeits- und Sozialrecht der EU* (Nomos, 1999) 15.

[31] See Lord Wedderburn, 'Labour Law: From Here to Autonomy' (1987) 16 *Industrial Law Journal* 1; A Bogg, C Costello, ACL Davies and J Prassl (eds), *The Autonomy of Labour Law* (Hart/Bloomsbury, 2015).

[32] H Collins, 'The Impossible Necessity of a European Labour Law' in S Muller, S Zouridis, M Frishman and L Kistemaker (eds), *The Law of the Future and the Future of Law* (Torkel Opsahl Academic ePublisher, 2011) 463.

[33] D Schiek, *Europäisches Arbeitsrecht*, 3rd edn (Nomos, 2007) 17.

[34] ibid.

European labour law is patchy in its coverage of rights.[35] For most of the twentieth century, national labour law systems were not affected by the European integration process which focused mainly on product market integration.[36] Although the EU's social policy competence, and with that the number of EU-derived social policy norms and labour laws, has increased over time, there remains an asymmetry between European social and market integration. At its heart, European labour law suffers from an equivocal purpose within the EU's framework. Article 3 TEU commits the EU to establishing 'a highly competitive social market economy, aiming at full employment and social progress' and 'combat[ing] social exclusion and discrimination, and [. . .] promot[ing] social justice and protection, equality between women and men, solidarity between generations [and among Member States]'. It is 'a political project of highly normative ambiguity' which is a 'key factor in legitimising European institutions'[37] and seeks to act as a counterweight to the economic dimension of European integration. However, it is marked by a 'constitutional asymmetry between policies promoting market efficiencies and policies promoting social protection and equality'.[38]

The following brief overview of the development of EU social policy norms over time illustrates that individual elements reflect different philosophies of economic and social integration, which move between the poles of 'social integration' and 'competitive fragmentation'.[39] There is no straightforward development towards more social integration and a coherent European labour law, just as there is no irreversible trend towards de-solidarisation.[40] Which orientation prevails depends on the political majorities in the Member States and the Union institutions, as well as the orientation and influence of the social partners at national and European level.[41]

The founding Treaty of the EEC was characterised by the near exclusion of social policy, reflecting a consensus which relied on market forces for growth and wealth creation while social policy largely remained the preserve of the Member States.[42] The Treaty limited EEC social policy competence to the free movement of workers, equal pay and co-operation in the area of social security.[43] The EEC mainly relied on the assumption that the 'approximation of living conditions by means of progress' (Article 151 Treaty on the Functioning of the European Union (TFEU), in this respect identical to the

[35] As evidenced, for example, if one looks at the subjects covered in a textbook on 'European labour law', see C Barnard, *EU Employment Law*, 4th edn (Oxford University Press, 2012). See also C Barnard, 'EU "Social" Policy from Employment Law to Labour Market Reform' in P Craig and G de Búrca (eds), *The Evolution of EU Law* (Oxford University Press, 2021).

[36] M Höpner and A Schäfer, 'A New Phase of European Integration: Organized Capitalisms in Post-Ricardian Europe' (2010) 33 *West European Politics* 344.

[37] A Serrano Pascual and M Jepsen (eds), *Unwrapping the European Social Model* (Policy Press, 2006) 19, 25.

[38] FW Scharpf, 'The European Social Model: Coping with the Challenges of Diversity' (2002) 40 *Journal of Common Market Studies* 645, 645.

[39] See B Hepple, *Labour Laws and Global Trade* (Hart/Bloomsbury, 2005) 198. See also C Barnard, 'EU Employment Law and the European Social Model: The Past, the Present and the Future' (2014) 67 *Current Legal Problems* 199.

[40] See further Schiek and Zahn (n 29).

[41] See also S Simitis and A Lyon-Caen, 'Community Labour Law: A Critical Introduction to its History' in P Davies, A Lyone-Caen, S Sciarra and S Simitis (eds), *European Community Labour Law: Principles and Perspectives: Liber Amicorum Lord Wedderburn of Charlton* (Clarendon Press, 1997) 1, 6.

[42] For a recent historical discussion of the evolution of European integration, see K Patel, *Project Europe: A History* (Cambridge University Press, 2020).

[43] See Arts 117–128 Treaty establishing the European Economic Community [1957].

original Article 117 EEC) would follow from market integration without the need for specific additional measures.[44] This optimism was shaken by the political upheavals of the 1960s, particularly in France and Germany, and the economic fallout from the twin oil shocks in the 1970s, which convinced political leaders that:

> [t]he Community has to be seen to be more than a device to enable capitalists to exploit the common market; otherwise it might not be possible to persuade the peoples of the Community to accept the disciplines of the market.[45]

The result was the adoption of an ambitious Social Action Programme (1974).[46] Although a downward economic cycle as well as domestic political pressures meant that the programme's aims were largely unrealised,[47] this period appeared, in retrospect, as the 'golden age of harmonization',[48] in which the need for harmonisation of labour rights in the common market was recognised.

The boom in European social policy was, however, short-lived. At the beginning of the 1980s, it became clear that the economic crisis was anything but temporary. Unemployment continued to rise or remained at a high level in all EEC Member States. The idea that unemployment was due to the 'over-regulation' of the labour market came to prevail in the political arena, with deregulation and flexibilisation also becoming the guiding principles of EC social policy until the late 1990s.[49] In contrast to the economic liberalism of the 1950s and 1960s, which believed that social progress went hand in hand with economic prosperity, the neoliberalism of this phase called for social regression in order to (re)enable economic prosperity.[50] The costs of social policy were to be examined in terms of 'competitiveness' and the aggressive promotion of new technologies during this period also reflected the tendency to place social policy primarily at the service of economic policy.[51]

Following the election victories in France (1996), the UK (1997) and Germany (1998) of governments which sought to combine social democratic policies with modernisation and flexibility, and the adoption of the Treaty of Amsterdam (1997) which inserted social policy into the primary law of the treaties (Article 136 EC, now 151 TFEU), the rationale for European labour law changed again. A reorientation of legislation in labour law could be observed, which the European Commission described as a 'triangle of tension: social

[44] See A Crespy, 'Social and Health Policy' in S Faure and C Lequesne (eds), *The Elgar Companion to the European Union* (Edward Elgar, 2023) 271–83.

[45] Michael Shanks, 'The Social Policy of the European Communities' (1977) 14 *CML Rev* 375, 377. See also J Kenner, *EU Employment Law. From Rome to Amsterdam and Beyond* (Hart/Bloomsbury, 2002) ch 2; A Hartzén, 'Improved Working Conditions and Paths to Worker Solidarity in an Increasingly Diversified EU' in P Ekman, B Lundqvist, A Michalski and L Oxelheim (eds), *The Depth and Size of the European Union in a Time of War* (Springer, 2025) 151–76, 154–55.

[46] Council of the European Communities, 'Council Resolution of 21 January 1974 concerning a social action programme' [1974] OJ C13/1.

[47] See further Kenner (n 45) ch 2.

[48] See R von Blanpain, M Schmidt and U Schweibert, *Europäisches Arbeitsrecht* (Nomos, 1996).

[49] Schiek and Zahn (n 29).

[50] See FW Scharpf, 'Politische Optionen im vollendeten Binnenmarkt' in M Jachtenfuchs and B Kohler-Koch (eds), *Europäische Integration* (Leske und Budrich, 1996) 109, 130–36.

[51] See further S Deakin, 'Labour Law as Market Regulation' in P Davies, A Lyone-Caen, S Sciarra and S Simitis (eds), *European Community Labour Law: Principles and Perspectives: Liber Amicorum Lord Wedderburn of Charlton* (Clarendon Press, 1997). See also W Sengenberger, 'Labour Standards: An Institutional Framework for Restructuring and Development' in W Sengenberger and D Campbell, *Creating Economic Opportunities: The Role of Labour Standards in Industrial Restructuring* (International Institute for Labour Studies, 1994).

quality, competitiveness, full employment'.[52] Labour law was viewed more as an instrument of employment policy, which was characterised by the buzzwords 'employability' and 'flexicurity' (flexibility with security). Liberalisation was increasingly emphasised in the reconciliation of the internal market and competition law with labour law.[53] The European Commission also devised a new method of policy-making to implement the strategic goal of making the EU 'the most competitive and dynamic knowledge-based economy in the world capable of sustainable economic growth with more and better jobs and greater social cohesion'.[54] New forms of governance, such as the flexible, non-binding processes of the Open Method of Coordination were to foster policy convergence.[55]

The 2008 global economic and financial crises put an abrupt end to the social policy/liberalisation movement. In its response to the crises, the EU institutions pushed for lower levels of social assistance, employment protection and the reduction or freezing of wages across a number of Member States.[56] Rather than acting as a corrective to market integration, the European social dimension was incorporated into the logic of a market-driven process of European integration.[57] The consequence is that, for many citizens, the EU came to be seen:

> as a machine for divergence, inequalities, and social injustice. A project associated for decades with convergence, prosperity, and progress is now being blamed for downgrading of welfare systems and seen as a threat to people's well-being.[58]

Coupled with the shadow of Brexit (2016) and the 'migration crisis' (2015), the revitalisation of European social policy eventually became a focus for the European Commission from 2016 onwards. The European Pillar of Social Rights, launched in 2017, sought to increase the prominence and visibility of the European social dimension.[59] The Pillar is a declaration which contains 20 principles and rights that are grouped into three themes which should guide future EU policy-making: (i) equal opportunities and access to the labour market; (ii) fair working conditions; and (iii) social protection and inclusion.[60] In practice, the Pillar is implemented using a threefold approach. First, there is a focus on reinforcing and scrutinising the existing social acquis and, where necessary, updating it. This has led to the adoption of several Directives on, for example, improving the working

[52] Communication from the Commission to the Council, the European Parliament, the Economic and Social Committee and the Committee of the Regions, 'Social Policy Agenda' COM(2000) 379, 6.

[53] Schiek and Zahn (n 29).

[54] European Council, 'Presidency Conclusions — Lisbon European Council', 23–24 March 2000.

[55] See generally, P Pochet, *À la recherche de l'Europe sociale* (Puf, 2019) and A Crespy, *L'Europe sociale: acteurs, politiques, débats* (ULB Press, 2019).

[56] This took place through either the European Semester framework for macroeconomic governance (instituted as part of the Europe 2020 Strategy) or, in the case of Euro-zone states receiving financial assistance from the Troika of the International Monetary Fund, European Commission and the European Central Bank, through direct intervention. See P Copeland, *Governance and the European Social Dimension: Politics, Power and the Social Deficit in a Post-2010 EU* (Routledge, 2020) ch 1; Hartzén (n 45) 162–64.

[57] Copeland (n 56) ch 1.

[58] European Parliament, 'Report on a European Pillar of Social Rights' (Publications Office of the European Union, 2016) 25.

[59] European Parliament, Council and Commission, 'Interinstitutional Proclamation on the European Pillar of Social Rights' [2017] OJ C428/10–15. See further S Garben, 'The European Pillar of Social Rights: An Assessment of Its Meaning and Significance' (2019) 21 *Cambridge Yearbook of European Legal Studies* 101, 125 and Crespy (n 44) 275.

[60] European Commission, 'European Pillar of Social Rights' (Publications Office of the European Union, 2017); European Commission, 'The European Pillar of Social Rights Action Plan' (Publications Office of the European Union, 2021).

conditions of people working through platforms or on adequate minimum wages (on the latter, see section IV).[61] Second, the Pillar's implementation is facilitated through specific funding mechanisms designed to bolster initiatives and programmes that directly contribute to the realisation of the Pillar's objectives. Finally, the EU's socio-economic governance framework has undergone adjustments to accommodate the Pillar's principles. The La Hulpe Declaration adopted by the Member States in 2024[62] sees the Pillar as the main compass that should guide the EU's response. The Pillar's principles are to form the basis for building a more inclusive and sustainable growth model, focusing on social and territorial cohesion and helping to improve Europe's competitiveness.

It is difficult to assess how this will be achieved at a time when the EU is grappling with its response to geopolitical and economic shifts and uncertainties, and green and digital transitions.[63] European labour law and social policy only play a minor role in the European Commission's 2025 work plan which subordinates social policy regulation to the achievement of 'a more competitive, resilient, and growth-oriented Europe'.[64] Overall, the situation is therefore contradictory. The EU remains marked by a 'constitutional asymmetry between policies promoting market efficiencies and policies promoting social protection and equality'[65] exemplified both by the EU institutions' limited legal social policy competence and preference for new governance mechanisms in the social sphere, and continued prioritisation of measures which foster competitiveness. Yet the increased politicisation of the EU in recent years as a result of multiple crises has also led to an increase in European labour laws and a renewed interest in European labour law's potential to transform the increasingly unequal European economy and society.

Against this background, it is apt to consider what critical theory could offer scholars and policy-makers thinking about European labour law's development and future. In particular, this chapter uses the concept of a 'minor comparativism' in order to enable scholars and policy-makers to discover alternative starting points when reimagining the future of European labour law.

III. Introducing a Minor Comparativism

A 'minor comparativism'[66] is an approach which brings together insights from comparative law and 'minor' literature to unearth, for the purposes of this chapter, different

[61] See Directive (EU) 2024/2831 of the European Parliament and of the Council of 23 October 2024 on improving working conditions in platform work [2024] OJ L2024/2831 and Directive (EU) 2022/2041 of the European Parliament and of the Council of 19 October 2022 on adequate minimum wages in the European Union [2022] OJ L275/33.

[62] Council of the European Union, 'European Pillar of Social Rights: The La Hulpe Declaration on the Future of Social Europe', 15–16 April 2024.

[63] See Crespy (n 44) 277–78. For discussion of the link between the digital and green transitions and EU labour law and policy, see, eg, M Urbaniec (ed), *The Digital Economy and the European Labour Market* (Routledge, 2023) and E Ales, T Addabbo, Y Curzi, T Fabbri and I Senatori (eds), *Green Transition and the Quality of Work. Implications, Linkages and Perspectives* (Palgrave Macmillan, 2024).

[64] Communication from the Commission to the European Parliament, the Council, the European Economic and Social Committee and the Committee of the Regions, 'Commission work programme 2025. Moving forward together: A Bolder, Simpler, Faster Union', COM(2025)45.

[65] Scharpf (n 38) 645.

[66] See generally Munshi (n 11) 655 and R Zahn, 'Finding New Ways of "Doing" Socio-Legal Labour Law History in Germany and the UK: Introducing a "Minor Comparativism"' (2020) 21 *German Law Journal* 1378 where this is developed in relation to labour law specifically.

starting points for European labour law's development which have hitherto escaped the legal record. Coupled with the use of the comparative law method – observing something about one's own legal system by using the lens of another – a minor comparativism can both critique and reconstruct. This chapter treats a minor comparativism as a legal method through which EU legal scholars and policy-makers can operationalise some of the key tenets of critical theory and thus enhance their critical engagements with EU law.

The idea of 'minor' literature, a term used by Giles Deleuze and Felix Guattari[67] to reassess the influence of Franz Kafka's multilingual and multicultural formation on his writing, is to both seriously engage with the experiences of minority subjects while also providing a critical understanding of the majority discourse with a view to transforming that discourse to be more inclusive. In their analysis, Deleuze and Guattari suggest that Kafka's status as an 'outsider' or a 'minority'– born into a middle-class German- and Yiddish-speaking Czech Jewish family in Prague in the late nineteenth century – enabled him to observe life and society's complexities and expressively use language to depict these in uncanny ways. As Sherally Munshi explains, '[i]f we understand language to reflect or to structure consciousness, then minor literature is writing within a national culture but without absorption of national consciousness, morality, or world-view'.[68] Writing as a minority subject enables the depersonalisation of the narrative. At the same time, the minority perspective opens up the possibility 'to express another possible community[,] … another consciousness[,] … another sensibility'.[69]

Comparative law is helpful in order to discover that minority perspective. European labour law is no stranger to the comparative method. There is an everincreasing amount of literature comparing aspects of different (European) labour law systems and assessing the relationship between comparative law and European labour law.[70] A comparative perspective brings to light the similarities and differences between national, subnational and transnational legal systems as well as their socio-economic foundations. Used by the European courts and legislature, this results in the elevation of national legal traditions to the level of Union law, where they are interwoven into a new mixture of a Union law nature and applied with supranational validity.[71] Comparative law has thus been instrumental in the creation of European labour law as we know it; to achieve the 'economic and social interdependence'[72] of the Member States that the EU is striving for, without jeopardising the diversity on which the unity of the EU is based. As part of this process,

[67] G Deleuze and F Guattari, *Kafka: Toward a Minor Literature* (translated by D Polan, University of Minnesota Press, 1986).

[68] Munshi (n 11) 667.

[69] Deleuze and Guattari (n 67) 17.

[70] For an overview, see Encyclopedia of International and Comparative Labour Law, 'IEL Labour Law', available at www.kluwerlawonline.com/toc.php?pubcode=IELL; MW *Finkin and G Mundlak* (eds), *Comparative Labour Law. Research Handbooks in Comparative Law* (Edward Elgar, 2015).

[71] See M Kiikeri, *Comparative Legal Reasoning and European Law* (Springer, 2001); K Lenaerts, 'Discovering the Law of the EU: The European Court of Justice and the Comparative Law Method' in T Perišin and S Rodin (eds), *The Transformation or Reconstitution of Europe. The Critical Legal Studies Perspective on the Role of the Courts in the European Union* (Hart, 2018) 61–88.

[72] See C-646/15 *Trustees of the P Panayi Accumulation & Maintenance Settlements v Commissioners for Her Majesty's Revenue and Customs* [2016] ECLI:EU:C:2016:1000, para 27 and C-35/70 *S.A.R.L. Manpower v Caisse primaire d'assurance maladie de Strasbourg* [1970] ECLI:EU:C:1970:120, para 10.

however, comparative law has become an increasingly ahistoric field. As Frankenberg explains:

> Comparative law has started to recognise the need to look beyond law (see R Hirschl, 'Editorial: From Comparative Constitutional Law to Comparative Constitutional Studies' (2013) *International Journal of Constitutional Law* 1) but many of these debates are internal debates over theory and method. Notably in the post-1900 era, the comparison of laws and legal systems was open to information from the neighbouring sciences, especially philosophy, history and anthropology. But throughout the twentieth century, the interdisciplinary predisposition of comparative legal scholars got lost in the mainstream. The discipline became known for its 'entrenched ahistoricism'.[73]

This has led comparative lawyers to assume that the law of each modern jurisdiction forms a coherent system rather than an amalgam of solutions developed over time.[74] Recent scholarship in comparative law has sought to move away from what Legrand described as 'positivist' comparative law, towards the contextualised analysis of legal rules, their active interpretation, and engagement with interdisciplinary study.[75] As part of this trend, scholars have adopted different methodological lenses in order to give a voice to individuals and social groups whose views are not part of mainstream narratives;[76] to bring to light the different solutions that have been developed over time. Such an approach decentres the state and positive law as the focus of a comparison and recognises the legitimacy of multiple (historical) traditions and social orderings.[77]

In an article published in 2015, building on the trend of adopting methods for producing more historically situated critical comparative legal scholarship, Sherally Munshi borrowed from minor literature to propose the idea of a minor comparativism.[78] A minor comparativism retains the general tenor of comparative law, which is 'to reveal something about our immediate world that would not reveal itself but through the practice of adopting a foreign perspective', but it seeks that foreign perspective 'within' one's own country.[79] It 'sets the official image of a particular state *against* the reflections of its minority subjects'.[80] A minor comparativism acknowledges that the minority – to be understood in the sense of foreign or not belonging to the majority – is not

[73] G Frankenberg, *Comparative Law as Critique* (Edward Elgar, 2019) 13 (quoting P Legrand, 'The Return of the Repressed: Moving Comparative Legal Studies Beyond Pleasure' (2001) 75 *Tulane Law Review* 1033, 1037).

[74] See R Sacco, 'Legal Formants: A Dynamic Approach to Comparative law' (1991) 39 *The American Journal of Comparative Law* 1.

[75] See generally P Legrand, 'Jameses at Play: A Tractation on the Comparison of Laws' (2017) 65 *American Journal of Comparative Law* 1, as well as the other contributions in the 2017 special issue of the *American Journal of Comparative Law*.

[76] For an overview, see the *Decolonial Comparative Law* project led by Professor Ralf Michaels and Dr Lena Salaymeh at the Max Planck Institute for Comparative and International Private Law (Hamburg). R Michaels and L Salaymeh, '*Decolonial Comparative Law Project' (Max Planck Institute, 2020), available at www.mpipriv.de/decolonial.*

[77] Thus, there are some similarities between the arguments made in favour of transnational history to correct the focus by comparative historians on the nation-state. See generally J Kocka, 'Comparison and Beyond' (2003) 42 *History and Theory 39 and* I Tyrell, 'Reflections on the Transnational Turn in United States History: Theory and Practice' (2009) 4 *Journal of Global History* 453.

[78] Munshi (n 11).

[79] ibid 664.

[80] ibid 665.

peripheral but central to the formation of laws, the state, and the nation. A consequence of this is that a minor comparativism resists regurgitating authorised representations of the law. It seeks to complicate received understandings of the law and its development. For scholars of European labour law and for European policy-makers, the use of such an approach opens up traditional narratives on the subject's development to reinterpretation, and provides different starting points for the subject's future. A minor comparativism thus requires engaging with a minority discourse

> not only because it conveys the experience of the minority to a majority, but because it presents us with the possibility of transforming our understanding of the majority discourse. Put slightly differently, minor comparativism engages the reflections of the foreigner with the expectation that it might render the nation and its institutions foreign to itself, so that, in the end, we might imagine another, more inclusive form of community.[81]

Employing a minor comparativism enables EU legal scholars and policy-makers to operationalise key tenets of critical theory in order to enhance their critical engagements with EU law. Like critical theory, a minor comparativism counters the ahistoricism of critical legal scholarship and facilitates a genealogical critique of the law which examines the historical development of normative ideas underpinning the law and the impact of this development on different social groups. As it emerges in Foucault's work, genealogical critique 'allows us to cut into historical trajectories to look at how, at crucial junctures, certain options were discarded and certain options were *installed* as conditions of the range of further developments' (emphasis added).[82] It brings to light 'the possibilities and contingencies that might have been thereby passed over, elided or obscured'.[83] By adopting a minority perspective, a minor comparativism can examine the social embeddedness of the law and expose the power struggles (eg between political and/or ideological opponents, between workers and employers, between citizens and those holding political power) which underpin the law and its historical development.[84] Rather than accepting that the law is neutral or universal, it instead reveals the social, economic, and political interests of the 'majority' which have been portrayed and naturalised as such in the law. That is, a minor comparativism can reveal how the law constitutes certain social actors as dominant or normative actors (the 'majority') while 'othering' those who deviate from this norm (the 'minority', or the 'other'), often with the effect of marginalising, excluding, and discriminating the latter. An exposition of the processes of othering in the law is, of course, pivotal to unequivocally critical legal scholarship.[85]

Inherent, too, in a minor comparativism – as in critical theory – is a commitment to de-naturalising the majority perspective. By challenging majority discourse (ie the interests which are currently represented in the law), a minor comparativism offers ways

[81] ibid 669.

[82] Christodoulidis (n 8) 15. See also M Foucault, *Language, Counter-Memory, Practice: Selected Essays and Interviews* (edited by DF Bouchard, Cornell University Press, 1977) eg 144.

[83] Christodoulidis (n 8) 16.

[84] Lacey (n 5) 137; Neuvonen (n 4) 83. See further K Ng, 'Ideology Critique from Hegel and Marx to Critical Theory' (2015) 22 *Constellations* 393, 394, 399.

[85] See, eg, R West, 'Feminism, Critical Social Theory and Law' (1989) 1 *University of Chicago Legal Forum* 59 and V Corcodel, *Modern Law and Otherness. The Dynamics of Inclusion and Exclusion in Comparative Legal Thought* (Edward Elgar, 2019). See further Foucault (n 82) 148–50.

to rethink – and subsequently reform – the law from a minority perspective to, for instance, enhance equality and inclusion.[86] Thus, as Munshi explains:

> The purpose of [a minor comparativism] is not merely ethnographic or to thicken our account of a culture, but *liberatory*. By recognizing that authoritative declarations of law do not exhaust our own understanding or experience of law, we proliferate opportunities to transform the laws that give shape and meaning to our shared circumstances (emphasis added).[87]

A minor comparativism therefore carries with it the emancipatory potential characteristic of critical theory, namely liberation from social, economic, and political domination, in its rethinking of the law.[88] The next section applies a minor comparativism to European labour law, highlighting the value of solidarity as a central starting point for examining the development and rethinking the future of European labour law.

IV. Applying a Minor Comparativism

If we want to apply a minor comparativism to think critically about European labour law's development and future, then we first need to address the question of what is meant by 'the nation and its institutions'. The EU is not a nation state in the sense used by Munshi. Yet, its supranational character and its institutions' ability to create social policy norms which affect and shape national labour law systems – as outlined in section two above – mean that European labour law nonetheless lends itself to a minor comparativism. The purpose of the minor comparativism is to set the traditional narrative of its development to the reflections of its 'minority' subjects. The second question that we therefore need to consider is who is meant by 'the minority' for European labour law scholars and policy-makers. The positioning of a majority and minority in a minor comparativism presumes the existence of a power imbalance or struggle underpinned by political, economic, or social tension between social groups. As a first step, centring the minority perspective thus necessitates recognising that European labour law's shape – like that of national labour law – is dependent on

> the outcome of a process of struggle between different social groups – monarchy, bureaucracy and middle class; bourgeoisie and working class; townspeople and countryfolk – and of competing ideologies of conservatives, liberals and socialists, as well as religious and secular groups.[89]

Here, labour law scholarship has already reflected, or been influenced by, insights of critical theory and genealogical critique exposing the social, economic, and political tensions underpinning labour law.[90] As outlined in section II above, similar tensions have also permeated European labour law. Hepple explains that the development of

[86] See, eg, Lacey (n 5) 137.
[87] Munshi (n 66) 669.
[88] N Fraser and R Jaeggi, *Capitalism. A Conversation in Critical Theory* (edited by B Milstein, Verso, 2023) 124. See M Horkheimer, 'Traditional and Critical Theory' in M Horkheimer, *Critical Theory. Selected Essays* (translated by MJ O'Connell and others, Continuum, 2002) 188–243.
[89] Dukes (n 4) 353.
[90] ibid.

labour law in capitalist societies 'is the product of a variety of historical factors, which are neither "necessary" nor "natural" [. . .]. The choices made were not inevitable solutions to the social problems created by the workings of the market'.[91] For Hepple,

> [m]any of the demands made by labour movements and social reformers were unsuccessful because they were unacceptable to those with greater economic and political power [. . .]. [T]he powerfulness of the opponents of reform was the decisive factor in the making of labour law.[92]

The views of the individuals or groups which did not become represented in the law – including social reformers and labour movements who were unsuccessful – have been erased from the legal record and, by extension, are the subject of study of legal or labour historians but often neglected by legal scholars. Yet, their demands held sway at particular moments in history even if they were not in the end translated into law – the outcome of power struggles was neither inevitable nor predetermined. Rediscovering these minority viewpoints disrupts and complicates received understandings of (European) labour law's historical development. Such an exercise requires scholars and policy-makers to engage seriously with the discourse of minorities and to set it against the traditional narrative. This, in turn, enables them to identify, question, and challenge conventional assumptions about the legal system by rendering those conventional assumptions foreign to themselves.

To recover those voices that are not represented in traditional narratives of the development of European labour law so that different starting points for its future may be identified, the remainder of this chapter considers one example: the 1931 proposal written by French socialist Albert Thomas, the first Director General (1919–1932) of the International Labour Organisation (ILO), on labour questions for submission to a Commission of Inquiry for European Union.[93] This provides an illustrative example for the purposes of this chapter because it provides not only a rationale for social integration (ie to create solidarity between nation-states and their citizens) but also practical suggestions for its operationalisation; both of which remain relevant today. Although elements of Thomas's proposal were later incorporated into the European Coal and Steel Community (ECSC), they were not given effect in the EEC Treaty. Political tensions between European policy-makers who, like Thomas, favoured social integration as a necessary complement to economic integration and those (mostly of the centre-right conservative persuasion like Swedish economist Bertil Ohlin, see section IV.A below) who rejected the idea for being too politically controversial to form a foundation for the EEC were ultimately resolved in favour of the latter. Thomas's perspective on labour questions therefore represents a minority perspective in European labour law because it did not become represented in early European labour law and has subsequently largely

[91] B Hepple (ed), *The Making of Labour Law in Europe. A Comparative Study of Nine Countries up to 1945* (Mansell, 1986) 4.

[92] ibid 5.

[93] The following paragraphs summarise parts of Zahn (n 28). The Commission of Inquiry for European Union held six meetings between September 1930 and October 1931. However, international events of the 1930s – the Great Depression, rising nationalism across a number of European states, and the League of Nations' (and its Member States') failure to deliver disarmament and collective security – hampered the Commission's work and it stopped convening after its Chairman's (Aristide Briand) death in 1932.

disappeared from legal scholars' and European policy-makers' consciousness. We have selected Thomas's perspective as a minority perspective to be recovered particularly because it offers a desirable perspective on solidarity which is absent in the current conception and practice of European labour law and social policy.[94] The current economic framing of solidarity which favours solidarity-building between Member States is misplaced and, to help legal scholars and policy-makers to rethink the future of European labour law and social Europe in this regard, a recovered minority voice must exhibit a commitment to a more social conception of solidarity between European citizens (ie workers), which we observe in Thomas's early perspective.

A. The Memorandum from the ILO on Questions of Special Interest to European States

The Commission of Inquiry for European Union, established by the League of Nations between 1930 and 1931, was tasked with considering the possible creation of a European Federal Union – a project different from the current European Union – whose purpose was to create a 'permanent union of solidarity' and to co-ordinate European interests so that European states could represent their views more effectively, with one voice.[95] Thomas's 'Memorandum from the ILO on questions of special interest to European states'[96] considered a number of 'labour questions' particular to Europe which could undermine economic co-operation if left unresolved, principally the conditions of workers in industries which were either vital to the European economy (coal) or which crossed European borders (river shipping and railways), and recommended the adoption of ILO conventions (to be applied initially within Europe) to set standards for these industries. Resolution of these labour questions was considered essential for economic integration to succeed. Other areas of concern raised in the ILO's Memorandum include the free movement of labour, unemployment and agriculture. The free circulation of labour was considered essential to the realisation of 'a real Union, or even an economic Union'.[97] However, its success could not be left to 'chance impulses or interests of individuals or even nations. It must be regulated, and, indeed, systematically organised'[98] so as to ensure that labour standards were upheld and labour rights of migrants were properly enforced in their host countries.

The ILO's Memorandum accepted the premise that in the long-term, trade liberalisation would raise living standards which would in turn create social stability and solidarity amongst states. A precondition of European integration, though, was acceptance by its

[94] In future work, consideration should be given more fundamentally to which minority perspectives are 'worthy' of recovering. The authors would like to thank the editors for raising this point during the editorial process. Space constraints prevented a broader discussion at this stage.

[95] *Memorandum sur l'Organisation d'un Régime d'Union Fédérale Européenne*, Series of League of Nations Publications, VII. Political, 1930, II. 4, 10 and *Memorandum from the ILO on questions of special interest to European states*, See also S Schirmann (ed), *Organisations internationales et architectures europées 1929-1939* (Metz, 2003).

[96] Commission of Enquiry for European Union, Minutes of the Second Session of the Commission, held at Geneva from January 16th to 21st, 1931, Annex 2.

[97] ibid 75.

[98] ibid 75–76.

citizens. The Memorandum's author – Albert Thomas – had been Minister of Armaments and War Production during World War I. As Mechi explains, 'the wartime economy had allowed him to see the advantages of closer collaboration among the social classes and of rationalisation and productivity increases for promoting growth and prosperity in peacetime'.[99] Thomas had advocated the harmonisation of European labour laws in the field of working time since 1919 and had been interested in the pursuit of European unity, albeit within the framework of the League of Nations, since 1925.[100] He was aware that differences in labour and living standards between European countries would undermine solidarity particularly between European citizens.[101] The key driving force behind his proposals was not ideological in the sense of pursuing a vision of European unity, but the practical conviction that *future prosperity and peace* on the continent depended on European states giving up parts of their sovereignty and co-operating.[102] He was convinced that 'if there is the constant respect for national sovereignties, no League of Nations is possible, no Organization is possible'.[103] However, co-operation would only be possible if European citizens became enthusiastic supporters of European unity; this was to be achieved through concrete transnational works and projects which would increase co-operation and mutual dependence.[104] Although Thomas did not list specific projects as examples, he recognised that the elimination of tariffs (inherent in closer economic integration) and cross-border cooperation may undermine national industries. To counter negative effects of such rationalisation, he called for transnationally organised measures of compensation and adaptation for the protection of affected workers. More specific details were to be worked out by an expert committee under the auspices of the ILO. In essence, therefore, the ILO's Memorandum provided the practical plan which would create solidarity: large-scale, cross-border public works which would not only tackle the main issue of the day – large-scale unemployment – but, in the longer term, would encourage European integration and European society-building.

Thomas's proposals have largely disappeared from legal scholars' and policy-makers' consciousness, yet there was some continuity in thinking in the immediate post-World War II period. The recognition that solidarity was essential *and* had to be actively created was enshrined in the Preamble of the Treaty of Paris establishing the predecessor of the EEC, the ECSC.[105] In 1953, the ECSC and the ILO signed a co-operation agreement

[99] L Mechi, 'Managing the Labour Market in an Open Economy: From the International Labour Organisation to the European Communities' (2018) 27 *Contemporary European History* 221, 225.

[100] See generally D Guérin, *Albert Thomas au BIT, 1920–1932. De l'internationalisme à l'Europe* (Euryopa, 1996).

[101] Commission of Enquiry for European Union, Minutes (n 96) Annex 2, 75.

[102] This vision was different from the current EU where the idea was that Member States did not give up their sovereignty in the social sphere. Rather, the EU would provide for economic integration which would lead to ever increasing living standards, while national welfare states would provide the safety net. This can be distinguished from the ECSC where there was some pooling of sovereignty and co-operation. See Zahn (n 28).

[103] Commission of Enquiry for European Union, Minutes (n 96) Annex 2, 91.

[104] ibid 72 citing Lettre à Raoul Richard, fin mai 1931, AN 94 AP 392: 'Je crois vraiment qu'on ne pourra faire une Europe que si on fait travailler tous les pays qui la composent à un certain nombre de projets d'intérêts communs, que si on multiplie les moyens d'échanges et de communication, de circulation des hommes et des choses.'

[105] The Preamble states that '[l] Europe ne se construira par les realisations concrètes créant d'abord une solidarité de fait.' See further Hartzén (n 45) 154 and A Hartzén, A Iossa and E Karageorgiou (eds), *Law, Solidarity and the Limits of Social Europe. Constitutional Tensions for EU Integration* (Edward Elgar, 2022).

which regulated mutual consultation between the two bodies and formally committed the ILO to provide technical assistance to the Community.[106] ILO personnel made a major contribution to drafting concrete regulations for the ECSC on free movement of workers and providing technical assistance on vocational training and the recognition of professional qualifications. Although there are no explicit references, many of the outcomes of collaboration between the ILO and the ECSC concretely implemented proposals made by Thomas in his 1931 Memorandum to ease negative effects of the creation of a common market.[107] For example, an adaptation fund was created to facilitate the re-entry of workers into the labour market which provided for retraining and, if needed, re-location of unemployed workers.

The question of a social dimension posed by Thomas also permeated the discussions on the future shape and form of European integration which occurred in 1952–53 and which resulted in proposals on a European Political Community (EPC) and a European Defence Community (EDC).[108] European trade unions increasingly advocated European integration to be coupled with social integration; specifically the harmonisation of social conditions in European countries, so as to reduce the impact of trade liberalisation on the competitiveness of national production systems. Harmonisation in this context was to be understood as 'working "upwards" – that is, based on a general adjustment to the wage and social standards of the most-advanced countries'.[109] However, following the French rejection of the EDC Treaty and the subsequent abandonment of the EPC Treaty (the EDC's institutional corollary) in 1954, the European socialist movement distanced itself from the integration debates.[110] The Intergovernmental Committee set up in 1955 to study the future shape and form of European integration, in its Spaak Report (published in April 1956) negated the need for social harmonisation. Spaak, the Committee's chairman, 'was determined to avoid [. . .] the many controversial and political issues that arguably led to the downfall of the EDC and EPC treaties'.[111] Social integration was identified as one of those issues and the Spaak Committee had therefore tasked the ILO with investigating the feasibility of the subject.[112] The resulting Ohlin Report denied the need for social harmonisation and recommended the now well-known general exclusion of social policy from the EEC Treaty on the basis that:

[106] ILO, Minutes of the 122nd session of the Governing Body, Geneva, May–June 1953, 96.

[107] L Mechi, 'Economic Regionalism and Social Stabilisation: The International Labour Organization and Western Europe in the Early Post-War Years' (2013) 35 *International History Review* 844, 852.

[108] For the background to the EPC, see RT Griffiths, *Europe's First Constitution* (Federal Trust, 2001).

[109] L Mechi, 'A Prediction for Economic Integration? European Debates on Social Harmonisation in the 1950s and 1960s' in L Coppolaro and L Mechi, *Free Trade and Social Welfare in Europe* (Routledge, 2020). See also P Pasture, 'The Interwar Origins of International Labour's European Commitment' (2001) 10 *Contemporary European History* 221 and B Shaev, 'Liberalising Regional Trade: Socialists and European Economic Integration' (2018) 27 *Contemporary European History* 258.

[110] See RT Griffiths, 'European Utopia or Capitalist Trap? The Socialist International and the Question of Europe' in RT Griffiths, *Socialist Parties and the Question of Europe in the 1950s* (Brill, 1993) 21. See further AD Andry, 'The "Social Dimension" of Postwar Europe' in AD Andry, *Social Europe, the Road not Taken. The Left and European Integration in the Long 1970s* (Oxford University Press, 2022) 27–59.

[111] G De Búrca, 'The Road Not Taken: The European Union as a Global Human Rights Actor' (2011) 105 *American Journal of International Law* 649, 664–65.

[112] See L Mechi, 'Managing the Labour Market in an Open Economy: From the International Labour Organisation to the European Communities' (2018) 27 *Contemporary European History* 221.

> So long as we confine our attention to international differences in the general level of costs per unit of labour time, we do not consider it necessary or practicable that special measures to 'harmonise' social policies or social conditions should precede or accompany measures to promote greater freedom of international trade.[113]

It was assumed that closer economic co-operation would lead to 'more rapid growth of productivity [. . .] This would be amply sufficient [. . .], when account is taken of the strength of the trade union movement and of the sympathy of European governments for social aspirations, to ensure that labour conditions would improve and not deteriorate'.[114] Notwithstanding subsequent interventions by the French Government in favour of harmonisation of certain working regulations, the final version of the EEC Treaty effectively adopted the Ohlin Report's underlying philosophy with its reliance on market forces for growth and wealth-creation leading to upward, improved living and working conditions and regulatory activities at EU level limited to remedying distortions of competition.[115]

This approach, as outlined in section II above, continues to dominate much of the EU's social policy approach. Thus, the political decision to decouple economic and social policies (with competence for the latter largely residing at the national level) created a functional complementarity between the welfare state and the supranational level.[116] Yet this exclusion of those voices who had pushed for a social side to European integration – like that of Albert Thomas – had ramifications for the feasibility of the integration process; it created an 'unstable chemical compound'.[117] Eventually, the incomplete design of European monetary integration, brought into sharp relief by the 2008 banking and subsequent Euro-zone crisis, turned the already disintegrating functional complementarity between social policy and economic integration into a structural conflict, creating a constitutional crisis at national and EU level. This crisis has still not been resolved and rather than building solidarity between EU citizens, '[the] deficit of social cooperation'[118] at EU level has the practical effect of alienating the EU's citizens from the broader integration project and from each other.[119]

Against that background, Thomas's Memorandum and its limited realisation within the ECSC framework is helpful in envisioning how the normative commitment to solidarity at EU level, outlined in section I above, could be translated into European labour law in practice. For Thomas, solidarity operated on two levels: between states; and between European citizens. Top-down economic co-operation alone is not sufficient

[113] ILO, *Social Aspects of European Collaboration (Ohlin Report)* (ILO Studies and Reports, 1956) 40–41.

[114] ibid, para 210.

[115] S Simitis and A Lyon-Caen, 'Community Labour Law: A Critical Introduction to its History' in P Davies, A Lyone-Caen, S Sciarra and S Simitis (eds), *European Community Labour Law: Principles and Perspectives: Liber Amicorum Lord Wedderburn of Charlton* (Clarendon Press, 1997).

[116] S Giubboni, *Social Rights and Market Freedom in the European Constitution* (Cambridge University Press, 2006) ch 1.

[117] ibid 18. This came to the fore eg in the European Court of Justice case law on the Posted Workers' Directive, see R Zahn, 'Revision of the Posted Workers Directive: A Europeanisation Perspective' (2017) 19 *Cambridge Yearbook of European Legal Studies* 187.

[118] R Jaeggi, 'Solidarity and Indifference' in R ter Meulen, W Arts and R Muffels (eds), *Solidarity in Health and Social Care in Europe* (Springer, 2001) 287–309, 288. See further R Jaeggi, *Alienation* (translated by F Neuhouser and AE Smith, Columbia University Press, 2014) 219.

[119] S Giubboni, 'Stato Sociale e Integrazione Europea: Una Revisitazione Teorica' (2017) 46 *Quaderni Fiorentini* 553; Jaeggi, 'Solidarity and Indifference' (n 118) 302.

to resolve the tensions that inevitably arise between European states and which, if left unchecked, threaten social stability. Solidarity implies that one state will act in the interests of all states and that states will speak with one voice in times of crisis. For citizens, solidarity implies that individuals see the benefits of European integration in order to feel inter-connected; to be part of what Thomas terms a 'moral community'. In a labour law context, such a moral community has precedence in the form of trade unions. The importance of collective representation in labour law's development to address the power imbalance inherent in the worker-employer or capital-labour relationship underpins much of Thomas's proposals and is exemplified in the tripartite (involving trade unions, employers and governments) ILO system of decision-making. While the ECSC replicated such a tripartite structure, trade unions were not formally included in decision-making in the EEC until the introduction of the (incomplete) process of European social dialogue by the Treaty of Maastricht (1992).[120] Although the social dialogue has given trade unions and employer representatives a role in a complex process of law-making, the persistent asymmetry between European social and market integration since the EU's inception has undermined the effectiveness of the dialogue and the social partners' ability to negotiate agreements which address the pan-European concerns of workers. It thus falls short of contributing to the establishment of a 'moral community'.

Thomas also recognised that solidarity would not come about organically but required concrete actions, hence his proposal for large, genuinely European projects; the negative effects of which on national labour law systems would have to be actively managed. Such projects would serve the purpose of creating inter-dependencies and reducing alienation; making individuals supporters of integration.[121] This chapter closes with two examples of how solidarity has recently been operationalised in European labour law, reflecting on the insights gained from the minor comparativism undertaken in this chapter.

B. The Minimum Wage Directive and Temporary Support to Mitigate Unemployment Risks in an Emergency (SURE)

An example of a way in which solidarity has been operationalised at EU level in recent years is the European Instrument for Temporary Support to Mitigate Unemployment Risks in an Emergency (SURE).[122] Introduced in May 2020 in response to the COVID-19 pandemic, it set up a system of voluntary guarantees for financial assistance between EU Member States, provided by way of loans through the EU.[123] The funding was to

[120] On the social dialogue's origins, see B Bercusson, *European Labour Law* (Cambridge University Press, 2009). For a recent assessment, see S Rainone, 'EU Social Dialogue Revitalisation: Between Rhetoric New Rights, Political Commitments and Historical Caution' (2024) 15 *European Labour Law Journal* 900–11.

[121] Guérin (n 100).

[122] Council Regulation (EU) 2020/672 on the establishment of a European instrument for temporary support to mitigate unemployment risks in an emergency (SURE) following the COVID-19 outbreak [2020] OJ L159/1.

[123] European Commission, 'Report on the European instrument for Temporary Support to mitigate Unemployment Risks in an Emergency (SURE) following the COVID-19 outbreak pursuant to Article 14 of Council Regulation (EU) 2020/672. SURE: Taking Stock After Six Months' COM(2021) 148 final, 6.

> enable the Union to respond to the crisis in the labour market in a coordinated, rapid and effective manner and *in a spirit of solidarity among Member States*, thereby alleviating the impact on employment for individuals and the most affected economic sectors and mitigating the direct effects of this exceptional situation on public expenditure by the Member States (emphasis added).[124]

The Instrument's claim to solidarity was grounded in the Member States' voluntary commitment to supporting each other through the Union. As such, it was not dissimilar to the type of measures proposed by Thomas in his Memorandum. However, the measure was time-limited in that its use ended in December 2022 and it was not a social policy initiative as such – rather, it emphasised a monetary form of solidarity between Member States.[125] Its ability to contribute to building a moral community between European citizens was therefore limited.

A potentially more effective example of how solidarity could begin to be operationalised in European labour law can be found in the 2022 Minimum Wage Directive which 'highlights the challenges the EU faces in promoting solidarity between workers from different Member States and generating support for the Union among its citizens'.[126] Described as 'historic',[127] it is the first EU legislation ever to explicitly aim to ensure adequate minimum wages and strengthen collective bargaining.

The Directive was a response to the increasing 'polarization of labour markets' in the wake of globalisation, digitalisation, and the growth of atypical employment, particularly in the service sector, as well as the increase in 'low-wage jobs and jobs with low skill requirements' and the 'undermining of traditional collective bargaining structures'. This has 'widened the gap between low wages and other wages in many Member States', resulting in an increase in 'in-work poverty and wage inequality'.[128] According to the Commission, adequate minimum wage protection should, among other things, ensure a decent life for workers, support domestic demand, and promote gender equality. Erne explains that the EU legislator's 'aim was not merely to secure fair wages, but also to restore popular legitimacy to the European integration project'.[129] The Directive thus provides a framework aimed at improving the adequacy of minimum wages and access to minimum wage protection for workers with the goal of achieving adequate living and working conditions across the EU. Article 1 also explicitly mentions the promotion of collective bargaining for wage-setting. Another key innovation is the recognition of the importance of collective bargaining for adequate minimum wages. Provisions designed to strengthen the role of trade unions include an article which explicitly promotes

[124] Regulation 2020/672 (n 122), Preamble at recital (6).

[125] V Lindner, 'Solidarity without Conditionality. Comparing the EU Covid-19 Safety Nets SURE, Pandemic Crisis Support, and European Guarantee Fund' (2022) Leibniz Institute for Financial Research, SAFE Working Paper No 333, 19.

[126] Hartzén (n 45) 164.

[127] T Müller and T Schulten, 'Die Europäische Mindestlohnrichtlinie – Paradigmenwechsel hin zu einem Sozialen Europa' (2022) 48 *Wirtschaft und Gesellschaft* 335–64, 335. See, more broadly on the Directive, L Ratti, E Brameshuber and V Pietrogiovanni (eds), *The EU Directive on Adequate Minimum Wages. Context, Commentary and Trajectories* (Hart, 2024).

[128] All quotes are from European Commission, 'Proposal for a Directive of the European Parliament and of the Council on adequate minimum wages in the European Union' COM(2020) 682 final.

[129] R Erne, 'The EU Minimum Wage Directive: To Be or Not to Be?' (Social Europe, 24 February 2025), available from www.socialeurope.eu/the-eu-minimum-wage-directive-to-be-or-not-to-be.

collective bargaining, and the explicit reaffirmation of trade unions' prerogative to engage in collective bargaining (Arts 3(3) and 4(1)). There is thus explicit recognition of the importance of social partner involvement.

However, the legislative process was complicated by tensions between Member States with different labour market regulatory models (ie between countries which legally regulate minimum wages and countries where minimum wages are regulated by collective agreements) which undermine solidarity between Member States by instilling a lack of trust in the other regulatory model's ability to ensure equal or better protections for workers.[130] Although it was supported by the European Commission, the European Parliament, 24 national governments, nearly all trade unions and even the French employers' association (MEDEF), Denmark and Sweden challenged the Directive's legal basis before the European Court of Justice.[131] The complaint was upheld by Advocate-General Emiliou who recommended the Directive's annulment in full on the grounds that pay is excluded from the competence of the EU legislator under Art 153(5) TFEU.[132] It is interesting to note that the Advocate-General, at the outset, stressed that the EU can act only within the limits of the competences conferred upon it by the Member States in the Treaties. In the area of EU social policy, this is rendered more complex as a result of the division of competence between the EU and national level, and it is the Court's role to resolve these ambiguities in line with the rule of law enshrined in Art 2 TEU. However, the Advocate-General did not mention or engage with the other principles (such as democracy) or foundational values, including solidarity, also contained in that Article.

The Opinion has been heavily criticised by European trade unions and by European labour law academics,[133] who point out that the EU has intervened in pay-setting in the context of making bailout funding conditional on wage and pension cuts and labour market de-regulation during the 2008 financial crisis.[134] But the Opinion (and the challenge by Denmark and Sweden itself) must be seen in its broader political context. As Erne summarises, 'from a labour politics perspective, the lawsuit's outcome remains uncertain due to the powerful lobbying forces aligned against the directive'.[135] Repeated (successful) lobbying by employers and their umbrella organisations since at least the early 2000s has 'paved the way for what former Commission President José Manuel Barroso described as a "silent revolution", marking a shift from a predominantly market-driven (horizontal) mode of European integration to a more politically driven approach (vertical), particularly in wage policy'.[136]

[130] Hartzén (n 45) 170–71.

[131] See C-19/23 *Kingdom of Denmark v European Parliament and Council of the European Union*, Opinion of Advocate-General Emiliou delivered on 14 January 2025.

[132] For a discussion of the Opinion, see C Kilpatrick and M Steiert, 'A Little Learning is a Dangerous Thing: AG Emiliou on the Adequate Minimum Wages Directive (C-19/23, Opinion of 14 January 2025)', EUI Working Paper, 2025/02.

[133] For an overview see Erne (n 129).

[134] See R Erne, S Stan, D Golden, I Szabó and V Maccarrone, 'Contextualising the EU's NEG Prescriptions and Research Design' in *Politicising Commodification: European Governance and Labour Politics from the Financial Crisis to the Covid Emergency* (Cambridge University Press, 2024) 73–92.

[135] Erne (n 129).

[136] ibid.

The Minimum Wage Directive provides an opportunity to begin to counter this revolution; its annulment by the Court is not a foregone conclusion. The ambiguity inherent in the EU's competence in this field was deliberate, 'to paper over conflicting interests across countries and social classes'.[137] The Directive itself, to facilitate solidarity at EU level, had included a built-in exception (Art 1(4)) so that the procedure for setting statutory minimum wages (Arts 5–8) did not apply to Member States with the collective bargaining-based regulatory model (ie Austria, Cyprus, Denmark, Finland, Italy and Sweden). Furthermore, the Directive set out information, statistics and review procedures (Arts 11–15) to generate knowledge with a view to 'in the long run, create better opportunities for stronger solidarity and trust between Member States with different regulatory models'.[138] The Court could thus still decide to interpret the Directive in such a way that allows it to facilitate solidarity between workers and Member States; to begin to build a moral community between European workers, and workers and the state, through pan-European action.

V. Conclusion

The need to rethink European labour law situates against the increased politicisation of the EU in recent years as a result of multiple crises which has led to a renewed interest in European labour law's potential to transform the increasingly unequal European economy and society. In this chapter, we have employed a minor comparativism – a legal method operationalising some of the key tenets of critical theory – to recover those voices that are not represented in traditional narratives of the development of European labour law in order for different starting points for its future to be identified. The genealogical critique facilitated by the minor comparativism has revealed how economic interests displaced social interests in the development of European labour law and the broader process of European integration. Then, comparing the standard narrative of European labour law's development with the scheme proposed by Albert Thomas in 1931 has brought to light how important solidarity is to remedying the continued asymmetry between European social and market integration. However, in order to embed solidarity between states and between European citizens, any pan-European projects need to be coupled with a social dimension and adequate protections and opportunities for building moral community between workers – moving beyond top-down regulation – so that individuals see the benefits of European co-operation.[139] Here, insights from critical theory and minor comparativism are particularly helpful to support legal scholars and policy-makers rethinking the future of European labour law by stressing the foundational value of solidarity in connecting citizens with the broader European project.

[137] ibid.

[138] Hartzén (n 45) 171.

[139] R Banakar, 'Law, Love and Responsibility A Note on Solidarity in EU Law' in R Banakar, K Dahlstrand and L Ryberg Welander (eds), *Festskrift till Håkan Hydén* (Juristförlaget i Lund, 2018) 69–83, 83.

7

EU Anti-Discrimination Law through the Lens of Critical Theory

RAPHAËLE XENIDIS[1]

I. Introduction

Equality and non-discrimination are central principles of the European Union (EU) legal order.[2] Arguably, these two principles serve as a distributional key which conditions access to resources, opportunities and solidarity in social Europe.[3] As a result, equality and non-discrimination are two of the most polysemous legal principles in the realm of EU law. The spectrum of claims that they are invoked to respond to spans distributive, representational, symbolic, moral or procedural concerns, to name just a few.[4] In a context of unravelling national welfare states and fading of the European promise of embedded liberalism,[5] EU anti-discrimination law has come to be regarded as one of the main guardrails of social Europe.[6] It holds the emancipatory promise of freeing individuals and groups from (selected) social structures of domination, subordination, oppression, exploitation and inequality. For some scholars, it does so by removing social stigma that individuals bear because of the social groups they belong

[1] The author is grateful to the editors of this volume, Päivi Neuvonen and Paul Linden-Retek, and to Helena Alviar, for their thoughtful comments on earlier versions of this chapter, as well as to the participants of the workshop 'Critical Theory and European Union Law' held at Durham Law School in September 2024.

[2] See C-43/75 *Gabrielle Defrenne v Société anonyme belge de navigation aérienne Sabena* EU:C:1976:56, paras 10–12: '[Article 119 EEC] forms part of the social objectives of the Community, which is not merely an economic union, but is at the same time intended, by common action, to ensure social progress and seek the constant improvement of the living and working conditions of their peoples, as is emphasized by the Preamble to the Treaty.' ; 'This double aim, which is at once economic and social, shows that the principle of equal pay forms part of the foundations of the Community.'

[3] See A Somek, *Engineering Equality. An Essay on European Anti-Discrimination Law* (Oxford University Press, 2011); CM Rieder, 'The Construction of Social Europe through Transnational Equality' (2024) 15 *Transnational Legal Theory* 236. See also HW Micklitz, *The Politics of Justice in European Private Law: Social Justice, Access Justice, Societal Justice* (Cambridge University Press, 2018), who characterises the principle of non-discrimination as a right to 'access' various social goods and institutions.

[4] On the polysemy of the principle of non-discrimination, see, eg, R Xenidis, 'The Polysemy of Anti-Discrimination Law: The Interpretation Architecture of the Framework Employment Directive at the Court of Justice' (2021) 58 *CML Rev* 1649.

[5] See D Ashiagbor, 'Unravelling the Embedded Liberal Bargain: Labour and Social Welfare Law in the Context of EU Market Integration' (2013) 19 *European Law Journal* 303.

[6] See, eg, Rieder (n 3).

to.[7] For others, anti-discrimination law protects subjects' autonomy.[8] For others yet, it is a tool of distributive justice that offsets the disadvantages of less privileged social groups.[9] It can also be conceived as a regime protecting 'deliberative freedoms', that is insulating 'decisions about how to live [. . .] from the effects of normatively extraneous features of [people], such as our skin color or gender'.[10] Yet, when assessed against such axiological and distributive commitments, the legal regime of non-discrimination seems to fall short of its emancipatory promise.

A. The Critique

In fact, EU anti-discrimination law has been a subject of choice for critiques from various disciplines. In particular, it has been described as overly 'formalistic'. Such a critique stems from the distinction between 'formal' and 'substantive' equality, which has been an influential and durable motive in the critical analysis of EU equality law in the past decades.[11] Applying the analytical dichotomy between formal and substantive equality has led scholars to address the discrepancy between the 'actual' normative mandate of EU anti-discrimination law and its jurisprudential construction by the Court of Justice. Fredman suggests that substantive equality can be achieved by entrusting non-discrimination law with a four-dimensional mandate: to 'redress disadvantage; address stigma, stereotyping, prejudice, and violence; enhance voice and participation; and accommodate difference and achieve structural change'.[12] The polysemous nature of the principle of non-discrimination, and its central role in shaping social relations, appear clearly in Fredman's model. By contrast, formal interpretations of the principle of equality – so the critique goes – fail to apply such a model and mostly fall back on a conception of equality as sameness of treatment. Following these critical voices, this failure stems from the flattening of the principle of non-discrimination and its reduction to a negative entitlement to equal treatment. Such conceptions of discrimination, which foreground symmetry of treatment in a social void, ignore hierarchies and power asymmetries, and lack a normative vision as well as theoretical and social grounding.[13]

Though a productive lens of analysis, such a critique remains implicit in its engagement with social theory, leaving these references largely unexplored. Though parallels with Young's and Fraser's theories of justice can be established, current versions of the substantive equality critique – now widespread in critical analyses of anti-discrimination and gender equality law – often fail to spell out the theorisation of society that underpins their normative commitments.[14] A critical approach to anti-discrimina-

[7] See I Solanke, *Discrimination as Stigma: A Theory of Anti-Discrimination Law* (Hart Publishing, 2017).
[8] See T Khaitan, *A Theory of Discrimination Law* (Oxford University Press, 2015).
[9] See, eg, D Hellman, 'Two Concepts of Discrimination' (2016) 102 *Virginia Law Review* 895.
[10] S Moreau, 'What is Discrimination?' (2010) *Philosophy & Public Affairs* 143, 147.
[11] S Fredman, 'Substantive Equality Revisited' (2016) 14 *International Journal of Constitutional Law* 712.
[12] ibid.
[13] See CA MacKinnon, 'Substantive Equality: A Perspective'(2011) 96 *Minnesota Law Review* 1.
[14] See IM Young, *Justice and the Politics and Difference* (Princeton University Press, 1990); N Fraser, *Social Justice in the Age of Identity Politics: Redistribution, Recognition, Participation*, (Wissenschaftszentrum Berlin für Sozialforschung, 1998).

tion law must be concerned with the vision of society that such rules embody and the values which they reflect. This conditions any attempt at an immanent critique of EU anti-discrimination law: asking which society, societal forms and social relations this legal regime constructs, renders and precludes is necessary to assess those rules against their emancipatory promise. How does the principle of non-discrimination condition, mediate and construct specific forms of individual subjectivity, interpersonal relationships, institutional arrangements, material and spatial organisation and ultimately social order? How does it authorise the existence of certain subjects and groups while excluding and rendering others invisible? What 'forms of life' does EU anti-discrimination law and its jurisprudential construction by the Court enable or preclude?[15] Answering these questions also require understanding the distributional effects of this body of law, ie how this 'legal regime distributes surpluses' of different nature (wealth but also social recognition, power, opportunities, etc).[16]

B. Objective and Structure of the Chapter

Inspired by Päivi Neuvonen's recent contributions on EU law and critical theory, the chapter asks what 'rationalisations of society' and 'unpronounced assumptions of political reality' condition and guide the operation of EU anti-discrimination law?[17] The chapter proposes to examine the principle of non-discrimination and its avatars (equal treatment, equality) as instruments of social engineering at three levels: the micro-level of the embodied subject, the meso-level of legal proxies for social membership, and the macro-level of social order.[18]

The chapter first elaborates on why this reflexive moment must take place. Against the backdrop of a 'methodological turn' in EU law,[19] research in this field appears ripe for a reflexive introspection. This chapter thus proposes to unpack the role of critical theory

[15] Jaeggi defines 'forms of life' as 'historically situated problem-solving processes' and 'a culturally informed order of human co-existence' that encompasses an 'ensemble of practices and orientations' as well as their institutional manifestations and materialisations. See R Jaeggi, 'Towards an Immanent Critique of Forms of Life' (2015) 57 *Raisons politiques* 13, 15. In the context of EU law, see L Azoulai, 'The Critical Turn in EU Legal Studies' (2015) 52 *CML Rev* 881.

[16] D Kennedy, 'Law Distributes: Ricardo, Marx, CLS' in K Engle and N Hoad (eds), *Hierarchies at Work: Racial Capitalism, World-Systems Theory, and Legal Distributional Analyses* (Columbia University Press, 2025).

[17] See PJ Neuvonen, 'A Way of Critique: What Can EU Law Scholars Learn from Critical Theory?' (2022) 1 *European Law Open* 60, 62, 68.

[18] While scholars have theorised the differences between those terms, and in particular non-discrimination vs equality, the Court of Justice tends to use them interchangeably.

[19] See, eg, the conference series 'Controversies over Methods in EU Law' organised by Vincent Reveillère from 2022 to 2024 at the University of Aix-Marseille and the resulting symposia on Verfassungsblog, in particular: V Réveillère, 'Controversies over Methods in EU Law' (*VerfBlog*, 18 March 2024, available at https://verfassungsblog.de/controversies-over-methods-in-eu-law/. See also V Réveillère. 'Un moment réflexif pour les études européennes' (2024) 3 *Cahiers de Méthodologie Juridique* 1261. Other initiatives have flourished recently, see, eg, I Isailović, 'Introduction: Critical Legal Approaches in EU Law – Reflections on New Research Directions' (2024) 15 *Transnational Legal Theory* 493 and the corresponding special issue or M Rask Madsen, F Nicola and A Vauchez (eds), *Researching the European Court of Justice: Methodological Shifts and Law's Embeddedness* (Cambridge University Press, 2022).

and the methods of inquiry of critical approaches to EU anti-discrimination law.[20] It then outlines three methodological and theoretical interventions inspired by critical theory. At the micro-level, the chapter seeks to *reembody* EU law by excavating the forms of subjectivity and subjectivation that it validates or erases. It tells a story of how certain bodies appear or disappear when EU anti-discrimination law engineers subjects. At the meso-level, the chapter sets out to *trouble* the categories of EU anti-discrimination law to highlight how its classification operations and boundary work fix meaning and render legible or illegible certain interpersonal relations and forms of sociality. Finally, at the macro-level, the chapter attempts to *disenchant* EU law by exposing – beyond the enchanted metanarrative of EU integration – the choice of 'European society' fostered by the operation of anti-discrimination law and its implications in terms of excluding alternative forms of social order. This is the condition for imagining alternative – re-enchanted – futures.

It is hoped that the three methodological moves which this chapter relies on – embodying, troubling and disenchanting – can help shed light on, and question, the epistemological commitments of EU anti-discrimination law. While embedded in legal analysis, such an interdisciplinary account helps understanding that anti-discrimination law is not neutral but historically and socially situated, that its rules affect the allocation of power and resources in society, and that they shape the lives and experiences of Europeans. The aim is to expose the material realities and the forms of socialisation that are enacted, enforced, constrained or foreclosed by the legal arrangements and devices that constitute EU anti-discrimination law. Ultimately, the chapter reflects on how EU anti-discrimination law contributes to assembling an imagined subject and a fantasised and disembodied European society, otherwise rendered invisible by the leitmotiv of European integration.

C. The Case Study

Rather than aiming to systematically explore EU anti-discrimination law and its jurisprudential construction, the chapter aims to illustrate and theorise how selected interventions of this corpus of norms engineer the European society and its subjects. To conduct this enquiry, the chapter examines the jurisprudential saga in which the Court of Justice of the EU (CJEU) has ruled on the legality of workplace rules and practices prohibiting the wearing of religious clothing. While the Court has examined six cases since 2015,[21] the focus is placed on the most recent decisions: *LF v SCRL* and

[20] Morrow and Brown describe 'critical theory as a kind of conflict theory' because it 'has a more specific focus on the substantive problematic of domination, a complex notion based on a concern with the ways social relations also mediate power relations to create various forms of alienation and inhibit the realization of human possibilities'. They identify several aspects of critique, including a 'concern with unveiling ideological mystifications in social relations', a 'methodological [. . .concern. . .] involving establishing the presuppositions of approaches to the nature of reality, knowledge, and explanation' and another 'associated with the self-reflexivity of the investigator and then linguistic basis of representation'. See RA Morrow and DD Brown, *Critical Theory and Methodology* (Sage, 1994) 7, 10.

[21] The four previous decisions are C-157/15 *Samira Achbita and Centrum voor gelijkheid van kansen en voor racismebestrijding v G4S Secure Solutions NV* EU:C:2017:203; C-188/15 *Asma Bougnaoui et Association de défense des droits de l'homme (ADDH) contre Micropole SA* EU:C:2017:204; Joined Cases C-804/18 and C-341/19 *IX and MH Müller Handels GmbH v WABE eV and MJ* EU:C:2021:594.

Commune d'Ans.[22] In *LF*, a private company withdrew an internship offer it had made to an applicant once she informed the managers that she would not renounce wearing an Islamic headscarf in the workplace. In *Commune d'Ans*, a lawyer employed by a Belgian municipality started wearing an Islamic headscarf in the course of her employment and challenged the municipality's so-called 'strict' neutrality policy, which imposed neutrality not only in interactions between municipal employees and users of the public service, but also amongst employees themselves.[23] The Court of Justice examined both cases through the doctrinal lens of 'indirect discrimination', defined as a situation

> where an apparently neutral provision, criterion or practice would put persons having a particular religion or belief [. . .] at a particular disadvantage compared with other persons unless [. . .] that provision, criterion or practice is objectively justified by a legitimate aim and the means of achieving that aim are appropriate and necessary.[24]

As apparent from the definition, the framework of indirect discrimination automatically embeds a balancing exercise by way of a proportionality assessment weighing the allegedly discriminatory measure against other considerations. In cases of religious discrimination, competing interests have traditionally included the principle of neutrality and the freedom to conduct a business. Indeed, in *LF* and *Commune d'Ans*, the Court considers that 'an employer's desire to display, in relations with both public- and private-sector customers, a policy of political, philosophical or religious neutrality'[25] and 'an entirely neutral administrative environment'[26] are valid legitimate aims. In both cases, the Court concluded that the neutrality rules of the private company and the public municipality could be justified, respectively if the company could show a 'genuine need' and if the municipality pursued the neutrality objective 'in a genuinely consistent and systematic manner with regard to all employees'.[27] These two decisions serve as illustrations throughout the chapter because they offer a fertile ground for thinking about questions related to diversity, accommodation, subjectivity, autonomy, neutrality, etc, and the type of social arrangements that anti-discrimination law enables, engineers and protects.

II. What is 'Critical' in Critical Approaches to EU Anti-Discrimination Law?

What can a reflexive endeavour bring to critical engagements with EU anti-discrimination law? Clearly articulating what is critical in critical approaches to EU anti-discrimination

[22] C-344/20 *LF v SCRL* EU:C:2022:774 and C-148/22 *OP v Commune d'Ans* EU:C:2023:924. This chapter is based on a more extensive comment of these decisions, see R Xenidis, 'From Religious Neutrality to Religious Discrimination in the Public and the Private Sector: Commune d'Ans and SCRL' (2025) 62 *CML Rev* 513.

[23] For detailed analyses of this decision, see E Howard, 'OP v Commune d'Ans: Another Step in the Wrong Direction for Headscarf-Wearing Women' (2024) 53 *Industrial Law Journal* 305. N Dube, 'OP v. Commune d'Ans: When Equality, Intersectionality and State Neutrality Collide' (2024) 31 *Maastricht Journal of European and Comparative Law* 433.

[24] See Article 2(2)(b) of Council Directive 2000/78/EC establishing a general framework for equal treatment in employment and occupation [2000] OJ L303/16.

[25] *LF v SCRL (Vêtement à connotation religieuse)* (n 22) para 39.

[26] *Commune d'Ans* (n 22) para 33.

[27] *LF v SCRL (Vêtement à connotation religieuse)* (n 22) para 40 and *Commune d'Ans* (n 22) paras 38–39.

law can advance research on three levels. First, such engagements have sometimes provoked backlash and have been dismissed as activist interventions.[28] Morrow and Brown note that charges casting critical theory as 'antiscientific' are widespread.[29] What underpins these depictions of critical interventions as lacking 'neutrality' are in fact fundamental disagreements over methods of inquiry and epistemic production. Hence, making the role and methods of critical theory explicit is necessary to rebut these accusations.

On the one hand, critical theory is a social theory which accounts for, and analyses, social institutions and their evolutions. When such an interdisciplinary approach enriches legal analysis, explicit references to the mandate and methods of disciplinary companions can help ground contributions in accepted scientific canons. On the other hand, the strength of critical theory is precisely to make 'ideological assumptions [in the law] explicit, [so that] they can be subjected overtly to rational debate in terms of the legitimacy of the values they embody and the social forms through which they might be brought to life'.[30] For this to happen, the theorisation of society and the methods and moves inhering in critical theoretical analysis must be spelled out clearly.

Second, as Morrow and Brown note, 'critical theory [is] concern[ed] with the simultaneous critique of society and the envisioning of new possibilities'.[31] Hence, sociological imagination is part and parcel of the mandate of critical theory. 'Critique in this sense is concerned with *normative theory*, theory about values and what ought to be. Critical imagination is required to avoid identifying where we live here and now as somehow cast in stone by natural laws'.[32] Instead, the role of critical theory is to raise awareness of alternative modes of social organisation and futures. Again, this critical move must be made explicit in critical approaches to anti-discrimination law. It is only by dislodging assumptions of neutrality deeply engrained in EU anti-discrimination law that critical legal analysis can expose the social arrangements it maintains and propose alternative interpretations of existing rules or law reform.

Third, by articulating some of the methodological and analytical moves that characterise critical theory, the chapter also seeks to offer a methodological and theoretical companion for scholars embarking on critical journeys in the field of EU anti-discrimination law.[33] The chapter draws from different strands of critical theory – in particular materialist, post-structuralist and feminist accounts – without ambitioning to reconstruct the genealogies and articulations of these variations of critique. One central methodological move throughout the chapter is 'distributional

[28] Attacks pointing at the lack of 'neutrality' of critical scholarship are examples of such tensions. See Morrow and Brown (n 20) 22.

[29] ibid 6, 22: '[M]isleading' but 'popular images of science' and critical theory's 'explicit rejection of the traditional way the sciences have understood themselves and the so-called "scientific method"' play a large role in these accusations.

[30] ibid 22.

[31] ibid 10.

[32] ibid.

[33] For inspiring intellectual endeavours in the field, see also eg I Isailović, 'Gender in Political Economy and EU Law' (2024) 15 *Transnational Legal Theory* 525 and L Díez Sánchez, *Integration through Law and its Discontents: Unveiling the Distributive Impact of Judge-Made Law in the EU* (European University Institute, 2021).

analysis', a 'classic mode of work in critical legal studies', which Halley defines as 'oriented not to the symbolic "norm announcing" function of law and legal institutions but to their distributional consequences'.[34] The way this corpus of legal norms 'set[s] in motion a chain of further distributional changes in particular directions, for example, stagnation or growth, accumulation and impoverishment' can of course be understood in material terms.[35] Yet this chapter conceives of distribution in much broader ways, including how legal rules allocate not only resources, wealth and assets, but also visibility, power, opportunity, agency, space, prestige, voice, status, shame, pain, honour, etc, in line with feminist legal studies.[36] In fact, answering the question of 'what distributions [legal regimes] leave in place, and what distributions [they] shift?' is the condition for assessing the justice of such arrangements and for 'imagin[ing] [alternative] redistributions'.[37] This requires broadening the frame of analysis beyond the harm of discrimination to understand who are the 'winners' and the 'losers' of EU anti-discrimination law, what types of social goods are (re-) distributed through those legal rules, and how they create or modulate existing social arrangements and hierarchies.[38]

III. Re-Embodying EU Anti-Discrimination Law

Re-embodying EU anti-discrimination law aims to answer the following questions: Who are the 'protected' subjects of EU anti-discrimination law? What bodies, modes of existence and forms of subjectivity does EU anti-discrimination law 'see', render legible or construct? In turn, what epistemic erasures does EU anti-discrimination law perform? The move to re-embody EU law starts from what Fricker calls an 'epistemological reading [of structures of domination], which implies that the powerful have some sort of unfair advantage in "structuring" our understandings of the social world'.[39] It represents a strategy of hermeneutical resistance against 'epistemic oppression', namely an intervention to re-integrate the social and corporeal experiences of the most marginalised into 'collective understandings the social world'.[40] The move to re-embody EU law thereby responds to Fricker's injunction to 'start thought from marginalized lives [. . .] as a means to ensuring that no one's social experience is systematically obscured by unevenly informed collective interpretive practices'. That is what she calls 'hermeneutical affirmative action'.[41] The decisions in *LF* and *Commune*

[34] J Halley, 'Distribution and Decision: Assessing Governance Feminism' in J Halley and others (eds), *Governance Feminism: An Introduction* (University of Minnesota Press, 2018) 253.

[35] Kennedy (n 16).

[36] ibid; see also Halley (n 34) 256 and D Kennedy, 'Law and the Global Dynamics of Distribution', *A World of Struggle: How Power, Law, and Expertise Shape Global Political Economy* (Princeton University Press, 2016).

[37] Halley (n 34) 253.

[38] See ibid 257–58.

[39] M Fricker, 'Epistemic Oppression and Epistemic Privilege' (1999) 25 *Canadian Journal of Philosophy Supplementary Volume* 192. See also standpoint theory, eg S Harding, *Whose Science? Whose Knowledge?: Thinking from Women's Lives* (Cornell University Press, 1991).

[40] Fricker (n 39) 209.

[41] ibid 209–210.

d'Ans illustrate how the legal forms of EU anti-discrimination law produce disembodiment. In this context, re-embodying EU law gives visibility to excluded subjects and highlights, in the words of Benhabib, how 'women and their bodies become the object of disciplinary conflicts in culture, law and religion'.[42]

First, by constructing these cases purely as instances of religious discrimination, the Court fantasises a disembodied legal subject extracted from relevant power structures such as gender and race.[43] The question of intersectional discrimination came up in both cases. In *Commune d'Ans*, the national judge asked whether the municipality's strict neutrality policy could constitute indirect discrimination on grounds of sex 'where that prohibition appears mostly to affect women'.[44] The CJEU ruled the question inadmissible, explaining that

> the order for reference does not contain any information enabling ascertainment of the factual situation on which [that] question is based or of the reasons why an answer to that question [. . .] is necessary in order to resolve the dispute in the main proceedings.[45]

In *LF*, the national judge recognised the 'scientific interest' of 'the lengthy theoretical developments devoted by the plaintiff to the intersectional dimension of the alleged discrimination' but regretted that they 'complicate the judge's task'.[46] It nonetheless asked the CJEU about the existence of direct gender-based discrimination where

> a female worker who intends to exercise her freedom of religion by wearing a visible [religious sign], in this case a headscarf, is treated less favourably than another worker with the same beliefs who chooses to manifest them by wearing a beard (which is not specifically prohibited by the terms of employment, unlike manifestation through clothing).[47]

Although Advocate General Medina had recognised the possibility of 'double discrimination' that goes 'beyond religion and extend[s] also to gender', the Court did not address this question in its decision.[48] In so doing, the Court fragments the legal subjects and conditions their legibility under EU anti-discrimination law on their ability to fold themselves into a disembodied notion of religion. The Court's analysis obfuscates the predictable gendered effects of rules banning religious clothing on a 'very

[42] S Benhabib, 'The Return of Political Theology: The Scarf Affair in Comparative Constitutional Perspective in France, Germany and Turkey' (2010) 36 *Philosophy & Social Criticism* 451, 453.

[43] Scholars have also repeatedly drawn courts' attention to intersections of religion, race and gender in producing discriminatory disadvantage. See, eg, S Atrey, *Intersectional Discrimination* (Oxford University Press, 2019); I Solanke, 'Putting Race and Gender Together: A New Approach to Intersectionality' (2009) 72 *MLR* 723; and in the specific context of religious clothing, see Dube (n 23) and R Xenidis, 'Intersectionality from Critique to Practice: Towards An Intersectional Discrimination Test in the Context of "Neutral Dress Codes"' (2022) 2 *European Equality Law Review* 21, drawing from eg PM Caldwell, 'A Hair Piece: Perspectives on the Intersection of Race and Gender Frontiers of Legal Thought: Gender, Race, and Culture in the Law' (1991) *Duke Law Journal* 365, 387; K Crenshaw, 'Demarginalizing the Intersection of Race and Sex: A Black Feminist Critique of Antidiscrimination Doctrine, Feminist Theory, and Antiracist Politics' (1989) *The University of Chicago Legal Forum* 139.

[44] *Commune d'Ans* (n 22) para 42.

[45] ibid paras 49 and 42–50.

[46] Order for reference in *LF v SCRL* (*Vêtement à connotation religieuse*) (n 22) paras 40–43.

[47] ibid para 23 (question 3(f)).

[48] Opinion of Advocate General Medina, *LF v SCRL* (EU:C:2022:328) para 66.

clearly identifiable minority grou[p]'.[49] In turn, the separation of protected categories of religion and race renders illegible the racialisation of given religious practices and the negative perceptions associated therewith.[50] By contrast, re-embodying EU law is an experiential strategy that engages with intersectionality to capture the fact that 'the[se] major systems of oppression are interlocking'.[51]

Second, by legitimising so-called 'neutrality rules', the Court *de facto* effaces the bodies of Muslim women from the workplace, both through the effects of its decisions – applicants must choose between their religious practices and the workplace – and on a more epistemic level. It does so, on the one hand, by conflating the right not to be subjected to discrimination based on religion and the right to exercise freedom of religion.[52] Indeed, in *Commune d'Ans*, the CJEU invites the national court

> to weigh up the interests at stake, taking into account, on the one hand, the fundamental rights and principles at issue, namely, in this case, the right to freedom of thought, conscience and religion guaranteed by Article 10 of the Charter of Fundamental Rights [. . .] and, on the other hand, the principle of neutrality [put forward by] the public administration.

In this context, the 'prohibition of any discrimination based on religion' is described as only 'the corollary of' the right to freedom of religion.[53] As pointed out by Khaitan and Norton in another context, what the Court balances in the proportionality test that ensues from its analysis of indirect discrimination is therefore religious freedom 'understood as protecting [an individual's] interest in religious adherence (and non-adherence)' against the municipality's alleged interest in a 'neutral' working environment.[54]

[49] See the analysis by former AG Sharpston in earlier cases of *WABE and Müller Handels* (n 21), E Sharpston, *Shadow Opinion in Joined cases C-804/18 and C-341/19 IX v WABE e.V and MH Müller Handels GmbH v MJ* (EU Law Analysis, 2021), available at https://eulawanalysis.blogspot.com/2021/03/shadow-opinion-of-former-advocate.html para 265. The cases of *LF v SCRL* and *Commune d'Ans* come up against the background of rich discussions critiquing the Court's legal reasoning in previous rulings pertaining to the Islamic headscarf (*Achbita, Bougnaoui, Wabe and Müller*). Commentators have disputed the legal qualification of neutrality rules as instances of indirect discrimination and argued that they should rather fall under the notion of direct discrimination, that is a situation 'where one person is treated less favourably than another is, has been or would be treated in a comparable situation' on grounds of religion (Art 2(2)(a) of Directive 2000/78/EC (n 24)). Such distinction can appear technical but has important procedural consequences. As mentioned above, EU law foresees a closed regime of justifications in the case of direct discrimination and an open-ended regime in cases of indirect discrimination. Hence, a first stake in qualifying neutrality rules as direct or indirect discrimination relates to employers' ability to eschew liability for the discriminatory effects of such rules. See, eg, E Cloots, 'Safe Harbour or Open Sea for Corporate Headscarf Bans? Achbita and Bougnaoui' (2018) *CML Rev* 589 and E Howard, 'Headscarves and the CJEU: Protecting Fundamental Rights or Pandering to Prejudice' (2021) 29 *Maastricht Journal of European and Comparative Law* 648.

[50] On the intersections between racial and religious discrimination, see N Meer, 'Racialization and Religion: Race, Culture and Difference in the Study of Antisemitism and Islamophobia' (2013) 36 *Ethnic and Racial Studies* 385; B Etienne and I Wallerstein, *Race, Nation, Classe, les identités ambiguës* (La Découverte, 1988); see also R Kapur, 'Race-Making, Religion and Rights in the Post-Colony: Unmasking the Pathogen in Assembling a Hindu Nation' (2022) 18 *International Journal of Law in Context* 499; S Hennette-Vauchez, 'Neutralité religieuse, laïcité et colorblindness: essai d'analyse comparée' (2021) *Droit et societe* 351.

[51] The activists of the Combahee River Collective stated in their 1977 manifesto: '[t]he synthesis of these oppressions creates the conditions of our lives'. See Combahee River Collective, *The Combahee River Collective Statement: Black Feminist Organizing in the Seventies and Eighties* (Kitchen Table, Women of Color Press, 1986).

[52] See T Khaitan and J Calderwood Norton, 'The Right to Freedom of Religion and the Right against Religious Discrimination: Theoretical Distinctions' (2019) 17 *International Journal of Constitutional Law* 1125.

[53] *Commune d'Ans* (n 22) para 40.

[54] See Khaitan and Norton (n 52) 1125.

This analysis deflects from the rationale underpinning the right to non-discrimination on grounds of religion, that is 'protecting [the applicant's] non-committal interest in the unsaddled membership of [her] religious group'.[55] Through the proportionality test, the Court thus weighs 'the need to respect [the applicant's] decisional autonomy in matters of religious adherence', ie 'her ability to (intersubjectively) determine and [. . .] pursue her religious commitments'.[56] Instead, protecting the applicant from discrimination would have entailed balancing her 'interest in being unsaddled by the disabilities that accompany her religious group membership', in other terms 'the need to reduce any significant (political, sociocultural, or material) advantage gaps between different religious groups'.[57] This analytical confusion becomes immediately apparent when transposing the Court's analysis to other protected grounds than religion. The effect of such reasoning is to prioritise the municipality's alleged interest in 'neutrality' over the applicant's interest in being protected against the discriminatory projections associated with the religious garment at stake, and the consequences of these projections in terms of the applicant's inclusion in, or exclusion from, the workplace.

On the other hand, in *Commune d'Ans* and *LF* the Court reads religion as an immaterial, disembodied set of beliefs. Despite formally recognising that 'the concept of "religion" in Article 1 of Directive 2000/78 covers both the *forum internum*, that is the fact of having a belief, and the *forum externum*, that is the manifestation of religious faith in public',[58] the Court's reasoning around the notion of 'neutrality' negates the materiality of Muslim women's religious practices. Within its analysis of justifications in the context of indirect discrimination, the CJEU accepts that the municipality of Ans' strict neutrality policy 'may be regarded as pursuing a legitimate aim within the meaning of Article 2(2)(b)(i) of Directive 2000/78'.[59] In *LF*, the Court accepts the legitimacy of an employer's 'wish to project an image of neutrality towards customers' provided that it can show a 'genuine need'.[60] By accepting such notions of neutrality as legitimate aims capable of justifying *prima facie* discrimination, the Court suggests that the material practices manifesting religious beliefs are not neutral and can be subjected to limitations without necessarily infringing the principle of non-discrimination. Thereby it construes those practices as distinguishable from 'actual beliefs' and thus dispensable.

By separating religious beliefs and their material manifestations, the Court ignores the reality of mandated religious practices (*forum externum*) and promotes an assimilationist understanding of the principle of non-discrimination. Assimilation is described by Young as a 'logic of identity', which 'seeks to reduce the plurality of particular subjects, their bodily, perspectival experience, to a unity, by measuring them against the unvarying standard of universal reason'.[61] The power of defining such a standard sits in dominant social groups. As Young states, 'cultural imperialism is enacted partly through the ability of a dominant group to assert its perspective and experience as universal

[55] ibid.
[56] ibid 1125 and 1134–35.
[57] ibid.
[58] *Commune d'Ans* (n 22) para 22.
[59] ibid 36.
[60] *LF v SCRL (Vêtement à connotation religieuse)* (n 22) paras 39–40.
[61] Young (n 14) 112.

or neutral'.[62] This assimilationist approach also reflects what critical race theorists have described as 'colourblindness'.[63] It ignores how neutral dress codes implicitly accommodate the religious practices of majority groups while prohibiting or stimatising those of groups whose religion mandates the wearing of religious clothing. In fact, the Court fails to unpack the negative stereotypes that the notion of neutrality condones. It leaves undisturbed what Caldwell describes as the 'deeply-ingrained myths, negative images, and stereotypes that operate to define the social and economic position' of minority groups such as the applicants'.[64]

This assimilationist version of the principle of non-discrimination emerges again implicitly in *Commune d'Ans*, in the municipal authorities' justification for the strict neutrality policy and in the Advocate General's reasoning. The municipal policy states that '[w]orkers are required to observe the principle of neutrality, which means that they must refrain from any form of proselytising and that they are prohibited from wearing any overt sign which might reveal their ideological or philosophical affiliation or political or religious beliefs'.[65] It specifies that the 'rule applies both to their contacts with the public and to their working relationships with hierarchical superiors and colleagues'.[66] In one of its decisions, the municipal authorities state that the aim of the policy is to preserve peaceful relations between employees:

> without it being necessary to examine whether the wearing of a sign of conviction can be analysed as a mild form of proselytising, the neutrality of appearance imposed on all staff members not only serves as an example of the attitude to adopt towards the public, but also as a guarantee of the smooth running of the service and a way of avoiding tensions arising between staff members because of their respective positions on this sensitive issue or their convictions.[67]

In his Opinion in *Commune d'Ans*, Advocate General Collins deemed it necessary to probe whether 'strong community tensions or serious social problems', 'proselytising activities or a specific risk of conflicts between employees linked to such beliefs' justify the existence of a strict neutrality policy.[68] The Court, by contrast, simply accepts that the policy serves a legitimate aim without engaging with such justifications. While it does not endorse the argument concerning proselytism, this silence also risks condoning the negative stereotypes associated with the materiality of the religious beliefs at stake.

This section has shown how EU anti-discrimination law, through the concept of neutrality, performs epistemic oppression and marginalises subjects at the intersections of gender, religion and race. This leads to hermeneutical injustice when the disembodiment performed by EU anti-discrimination law denies subjects the right

[62] ibid 73–74. She also states that 'The culturally dominated undergo a paradoxical oppression, in that they are both marked out by stereotypes and at the same time rendered invisible.'

[63] See S Hennette-Vauchez, 'Neutralité religieuse, laïcité et *colorblindness* : essai d'analyse comparée' (2021) N° 108 *Droit et société* .

[64] Caldwell (n 43) 368.

[65] *Commune d'Ans* (n 22) para 15.

[66] ibid.

[67] Application for a preliminary reference to the CJEU in *Commune d'Ans* para 9.

[68] Opinion of Advocate General Collins, *OP v Commune d'Ans* EU:C:2023:378, para 73.

to be known on their own terms.[69] A critique of the modes of subject-making of EU anti-discrimination law should therefore aim to redistribute the power of definition. Importantly, re-embodying EU anti-discrimination law should not be understood, in an essentialising manner, as an attempt to fix or ascribe stable identities and roles to given minority groups and the individuals that are part of these groups (or perceived to be). Rather, this critical move should be used to highlight how the concept of neutrality naturalises and implicitly accommodates the religious practices of majority groups while rendering others as 'ab-normal'. Re-embodying, as a methodological intervention, gives visibility to the ways EU law excludes certain subjects and their modes of existence from the scope of protection of EU anti-discrimination law. In the context of the cases explored in this chapter, restoring subjects' corporeal dimensions helps contesting the subjective boundaries drawn by EU law, which are anchored in dominant social practices of religion. Hence, re-embodying anti-discrimination law is a strategy of epistemic resistance that can help re-institute pluralism and heterogeneity in EU law's subjectivation techniques and operations.

IV. Troubling the Categories of EU Anti-Discrimination Law

Categorisation is an inherent operation of EU non-discrimination law. Anti-discrimination law traditionally relies on social membership categories to seize the reality of inequalities.[70] Lived experiences must be subsumed into one of the protected categories of EU non-discrimination law – sex, race or ethnic origin, religion or beliefs, etc – to become legible as a form of unlawful discrimination. At the meso-level, these so-called protected grounds serve as proxies to capture vectors of discrimination. They can be regarded as enabling hermeneutical devices that should help make sense of experiences of injustice. Either the protected ground signals that the cause for unfavourable treatment is an individual's social membership, in the case of direct discrimination, or it points to a vector of group disadvantage, in the case of indirect discrimination.

Yet, these categories are frequently construed and operationalised to limit the scope of anti-discrimination law. While the previous section has demonstrated how the categories of EU anti-discrimination law can turn into limiting devices that restrict its personal scope and efface subjects – for example those who traverse the boundaries of several categories – this section focuses on the impact of this categorisation work on social groups. It shows how the categorising operations inherent in anti-discrimination law reflect a bias towards liberal individualism, which leaves communities of practices, modes of collective existence and 'forms of life' in a blind spot of legal protection. The section shows how, in the context of the cases studied in this chapter, EU anti-discrimination law conceptualises the members of protected social groups 'as a pure transcendental origin [which] has no foundation outside itself,

[69] See G Chakravorty Spivak, 'Can the Subaltern Speak?', *Imperialism* (Routledge, 2023).

[70] See D Pothier, 'Connecting Grounds of Discrimination to Real People's Real Experiences' (2001) 13 *Canadian Journal of Women and the Law* 37.

[and...] is self-generating and autonomous'.[71] This is because the law 'seeks to generate stable categories' and 'tends to conceptualize entities in terms of substance rather than process or relation'.[72] Troubling the categories of EU anti-discrimination law, as a methodological intervention, instead seeks to productively destabilise the ways in which these categories have been constructed and interpreted. This can help to diagnose how categorisation work produces alienation and assimilation and foster more relational and situated interpretations.

As explained above, the Court's use of the notion of neutrality in *LF* and *Commune d'Ans* construes religious practice as an individual 'choice', ie the choice (not) to wear an Islamic headscarf at work. Such a conceptualisation of religion reflects an individualistic understanding of protected categories: it reads religious practices from an individual standpoint – ie it is interested in 'workers *who intend to exercise their freedom* of religion and conscience through the visible wearing of a sign or an item of clothing with religious connotations' (emphasis added)[73] – but obfuscates their links to social communities. The Court does not operate the category of religion as capturing communities of practices or bundles of social relations. Rather, its balancing of neutrality rules against the applicants' freedom of religion results in conditioning access to non-discrimination rights to individual applicants' self-removal from a community of practices, namely the wearing of a headscarf. This epistemological individualism also leads the Court to minimise the consequences of such self-removal. In the proportionality analysis in *Commune d'Ans*, for example, it specifices that 'the [neutrality] rule [is] limited to the workplace, the users of its services and the members of its staff', thereby neglecting the importance of workplace relations in socialisation experiences.[74]

This individualistic bias in EU anti-discrimination law has been noted by scholars as pervading EU law more broadly. For Somek for instance, it translates in '[t]he European Union [putting] the individual at the centre and rest[ing] her hope in the wealth that accrues from competition', thus 'empower[ing] those who are agile and adaptable and reliev[ing] them from dependence on received social bonds and hierarchies'.[75] For Azoulai, 'affirm[ing] the sovereignty of the individual in the EU law context' cannot be entirely equated with 'affirm[ing] pure individualism' as EU law strives to re-create forms of sociality.[76] Yet, the highly selective forms of sociality that EU law recognises and co-constructs exclude the community of practices and forms of socialisation of the sort at stake in *LF* and *Commune d'Ans*. Indeed, the right to non-discrimination based

[71] Young (n 14) 112.

[72] ibid 111.

[73] *LF v SCRL (Vêtement à connotation religieuse)* (n 22) para 42.

[74] *Commune d'Ans* (n 22) para 40.

[75] A Somek, 'Alienation, Despair and Social Freedom' in L Azoulai, S Barbou Des Places and E Pataut (eds), *Constructing the Person in EU Law: Rights, Roles and Identities* (Hart Publishing, 2016) 52.

[76] See L Azoulai, 'The European Individual as Part of Collective Entities' in L Azoulai, S Barbou Des Places and E Pataut (eds), *Constructing the Person in EU Law: Rights, Roles and Identities* (Hart Publishing, 2016) : 'Pure individualism is the view that individuals are entirely inward-looking beings for whom only individual goods, and no collective goods, matter. In this perspective, group membership and a sense of community are of no intrinsic value. What we perceive with EU law is of a different nature. I should like to suggest that EU law strives to convert European individuals into members of social spheres external to the political system of the country of origin, with the possibility to circulate among these spheres, establishing links between them, occasionally pitting one entity against another. Hence, by this definition, EU law is not individualistic'. He cites 'market, family, society' of the host or home state.

on religion or belief, as construed by the Court, removes the negative consequences associated with exercising an internal, individual right to hold spiritual beliefs but leaves unaddressed those associated with signalling membership in a social community. In other terms, the right to non-discrimination excludes from its scope the relational and collective aspects of religious practices understood as a form of sociality.[77]

As Somek further writes,

> The rights that [EU law] protects are 'the rights of the egoistic man, of man separated from other men and from the community'. Their exercise does not give rise to that social solidarity which is conducive to universal individual self-realisation.[78]

Somek further diagnoses that '[s]olidarity is treated as a resource to be tapped by individuals' and that 'European Union law turns a blind eye to the link between individual agency and its facilitating social conditions'.[79] Troubling the categories of EU anti-discrimination law entails repositioning the individual rights bearer within social communities, relationships of interdependence, mutual vulnerability and equal needs in order to bring the social conditions that enable the exercise of individual agency within the scope of EU anti-discrimination law.[80]

Arguably, the epistemological individualism that underpins the readings of EU anti-discrimination law in *LF* and *Commune d'Ans* produces alienation on at least two levels, from self and from others.[81] Jaeggi proposes a multi-facetted definition of alienation:

> An alienated relation is a deficient relation one has to oneself, to the world and to others. Indifference, instrumentalization, reification, absurdity, artificiality, isolation, meaninglessness, impotence – all these ways of characterizing the relation in question are forms of this deficiency. [. . .] A distinctive feature of the concept of alienation is that it refers not only to powerlessness and a lack of freedom but also to a characteristic impoverishment of the relation to self and world.[82]

Two aspects in particular can be productively invoked to analyse the effects of the jurisprudential construction of discrimination by the Court of Justice here. On the one hand, alienation is the 'detachment from one's social involvements', for example when 'someone cannot identify with [. . .] the social or political institutions in which she lives'.[83] A 'symptom' of such alienation might be 'social alienation'. On the other hand, alienation is an 'impoverished' relation to self, or when 'one does not behave as one "genuinely" is but instead "artificially" and "inauthentically"'.[84] 'Role behavior and conformism' count

[77] This phenomenon is also observable in the Court's construction of religious discrimination in earlier cases dealing with neutrality requirements and the wearing of the headscarf at work.

[78] Somek (n 75) 36.

[79] See ibid 53.

[80] See ibid 42: 'Were we to take cognisance of our social existence explicitly, each of us would view herself as one human being with needs among equal others. We would realise that our social nature — our mutual dependence and complementation — represents what is universal about us.'

[81] ibid 41: 'alienation from others is the root of self-alienation'.

[82] R Jaeggi, *Alienation*, vol 4 (Columbia University Press, 2014) 7.

[83] ibid 6.

[84] ibid 5–6.

as alienation in this sense.[85] Both aspects are interdependent: 'Alienation is the inability to establish a relation to other human beings, to things, to social institutions and thereby also – so the fundamental intuition of the theory of alienation – to oneself.'[86]

In *LF* and *Commune d'Ans*, alienation ensues from religion being cast in terms of individual choice as opposed to a collective and relational form of identity and socialisation. The Court's operation of protected categories in these decisions enforces an individualistic conception of religion as a set of personal beliefs – a dominant social understanding of religion – and draws a boundary so as to render religion as a set of socio-cultural relations, interactions and collective practices illegible to non-discrimination law. This reduces the scope of the right to non-discrimination to the protection of discrete individuals – with the limits exposed in section III – and obscures their links to routinely disadvantaged social groups and communities, which produces alienation from self and from others. Moreover, social alienation ensues from the exclusion of the applicants' views on religion and neutrality from the community of meaning constructed by the Court of Justice. In *LF* and *Commune d'Ans*, but also in earlier cases pondering the legality of neutral dress codes, the applicants are not given an opportunity to 'resignify the wearing of the scarf', which prevents them from participating in the collective negotiation of the meaning and boundaries ascribed to religious discrimination.[87] This results in prioritising conflicting socio-economic interests in the form of employers' neutrality policies. Here the principle of non-discrimination therefore produces and even demands alienation.

This leads to a second problem in the form of assimilation. Showing discrimination entails comparing different demographic clusters to highlight that, but for a protected category, disadvantage would not exist. Scholars have pointed out that such a comparative understanding of discrimination conditions access to equality rights on sameness.[88] Since discrimination takes place when two groups in similar positions are treated or impacted differently because of a protected ground, a minority group must show likeness to a privileged group to be able to claim equal treatment.[89] In so doing, EU anti-discrimination does not protect difference meaningfully but rather creates assimilationist pressures. In the words of McColgan, '[c]onditioning equal treatment on "likeness", however defined, functions so as to grant less privileged actors access to the benefits enjoyed by the more privileged only to the extent that the former can prove "sameness" with the latter.'[90]

Assimilation contains a paradox: it is a necessary condition for claiming recognition and addressing discrimination but, at the same time, conforming to dominant norms does not produce equality.[91] Following Young, '[t]he irony of the logic of identity is that by seeking to reduce the differently similar to the same, it turns the

[85] ibid 6.
[86] ibid 5.
[87] Benhabib (n 42) 459.
[88] See, eg, P Westen, 'The Empty Idea of Equality' (1982) 95 *Harvard Law Review* 537; Hellman (n 9).
[89] Fredman (n 11) 719–20.
[90] A McColgan, *Discrimination, Equality and the Law* (Hart Publishing, 2014) 102, 118.
[91] See Young (n 14) 172. She 'criticize[s] an ideal of justice that defines liberation as the transcendence of group difference, which [she] refer[s] to as an ideal of assimilation'.

merely different into the absolutely other'.[92] Disadvantaged groups 'undergo a paradoxical oppression, in that they are both marked out by stereotypes and at the same time rendered invisible'.[93] Assimilation means that subject-making necessarily adopts the codes and norms of dominant groups and therefore reproduces and internalises power asymmetries. In order to participate in the European society – understood here as revolving around transnational market participation[94] – the individual is required to renounce her belonging to a community of socio-cultural practices and to assimilate into the dominant one, cast in *LF* and *Commune d'Ans* as 'neutrality' in the Court's and the defendants' language.

There is of course a material dimension to the alienation and assimilation that condition subject-making and legibility in EU anti-discrimination law. In fact, the applicants in cases such as *Achbita*, *Bougnaoui*, *Wabe*, *Müller*, *LF* and *SCRL* are faced with a dilemma: their participation into one of the major institutions of European sociality,[95] as framed by the CJEU, is conditioned by alienation and assimilation. Refusing to remove one's headscarf means being cut off from the workplace, a central tenet of the EU's market-based sociality, but also an important means of subsistence.

In this context, troubling the categories of EU anti-discrimination law means challenging an individualistic and essentialising understanding of protected grounds and proposing a more relational and collective reading of the legal protection against discrimination. An individualistic reading of protected categories yields what Freeman calls 'the perpetrator's perspective', an analytical lens that atomises structural inequalities by construing them as multiple but discrete instances of discrimination.[96] This goes against the promise of non-discrimination law as a tool for emancipation: whereas protected categories should serve as proxies for capturing social hierarchies, unequal power relations and structural inequalities, they instead become reified into individual identity traits. As a critical gesture, troubling these categories should help with making space to centre the standpoint, communities of practices and modes of existence of marginalised groups in the communities of meaning constructed by EU anti-discrimination law. Destabilising these categories, questioning their boundaries and contesting their scope should result in a more collective and relational understanding of sociality, power, privilege, disadvantage and discrimination. As a methodological intervention, troubling these categories allows diagnosing the systemic underpinnings of disadvantage and the deep-seated, institutionalised and naturalised hierarchies that maintain discrimination beyond individual cases. It expands the grasp of non-discrimination law to the social conditions surrounding and conditioning the exercise of individual preferences and freedoms. Troubling the categories of EU anti-discrimination law authorises a relational reading of privilege and disadvantage. Instead of construing protected categories as fixed individual identities, such a methodological move sheds light onto the social support nets that condition privilege. It aims to respond to the disconnect between EU legal studies and social reality which Azoulai diagnoses: '[i]f we need a method, it is

[92] ibid 112.

[93] ibid 73.

[94] See Somek (n 3).

[95] See Azoulai (n 76).

[96] See AD Freeman, 'Legitimizing Racial Discrimination Through Antidiscrimination Law: A Critical Review of Supreme Court Doctrine' (1978) 62 *Minnesota Law Review* 1049.

one that allows us to reconnect with European societies as a bustle of unsettled forms of life, from both an existential and social perspective'.[97]

V. Disenchanting EU (Anti-Discrimination) Law

This section brings the critical analysis proposed in this chapter to the macro-level, that of society and social ordering. EU law promises social integration.[98] For example, Article 1 of the Treaty on the European Union commits to 'a new stage in the process of creating an ever closer union among the peoples of Europe'. The leitmotiv of European integration has gained normative traction over the years. Barbou Des Places for instance diagnoses 'the rise of the notion of "integration"', which although always present in the first stage of EU law, has now become 'a central, free-standing and normative category of EU law'.[99] Azoulai describes EU integration 'not just as a grand political project but also as a genuine (largely damaged) "form of existence"'.[100] As an 'an order-building enterprise', EU law sets up 'a quasi-transcendental system, a sort of duplication of the "real" process of integration' that traditionally takes place at national level.[101] In this context, it has become important to interrogate this grand narrative of integration to understand the work that it performs in EU law.

The methodological intervention proposed in the term 'disenchanting' aims precisely to question the form of social order which legal integration promotes in the EU. In the spirit of critical social theory, disenchanting is a necessary condition for any normative project aiming to re-enchant EU law.[102] Disenchanting is also an invitation to question the 'enchanted' narrative of EU law's evolution beyond internal market law and its development into fundamental rights law. This narrative has prevailed, for example, to explain the Court's evolving approach to anti-discrimination norms in *Defrenne*, where Union law was entrusted not only with an economic but also a social purpose.[103] Beyond the dichotomy between 'the market' and 'the social' and the idea of a rights-driven European integration, the 'disenchanting' move proposed in this section raises the following questions: what society does the principle of non-discrimination in EU law construct? How does it order persons, relationships and institutions? What inclusions does it mandate and what exclusions does it legitimise? Arguably, disenchanting EU non-discrimination law can contribute to excavating the rationalisation of society underpinning the operations of the law.

An analysis of the legal techniques deployed by the Court to govern discrimination in the *LF* and *Commune d'Ans* decisions, as well as in previous cases of religious

[97] L Azoulai, *Reconnecting EU Legal Studies to European Societies* (*VerfBlog*, 19 March 2024), available at https://verfassungsblog.de/reconnecting-eu-legal-studies-to-european-societies/.

[98] 'Integration through law' has been an influential motive in the study of the EU. See, eg, M Cappelletti, M Seccombe and JHH Weiler, 'Integration through Law: Europe and the American Federal Experience. A General Introduction' in *Book 1 A Political, Legal and Economic Overview* (De Gruyter, reprinted 2013)

[99] S Barbou Des Places, 'The Integrated Person in EU Law' in L Azoulai, S Barbou Des Places and E Pataut, *Constructing the Person in EU Law: Rights, Roles, Identities* (Hart/Bloomsbury Publishing, 2016) 179.

[100] Azoulai (n 97).

[101] ibid.

[102] See Morrow and Brown (n 20) 13–14.

[103] See *Defrenne* (n 2).

discrimination against Muslim women, reveals potentially opposing visions of social integration. To understand how, it is first necessary to grasp the legal forms through which discrimination can be constructed. Under EU law, discrimination can be understood as either direct – essentially a form of differential treatment of comparable situations – or indirect – where an apparently *neutral* measure applied to different situations results in a particular disadvantage.[104] Albeit technical, this distinction is important because direct discrimination only suffers limited exceptions that are explicitly listed in anti-discrimination legislation and interpreted narrowly, while indirect discrimination can be justified on an open-ended basis via a proportionality test.[105]

Scholars have consistently criticised the Court's qualification of so-called neutrality rules or policies as indirect as opposed to direct discrimination. As explained in previous sections, the purported neutrality of these neutrality rules can be productively questioned when they serve as a proxy for entrenching existing social hierarchies through 'countless silent accommodations'.[106] Along with former Advocate General Sharpston, it can be argued that '"neutrality" that in reality predictably denies employment opportunities to particular, very identifiable, minority groups' cannot be considered neutral measures but should be treated as a direct form of discrimination.[107] A yet deeper questioning of the legal forms promoted by the Court of Justice reveals the rationalisation of society that informs the Court's construction of the principle of non-discrimination.[108] In particular, those qualifications engage different views on social diversity and homogeneity.

As highlighted by Advocate General Medina, qualifying a neutrality rule adopted by a private or a public employer as a form of direct discrimination places the burden of accommodating differences and minority practices onto those employers and ultimately onto clients or public service users.[109] When neutrality rules are construed as direct discrimination, the refusal to accommodate such practices suffers few legal exceptions. For example, an employer would need to show that a ban on religious symbols is 'a genuine and determining occupational requirement', that is, the targeting of religion by workplace regulations is necessary 'by reason of the nature of the particular occupational activities concerned or of the context in which they are carried out'.[110] Thinking with Moreau, the wrongful nature of discrimination then resides in the refusal or failure, by relatively privileged and powerful groups, to make reasonable accommodations for relatively disempowered or disadvantaged groups when such accommodation would not unduly burden them.[111] Such an understanding of discrimination normalises social diversity by calling out the prejudices and negative stereotypes that underpin, or are authorised by, so-called neutrality policies – understood as assimilatory injunctions – as (quasi-)unjustifiable discrimination. In *LF* and *Commune*

[104] See Art 2(2)(b) of Directive 2000/78/EC (n 24).

[105] For example, liability for direct discrimination can be discharged in case an employer can show a genuine and determining occupational requirement. By contrast, indirect discrimination can be 'objectively justified by a legitimate aim [when] the means of achieving that aim are appropriate and necessary'. See ibid.

[106] S Moreau, 'Discrimination as Negligence' (2010) 40 *Canadian Journal of Philosophy* 123, 146.

[107] See Sharpston (n 49) para 265.

[108] Opinion of Advocate General Medina, *LF v SCRL* (n 48) 44: 'the ethos underpinning Directive 2000/78 regarding discrimination based on religion or religious beliefs is manifested differently depending on whether employees concerned by religious clothing obligations are considered to be either directly or indirectly discriminated against by an internal neutrality rule'.

[109] ibid.

[110] See Art 4 of Directive 2000/78/EC (n 24).

[111] Moreau (n 106) 130–32. See also Hellman (n 9) 904.

d'Ans, a legal qualification of direct discrimination would have transferred the costs of social prejudice and the duty to suppress any negative consequence associated with religious clothing requirements, as well as the duty to accommodate such practices, from religious employees themselves to their employers, colleagues, clients and public service users.[112] This has a double effect. On the one hand, it normalises the expression of differences in society, promotes social diversity and protects a plurality of forms of life through the principle of non-discrimination.[113] On the other, such a legal approximation of discrimination places liability with the groups that enjoy sufficient social power to be in a position to redress it.[114]

By contrast, by choosing the framework of indirect discrimination in *LF* and *Commune d'Ans* as well as in previous cases on the legality of neutral dress codes, the Court pits the right to non-discrimination against the principle of neutrality via a proportionality test that entails a balancing exercise. As explained above, indirect discrimination can always be justified by a legitimate aim when measures are appropriate and proportional. Viewing neutrality rules through the lens of indirect discrimination rests on a homogenous vision of society where religious 'differences' can – but need not – be accommodated depending on how they are balanced against other interests. The balancing test inherent in indirect discrimination allows employers to accommodate 'a certain degree of prejudice of the public towards religious differences' in order to avoid 'severe adverse economic [or other, eg, in terms of *ordre public* or peaceful social relations] consequences'.[115] In so doing, EU anti-discrimination law, as mediated by the Court of Justice, engineers a social order revolving around social homogeneity.

When employers are not mandated to internalise the costs of social prejudice, the long-term effect is twofold. On the one hand, at a structural level prejudice remains tolerated. On the other hand, at a micro-level, the costs thereof must be borne by the employees themselves, either through conforming to majority preferences (in *LF* and *Commune d'Ans* through removing religious clothing) or through social isolation (eg, leaving a given employer or the labour market altogether). Where EU integration resides in transnational market participation[116] and associated social interactions, such consequences directly affect available forms of European sociality. Hence, disenchanting EU anti-discrimination law, and more broadly the grand narrative of European integration, is a necessary step towards un-packing, and contesting, the social order enacted by the legal and jurisprudential construction of EU anti-discrimination norms. It renders visible who can inhabit EU law and the forms of society that EU law protects.

VI. Conclusion

This chapter has argued that deeper-reaching engagements with critical theory and its methodological prescriptions can help give visibility to the ways in which EU law

[112] See also C-54/07 *Centrum voor gelijkheid van kansen en voor racismebestrijding v Firma Feryn NV* EU:C:2008:397.
[113] Opinion of Advocate General Medina, *LF v SCRL* (n 48) paras 45, 59–60.
[114] Freeman (n 96) 1055–56.
[115] Opinion of Advocate General Medina, *LF v SCRL* (n 48) para 59.
[116] See Somek (n 3).

perpetuates, challenges or re-instates social hierarchies. It has described three methodological interventions that can mediate such engagements with critical theory. At the micro-level, this chapter has described how re-embodying EU anti-discrimination norms represents a strategy of epistemic resistance against subjective erasures and re-institutes pluralism and heterogeneity in EU law's subjectivation techniques. At the meso-level, this chapter has invited to trouble the categories of EU anti-discrimination law, and in particular the proxies it uses to seize vectors of inequality. It has argued that such trouble can productively interrogate the boundary work performed by these categories and foster a more relational understanding of disadvantage, privilege, and the social conditions in which individual autonomy can be exercised. Finally, at the macro-level, this chapter has argued that disenchanting the narrative of integration through anti-discrimination law – and in particular framings of non-discrimination rights as 'access rights' – is necessary to excavate the forms of social order which result from its application. Such a critical move helps reveal how EU anti-discrimination law contains, frames, excludes and validates given forms of sociality, what counts as injustice and harm, and ultimately who can inhabit EU law.

8

Critical Legal Feminism in EU Law

A Post-State-Socialist Perspective

BARBARA HAVELKOVÁ*

I. Introduction

Has the European Union (EU) been good to women?[1] Is the EU better than the Member States (MSs) at 'including'[2] women? As feminists, should we be for or against the EU?[3] These are likely to be the questions many a European feminist has asked herself.[4] Complete, clear, unequivocal, and universal answers are impossible to give. The following contribution suggests which aspects of these questions could be answered, and how, by (critical) feminist legal scholarship.

This chapter started as a typical academic paper, not a positioned, personal reflection. In the process of writing, it became apparent that I have had ideas percolating about what a self-consciously post-state-socialist Central-European feminist legal scholar's take on EU law would look like. I decided to use this opportunity to clarify them for myself and share them. This chapter therefore draws on the post-socialist Central-European experience and is written as a reasoned but nonetheless personal account. I, of course, neither speak for Central and Eastern European (CEE) women as a group, nor are my observations necessarily only applicable to this region (they might be relevant more widely for civil-law or Germanic countries, or the Mediterranean). In terms of scholarly writing, I allow myself an element of subversion of genre.[5]

* I would like to thank the editors, Päivi and Paul, as well as Rosario Grima Algora, Jonathan Herring, Ruth Houghton, Ivana Isailović, Mathias Möschel, Jo Shaw, Nicole Štýbnarová, and Steve Weatherill, for their insightful comments and feedback on early drafts, and Jwalika Balaji and Adrija Ghosh for research assistance; all remaining mistakes are, of course, mine.

[1] These questions can be formulated at different levels of sophistication, of course. 'Has the post-national concept of sovereignty of the EU been infused with a self-conscious gender dimension?' is a more serious way of putting it. Paraphrasing J Shaw, 'Importing Gender: The Challenge of Feminism and the Analysis of the EU Legal Order' (2000) 7 *Journal of European Public Policy* 406, 411.

[2] In the sense of addressing their needs, preferences, and recognising their experiences. For the broad concept of 'exclusion', see D Réaume, 'What's Distinctive About Feminist Analysis of Law?: A Conceptual Analysis of Women's Exclusion from Law' (1996) 2 *Legal Theory* 265.

[3] The last was already asked by Shaw (n 1) 411.

[4] I am allowing myself a generic feminine in this instance, to include all genders.

[5] This disruption of the apparently objective 'view from nowhere' of traditional legal scholarship has rich antecedents in feminist writings. See R Hunter, 'Critical Legal Feminisms' in E Christodoulidis, R Dukes and M Goldoni (eds), *Research Handbook on Critical Legal Theory* (Edward Elgar Publishing, 2019) 52 and the references therein.

I could not perform a feminist critique of the EU legal order in this chapter without clarifying what that means, in terms of positions taken and questions asked;[6] a subject which has received surprisingly little attention from legal scholars.[7] In the end, rather than fully performing a feminist critique of EU law, I explore its methodology and suggest its possibilities, contours, challenges, and limits.

The chapter thus starts by asking what makes scholarship 'feminist', 'critical', and 'legal' (section II). In particular, I explore how 'critical legal feminisms' might differ from 'feminist legal scholarship', noting potential contentions, especially around structuralism versus post-structuralism, the material versus the symbolic, and theory and praxis. I identify my position as structuralist and radical in analysis but pragmatic in prescription, where the pragmatism in praxis requires a theory connected to the material realities of the lives of women.

Section III identifies four – existing and prospective – objects of feminist study of EU law (ie a typology of research agendas): 1) women as EU law-makers; 2) gender equality *acquis*; 3) gender in other EU substantive law; 4) gender in the EU legal order. It notes a gap when it comes to critical legal feminist engagement with EU law, especially when it comes to the legal order's fundamentals.

If sections II and III assess what critiques already exist and which are possible, Section IV then offers a rudimentary exploration of the questions about feminist attitudes to EU law asked above, noting that different answers depend on which lens one applies or prioritises. It observes that the most plausible answer to whether the EU has been good to women is a 'yes, but', although the enthusiasm about 'yes' depends on the approach taken: whether legal, whether critical, and/or whether pragmatic (section IV.A). Using the benchmark of the MSs, it can also be said that the EU has likely contributed to greater gender equality in most of its MSs, especially when viewed from post-state-socialist CEE (section IV.B).

II. A 'Feminist', 'Critical', and 'Legal' EU Scholarship?

Individual scholars' understandings of feminism vary considerably. There can therefore never be a definitive definition of a feminist critique of EU law. In the following, I nonetheless discuss what I consider the features of a 'feminist', 'critical', and 'legal' EU scholarship. Throughout, I share three main characteristics of my own feminism: inclusiveness in asking the woman question; radicalism and structuralism in going to the roots of gendered power hierarchies; combined with pragmatism.

[6] I have critiqued circumscribed areas of EU gender equality law before (see, for eg, B Havelková, 'Women on Company Boards: Equality Meets Subsidiarity' (2019) 21 *Cambridge Yearbook of European Legal Studies* 187) but have not reflected on the EU legal order more generally.

[7] The exception being several works by Jo Shaw, most now quarter-of-a-century-old. See especially Shaw (n 1); more recently, Ivana Isailović (cited throughout) explicitly aims to follow in Jo Shaw's footsteps, eg I Isailović, 'Gender in Political Economy and EU law' (2024) 15 *Transnational Legal Theory* 525.

A. What Makes a Project 'Feminist'?

i. *Feminist Questions and Methods*

Feminists overwhelmingly agree that what unites them is, first, the interest in the situation of women. For legal feminists, it is women's exclusion from 'the design of the legal system or the application of law'.[8] Second, that the way to learn about it is to talk to women.[9] I elaborate on these two aspects of feminist method in turn before discussing borders and types of feminism.

'Asking the woman question' has been a paradigm-changing addition to Western legal and political thought which had always, unreflectively, taken man as its norm. Nonetheless, it entails a danger that the general category itself becomes exclusionary, by ignoring other social axes of disadvantage.[10] In my feminist thought and practice, I aim to be inclusive. The gender order – patriarchy – that oppresses women also oppresses others: those non-conforming to patriarchy's gender expectations, especially queer people but also many men. Furthermore, there are other axes of social disadvantage – race, class, age, religion, etc – intersecting with[11] gender, which can alter the importance of gender in the experience of oppression. These perspectives ought to be looked at by feminists, although their relevance for any research project will vary depending on the particular issue and research questions asked.[12]

An inclusive approach does not mean a methodological requirement of 'completeness'; no research is truly complete and needs focus. Rather, it means that feminist research should not make assumptions about a norm. In other words, it should not base itself on a limited sample of experiences, especially not ones which correlate with privilege (of white, Western or Northern, educated, straight, professional women).[13] In the context of the EU, this can mean not forgetting the specific situation of Roma women,[14] third-country-national migrant women,[15] or CEE women as internal market migrants.[16]

[8] Réaume (n 2) 273. Internal citations omitted.

[9] Katharine Bartlett identifies three: (1) asking the woman question; (2) feminist practical reasoning; and (3) consciousness-raising. K Bartlett, 'Feminist Legal Methods' (1990) 103 *Harvard Law Review* 829.

[10] ibid 847–48 and references therein.

[11] See also chapter 7 by Raphaële Xenidis in this book.

[12] For example, it would be methodologically legitimate to discuss the issue of pregnancy separately for women assigned female at birth and trans men, as they raise different issues.

[13] Isailović offers an excellent example of applied intersectional perspective when she makes the point that work-life balance measures are likely to benefit high-skilled workers but leave low-skill, low-paid women behind. I Isailović, 'Gender Equality as Investment: EU Work-Life Balance Measures and the Neoliberal Shift' (2021) 46 *Yale Journal of International Law* 277.

[14] For eg E Vincze, 'The Racialization of Roma in the "New" Europe and the Political Potential of Romani Women' (2014) 21 *European Journal of Women's Studies* 435.

[15] A Bloch, T Galvin and B Harrell-Bond, 'Refugee Women in Europe: Some Aspects of the Legal and Policy Dimensions' (2000) 38 *International Migration* 169. See also R Cavanagh and A Elomäki, 'Feminist Political Economy and its Explanatory Promise' in Gabriele Abels et al (eds), *The Routledge Handbook of Gender and EU Politics* (Routledge, 2021).

[16] For eg P Scholten and M van Ostaijen (eds), *Between Mobility and Migration: The Multi-Level Governance of Intra-European Movement* (Springer Open, 2018).

For me, in terms of a political project, this translates into aspirational prioritarianism[17] – focusing on those worst off or worse off.

Talking among women and listening to women – referred to in different ways, from 'consciousness-raising'[18] to 'feminist conversations'[19] – seems to be a widely agreed-upon feminist method. When this is meant as conversations among scholars, some inequalities in knowledge production within the EU ought to be noted, relevant in particular for CEE, but not only. The problem of the coloniality of knowledge production, epistemic imperialism, and not letting 'the subaltern speak'[20] has been well made by minority feminists from within the 'first world' and from the 'third world' (many from common-law countries with English-speaking academia). Neither the 'first world' nor the 'third world' scholarship always understands or allies with 'second world'[21] concerns, however. The most notable example of this was the long-term, unwavering support that Angela Davis – an African-American Marxist feminist – gave the USSR, despite numerous attempts by those oppressed by the socialist states to tell her otherwise.[22] The experience of 'Westsplaining'[23] is common among CEE scholars.

ii. Borders and Types of Feminism

It is beyond the scope of this chapter to examine the borders of feminism, and at what point it crosses into post-feminism, non-feminism, anti-feminism, or un-feminism.[24] Even within what is generally understood to be a 'feminist' approach, differences and disagreements are both common and profound. In relation to law,[25] the following main strands can be identified: 1) liberal (women should have the same rights as men; eg Betty Friedan[26]); 2) 'feminism of care' (requiring proper valuation of care; eg Carol

[17] D Parfit, 'Equality and Priority' (1997) 10 *Ratio* 202. For a recent application of the prioritarian perspective to intersectional gender equality, see S Atrey, 'A Prioritarian Account of Gender Equality' in RJ Cook (ed), *Frontiers of Gender Equality Transnational Legal Perspectives* (University of Pennsylvania Press, 2023).

[18] CA MacKinnon, *Toward a Feminist Theory of the State* (Harvard University Press, 1989) 83–105.

[19] R Houghton, 'Feminist Approaches to Global Constitutionalism' in AF Lang Jr and A Wiener (eds), *Handbook on Global Constitutionalism*, 2nd edn (Edward Elgar, 2023) 198–200.

[20] G Chakravorty Spivak, 'Can the Subaltern Speak? Speculations on Widow Sacrifice' (1985) 7 *Wedge* 120.

[21] A Cold War terminology developed by the United Nations in the late 1940s is now considered obsolete, but for discussions of path dependencies, is still relevant for analyses of CEE. See also Wallestein's world systems theory, where the 'second world' constitutes a semi-periphery. IM Wallerstein, *World-Systems Analysis: An Introduction* (Duke University Press, 2004).

[22] T Hendl and S Durdiyeva, 'On Collateral Damage, Selective Anti-Imperialism and the Path to Liberation'(2025) *American Communist History* 24(1–4), 53–83, available at www.tandfonline.com/doi/full/10.1080/14743892.2025.2501407

[23] In the context of International Relations and the Russian invasion of Ukraine, see T Hendl et al, '(En) Countering Epistemic Imperialism: A Critique of "Westsplaining" and Coloniality in Dominant Debates on Russia's Invasion of Ukraine' (2023) 45 *Contemporary Security Policy* 171.

[24] These are well explored by the different authors in B Cossman et al, 'Gender, Sexuality and Power: Is Feminist Theory Enough?' (2003) 12 *Columbia Law Review* 601.

[25] Some strands of feminism, such as psychoanalytic feminism, have not found an equivalent in feminist legal theory. For a more general classification, see eg,, R Tong, *Feminist Thought* (Westview, 2009). For legal feminism typology, see eg, M-B Dembour, *Who Believes in Human Rights? Reflections on the European Convention* (Cambridge University Press, 2006).

[26] B Friedan, *The Feminine Mystique* (WW Norton, 1963).

Gilligan[27]); 3) radical (arguing for the abolition of the gender hierarchy; eg Catharine MacKinnon[28]); 4) Marxist, socialist, or materialist[29] (focused on the intersection of class and gender; eg Angela Davis[30]); 5) post-modern (focused on language and culture; eg Judith Butler[31] or Mary Jo Frug[32]).

My personal feminism is best understood as 'radical', focused on the roots of the gender power hierarchies. This can be seen as an attachment to 'second wave' feminism,[33] and I am happy to identify it as such. In this, my position is, again, informed by my CEE heritage. I have noted elsewhere[34] that despite the common perception of them as progressive on women's rights, the socialist states of Central Europe pursued 'public equality' at best but were content to perpetuate 'private difference' – no changes were made to the roles of women in the family.[35] Moreover, at least in Czechoslovakia, there was 'first equality, then difference': whatever transformative ambitions the regime had in the late 1940s and 1950s fizzled out from the 1960s onwards. The experience of 'real existing socialism' should be understood as showing us that gender, as an axis of disadvantage, and patriarchy, as a system of oppression, survive even in a classless society and are thus separable from class and capitalism.

While the bottom-up 'second wave' feminist movement of the 1960s, 70s, and 80s was identifying new forms of patriarchal oppression and discussing ways to challenge them, Czechoslovakia was re-traditionalising in gender terms. Czechoslovakia participated (or experienced) neither the intellectual and activist political developments of the 'second wave' of feminism,[36] nor did it have its own truly feminist scholarly or intellectual moment of focus on women, a shift from biological determinism to social-constructivism, or an acknowledgement of the gender order as a structure which creates important limitations on individual life choices.[37]

This gap has not really been remedied since and has had real impact on CEE states' (negative) attitudes to EU gender equality *acquis*. For example, in the process of

[27] Her early work has been sometimes termed 'difference feminism', see C Gilligan, *In a Different Voice: Psychological Theory and Women's Development* (Harvard University Press, 1982); increasingly, the focus has been on valuing care, in Gilligan's own work, but also in the work of others, see eg, S Fredman, 'Care as a Constitutional Value' (2024) 22 *International Journal of Constitutional Law* 741.

[28] MacKinnon (n 18).

[29] A position taken on EU law in, eg Isailović (n 7).

[30] A Davis, *Women, Race and Class* (Random House, 1981).

[31] J Butler, *Gender Trouble: Feminism and the Subversion of Identity* (Routledge, 1990).

[32] MJ Frug, *Postmodern Legal Feminisms* (Routledge, 1992).

[33] The metaphor of waves or phases is not perfect but has been heuristically used both for feminism and for Critical Legal Studies more generally. For feminism, see eg NA Hewitt, 'Feminist Frequencies: Regenerating the Wave Metaphor' (2012) 38 *Feminist Studies* 658; or, more critically, L Nicholson, 'Feminism in "Waves": Useful Metaphor or Not?' (2010) 12 *New Politics* 34; for Critical Legal Studies, see discussion in PJ Neuvonen, 'Retrieving the "Subject" of European Integration' (2019) 25 *European Law Journal* 6.

[34] B Havelková, 'The Three Stages of Gender in Law' in H Havelková and L Oates-Indruchová (eds), *The Politics of Gender Culture under State Socialism: An Expropriated Voice* (Routledge, 2014).

[35] ibid.

[36] With radical feminism being the least present. I have previously noted that 'difference feminism' is perhaps the closest thing to existing, because of an essentialist understanding of women and the feminine; 'liberalism' would need to be applied to women, in order to speak of 'liberal feminism'; Marxism/socialism would need to be de-discredited (re-credited?) in order to be able to be able to speak of Marxist/socialist feminism; and 'radical feminism' is missing entirely. B Havelková, *Gender Equality in Law: Uncovering the Legacies of Czech State Socialism* (Hart/Bloomsbury, 2017) 292–94.

[37] ibid.

adoption of the 'women on company boards' Directive,[38] the reasoned opinions coming from CEE MSs' parliaments challenged the EU's understanding of gender equality in at least two ways. First, in viewing low numbers of women in decision-making positions as a natural and therefore justified consequence of women's life choices – notably motherhood – they clashed with the more substantive EU understanding of equality, whereby difference should not automatically lead to disadvantage. Second, a lack of awareness and critical attitude to androcentrism was discernible in an unproblematised emphasis on merit and the perceived fairness of selection processes.[39] As I note in section IV below, this makes almost any of the EU's gender equality law ground-breaking in CEE, in terms of legal guarantees as well as narratives that they rest on.

B. What Makes a Feminist Project 'Critical'?

It is a feminist legal endeavour to look at legal norms and how they serve women and how they could serve women better. It is also a feminist endeavour to expose androcentrism in seemingly neutral concepts. So is to analyse the gendered-ness of the legal concepts and ideas that underpin the legal order,[40] to look at the law's deeper normative underpinnings and the understandings about the gender order they draw on, convey, and often, consequently, perpetuate, and to 'interrogate the deeper political, historical, and philosophical logics which underpin the power of law'.[41] As Jo Shaw put it for EU law:

> neither the existence nor the nature of [. . . the EU's] norms and practices should be taken for granted. On the contrary, it is important to see how the gendered identities instantiated in concepts such as sovereignty, democracy and citizenship are themselves the products of particular political and legal discourses.[42]

Are all these layers of feminist legal scholarship 'critical'?

First, 'critical' should be understood as relating to 'critique', rather than 'criticism'.[43] It does not necessitate a negative assessment in substantive terms; it necessitates a questioning attitude. As Päivi Neuvonen has observed, this has been an under-appreciated distinction in EU (legal) scholarship, as criticism seems to be both more common and methodologically conflated with critique.[44] Second, the term should not be confused with 'gender-critical feminism', which sees sex as an unchangeable fact of biology, is

[38] Council Directive (EU) 2022/2381 of 23 November 2022 on improving the gender balance among directors of listed companies and related measures [2022] OJ L315/44.

[39] Havelková (n 6).

[40] See, eg, A O'Donoghue and R Houghton, 'Can Global Constitutionalisation be Feminist?' in S Harris Rimmer and K Ogg (eds), *Research Handbook on Feminist Engagement with International Law* (Edward Elgar, 2019); Houghton (n 19) 188.

[41] PJ Neuvonen, 'A Way of Critique: What Can EU Law Scholars Learn from Critical Theory?' (2022) *1 European Law Open* 60, 61.

[42] Shaw (n 1) 416.

[43] Neuvonen (n 41) 68–69.

[44] ibid.

sceptical of self-defined gender identity, and – especially in the United Kingdom (UK) – has clashed with pro-trans-rights activism.[45]

Critique also means slightly different things in natural language and in social science. Natural language contains a broad understanding of critique: an evaluation or assessment which has a questioning attitude to what it sees. In this broad sense, all feminist legal scholarship would be critical because it searches for instances and mechanisms of exclusion of women in the law.[46] A narrow understanding – the one adopted in this book – references Critical Theory. This means a deeper 'not-taking-for-granted', an analytical and methodological open-endedness,[47] the aim of uncovering assumptions about policy, ideology (or 'ideation'[48]), and assumptions about the law and/or the legal order.[49] It 'engages in continued discourse and debate about meanings and effects of legal rules, categories, institutions and processes'.[50]

Does critical legal feminism have further unifying characteristics? Are 'critical legal feminisms' distinguishable from feminisms, writ large? They are to Rosemary Hunter, who noted that:

> the key commonality among critical legal feminisms is that they engage in critique in three dimensions simultaneously: critique of law, critique of other ('malestream') critical theories (critical legal theory, critical race theory, left political theory generally) and critique of other ('mainstream') feminisms (white/middle class/liberal and structuralist feminisms).[51]

Hunter, moreover, sees critical legal feminisms as characterised by scepticism of feminist law reform efforts and as integrating post-structuralism:

> [P]oststructuralist feminists argued that all subjects are unstable and contingent, and are constructed in discourse rather than possessing fixed identities. While liberal, radical and some materialist legal feminists found these arguments destabilizing and dangerous, posing a threat to the very possibility of feminist legal politics, critical legal feminisms have embraced them and worked through their implications.[52]

This creates a twofold tension: 1) within the relationship between the material or socio-economic[53] on the one hand and the symbolic or socio-cultural[54] on the other (I discuss this in the following section in relation to structural and post-structural positions); and 2) between theory and praxis.

[45] On the UK situation and debates, see E Sarter, P Hegarty and A Casini, 'Gender-Critical or Gender-Inclusive?: Radical Feminism is Associated with Positive Attitudes toward Trans* People and Their Rights' (2024) 90 *Sex Roles* 1301.

[46] To use Réaume's definition. Réaume (n 2) 273.

[47] For eg, on the necessity of ongoing feminist contestation as a way of conceiving 'feminist constitutionalism', see S Atrey, 'Feminist Constitutionalism: Mapping a Discourse in Contestation' (2022) 20 *International Journal of Constitutional Law* 611.

[48] Suggested as 'less politically charged' in Neuvonen (n 41) 67–68.

[49] Hunter (n 5) 45–46.

[50] Shaw (n 1) 414.

[51] Hunter (n 5) 45.

[52] ibid 48.

[53] That is, 'redistribution' in Fraser's terminology, N Fraser and A Honneth, *Redistribution or Recognition* (Verso, 2003).

[54] ibid, ie, 'recognition'.

My mention of 'second wave feminism' above related to the fact that one's feminist positions are typically formed in relation to what one reacts to.[55] I view myself as a structuralist, mainly because in the CEE context, the public discourse still very much sees individuals as masters of their own destiny, which leads to very dismissive attitudes towards negative consequences of women's 'free choices', such as financial and mental health struggles caused by motherhood.[56] Structuralism – the seeing of patterns of (gender) power which limit people's (especially women's) options – is thus, to me, still important as a reaction to liberal individualism.[57]

The structuralism of 'second wave' feminism is taken to contrast with the more recent shift to post-structuralism and post-modernism, which has moved the 'starting point of analysis from "women's experience" to the discursive processes by which gender and women's experience are constructed'.[58] This 'deconstructive' approach and focus on language and culture can be diagnostically enlightening. I do share Catherine MacKinnon's and Martha Nussbaum's scepticism, however, that it is an inadequate platform for real-life action: they both see 'subversion' as insufficient in transformative terms.[59] A similar doubt is apparent in the work of many feminist Critical Theorists. Seyla Benhabib noted that the 'death of metaphysics' meant a retreat from feminist Utopia, ie abandoning any plan for a better world.[60] Nancy Fraser has criticised postmodernism for its over-emphasis on identity politics and decentring of class.[61]

Can permanent postmodern 'deconstruction' ever lead to the 'construction' of anything new? Can a sole focus on discourse inform praxis in the real world? Intellectually, I can see poststructuralism's point about the dangers of 'using the Master's tools to dismantle the Master's house'.[62] As an academic argument, I can accept that the law needs to be critically viewed not as a tool, but as a site of struggle.[63] But for the purposes of praxis, in real life, where the law continues to have great impact on the lives of women, it is hard to ignore it as – flawed and limited, but nonetheless – a tool against oppression.

There are three possible settlements of these tensions. First, if critical legal feminism goes hand in hand with a post-structural dismissiveness of law reform projects – seeing

[55] A similar point can be made in relation to the concept of anti-essentialism: for me it means primarily social constructivism, i.e., an opposition to biological determinism which is still prominent in CEE, while I view the more current uses of the term 'anti-essentialism' as against a singular notion of a 'woman' better understood in terms of inclusiveness, anti-homogenisation, and intersectionality. B Havelková, 'The Struggle for Social Constructivism in Postsocialist Central and Eastern Europe' (2020) 18 *International Journal of Constitutional Law* 434.

[56] See, eg, Havelková (n 36) 190.

[57] See eg Robin West's powerful critique of the ideal of 'independence' in Western liberal thought, while women experience lives of 'interdependence'. R West, 'The Right to Care' in E Feder Kittay and E Feder (eds), *The Subject of Care: Feminist Perspectives on Dependency* (Lanham, 2002).

[58] Hunter (n 5) 54.

[59] MC Nussbaum, 'The Professor of Parody: The Hip Defeatism of Judith Butler' (*The New Republic*, 22 February 1999), available at https://newrepublic.com/article/150687/professor-parody; C MacKinnon, 'Points against Postmodernism' (2000) 75 *Chicago-Kent Law Review* 687.

[60] S Benhabib et al, *Feminist Contentions: A Philosophical Exchange* (Routledge, 1995).

[61] N Fraser, *Justice Interruptus: Critical Reflections on the "Postsocialist" Condition* (Routlege, 1997).

[62] A Lorde, *Sister Outsider* (Crossing Press, 1984).

[63] Drawing on Carol Smart, see Hunter (n 5) 49.

them as complacent[64] or labelling them 'governance feminism'[65] – I am not certain I can subscribe to it. Second, and more strongly, I wonder whether defining 'critical legal feminisms' as fully embracing post-structuralism does not clash with the requirement of theory being informed by praxis,[66] and the normative aim of the abolition of social injustice,[67] both fundamental tenets of Critical Theory. Or, third, a conciliatory stance – a 'big tent' approach – could be taken. This would see critical legal feminisms as containing a spectrum of levels of adoption of deconstructivist approaches, where critical could perhaps be capitalised if a connection to Critical Theory – with its attachment to socio-economic emancipation and praxis – wanted to be emphasised. In this sense, I would consider myself a Critical legal feminist; one very much focused on the real lives of women, the structures that oppress them, while also being pragmatic and aware of real-life constraints of any proposed solutions. A sense of these tensions is important for a feminist (Critical?) discussion of EU law in section IV.

C. What Makes a Feminist Critique of the EU a 'Legal' One?

Does this question even need a section? I believe it does, as any literature review on gender, feminism, and the EU, overwhelmingly yields results from disciplines other than law. Even EU gender-relevant *law* itself is often studied by social and political scientists, economists, or philosophers. At the same time, feminist legal scholarship often shuns the doctrinal legal method – the only approach truly distinct from other disciplines' –, seeing it as limiting. Because of its interest in real life as well as the hidden or unattended-to, feminist legal scholarship almost invariably tends to take an 'external'[68] view on the law, drawing on historical, socio-legal, or jurisprudential methods. In transcending the doctrinal ('internal'[69]) approach to law, feminist legal scholarship can be seen as coming very close to what other disciplines already offer.

It is, nonetheless, legal scholarship's 'internal' take, its ability to see the law not merely as 'a datum, as fact, unproblematic, and one-dimensional', but instead as 'complex, nuanced, [. . .] contested, and constantly evolving'[70] that distinguishes legal scholarship and maintains its usefulness. To give an example, the domestic implementation of the

[64] I Isailović, 'Introduction: Critical Legal Approaches in EU Law: Reflections on New Research Directions' (2024) 15 *Transnational Legal Theory* 493.

[65] See, eg, Isailović (n 13) 286.

[66] On the unity of theory and praxis in the Marxist method, in a discussion of the legal project, see, eg, E Christodoulidis, 'Critical Theory and the Law: Reflections on Origins, Trajectories and Conjunctures' in E Christodoulidis, R Dukes and M Goldoni (eds), *Research Handbook on Critical Legal Theory* (Edward Elgar Publishing, 2019) 9.

[67] For eg M Horkheimer, 'Traditionelle und kritische Theorie' (1937) 6 *Zeitschrift für Sozialforschung* 245; see also, recently, the feminist critique of capitalism in C Arruzza, T Bhattacharya and N Fraser, *Feminism for the 99%: A Manifesto* (Verso, 2019).

[68] C McCrudden, 'Legal Research and the Social Sciences' (2006) 122 *Law Quarterly Review* 632.

[69] ibid. Although McCrudden himself does not cite Hegel, this distinction largely tracks the Hegelian difference between 'immanent' and 'external' critique.

[70] ibid, 647–50.

EU's anti-discrimination directives has been studied by political and social scientists.[71] Their assessment of the politics of the transposition of directives, and the interpretation and theorisation of the surrounding contestation, has offered important context as to who is embracing or resisting the EU gender equality *acquis* and why.[72] What non-legal scholarship did not do – and likely could not do for lack of methodological expertise – was examine in detail the quality and clarity, the language, and the position of the EU-originating rules within the domestic legal systems.[73] And yet, in order to understand anti-discrimination law's fit in individual MSs and grasp why it has had limited effectiveness, one has to look to both legal and extra-legal factors. Many continental civil-law jurisdictions' rebuffs of EU anti-discrimination norms cannot be understood by looking at politics or mobilisation alone. One would also have to consider pre-existing law and its interpretation (eg the origins of norms on harassment in French criminal law which makes a shift to anti-discrimination law's no-fault approach foreign) as well as constitutional and legal foundations and narratives in the various MSs (such as the German right of freedom of business).[74]

III. The Four Objects of Feminist Study of EU Law

How is gender analysis relevant for EU law? What have feminists (whether 'critical' or not) studied about the EU? And, more specifically, what role does feminist scholarship currently play and could play in EU studies? In order to answer these questions, I distinguish four objects[75] of feminist legal analysis of EU law: 1) women as EU law-makers; 2) gender equality *acquis* (women-specific law and policy); 3) gender in other EU substantive law (gender aspects of non-women-specific policies); 4) gender in the EU legal order (the gender of the system's set-up). I make two main points. First, there tends to be a correlation between the type of objects of study and how 'Critical' their analysis would be (in increasing order). Second, relatedly, legal scholarship that looks at the EU legal order (object four) as a system, is feminist, and is critical, has been relatively sparse.

The first possible object of study is 'women as EU lawmakers'. This question of representation and participation of women can be asked at two levels: constitution-making

[71] Often under the heading of 'Europeanization', meaning the impact of European integration on MS policies, practices, and politics. J Kantola, 'The Paradoxical Gendered Consequences of the EU Policy on Multiple Discrimination: The Nordic Case' (2014) 18(7) *European Integration Online Papers* 1, 3; see also, for an overview and problematisation of the term, M Forest, 'Europeanization' in G Abels et al (eds), *The Routledge Handbook of Gender and EU Politics* (Routledge, 2021).

[72] See, eg, U Liebert, 'Gendering Europeanization: Patterns and Dynamics' in U Liebert (ed), *Gendering Europeanization* (Presses Interuniversitaires Européennes, 2003); TE Givens and R Evans Case (eds), *Legislating Equality: The Politics of Antidiscrimination Policy in Europe* (Oxford University Press, 2014).

[73] B Havelková and M Möschel, 'Introduction: Anti-Discrimination Law's Fit into Civil Law Jurisdictions and the Factors Influencing It' in B Havelková and M Möschel (eds), *Anti-Discrimination Law in Civil Law Jurisdictions* (Oxford University Press, 2019).

[74] ibid, see the typology of factors.

[75] Other similar typologies of objects of study exist. In 1996, Catherine Hoskyns identified three: 1) substantive content of EU policy; 2) organisation and mobilisation among women; 3) structural development of the EU. C Hoskyns, *Integrating Gender: Women, Law and Politics in the European Union* (Verso, 1996).

and ordinary law-making.[76] As for the former, it is a current topic – Ruth Rubio-Marin has observed a more general 'participation turn' within feminist comparative constitutional scholarship.[77] The sporadic process of EU Treaty-amendment has meant that this has not been a particular focus in EU legal scholarship. The last constitutional moment – the Constitutional Convention of 2001[78] – has, however, been noted for considerable gender imbalance,[79] as only 17 out of 104 full members were women (16 per cent).[80]

In ordinary law-making, women tend to be better represented at the EU level than they are in the MSs. For example, in the European Parliament, women made up 40 per cent of the Members of the European Parliament (MEPs) after the 2019 elections and 39 per cent since 2024,[81] while the national average is 33 per cent.[82] Moreover, this higher representation is often the result of a conscious effort. Thus, for example, political pressure[83] on including women amongst national Commissioner candidates, and the increased role of the European Parliament in their elections,[84] saw their proportion rise from zero in the 1980s to 40 per cent in both 2019 and 2024.[85] The Court of Justice used to be criticised for its maleness,[86] but even there, women now constitute approximately a third of its members.[87]

While essential to understanding who creates the law and how, the research on women in the EU's decision-making has been – unsurprisingly, given the necessary methodologies – a preserve primarily of social and political scientists.[88] For lawyers, the Court of Justice has been the obvious focus of interest,[89] although a feminist lens

[76] More broadly, it can also be asked, in terms of women's external influence on law-making, whether via lobbying or litigation.

[77] R Rubio-Marín, 'Women and Participatory Constitutionalism' (2020) 18(1) *International Journal of Constitutional Law* 235.

[78] Otherwise innovative and inclusive. C Closa, *The Convention Method and the Transformation of EU Constitutional Politics* (Routledge, 2004) 196.

[79] See also A Scheele, 'Economic and Monetary Union' in G Abels and J Marie Mushaben (eds), *Gendering the European Union New Approaches to Old Democratic Deficits* (Palgrave Macmillan, 2012) 13 and references therein.

[80] Closa (n 78) 196.

[81] European Commission, 'European Elections 2024', available at https://results.elections.europa.eu/en/mep-gender-balance/2024-2029/.

[82] '33.4% of parliamentarians across EU are women' (*Eurostat*, 7 March 2025), available at https://ec.europa.eu/eurostat/web/products-eurostat-news/w/edn-20250307-1.

[83] See, eg, N Vinocur and B Moens, 'Von der Leyen Pressures EU Countries to Swap Women in as Commissioner Picks' (*Politico*, 3 September 2024), available at www.politico.eu/article/von-der-leyens-gender-problem-the-fightback-has-begun/.

[84] M Hartlapp, H Müller and I Tömmel, 'Gender Equality and the European Commission' in Gabriele Abels and others (eds), *The Routledge Handbook of Gender and EU Politics* (Routledge, 2021) 134–35.

[85] European Commission, 'College of Commissioners', available at https://commission.europa.eu/about/organisation/college-commissioners_en.

[86] RD Gill and C Jensen, 'Where are the Women? Legal Traditions and Descriptive Representation on the European Court of Justice' (2020) 8 *Politics, Groups, and Identities* 122; see also, earlier, SJ Kenney, *Gender and Justice: Why Women in the Judiciary Really Matter* (Routledge, 2013).

[87] As listed at 'Presentation of Members' (*Court of Justice of the European Union*), available at https://curia.europa.eu/jcms/jcms/Jo2_7026/en/.

[88] Hartlapp, Müller and Tömmel (n 84) Part II; see also Special Issue on 'Gender Equality, Legal Mobilization, and Feminism in a Multilevel European System' (2013) 28(2) *Canadian Journal of Law and Society / La Revue Canadienne Droit et Société*.

[89] For eg S Rodin and T Perišin, 'Transformation or Reconstitution of Europe: The European Critical Legal Studies Perspective' in S Rodin and T Perišin (eds), *The Transformation or Reconstitutional of Europe* (Hart, 2018).

has been rarer[90] until recently.[91] For feminist legal scholars, the questions of 'gender and judging' – the impact of sex/gender on reasoning and outcomes – is a fruitful avenue of research, whether asking the question substantively (cutting across the following two categories, gender equality *acquis* and gender in other EU substantive law) or institutionally (and thus falling under this first object, or informing the fourth, ie, gender in the EU legal order).[92]

The second object of study is the 'gender equality *acquis*' – what the EU does specifically to women and to the gender order. This scholarship looks at laws and policies which, mostly explicitly, mention women/men or sex/gender: equal pay legislation; anti-discrimination law; pregnancy, maternity, paternity and parenthood protections and rights; gender-based violence, etc. The Gender Equality Strategy 2020–25[93] clusters these into three substantive areas: 1) Being free from violence and stereotypes; 2) Thriving in a gender-equal economy; and 3) Leading equally throughout society.

Much of the existing feminist legal scholarship on the EU has focused on the gender equality *acquis*.[94] Feminist legal scholars have analysed specific legal instruments and doctrines,[95] as well as their conceptual underpinnings.[96] For reasons of space, I cannot introduce or map this literature, but I draw on examples from the debates surrounding the gender equality *acquis* throughout the text.

The third object of study is 'gender in other EU substantive law': looking at how concerns of women and the aim of gender equality are addressed in the EU's non-gender-specific laws and policies, including economic integration, migration, agriculture, climate, environment, health, research, etc. The EU itself specifically commits to 'aim[ing] to eliminate inequalities, and to promote equality, between men and women' 'in all its activities'.[97] The Gender Equality Strategy 2020–25[98] addresses this in its last three heads: 4) Gender mainstreaming and an intersectional perspective in EU policies; 5) Funding actions to make progress in gender equality in the EU; and 6) Addressing gender equality and women's empowerment across the world.

This process of 'gender mainstreaming',[99] as well as the substantive question of the place of women in seemingly 'neutral' laws and policies,[100] have both been the subject of

[90] A few notable exceptions have been J Shaw, 'Gender and the European Court of Justice' in G de Búrca and JHH Weiler (eds), *The European Court of Justice* (Oxford University Press, 2001); Hoskyns (n 75); SJ Kenney, 'Breaking the Silence: Gender Mainstreaming and the Composition of the European Court of Justice' (2002) 10 *Feminist Legal Studies* 257.

[91] J Guth and S Elfving, 'The Court of Justice' in Gabriele Abels and others (eds), *The Routledge Handbook of Gender and EU Politics* (Routledge, 2021).

[92] ibid, Guth and Elfving suggest it as future direction of research.

[93] European Commission, 'A Union of Equality: Gender Equality Strategy 2020-2025' (5 March 2020), available at https://ec.europa.eu/newsroom/just/redirection/document/68222.

[94] The literature is too numerous to cite here, but I refer to many examples throughout.

[95] For eg E Ellis and P Watson, *EU Anti-Discrimination Law* (Oxford University Press, 2012).

[96] For eg E Caracciolo di Torella and A Masselot, *Caring Responsibilities in European Law and Policy: Who Cares?* (Routledge, 2020); or Isailović (n 13).

[97] Consolidated version of the Treaty on the Functioning of the European Union (TFEU) [2012] OJ C326/47, Art 8, originally inserted in 1999 by the Treaty of Amsterdam Amending the Treaty on European Union, The Treaties Establishing the European Communities and Related Acts (TEC) [1997] OJ C 340/1, as Art 3(2) of the TEC.

[98] 'Gender Equality Strategy 2020-2025' (n 93).

[99] For eg J Shaw, 'Mainstreaming Equality and Diversity in the European Union' (2005) 58 *Current Legal Problems* 255; S Mazey, 'Gender Mainstreaming Strategies in the EU: Delivering on an Agenda?' (2002) 10 *Feminist Legal Studies* 227; J Rubery, 'Gender Mainstreaming and Gender Equality in the EU: The Impact of the EU Employment Strategy' (2002) 33 *Industrial Relations Journal* 500–22; C Bretherton, 'Gender Mainstreaming and EU Enlargement: Swimming against the Tide?' (2001) 8 *Journal of European Public Policy* 60.

[100] See chapters in Part IV of Forest (n 71).

feminist EU scholarship. An example of the latter – a substantive legal feminist critique from the early days of the EU but still relevant today[101] – is the observation that the concept of worker, in free movement[102] law, has been tied to economic activity outside of the home and has not included domestic work, a highly feminised job.[103] As new areas of legal regulation emerge, so does the need to include concern for gender equality, such as in the EU's post-crisis Recovery and Resilience Facility,[104] or the 2024 'AI Act'[105] and its provisions to prevent discrimination.[106]

The study of 'gender equality *acquis*' (the previous, second object) and 'gender in other EU substantive law' (this third object on my list) are not entirely distinct. Rather, they are on a spectrum, with areas we would expect to have an important gender dimension, such as employment law, on one end, and those much less obviously gendered, such as monetary policy, on the other (although even monetary policy, as it relates to having requirements on domestic fiscal policy and national budget allocation, can certainly be gendered[107]). Furthermore, topics can move from the area of mainstreaming into specific, direct action. This can be seen with the EU's asylum system, for example, where gender equality was not an explicit prominent aim[108] – although it has always been a subject of gender analysis and feminist critique[109] – until the EU signed up to the Istanbul Convention.[110]

The fourth object, 'gender in the EU legal order', consists of asking the more fundamental questions of whether and how gender relations are affected by the EU's constitutional set-up of multilevel democracy, its political economy, the structure of its institutions, etc. Much of the feminist analyses of the EU as a system have happened outside of legal scholarship, however.[111] Scholars have discussed various aspects of the

[101] See notably the case of *Dano*, which is often seen as the Court of Justice of the European Union (CJEU) reversal of a trend of generosity in finding entitlement of EU internal migrants on the basis of EU citizenship (ie without strong economic activity). The applicant, Elisabeta Dano, was a home-maker single parent (thus 'economically inactive'); her Romanian origin is also worth noting. Case C-333/13 *Elisabeta Dano, Florin Dano v Jobcenter Leipzig* EU:C:2014:2358 [2014] ECR I-2358.

[102] A critical, albeit not feminist, perspective is well put in F de Witte, 'The Liminal European: Subject to the EU Legal Order' (2021) 40 *Yearbook of European Law* 56.

[103] V Pavlou, 'Domestic Work in EU law: The Relevance of EU Employment Law in Challenging Domestic Workers' Vulnerability' (2016) 41 *European Law Review* 379.

[104] European Commission, 'Recovery and Resilience Committee', available at https://commission.europa.eu/business-economy-euro/economic-recovery/recovery-and-resilience-facility_en. For a discussion, see R Guerrina, H MacRae and A Masselot, 'Between a Rock and a Hard Place: The EU's Gender Regime in Times of Crisis' (2023) 99 *Women's Studies International Forum*.

[105] Council Regulation (EU) 2024/1689 of 13 June 2024 laying down harmonised rules on artificial intelligence and amending Regulations (Artificial Intelligence Act) [2024] OJ L2024/1689.

[106] For a discussion, see, eg, L Bosoer, M Cantero Gamito and R Rubio Marin, 'Non-discrimination and the AI Act' in F Pedrini (ed), *Law in the Age of Digitalization* (Arazandi, 2024) .

[107] Scheele (n 79) 271 ff; see also discussion at (n 160).

[108] The European Agenda on Migration 2015 did not mention gender at all. J Freedman, 'Mainstreaming Gender in EU Immigration and Asylum Policy' in H MacRae and E Weiner (eds), *Towards Gendering Institutionalism Equality in Europe* (Rowman & Littlefield International, 2017) 145.

[109] For eg J Bastaki, '"Not Without My Daughter": EU Asylum Law, Gender, and the Separation of Refugee Families' (2019) 38 *Refugee Survey Quarterly* 266; For a general overview, see C Briddick, 'When Does Migration Law Discriminate Against Women?' (2021) 115 *AJIL Unbound* 356.

[110] C Warin, 'Gender in European Union Asylum Law: The Istanbul Convention as a Game Changer?' (2024) 36 *International Journal of Refugee Law* 93.

[111] On the relative lack of legal scholarship in analysing the largely gender-neutral vision of the rule of law in the EU (and its particular relevance for CEE), see S Suteu, 'The Rule of Law Crisis Was Always Gendered: The Anti-Gender Playbook in Europe' (2025) 21 *European Constitutional Law Review* 58.

project of post-nationalism,[112] economic integration,[113] Europeanisation,[114] enlargement,[115] governance,[116] etc. In terms of legal scholarship, many of these could be understood as 'constitutional questions': division of competences between the Union and its MSs, conditionality in enlargement, implementation of directives and enforcement of directly effective law, etc. There is scope for more feminist (critical) legal research on these questions (I touch briefly on competences in section IV).

There tends to be a correlation between the three latter objects of study and how 'C/critical' their analysis would be: feminist discussions of the gender equality *acquis* (object 2) might do without going deeper into ideologies and underlying assumptions; the analysis of other EU substantive law (object 3) would require an ability to look behind seeming gender neutralities; and, finally, feminist theorising of the EU legal order, because of its scope, would likely be 'C/critical'.

What emerges from this overview is that there is a relative gap at an intersection of several areas of scholarship. There is plenty on the EU by legal scholars, of course, even on constitutional issues. Feminist legal scholars, however, have largely examined the EU gender *acquis*, or assessed mainstreaming (objects 2 and 3); much less have the 'legal order' questions been asked (object 4). The increasingly rich feminist constitutionalism literature, as well as feminist public international law, have largely overlooked the EU so far. Beyond legal scholarship, a varied feminist work on the EU exists in social and political science, economics, and even philosophy. But legal scholarship that looks at the legal order as a system, and is feminist, critical, and focuses on the EU, has been relatively rare.[117]

IV. As Feminists, Should We Be For or Against the EU?

Catherine MacKinnon has argued that 'women may receive more recognition of rights from distant than near authorities'.[118] As with other public international law instruments,[119] as long as the international – or, in the case of the EU, supranational – level

[112] For eg R Braidotti, 'Gender and Power in a Post-Nationalist European Union' (2004) 12 *NORA - Nordic Journal of Feminist and Gender Research* 130.

[113] For eg Cavanagh and Elomäki (n 15).

[114] For eg Liebert (n 72); R Süleymanoğlu-Kürüm and F Melis Cin (eds), *Feminist Framing of Europeanisation: Gender Equality Policies in Turkey and the EU* (Palgrave Macmillan, 2021).

[115] For eg C Chiva, 'Enlargement' in G Abels and others (eds), *The Routledge Handbook of Gender and EU Politics* (Routledge, 2021) .

[116] For eg A van der Vleuten, *The Price of Gender Equality. Member States and Governance in the European Union* (Ashgate, 2007).

[117] Ivana Isailović's recent work being the exception.

[118] Discussed for constitutions in C MacKinnon, 'Gender in Constitutions' in M Rosenfeld and A Sajo (eds), *The Oxford Handbook of Comparative Constitutional Law* (Oxford University Press, 2012) 399; and previously for international law in C MacKinnon, *Are Women Human? And Other International Dialogues* (Belknap Press, 2006) 1–14.

[119] For Convention on the Elimination of All Forms of Discrimination Against Women (CEDAW), see, eg, R Rubio Marin and ML Morgan, 'Constitutional Domestication of International Gender Norms: Categorizations, Illustrations, and Reflections from the Nearside of the Bridge' in K Knop (ed), *Gender and Human Rights* (Oxford University Press, 2004).

offers more or something different, there will be potential to use it for domestic advocacy to advance women's rights,[120] or, as EU law powerfully allows, even use it directly. In the following, I first explore the EU on its own merit, without accounting for what happens in the MSs.[121] I note that the EU, via its laws, has been good for women, but that it has been limited by its focus on market-making to practice a constrained, 'neo-liberal feminism' at best (section IV.A).[122] Second, I note that the domestic benefit of the EU will vary depending on what had already been achieved in each individual MS, with many winners found especially in CEE (section IV.B). Drawing on the typologies and definitions presented in the previous section, I structure the discussion around four approaches/perspectives in turn: asking the law question, the critique question, and the pragmatic question, and finally foregrounding the CEE experience.

A. Has the EU, via its Laws, Been Good for Women?

Looking at EU law, its addressing of gender inequality has an upward trajectory. The (her)story told is that the EU started with one provision – on equal pay[123] – which was economically motivated, adopted to mitigate the economic comparative disadvantage due to the French textile industry's pre-existing equal pay laws.[124] In mid-1970, the social aims of the provision were recognised by the Court of Justice of the European Union (CJEU),[125] and later became seen as the primary ones.[126] It also acquired the status of a fundamental right,[127] with horizontal application.[128] The EU's gender equality *acquis* has undeniably been expanding and becoming more comprehensive and substantive.[129] For example, EU anti-discrimination law has gone from a formal prohibition of direct discrimination, to incorporate the more substantive doctrines of indirect discrimination, positive action, or shift of the burden of proof.[130] An acknowledgement of the limits of individual judicial enforcement of anti-discrimination provisions has led to legislation focusing on the preventative, structural

[120] For a similar point about the use of CEDAW as leverage, domestically, see Houghton (n 19) 190.
[121] There is a rich debate in the political and social sciences about whether the EU can be seen as an independent gender regime from the MSs or not. See, eg, S Walby, 'The European Union and Gender Equality: Emergent Varieties of Gender Regime' (2004) 11 *Social Politics: International Studies in Gender, State & Society* 4. But here I ask a slightly different question and focus on the law only.
[122] Isailović (n 13).
[123] Treaty establishing the European Economic Community (TEEC) (Rome, 25 March 1957) Art 119.
[124] C Barnard, 'The Economic Objectives of Article 119' in T Hervey and D O'Keeffe (eds), *Sex Equality Law in the European Union* (Wiley, 1996); G More, 'The Principle of Equal Treatment: From Market Unifier to Fundamental Right' in P Craig and G de Burca (eds), *The Evolution of EU Law* (Oxford University Press, 1999).
[125] Case 43/75 *Defrenne II* EU:C:1976:56 [1976] ECR 455.
[126] Case 50/96 *Deutsche Telekom AG v Schröder* ECLI:EU:C:2000:72, [2000] ECR I-00743 para 57.
[127] Case 149/77 *Defrenne III* ECLI:EU:C:1978:130, [1978] ECR 1365 para26. This was confirmed by the insertion of Art 23 into the European Charter. See also C Barnard, 'Gender Equality in the EU: A Balance Sheet' in P Alston (ed), *The EU and Human Rights* (Oxford University Press, 1999).
[128] *Defrenne II* (n 125).
[129] For eg C Barnard and B Hepple, 'Substantive Equality' (2000) 59 *The Cambridge Law Journal* 562
[130] See on this, recently, several chapters in T Giegerich (ed), *The European Union as Protector and Promoter of Equality* (Springer, 2020).

obligations of duty bearers: transparency for equal pay,[131] and giving clearer tasks and greater powers of enforcement to equality bodies.[132] There has also been a realisation that discrimination in the labour market is only one of the causes of gender inequality,[133] and the EU has thus adopted measures focused on equalisation of care and on work-life balance.[134] A similar story can be told around measures on gender-based violence.[135] The EU has also shifted away from the measures protecting motherhood in the early 1990s to a more gender-neutral and inclusive approach to parenthood;[136] which a critical perspective has identified as a move from the 'dominant ideology of motherhood' to a less essentialist approach.[137]

In terms of legal guarantees and rights, it would be hard to argue that there has been regress in the EU. A comprehensive verification of this would be a worthy project, however, as this might not be true of all areas of legal regulation; for example for budgetary rules, especially in relation to the financial crisis.[138] The story of upward trajectory might also not be true for the ideologies underlying the law; this brings us to the question of 'critique'.

The main feminist critique of the EU has been of the fact that the EU 'favours deregulation and market liberalization over market correction and social regulation';[139] or, in more legal terms, there is focus on economic integration, to the detriment of social solidarity, democracy, or individual rights. It has often been noted that EU action has been constrained and/or determined by economic arguments. The EU has been seen as practicing 'neo-liberal feminism',[140] one that benefits otherwise privileged women, while those at the intersections of various disadvantages are left behind. For example, Ivana Isailović has argued that the recent post-financial-crisis development has been marked

[131] Council Directive (EU) 2023/970 to strengthen the application of the principle of equal pay for equal work or work of equal value between men and women through pay transparency and enforcement mechanisms [2023] OJ L132/21.

[132] Council Directive (EU) 2024/1499 on standards for equality bodies in the field of. . .equal treatment between women and men in matters of social security and in the access to and supply of goods and services [2024] OJ L2024/1499; Council Directive (EU) 2024/1500 on standards for equality bodies in the field of equal treatment and equal opportunities between women and men in matters of employment and occupation, and amending Directives 2006/54/EC and 2010/41/EU [2024] OJ L2024/1500.

[133] European Commission, 'The Gender Pay Gap Situation in the EU', available at https://commission.europa.eu/strategy-and-policy/policies/justice-and-fundamental-rights/gender-equality/equal-pay/gender-pay-gap-situation-eu_en.

[134] For eg Council Directive (EU) 2019/1158 on work-life balance for parents and carers and repealing Council Directive 2010/18/EU [2019] OJ L188/79.

[135] M Möschel, 'The European Union's Actions in the Domain of Combating Gender-based Violence' in E Brodeală, I Jelic and S Şuteu (eds), *Violence Against Women under European Human Rights Law From Supranational Standards to National Realities* (Edward Elgar, 2024).

[136] M Matero, 'Breadwinners and Primary Caregivers? A Feminist Critique of Gender Equality in the EU Parental Leave Framework' (2021) 24 *Trinity College Law Review* 69. More generally on care, see Torella and Masselot (n 96).

[137] *cf* (n 59).

[138] *cf* (n 3) and (n 108). For the domestic level, see, eg, A Kosyfologou, 'Austerity, Gender Inequality and Feminist after the Crisis: The Gendered Aspects of the Austerity Regime in Greece: 2010 – 2017' (*Rosa-Luxemburg-Stiftung*), available at https://rosalux.gr/en/publication/the-gendered-aspects-of-the-austerity-regime-in-greece-2010-2017/.

[139] R Cavaghan and M O'Dwyer, 'European Economic Governance in 2017: A Recovery for Whom?' (2018) 56 *Journal of Common Market Studies* 96.

[140] Isailović (n 13); see also A Elomäki, 'The Economic Case for Gender Equality in the European Union: Selling Gender Equality to Decision-Makers and Neoliberalism to Women's Organizations' (2015) 22 *European Journal of Women's Studies* 288.

by a deregulatory shift and an instrumentalisation[141] of the EU's work-life balance measures for market-making, as opposed to the previously regulatory market-correcting project.[142] I noted elsewhere, in relation to the Directive on women on company boards, that the Commission used economic rather than principled arguments of democratic participation or gender equality, which not only does not fit with the measure, but could backfire when the promised economic benefits do not materialise.[143]

Can this criticism be countered by the pragmatic argument of the 'constitutive limitations of the institutional'?[144] The constitutional limits of the EU's competences contained in the Treaties – the principles of conferral (the EU only has competences explicitly given), subsidiarity (the EU should only exercise it if and insofar as the objectives cannot be sufficiently achieved by the MSs) and proportionality (only insofar as necessary)[145] – can explain why the EU is not doing more. For example, due to the limitations[146] of its competence, the EU can legitimately support reconciliation of work and family life in the standard labour market, but it might not have the power to help those outside it – admittedly those more vulnerable and typically intersectionally disadvantaged. It has no ability to directly address inequalities of care happening within the family. Even if insufficiently inclusive and/or prioritarian,[147] however, I believe improving the situation of women within the EU's competence is still worth doing and better than doing nothing at all.

The EU, and consequently EU law, is obviously a flawed project; the result of ongoing transnational compromises, changing political circumstances, national grievances (de Gaulle's vetoes of UK entry), popular moods (eg constitutional referenda or Brexit), etc. It is a bundle of tensions: technocracy vs democracy, economic liberalism vs social solidarity, centralisation vs national diversity, etc.[148] On the one hand, the EU is likely the best way Europe has for managing interdependence; on the other, the specific ways in which this is done can be subject to legitimate criticisms. It is far from an ideal set-up. Importantly, the set-up is fragile, and MSs do not look kindly at what can be perceived as 'competence creep'.[149] There is need for pragmatism and strategy and doing what is possible given the constitutional and political constraints: an all-things-considered attitude. Not only would an 'EU should be different' type of argument require a different paper, but I also do not actually believe it would be a plausible one. I do, however, concede that the EU should be better in remembering that gender equality is now a value and a right and should shine through all law and policy (*cf* the handling of the economic crisis[150]), and that the EU comes with a range of competences now[151] which

[141] Isailović (n 13); similarly, J Shaw has suggested that gender equality has been merely an institutional legitimising strategy for the CJEU, Shaw (n 90) 142; see also M O'Dwyer, 'Expertise in European Economic Governance: A Feminist Analysis' (2019) 15(2) *Journal of Contemporary European Research* 162.

[142] Isailović (n 14).

[143] Havelková (n 6) 205.

[144] Christodoulidis (n 66) 23.

[145] For a discussion, see Havelková (n 6).

[146] Aside from legal constitutional limitations, there are political ones, such as anticipating resistance and backlash.

[147] *cf* (n 16).

[148] Explored in S Weatherill, *Law and Values in the European Union* (Oxford University Press, 2016).

[149] S Weatherill, 'Competence Creep and Competence Control' (2004) 23 *Yearbook of European Law* 1; for assessment of recent developments, see Weatherill (n 148) ch 2.

[150] Weatherill (n 148) 409–15.

[151] TFEU, Arts 19, 153, 157(1) and (3).

should be used boldly, with gender equality being seen as its own project that does not need to hide behind or serve economic purposes.

B. Has the EU Been Better for Women than the MSs?

Here, the post-state-socialist perspective matters. In most CEE countries, EU law has been essential for the development of various domestic protections, aided by the EU's distinctive (stricter) gender equality membership conditionality towards post-state-socialist candidates.[152] Even if, admittedly, the external origin of the measures has caused a range of issues relating to lack of understanding of aims and doctrines and subsequently effectiveness.[153] In many 'old' MSs too, however, EU membership led to the adoption of measures which would not have been proposed domestically. On the continent, this applies to anti-discrimination provisions,[154] in the UK, this was true for employment rights.[155] In some countries, this process even led to new legislation guaranteeing minority rights, which were not even required by the EU, such as LGBTQ+ guarantees in Croatia.[156] On the other hand, viewed from the Nordic countries, the introduction of other protected grounds has been noted as challenging the central place of gender equality in its welfare systems.[157]

V. Concluding Remarks

As I reviewed the existing literature for this contribution in several databases of legal publications,[158] a temporal high point in the feminist (critical) legal scholarship on the EU jumped out, around the start of the millennium.[159] This likely had to do with the innovations contained in the Amsterdam Treaty, including the introduction of gender mainstreaming, the work on new directives, as well as the start of the Constitutional Convention process in 2001. However, this interest has tapered off since. Even the recently founded journal 'European Law Open' (2022), aiming to publish 'slow', considered, 'contextual and critical approaches to EU Law'[160] has, as of April 2025, yet to see a feminist contribution.[161] Part of the reason is likely that scholars mainstreamed their feminist commitment into work closer to the ground, which would often centre

[152] Chiva (n 115) 183.
[153] Havelková (n 36) 255 ff.
[154] For eg M Wrase, 'Anti-Discrimination Law and Legal Culture in Germany' in B Havelková and M Möschel (eds), *Anti-Discrimination Law in Civil Law Jurisdictions* (Oxford University Press, 2019) 136, and references therein.
[155] S Walby, 'Changes in Women's Employment in the United Kingdom' (1999) 4 *New Political Economy* 195.
[156] A Horvat Vuković and A Samobor, 'Constitutional Construction of Reproductive Rights and Family in Croatia and Slovenia' (2025) *International Journal of Constitutional Law*.
[157] Kantola (n 71).
[158] I looked through prominent EU law journals and Westlaw, using search words 'EU law'+'gender' and 'EU law'+'feminism'.
[159] See especially Jo Shaw's work cited throughout.
[160] D Ashiagbor et al, 'Introducing European Law Open' (2022) 1 *European Law Open* 1.
[161] This is not meant as a criticism of the editorial board, but it does illustrate my point.

experiences of women, rather than more general theoretical work; and that women scholars became more visible in EU law scholarship as a whole.[162]

Now, however, a theoretical, critical feminist debate on EU law seems to be experiencing a generational and geographic renewal.[163] This is a welcome development, as much about the EU – especially going beyond the gender equality *acquis* and substantive areas of EU action to the EU legal order as a system – is still yet to be subjected to comprehensive feminist critique.

[162] I thank Jo Shaw for this reflection.

[163] See work by Ivana Isailović or Silvia Suteu cited above, among others.

9

A Critique of EU Data Protection Law

Focusing on Data Instead of Individuals

SUSANNA LINDROOS-HOVINHEIMO

I. Introduction

In this chapter, I engage in a critique of European Union (EU) data protection law. Recent scholarship has recognised that the privacy provided by one of the most effective legal instruments in the EU today, the General Data Protection Regulation (GDPR), is of a very special kind. It is rooted in an understanding of people, foremost, as individuals rather than relational beings.[1] This comes at a cost. When the law focuses so strongly on the protection of individuals, other interests and societal concerns are largely forgotten. Legislators are not primarily to blame for this. The case law of the Court of Justice of the EU (CJEU) shows a lack of collective or communal interest in data protection.

The purpose of this chapter is to consider data protection law in a critical theoretical framework. It will be done by analysing the fundamental tenets of the law as well as the ways in which the CJEU has developed law in practice. I will consider some of the shortcomings of the GDPR and analyse how they manifest in case law. The critique entails many layers, and the chapter is structured accordingly. I will consider individualism first, then data capitalism and political economy, and finally the deeper philosophical question of the nature of data. Towards the end of the chapter, I will consider alternative ways of thinking about data protection.

I argue that the GDPR is not well suited to addressing the hard questions that derive from mass data gathering, shared meaning-making and unidentifiable data. Various power relations shape the gathering and processing of data and the GDPR is not the best instrument to control them. However, if we would concentrate on regulating data, not merely data linked to an individual, we could think differently and solve some of the problems.

[1] S Lindroos-Hovinheimo, *Private Selves: Legal Personhood in European Privacy Protection* (Cambridge University Press, 2021); F Bieker, *The Right to Data Protection: Individual and Structural Dimensions of Data Protection in EU Law* (Springer, 2022); N Richards and W Hartzog, 'Relational Turn for Data Protection?' (2020) *European Data Protection Law Review* 492–97.

II. Critical Framework

This chapter situates itself within the tradition of critical theory by analysing the ideological context in which data protection law operates. Rather than representing a unified theory, here critical theory is understood as a theoretical outlook that dates back to Hegel and Kant. The starting point for this chapter is French critical thinking inspired by the works of Jean-Luc Nancy and Jacques Rancière.[2] This framework was chosen because of its potential to show how data protection law works in societies embedded in liberalist and individualistic ways of thinking. It will help us analyse the questions of individualism, democracy, data capitalism and the nature of data that this chapter focuses on.

Many, though not all, French critical theorists of the late twentieth century either worked within a structuralist paradigm or attempted to distinguish themselves from it.[3] Most also worked with Marxist ideas.[4] Both structuralism and Marxism place importance on social and economic structures, the divisions of power, the real conditions of life or the ideological boundaries within which people spend their lives.[5] Structures and forces, rather than, primarily, individuals, are significant when we attempt to understand societies.

The theoretical framework for the analysis includes a critical stance towards liberalism and individualism. The former is suspicious not because of an inherent problem with liberty, or freedom, but because so often the social and political drive for liberty results in inequality. The latter is suspicious because individuals never exist in society as individuals, and if we base a political ideology on the idea that they do, we run the risk of forgetting the ways in which individuals are intertwined and the value of them being so.

Of the philosophers mentioned, Nancy comes closest to indicating an interest in individuals. However, his theory, too, emphasises the general nature of the singular. Developing a complex theory, which includes an astonishingly simple core, he argues that being is always being-with.[6] No being in the world is a completely independent being. There is no individual, only singular plural people, who are entwined in ontological, psychological, social and political ways.[7] Thus, the task of political philosophy is to question the manner in which our relations are defined and shaped in society.

[2] See J-L Nancy, *The Inoperative Community* (University of Minnesota Press, 1991); J-L Nancy, *Being Singular Plural* (Stanford University Press, 2000); J Rancière, 'The Community of Equals' in J Rancière, *On the Shores of Politics* (Verso, 1995); J Rancière, *Disagreement: Politics and Philosophy* (University of Minnesota Press, 1999); J Rancière, *Hatred of Democracy* (Verso, 2009); J Rancière, *Dissensus – On Politics and Aesthetics* (Continuum, 2010).

[3] See, eg, J-P Deranty, D Petherbridge, J Rundell, 'Themes and Dialogues in Contemporary French Critical Theory' in J-P Deranty, D Petherbridge, J Rundell, Robert Sinnerbrink (eds), *Recognition, Work, Politics: New Directions in French Critical Theory* (Brill, 2007) 1–26.

[4] This position can be called post-Marxism, where the focus is not so much on class struggle, as in traditional Marxism, but rather on various other societal inequalities. Post-Marxist scholarship also tends to be guided by a general suspicion of both capitalism and liberalism. See, eg, S Sim, *The Edinburgh Companion to Critical Theory* (Edinburgh University Press, 2016) 47–50.

[5] For a recent discussion on the role of ideas versus economic forces in history, see P Anderson, 'Idées-forces' (2025) *New Left Review* 151.

[6] J-L Nancy, *Being Singular Plural* (Stanford University Pres, 2000) 7, 35, 66.

[7] See also E Hobsbawm, *How to Change the World: Reflections on Marx and Marxism* (Yale University Press, 2011) 130–32. He argues that it is an important feature for Marx's theory as well that man is a social animal.

Nancy and Rancière emphasise equality. The entire body of Rancière's work is centred on a profound commitment to the idea of radical equality.[8] People are equal in their mental capacities, ethical worth and political importance, even though this is seldom evident in society. Rancière is not primarily interested in investigating equality from the perspective of individual participants or social outcasts. Rather, his analyses focus on the ways societies are organised and the kinds of ideological underpinnings that direct politics. For him, politics essentially represents the struggle of those excluded or silenced to become visible and heard. It is a struggle against unequal structures, which he calls the distribution of the sensible. When politics happens, the distribution of the sensible changes. In such actions and instances the excluded become equals to those who hold power and are seen and heard. When such disruption is achieved, the sensible is redistributed, which means that new subjects can be seen and heard in novel ways.[9]

For Nancy, equality is an undercurrent of his analysis of community, although he approaches it more hesitantly than Rancière. Nancy focuses on the social rather than the political, and, for him, the task of philosophy is to enquire about the conditions for community and 'being-with'. Nancy emphasises the need for more profound analysis of our shared lives and co-existence in society. His ontology of being-with can be translated into ethics, as he advocates respect for the ways we always share our being. Such respect also entails a respect for difference.[10]

Democracy is an important theme in the writings of both thinkers, and they consider it valuable in many ways.[11] First, it may be the only political system that can enable the kind of radical equality that Rancière posits. Second, it is a way of being together in community where differences are respected and the singular-plural nature of people is not repressed under some common super value or unifying thought.

Neither Nancy nor Rancière, the most important reference points for the critique presented here, are legal theorists.[12] This is important. When drawing on their ideas, it is necessary to acknowledge their lack of interest in the law. This gap must be filled with something else, which is a challenging task. Hence, these theories do not offer a ready-made model that could be applied to a legal phenomenon or a specific legal problem.[13]

[8] Rancière, *Dissensus* (n 2) 213.

[9] Rancière, *Hatred of Democracy* (n 2) 117; J Ranciere et al, 'Jacques Rancière – Literature, Politics, Aesthetics – Approaches to Democratic Disagreement' (2000) 2 *SubStance* 3–24; J Rancière and D Panagia, 'Dissenting Words – A Conversation with Jacques Rancière' (2000) 2 *Diacritics* 30, 113–26.

[10] See, eg, A Norris, 'Jean-Luc Nancy and the Myth of the Common' (2000) 7 *Constellations* 272–95.

[11] However, some readers, like J Habermas, have been critical of French thinkers for failing to have coherent political positions. For a discussion, see T May, 'Jacques Rancière and the Ethics of Equality' (2007) 36 *SubStance* 20–36. On the other hand, for the purposes of this chapter, it is important to note the critique directed at Jürgen Habermas's theory for not resisting the de-democratisation of the economy through the rise of economic constitutionalism from the 1980s onwards. See, eg, B Roth, 'The Welfare State Between Juridification and Commodification: How the Frankfurt School Gave Up on Economic Democracy' (2023) 2 *European Law Open* 386–404.

[12] Nor are they perhaps theorists in any other sense of the term. The writings of both constitute engagements with various themes such as politics and society, but they do not form any coherent theories or systematic thought. On this, see, eg, J-L Nancy, 'Politics and Beyond: An Interview with Jean-Luc Nancy' (2025) 43 *Diacritics* 90–108; I Devisch, 'Thinking Nancy's "Political Philosophy"' in S Dejanovic (ed), *Nancy and the Political* (Edinburgh University Press, 2015) 116–36; J Rancière, L Jeanpierre, D Zabunyan, *The Method of Equality: Interviews with Laurent Jeanpierre and Dork Zabunyan* (Polity Press, 2016) 1–92.

[13] See also E Christodoulidis, 'Critical Theory and the Law: Reflections on Origins, Trajectories and Conjunctures' in E Christodoulidis, R Dukes, and M Goldoni (eds), *Research Handbook on Critical Legal Theory* (Elgar, 2019) 2–26.

Consequently, they can get us only so far. We can draw on them for the first steps, but after that, we are on our own.

I argue that data protection law is a field strongly influenced by individualism and liberalism. Theoretically, these notions contain two major flaws. Individualism tends to be reductionist in the sense that it forgets the societal, economic and political context of the individual. This can result in misleading conclusions at best or an inability to recognise the structural flaws of society at worst. Combined with liberalism, it tends to over-emphasise the freedom and autonomy of people, which can result in a disregard for equality.

It is perhaps unsurprising that data protection in EU law is a project with individualism at its heart. This is true for many rights. When this chapter criticises data protection rights, it hence aligns itself with many other critiques of rights, for example the works of Susan Marks and Samuel Moyn, who also draw inspiration from Marxist traditions.[14] Their critique, too, is essentially that rights are founded on liberalism and individualism. For instance, Moyn argues that

> The tragedy of human rights is that they have occupied the global imagination but have so far contributed little of note, merely nipping at the heels of the neoliberal giant whose path goes unaltered and unresisted. And the critical reason that human rights have been a powerless companion of market fundamentalism is that they simply have nothing to say about material inequality.[15]

When tracing the development of human rights over time, Moyn demonstrates, in a fascinating way, that rights conform to the political economy of the age, not defining but reflecting it. He analyses the ways pluralism and tolerance have increased but equality has not. The manner in which human rights have been intertwined with market fundamentalism has, in fact, paved the way for more inequality.

The EU has been keen to incorporate rights into its legal system. The EU Charter of Fundamental Rights is the instrument that defines which rights are to be respected in the Union. Some rights are also enshrined in one way or another in the Treaties of the Union. Personal data protection enjoys double protection in this regard because it appears in both. Indeed, it is undoubtedly one of the strongest rights in the EU today. One only need glance at the 99 articles of the GDPR, where detailed rules on data protection are defined, to note that the right is comprehensively regulated.[16] In addition, the CJEU has developed practice where data protection is strongly enforced.

This chapter explores the ways data protection is individualistic. The main focus is the effects of this logic, which undergirds the law. Hence, the purpose is not to investigate potential failures in data protection law. Rather, the aim is to scrutinise how it

[14] S Marks, 'Four Human Rights Myths' in D Kinley, W Sadurski and K Walton (eds), *Human Rights: Old Problems New Possibilities* (Edward Elgar Publishing, 2013); Rancière, *Dissensus* (n 2); S Moyn, *Not Enough: Human Rights in an Unequal World* (Harvard University Press, Belknap Press, 2018). See also Z Manfredi, 'An Unlikely Resonance? Subjects of Human Rights and Subjects of Human Capital Reconsidered' in B Golder and D McLoughlin (eds), *The Politics of Legality in the Neoliberal Age* (Routledge, 2017); M Lopez Lerma, J Etxabe (eds), *Rancière and Law* (Routledge, 2017).

[15] Moyn (n 14) 216.

[16] Regulation (EU) 2016/679 of the European Parliament and of the Council on the protection of natural persons with regard to the processing of personal data and on the free movement of such data, and repealing Directive 95/46/EC (General Data Protection Regulation) [2016] OJ L119/1.

works and what it produces in its everyday operation.[17] Hence, the chapter attempts to cast a critical gaze on the ideological underpinnings of data protection law. This strand of critical legal research aims to criticise and contest the background rules of law and work to alter them in order to envisage a more just and egalitarian world.[18]

III. How Did It Come to This?

The GDPR has been the target of much criticism. Some claim it is ineffective;[19] some argue that it is doing the wrong thing;[20] and some complain that it is too vague and broad in its application.[21] I argue, however, that even though data protection law is rather effective and often functions as intended, it is not enough. And in some respects, it is the wrong instrument to use in regulating and controlling contemporary digital societies.

The GDPR is an extremely ambitious piece of legislation that came at an opportune moment. The world – or at least Europe – was experiencing a perceived lack of privacy and personal security in technological settings due to the Snowden revelations and the subsequent Cambridge Analytica scandal. EU legislators then responded to the political pressure to act. Hence, the GDPR legislation process occurred in the context of rapidly developing technology combined with suitable political and geopolitical conditions. Many people, even some companies, were ready for more stringent data protection rules.

Nevertheless, the GDPR represents a compromise reached after long negotiations between the different legislators. Moreover, the importance of various lobbying endeavours during the legislative process should not be forgotten. Multiple conflicting interests were at stake, some aiming for strong fundamental rights protection, others seeking regulation that would enable innovation in a data-driven internal market. This is one reason for the overall complexity of the GDPR. As with most laws, it represents a compromise. The text leaves room for interpretation due to an abundance of technicalities, vague definitions and occasional inconsistencies. For this reason, the role of the CJEU has become important. It is the most significant institution – in addition to the national data protection authorities – that shapes the content of the law.

The CJEU had already been active in enforcing personal data rights before the GDPR was passed. Thus, in this regard, the Court can be seen as an important actor influencing the legislation.[22] Moreover, the Court has continued to take a strong stance on data

[17] See also R Fine, 'Marxism and the Social Theory of Law' in R Banakar and M Travers (eds), *Introduction to Law and Social Theory* (Hart Publishing, 2002) 101–17.

[18] DM Davis and K Klare, 'Critical Legal Realism in a Nutshell' in E Christodoulidis, R Dukes, and M Goldoni, *Research Handbook on Critical Legal Theory* (Elgar, 2019) 27–43.

[19] See, eg, A Bradford, *Digital Empires: The Global Battle to Regulate Technology* (Oxford University Press, 2023).

[20] See, eg, J Cohen, *Between Truth and Power: The Legal Constructions of Informational Capitalism* (Oxford University Press, 2019).

[21] See, eg, N Purtova, 'The Law of Everything. Broad Concept of Personal Data and Future of EU Data Protection Law' (2018) 10 *Law, Innovation and Technology* 40–81.

[22] Indeed, one of the most privacy-friendly decisions of the Court, the *Google Spain* ruling (Case C-131/12 *Google Spain* ECLI:EU:C:2014:317) was delivered before the GDPR came into force. In this ruling, the Court argued that citizens enjoyed the right to be forgotten even though the Data Protection Directive applicable at the time did not recognise such a right. Unsurprisingly, the right to be forgotten made its way into the text of the GDPR.

protection ever since. Whether it has overstepped the limits of its discretion remains, however, an open question. In some issues, the text of the Regulation is rather clear and the Court's leeway narrow. In such situations, one can reasonably argue that the Court could not have reached a different conclusion. Nonetheless, it should be noted that the method and boundaries of interpretation have been created by the very same Court.[23] However, in such rulings, which often concern technical definitions, the result of the interpretation has been logical, taking into account the context of the case. In other cases, the Court has enjoyed much more room to manoeuvre. These cases include, at least, the rulings in *Breyer*, *Nowak*, *Wirtschaftsakademie*, *Schufa Holding*, *Norra Stockholm bygg* and *Endemol Shine*.[24] In many of these rulings, the Court has openly admitted that it favours an interpretation that best serves the privacy rights of individuals. It engages in little balancing of data protection with other rights and values, nor does it discuss the practical consequences of its interpretations.

In data protection law, there are many issues open to interpretation. For instance, the meaning and implication of the data protection principles in Article 5 of the GDPR, which are a core issue, have been left to the Court to clarify. The same is true for the important relationship between Article 6, which lists the lawful conditions for data processing, and Article 9, which regulates the processing of special categories of data, such as data concerning health.[25] Another example is the meaning and scope of the purpose limitation principle, according to which data can only be processed for a specific purpose and not reused freely.[26] Here, too, the text is ambiguous and requires interpretation, ultimately by the CJEU. In addition, while the overall amount of discretion left to the Member States to legislate on different data protection issues varies, in some instances, it is rather extensive.

In data protection case law, the CJEU has commonly sought to solve interpretation problems by referring to the purpose of the Regulation.[27] This is normal in EU law and should come as no surprise. What is surprising, however, is that while the legislators decided that the Regulation serves *two purposes*, to protect the fundamental right to personal data and to enable the free flow of data, the CJEU only tends to recognise one objective, the former.[28] Hence, practical interpretation issues are solved by adhering to

[23] See S Lindroos-Hovinheimo, 'Who Controls our Data? The Legal Reasoning of the European Court of Justice in Wirtschaftsakademie Schleswig-Holstein and Tietosuojavaltuutettu v Jehovan todistajat' (2019) *Information & Communications Technology Law* 28.

[24] Case C-582/14 *Breyer* ECLI:EU:C:2016:779; Case C-434/16 *Nowak* ECLI:EU:C:2017:994; Case C-210/16 *Wirtschaftsakademie* ECLI:EU:C:2018:388; C-634/21 *Schufa Holding* ECLI:EU:C:2023:957; Joined Cases C-26/22 and C-64/22 *Schufa Holding* ECLI:EU:C:2023:958; Case C-268/21 *Norra Stockholm Bygg* ECLI:EU:C:2023:145; Case C-740/22 *Endemol Shine Finland* ECLI:EU:C:2024:216.

[25] See Case C-667/21 *Krankenversicherung Nordrhein* ECLI:EU:C:2023:1022.

[26] See, eg, Case C-439/19 *Latvijas Republikas Saeima (penalty points)* ECLI:EU:C:2021:504.

[27] Case C-579/21 *Pankki S* ECLI: EU:C:2023:501, para 38 and C-487/21 *Österreichische Datenschutzbehörde and CRIF* ECLI: EU:C:2023:369, para 19 and the case law cited. The Court states in these paragraphs that the interpretation of a provision of EU law requires that account be taken not only of its wording, but also of its context and the objectives and purpose pursued by the act of which it forms part.

[28] For recent examples, see, eg, Case C-634/21 *Schufa Holding* ECLI:EU:C:2023:957; Case C-203/22 *Dun & Bradstreet Austria* ECLI:EU:C:2025:117. In the latter, para 51, the Court states that 'As regards, lastly, the purposes of the GDPR, it should be recalled that the objective of that regulation consists, inter alia, in ensuring a high level of protection of the fundamental rights and freedoms of natural persons, in particular their right to the protection of personal data, enshrined in Article 16 TFEU and guaranteed as a fundamental right in Article 8 of the Charter, which supplements the right to private life guaranteed in Article 7 thereof (see, to

the principle of individuals' rights to privacy and personal data protection. The teleological interpretation that the Court utilises is hence rather problematic as it includes the choice of one purpose above another, that choice being based on nothing except the Court's own argumentation. This raises difficult questions about the ideology and value base of data protection law.

IV. Data Protection or Democracy?

The protection of individuals' data is not the only value in the world, nor is it perhaps a right more important than others. As the CJEU often states, this right must be balanced with others. This is, however, a principle that the Court expresses but does not always follow. For instance, we can consider two communal values that have been sidelined in the name of the individual-centred data protection rights: access to documents and the publicity of trials. Both are important for democracy, the former being a prerequisite for transparency and accountability of government, the second an element of the democratic legitimacy of the legal system.

In the case of access to documents, the legal landscape at the EU level is structurally problematic because only personal data is protected in primary law, including the Charter, in a way that obliges the Union and the Member States to protect the right. Access to documents, which is ultimately a prerequisite for transparency of government, does not enjoy the same status. It is protected, but only as far as Union institutions are concerned.[29] Member States naturally have their own legislation on access to documents, which is acknowledged in Article 86 of the GDPR.[30] However, when practical problems of balancing the right to personal data protection with the more common good of public access to documents, EU law leans strongly towards data protection, it being explicitly protected in primary law.[31] Hence, individualistic concerns override the need for transparency in democratic government.[32]

Another more recent development concerns the right to public trials, which is enshrined in Article 47 of the Charter and applies to the Union and Member States

that effect, judgment of 4 October 2024, Schrems (Communication of data to the general public), C-446/21, EU:C:2024:834, paragraph 45 and the case law cited).' Even though 'inter alia' appears in this paragraph, the Court does not consider any other purpose of the GDPR. For a recent discussion, see also H Kranenborg, 'About Profiles, Profiling, Data Availability and AI' (2025) *European Data Protection Law Review* 11, 9–18.

[29] Article 42 Charter of Fundamental Rights of the European Union [2012] OJ C326/391.

[30] Article 86 GDPR stipulates that personal data in official documents held by a public authority or a public body or a private body for the performance of a task performed in the public interest may be disclosed by the authority or body in accordance with Union or Member State law to which the public authority or body is subject in order to reconcile public access to official documents with the right to the protection of personal data pursuant to this Regulation.

[31] See, eg, G Meo, 'Har offentlighetsprincipen blivit en gemensam konstitutionell tradition? En jämförelse mellan Sverige, England och Italien' (2020) *Europarättslig tidskrift* 391–409; D Wyatt, 'The Anaemic Existence of the Overriding Public Interest in Disclosure in the EU's Access to Documents Regime' (2020) 21 *German Law Journal* 686–702; P Leino, 'Just a Little Sunshine in the Rain: The 2010 Case-Law of the European Court of Justice on Access to Documents' (2011) 48 *CML Rev* 1215–2011.

[32] See Case C-439/19 *Latvijas Republikas Saeima (Penalty points)* ECLI:EU:C:2021:504; Joined Cases C-37/20 and C-601/20 *Luxembourg Business Registers* ECLI:EU:C:2022:912; Case C-184/20 *Vyriausioji tarnybinės etikos komisija* ECLI:EU:C:2022:601.

alike.[33] There is scant case law on conflicts between data protection and public trials, but the little there is proves disconcerting. For instance, in the *Endemol Shine* case, the CJEU discussed the matter of providing information from a court register primarily as a matter of public access to documents, sidestepping the issue of public trials.

The case concerned a company's request to a court of first instance for information on any pending and concluded criminal convictions of a private individual.[34] Even though public access to documents is protected in Article 86 of the GDPR, the CJEU did not engage in an analysis of the Article. It largely failed to balance the right to data protection with public access to documents, nor did it take into consideration the trial setting of the case. The Court simply repeated its earlier stance, according to which the fundamental rights to respect for private life and to the protection of personal data must be considered in relation to their function in society and be weighed against other fundamental rights. Nonetheless, it performed no such weighing. The Court argued that in the light of the sensitivity of data relating to criminal convictions, it must be held that privacy rights prevail over the public's interest in access to documents.[35] Hence, the CJEU concluded that, in this case, data protection was more important than any other rights or values.

It is interesting that in the *Endemol Shine* case, the Court neglected to consider Article 47 of the Charter or the principle of public trials. In this regard, its interpretation is restrictive and narrow. The Court understood the case to concern personal data protection, without considering the context. In judicial proceedings, it is of course necessary to process large amounts of personal data. If trials are to be public, it is necessary that some data is made publicly available, and this usually occurs through access to court documents. By restricting that access, the Court promoted an understanding of data protection that may limit transparency and therefore also the legitimacy of trials. Hence, the judgment shows that transparency, openness and democratic oversight are not as important as individuals' data protection.

These rulings leave us with an uncomfortable feeling that data protection has gone awry or simply too far in protecting individuals' rights. Privacy has traditionally been seen as a right to personal freedom and autonomy, and as such a prerequisite for many social values.[36] Among these, the freedom to form one's opinion, have a say in government, and participate in political movements are freedoms required by a functioning democracy. Privacy rights are thus intended to be an instrument that protects democracy. Without them, the political system would be undemocratic, totalitarian at worst. The over-individualistic manner in which data protection law works today causes us to forget these other values that exist to safeguard democracy.[37] Understanding privacy

[33] According to Art 47(2), everyone is entitled to a fair and public hearing within a reasonable time by an independent and impartial tribunal previously established by law. Everyone shall have the possibility of being advised, defended and represented.

[34] On the ways in which data protection has begun to affect (national) procedural law, see Case C-245/20 *Autoriteit Persoonsgegevens* ECLI:EU:C:2022:216; Case C-268/21 *Norra Stockholm Bygg* ECLI:EU:C:2023:145. See also S Lindroos-Hovinheimo, 'The CJEU Delivers Controversial Ruling on Data Protection in Civil Procedure: Norra Stockholm Bygg' (2023) *European Data Protection Law Review* 9, 257–63.

[35] Case C-740/22 *Endemol Shine Finland* ECLI:EU:C:2024:216.

[36] See, eg, AF Westin, *Privacy and Freedom* (Atheneum Publishers, 1967); R Gavison, 'Privacy and the Limits of Law' (1980) 89 *The Yale Law Journal* 421–71.

[37] One more example of overly individualistic rulings would be those in which the CJEU maintains that data protection rules apply also in national parliaments. See, eg, Case C-272/19 *Land Hessen* ECLI:EU:C:2020:535; Case C-33/22 *Österreichische Datenschutzbehörde* ECLI:EU:C:2024:46.

simply as an individual right is an overly narrow interpretation that loses much of what is valuable in privacy.

In sum, a trend is emerging in case law. Communal values such as the transparency of government or publicity of trials are under-emphasised by the CJEU whenever the case concerns data protection. It sometimes appears that in data protection law it is unnecessary to take other rights and interests as seriously as data protection rights. One reason for this is the Court's interpretation of data protection almost solely as a means to protect individuals' personal data.

To analyse the operational logic of data protection law within Nancy's framework, we will recognise that the law emphasises the singular instead of the singular-plural. Contrary to Nancy's ideas, the individual rather than the shared being is the highest value of the law. In addition, democracy and community seem less valuable than the protection of individuals' data.

V. Dialectics of Individualism

In addition to the tendency to view societal concerns as secondary to data protection, the individualism inherent in the law also leads to other practical problems that data protection lawyers struggle to solve. For instance, where data is not tied to individuals, it is not protected. Such is the case when large amounts of data are processed if no individual can be identified. This is a result of the case law on the definition of personal data.[38] On the other hand, individualism also results in impasses when some data represents personal data for many people. In these situations, it is often extremely difficult to choose whose data should matter, whose consent is valid and who has rights to the data.[39] Such challenging instances of data protection law are a consequence of an individualistic outlook.

Unfortunately, they are not solved by delving into the theoretical infrastructure of the law because more individualism is usually found there. I argue that the individualism inherent in data protection law has a twofold nature that may be understood in dialectical terms. On the one hand, the practical application of the law in a way that prioritises individuals is so strong that it feeds into the understanding of data protection law as a whole, including the underlying purpose and foundational values of the whole area of law. Hence, there is a direct line of influence from case-by-case teleology to the more fundamental architecture of data protection law. The surface level of the law affects its underlying ideological foundation.[40]

On the other hand, the solutions to difficult cases are often sought in the foundational ideology and values of the law. When data protection law is dictated by liberalist and individualistic ideas about rights, then the whole idea of data protection law is understood in a very specific setting.[41] It is permeated by individualism. This fundamental

[38] The landmark ruling is Case C-582/14 *Breyer* ECLI:EU:C:2016:779.

[39] Case C-434/16 *Nowak* ECLI:EU:C:2017:994.

[40] See also K Tuori, *Critical Legal Positivism* (Routledge, 2017).

[41] Lindroos-Hovinheimo (n 1); K Nolan, *The Individual in EU Data Protection Law* (The London School of Economics and Political Science, 2023, forthcoming, manuscript with author); R Griffin, 'Rethinking Rights in Social Media Governance: Human Rights, Ideology and Inequality' (2023) 2 *European Law Open* 30–56.

ideology of the law, then, affects the surface level – the way cases are decided. Therefore, there is a direct line of influence also from the ideological foundation of the law to decisions in particular cases.

The dialectical movement means that individualism at the level of case law informs the fundamental ideology underlying the law, and vice versa. Such a circle is extremely compelling and difficult to break. There seems to be nothing wrong with individualism because it is supported by both the surface level instances of the law and the values upon which the law is based. What must be seen, though, is that this circular movement is a result of choices made by the Court and occasionally by supervising authorities and legal scholars. Choices can be remade.

One problem with the prevailing individualism of data protection law is that it is a way of thinking that obscures others. By understanding the law in a certain way, we are prevented from seeing it in an alternative light. Community and shared being are not recognised. Because of the specific subject matter of data protection legislation, the individualism inherent in the law can also affect the ways we understand society more generally. The law's individualistic view of people and their digital lives highlights the fact that only individual persons' data is valuable and in need of protection. This frames our understanding of digital society. If an individual's rights are not infringed, the situation often appears unproblematic from the perspective of EU law.

Alternative ways of conceptualising the law can be derived from Nancy, according to whom we must attend to the ways our social lives are defined and how we as people are defined in society. Data protection law functions as an index of our individualised existence. We are not primarily understood as social, relational beings. We need to ask what sort of digital society we live in when everyone is first and foremost an individual rather than a being in relation with others. What social effects does such an understanding exert?

It is relevant in this regard to consider the meaning of social existence, not only its ontology. In Nancy's theory, there is no meaning, or no sense, in the singular. We make meaning or, even, we are meaning, together. In a digital society, where data is a key commodity, this is even more self-evident than before. Nevertheless, the law is not attuned to the fact that meaning is shared. By regulating data within such a strong individualistic framework, the GDPR is ill-suited to addressing the hard questions that come from mass data-gathering, shared meaning-making and unidentifiable data. Nonetheless, such data is extremely important in a digital society – and digital capitalism – and the gathering and processing of it are shaped by various power relations.

Thus far, I have painted a critical picture of data protection law, arguing that its individualistic undercurrent leads to various problems. The counter argument would be to suggest that data protection is nevertheless extremely important, and I do not refute this. There is value in privacy, and there is value in personal data protection, but they are not the only values. Nor is individualism the only framing within which privacy and personal data protection are valuable.

Even though data protection is important for many reasons, I will only engage with one argument for it – the claim that the GDPR is a vital tool for combatting the worst side effects of contemporary digital capitalism. This is an interesting context for analysis because here the GDPR seems at first glance to be used contrary to its main aim, that is, contrary to the dominant individualistic view of its purpose.

VI. Data Protection and Digital Capitalism

A reason for protecting personal data is to the fight against the worst forms of economic exploitation practised by tech companies. In many ways, the EU has been a pioneer in this fight. However, it may be that the fundamentally individualistic logic of data protection law reduces its effectiveness as an instrument for resisting the various kinds of data exploitation predominant today.[42]

Let us take a step back and consider Lawrence Lessig's *Code*, where the Internet was still, at least partially, an anonymous place. People could participate in conversations and exchange information without the possibility of tracking their identity or location. Lessig foresaw that the inability to regulate the original Internet would pass. In fact, he called for more regulation of cyberspace in order to ameliorate some of the more troubling aspects of libertarian life on the web. He argued that it might be beneficial, at least in some instances, if the credentials of users and the nature of data were known. That knowledge could be layered onto the Internet without destroying its positive functionalities.[43] What he did not completely foresee, perhaps, was who would perform the layering. As later developments have shown, the identities of users are collected and stored not only by governments, but also – and in the West maybe to a larger degree – by big tech companies. The latter's business model is founded on data-gathering. The processing of this data – the personal data of internet users – is what the EU regulates.

As Henri Lefebvre notes, today information is a privileged commodity – it occupies a special place in our societies. Interestingly, it is, according to him, ubiquitous but also clearly situated. It is everywhere but also prominently in the hands of the few. Information has always existed, but it has now become an exchangeable product.[44] Lefebvre poses an acute question that pertains to the special status of data in today's capitalism:

> Is not information most deserving of the title of supreme commodity, commodity of commodities? Produced, it has material (technological) conditions; it requires investment and organized labour. It has a production cost. Once it is produced, it is bought and sold. But it is what makes possible all other exchanges: all the flows in which daily life is immersed.[45]

Perhaps, similar to Lessig, Lefebvre recognises a utopian undercurrent at the beginning of the technological age. The myth of freedom realised by information technology was an early driving force in the development of the Internet, as well as in the technological advances towards automation in the hope of ending work.[46] He asks, nevertheless, whether and how information society will advance towards freedom for all and the emancipation of workers. In Lefebvre's view, information technology has not begun a new era; it is perfecting the old: global capitalism.[47]

[42] We also must not forget that the GDPR itself is an instrument that is supposed to foster the economic aims of the union. More trust in digital markets means more money, and this trust is at least partly achieved by foreseeable and effective fundamental rights protection that works similarly in all the Member States.

[43] L Lessig, *Code And Other Laws of Cyberspace Version 2.0* (Basic Books, 2006) 33–37.

[44] H Lefebvre, *Critique of Everyday Life Volume 3 From Modernity to Modernism* (Verso, 2008) 55, 144–45.

[45] ibid 56.

[46] ibid 91. See also M Maroni, *The Right to Access The Internet: A Critical Analysis of The Constitutionalisation of The Internet* (University of Helsinki, 2022).

[47] Lefebvre (n 44) 145.

Later research has analysed the ways big tech companies profit from surveilling us online.[48] These companies are mostly interested in data for marketing purposes. Even though the economic structure of the business is complicated, its underlying idea is not. The more data companies possess, the better they can offer goods and services to those who are likely to buy them.[49] The GDPR was not drafted in a way that would prevent this.[50] For instance, it allows for two lawful grounds for processing people's data, consent and contract, which introduce the economic logic of commerce into data-gathering from the start.[51] Both are lawful, both are utilised.

When large companies collect infinite amounts of data through the various services that we use, they can draw extremely accurate pictures of us and influence our understanding of ourselves and the world around us. What is fascinating, though, is that even when companies know much less about us as individuals, they are often able to exploit us in many ways.[52] The profiling that is performed is not usually dependent on individual preferences. Rather, it groups us into segments and types. The capitalist logic is not necessarily individualistic. Hence, the primary problem with digital capitalism is not that an individual's data is processed but that data is processed and people are exploited.

It is here that the economic critique of the GDPR should be focused: the law misses opportunities to rein in digital capitalism if it only focuses on the protection of individuals' data. This is both a societal and an economic issue because they are intertwined, especially when it comes to equality.

Because so much data protection energy in the EU has focused on individuals' privacy concerns, the law has been unable to fully respond to the challenges posed by the economic power achieved by big tech. Indeed, the individualism of data protection law is one manifestation of the political economy of digital society.

In order to resist the capitalism of the Internet, it is neither necessary nor always helpful to focus the legal gaze solely on the rights of individuals. This is not to claim that the current EU model for regulating life online has exerted no effect on data capitalism. As we shall see below, in the absence of other instruments, the data protection regime has occasionally been used for this purpose as well. Being open to interpretation, the law can be operationalised in many ways.

In this regard, the *Meta Platforms* ruling from 2023 is an interesting example.[53] Originally, it was a competition law case that came to the CJEU in the form of a

[48] S Zuboff, *The Age of Surveillance Capitalism: The Fight for a Human Future at the New Frontier of Power* (Profile Books, 2019).

[49] See also the recent discussion in *New Left Review*: TE Ström, 'Capital and Cybernetics' (2022) *New Left Review*; E Morozov, 'Critique of Techno-Feudal Reason' (2022) *New Left Review*; C Durand, 'Scouting Capital's Frontiers' (2022) *New Left Review*; R Lucas, 'The Surveillance Business' (2020) *New Left Review*.

[50] See also A Jr Golia, 'Taxing Data as an Instrument of Economic Digital Constitutionalism: Elements for a Normative Agenda' (2024) 3 *European Law Open* 865–89. He argues at 888 that 'data taxation could be a crucial element to re-assert the centrality of *political* institutions in global governance, especially in the light of the historically genetic link between taxation, democracy, (popular) sovereignty, and modern constitutionalism'.

[51] These are the most important legal bases for processing data that private actors such as social media companies can use. For public actors, such as governments, there are other options in Art 6 GDPR.

[52] See, eg, J Cohen, *Between Truth and Power: The Legal Constructions of Informational Capitalism* (Oxford University Press, 2019); NP Suzor, *Lawless: The Secret Rules That Govern our Digital Lives* (Cambridge University Press, 2019); N Srnicek, *Platform Capitalism* (Polity Press, 2017); SM West, 'Data Capitalism: Redefining the Logics of Surveillance and Privacy' (2019) *Business & Society* 58.

[53] Case C252/21 *Meta Platforms and Others* ECLI:EU:C:2023:537.

preliminary reference request from Germany. The Court, sitting in Grand Chamber, was tasked with considering the relevance of data protection rules in competition law. From a competition standpoint, the issue was dominant position, which the German authorities were assessing.

As the Court recognised, the business model of Facebook is based on online advertising, which is tailored to the users of the social network according to their consumer behaviour, interests, purchasing power and personal situation. Such advertising is made possible by the production of detailed profiles of the network's users and the users of the other online services offered by the Meta group. Therefore, in addition to the data provided directly by users when they sign up for the online services, other user- and device-related data is also collected on and off Facebook and the online services provided by the Meta group. The aggregate data allows detailed conclusions to be drawn about users' preferences and interests.[54]

The German competition law authorities had prohibited Meta from processing Facebook users' off-Facebook data and from processing data without their consent according to the rules laid down in the GDPR. The authorities argued that the processing of user data constituted an abuse of Meta's dominant market position in Germany.[55] The CJEU agreed with most of the authorities' arguments, especially those related to the interpretation of the conditions for users' legally valid consent.

In the *Meta Platforms* case, data protection issues and the market behaviour of companies became intertwined. This was a rather uncommon scenario in CJEU case law at the time, which renders the judgment ground-breaking. The case demonstrates that data protection law can indeed be utilised for the purposes of controlling markets and business models. In this case, the focus on consent makes the dispute nevertheless a rather traditional data protection issue because it focuses on individuals' control over their data. From a pragmatic perspective, it is understandable that the German authorities pushed the argumentation in this direction because, in light of previous case law, it was likely that the CJEU would side with it. Perhaps it was insufficient to argue that the problem was really the huge amounts of data that Meta gathered and combined in its various services. The tipping point in the case was consent, or the lack thereof.

The judgment shows that data protection arguments can also be effective in dealing with some unwanted capitalist behaviour. Thus, it may be useful to continue utilising the data protection regime. However, the case also illustrates that it is not always the personal data of individuals that requires protecting. Rather, it is the power of big tech companies that must be restricted. Even though consent played a rather prominent role in the case, the most pressing issue was not whether some specific individual provided their consent. What was problematic was the way the company used huge amounts of data from numerous people for its own purposes. As the company was able to utilise data from several different services, it had the power to define many aspects of the digital surroundings of people.

From a Rancièrean standpoint, the most serious threat posed by capitalism is its inherent inequality. This feature is exaggerated in today's form of capitalism, where the

[54] ibid, para 27.
[55] ibid, paras 29–30.

very meanings of social life are mediated by large tech companies.[56] Even though a key starting point for an egalitarian society would be the equal capacity to participate, today that goal seems further away than ever. Even our access to knowledge is restricted and caused to function with the capitalist logic of ever-higher gains.

Digital capitalists, such as social media platforms, are increasingly influential in defining our contemporary social landscape. They collaborate in a distribution of the sensible, where the digitally mediated view of the world makes up a big part of what we see, hear and understand. As such, the tech giants play a fundamental role in shaping the social, political and economic conditions of contemporary life.[57] To disrupt this distribution of the sensible would be, for Rancière, the properly political act, but it is increasingly hard to imagine how such disruptions could be achieved. Data protection rights are ill-suited for such a task. In the *Meta Platforms* case, this is illustrated by the impotence of resistance based on the legal requirement of consent. Whether or not users express their consent to processing in legally valid ways is rather irrelevant when considering the overall dynamics of digital capitalism and the power imbalances between the companies and the service users.

Politics, for Rancière, is an aesthetic matter. It is associated with configurations of space, and today space is increasingly digital. Digital aesthetics is hence just as important as the traditional version. Equality has to do with the ways in which things can be seen and heard. In this sense, politics is about capabilities, visibilities and distributions of our digital surroundings, as well as struggles about power over them. This is to say that the aesthetics of power is relevant in digitalisation. And the economic power of tech companies is a very significant form of power precisely because of the way it influences aesthetics.

As Moyn argues, rights conform to the political economy of the age – so, too, data protection law. Even though the GDPR can be utilised to hamper certain forms of economic exploitation by big tech, it is not primarily intended for this purpose. As so many of the GDPR rules are centred around individuals and their consent, they are ineffective at protecting the kind of capitalist exploitation that occurs when people do consent to their data being collected, stored, harvested, sold, used and reused for various purposes. Other legal instruments are required to deal with the systemic threats to society posed by big tech and the capitalism that accompanies them.[58] These threats do not concern individuals but societies more generally, and thus an individualistic instrument like the GDPR is not ideal.[59]

[56] See Miikka Hiltunen on how the EU's internal market aims can be discerned in the regulation of platforms. M Hiltunen, 'Social Media Platforms within Internal Market Construction: Patterns of Reproduction in EU Platform Law' (2022) 23 *German Law Journal* 1226–45.

[57] On the commodification process in digital capitalism, see JA Prodnik, '3C: Commodifying Communication in Capitalism' in C Fuchs and V Mosco (eds), *Marx in the Age of Digital Capitalism* (Brill, 216) 233–321.

[58] See, eg, T Knapstad, *Market Power of Online Platforms: Analysing the Role of Article 102 TFEU, Particularly in Light of the Digital Markets Act* (University of Helsinki, 2025). For a rather pessimistic view, see S Veitch, 'The Perfect Storm: Artificial Intelligence, Financialisation, and Venture Legalism' (2024) 35 *Law & Critique* 609–33. See also I Lianos, 'Value Extraction and Institutions in Digital Capitalism: Towards a Law and Political Economy Synthesis for Competition Law' (2022) 1 *European Law Open* 852–90; M Eifert, A Metzger, H Schweitzer, G Wagner, 'Taming the Giants: The DMA/DSA Package (2021) 58 *CML Rev* 987–1028.

[59] One reason for the EU to keep up the rights-based approach is undoubtedly the aim of enabling free markets and fostering economic growth. From such a perspective, other ways of regulating digitalisation may prove threatening to Europe's possibilities of competing globally. See, eg, F Ferretti, 'The Consumer Image under EU law: Average, Rationally Bounded and Dispositionally Vulnerable. What are the Prospects for Protection in Digital Markets?' (2025) 62 *CML Rev* 121–46.

VII. Taking Data Seriously

Data and data processing are not innocent, as Zuboff and many others remind us.[60] However, what has been less emphasised is that by collecting data, various operators – both public and private – can see human nature for what it is – ambiguous, irrational and often unknowable. Big tech companies are arguably the first major capitalist enterprises in history that are able to exploit the opaqueness of people. They make money not on data as truth but rather on data as assumptions. People are constantly changing, counterintuitive and self-contradictory beings. Tech companies have revolutionised capitalism because they no longer need to know us as individuals; they can still make money from us, occasionally causing all kinds of harm. In fact, it is unnecessary for companies to distinguish one individual's data from another's. By contrast, the law is extremely keen on such distinctions.

One reason for this is the definition of personal data on which the whole GDPR rests. In case law, this definition has become extremely broad. Personal data is considered any data by which a natural person can be identified.[61] As such, any data that can be linked to an individual, or that somehow refers to an individual, represents personal data and thus falls within the scope of the GDPR. This includes a wide range of information, from IP addresses to people's names. However, if no person can be identified, the data is not personal and the GDPR does not apply. Hence, data sets from which no individual can be identified do not constitute personal data.

Because of the individualistic framework, often the consideration of a data protection case begins with the simple question of whose data is processed. In the recent case *Pankki S*, the CJEU was faced with some hard choices in this regard. The issue concerned whether log data constituted personal data. It was a difficult case because the GDPR provides no clear answer. However, considering the practice of the CJEU, it came as no surprise that the Court adopted a rather broad understanding of personal data.[62]

In *Pankki S*, the CJEU considered that log data was personal data, which led to the second question: whose data is it? The case concerned a bank employee who was also a customer of the bank. He had asked the bank to tell him the identity of the persons who had reviewed his personal data in the context of an internal investigation. The bank refused. It argued that the right of access under Article 15 of the GDPR did not apply to log data from the bank's data processing system, which included information on employees with access to the computer system containing customer data. The bank considered that the information requested related to the personal data of employees.

In this case, the personal data of one individual was protected under the right of access provided by Article 15, but the personal data of the employees who had processed the individual's data was also protected under the GDPR. In attempting to

[60] S Zuboff, *The Age of Surveillance Capitalism: The Fight for a Human Future at the New Frontier of Power* (Profile Books, 2019).

[61] According to Art 4 GDPR, '"personal data" means any information relating to an identified or identifiable natural person ("data subject"); an identifiable natural person is one who can be identified, directly or indirectly, in particular by reference to an identifier such as a name, an identification number, location data, an online identifier or to one or more factors specific to the physical, physiological, genetic, mental, economic, cultural or social identity of that natural person'.

[62] Case C-579/21 *Pankki S* ECLI:EU:C:2023:501.

solve this dilemma, the Court unfortunately made no effort either to revise its interpretation of personal data or discuss the nature of data relating to many people; instead, it introduced an essentiality test. It ruled that Article 15 did not provide the right of access to information relating to the identity of employees with access to the computer system unless that information was essential for the data subject to effectively exercise the rights conferred on him by the GDPR and provided that the rights and freedoms of those employees were taken into account.[63] Hence, the Court did engage in balancing, but it concerned solely the balancing of various individuals' data protection rights. It did not properly consider the fact that most data is always the personal data of many people.

The case elegantly illustrates the difficulty of distinguishing data from more data. One individual's data always refers to the data of others. This resonates with our nature as relational beings who never exist in the world on our own. As Nancy says, we are always *with*. However, because the GDPR is fixated on – and only on – individuals' personal data, situations where the same data or data set refers to many people becomes extremely difficult to solve. This brings us to an important question about the nature of data that has been addressed in neither the GDPR nor the case law of the CJEU.

Data pre-exists each person and often lasts much longer than they do. It is impossible for us to extract ourselves from the data that surrounds us. Paraphrasing Nancy, we are thrown into a world of data. Our being-in-the-world today is always being-with-data, including data about ourselves and data about others. Data is singular-plural, just as people are.

For instance, the most significant social signifier of a person – their name – is personal data in the eyes of the law. It is, however, never simply our own. It usually refers to a certain family and sometimes to a certain gender. A name has relevance only in relation to other names, other signifiers, other meanings. Likewise, health data links us to a pre-existing and endless mass of societal data, data about diagnoses and diseases, birth and death rates, anatomy, data in the innumerable blood and tissue samples of a limitless number of people, as well as aggregates of data stored in various biobanks. Similarly, our location data is combined from points, lines, polygons and pictures concerning cities, roads, mountains, forests or bodies of water.

To put it differently, we can consider data as a sign. Signs possess no fixed meanings. A sign denotes something only in a system of signs, where the way a sign differs from other signs creates its meaning. Meaning is thus based on differences. Every sign refers to other signs that can be present or absent at a given moment. The play of differences is an endless play of reference. All the elements in the endless play leave traces, and no element in the system of signs is ever purely present or absent. There are only differences, traces, and traces of traces.[64] The same goes for data. We are thrown into a web of data and have no escape because our every action generates more data.

If we consider personal data from such a perspective, it is clear that the individualistic undertones of the law do not correspond to the reality of digital societies. The way

[63] ibid, para 83. See also Case C-487/21 *Österreichische Datenschutzbehörde and CRIF* EU:C:2023:369; Case C-154/21 *Österreichische Post* ECLI:EU:C:2023:3.

[64] J Derrida, *Positions* (The University of Chicago Press, 1981); J Derrida, *Margins of Philosophy* (The University of Chicago Press, 1982).

digitalism operates is not individualistic, nor can it be successfully regulated with such instruments.

VIII. Unruly Data and the Power to Control It

A huge amount of data exists. Indeed, there is no end to it. The distinction between data and non-data is, from this perspective, impossible. Data can be distributed and reconstructed, collected, combined and collected again, thus forming new data with new meanings.[65] The GDPR is not completely blind to this. The principle of purpose limitation found in Article 5 and Article 6(4) is perhaps an attempt to come to terms with the ever-expanding multiplication and morphing of data. Nonetheless, the principle is difficult to apply because of the complexity of data itself. It is hard to demarcate where some data begins and other data ends, or where one processing situation starts and another stops.

Data can be copied and reproduced endlessly. Sometimes, disputes about origin and authenticity can arise. However, even forged data is data. Continuous reproduction is the normal state of data processing. Data is organised, analysed and moved around in technological systems and combinations of them. How does one then identify the original data and attribute it to the people to whom it refers? Data possesses certain special characteristics, then. Its use does not diminish what is left for others. There is always more. It is cumulative because use and reuse produce more data.[66] Moreover, it flows in ways that are difficult to control.

Data regulation in the EU can be understood as the regulation of movement and flow, the law torn between the need to let data loose and keep it in place. The links to global capitalism can be discerned in this struggle to control data movement. It is not only the accumulation of vast quantities of data that makes the capitalism of our era special. It is also the ability of certain entities to store data, stop its movement or push it into motion for their own benefit. The accumulation of wealth from data requires both the movement of data and the closure of data flows.[67] The actors who have power over data, power to make it move and keep it in place, have power over others.

This returns us to equality. As long as data protection law is an individualistic endeavour, it will be near impotent to further equality. Its underlying premises and case law appearance make it ill-suited to achieving any kind of egalitarian goals. Digital

[65] A paradoxical detail in the GDPR illuminates the complex nature of data and processing: deleting data is processing and must be performed in accordance with all the rules of the GDPR. According to Article 2, '"processing" means any operation or set of operations which is performed on personal data or on sets of personal data, whether or not by automated means, such as collection, recording, organisation, structuring, storage, adaptation or alteration, retrieval, consultation, use, disclosure by transmission, dissemination or otherwise making available, alignment or combination, restriction, erasure or destruction.'

[66] See also R Susskind and D Susskind, *The Future of the Professions: How Technology will Transform The Work of Human Experts* (Oxford University Press, 2015) 193.

[67] Of course, also states and governments attempt to find a balance between the two aims of the GDPR, data privacy and the free movement of data. Public bodies, such as security services, have an interest both in facilitating the movement of data and in holding it in place.

capitalists can continue their exploitation, and the people will have very little say in the matter. Individualistic rights are simply not powerful enough to rule over data.[68]

IX. Conclusions

This chapter has criticised EU data protection law for its individualism. It has focused on the most important legal instrument, the GDPR, and sought to understand the ways it is used in practice. The openness and ambiguities of the GDPR allow for different interpretations, where the *telos* in CJEU practice has become the protection of persons as individuals. This has led to clashes with other values or an ignorance of their importance. Moreover, even when other values are recognised, primacy has been assigned to individuals' personal data protection.

In addition to these issues that cause problems on the surface of the law, I have argued that the individualism of data protection law makes it a weak instrument for resisting problematic forms of digital capitalism. Where data is protected only when it refers to an individual, the mass usage of data goes unregulated. Nonetheless, mass usage is where much economic and social power resides.

Is there another way of understanding data protection? One possibility would be for the law to concentrate more on the regulation of data and less on the individualism of data protection rights. Such rethinking is possible if we consider data in more depth at a theoretical level. Flipping the perspective and focusing on data instead of individuals allows new ways of thinking to emerge. After all, people come into the world already saturated with data. Their data merges with all the other data in the world, building new data, producing innumerable combinations. This data-producing motion is the most prominent feature of our technology-infused lives. It precedes our being in the world, and it does not stop when we cease to exist as individuals.

The regulation should focus on data as that which is in between people, connecting them and distinguishing them from one another. Only in relation to others can we be unique, or singular plural in the words of Nancy. Only in relation to others can we exist as equal human beings. Perhaps the most obvious but often neglected issue in data protection law is that between people, there is data. Data is always about many people, and it defines us in our social being, not solely as individuals.

The benefit of this perspective is that there is no need to presuppose a person, any kind of person, with preferences, a will to control data or a capacity for rational choice as the basis of data protection law. If we concentrate on regulating data, not merely data linked to an individual, we may begin to think differently. It might also become easier to take account of other values and interests than individuals' data protection. Communal values such as transparency of government or public trials could then be considered just

[68] So far, the fundamental rights perspective has been the logic overriding other interests in EU law on digitalisation. Nonetheless, a potential shift is occurring. The Digital Markets Act, the Digital Services Act, the Digital Governance Act, the Data Act and to some extent also the Artificial Intelligence Act strive towards another kind of legal framework. Time will tell how they change the legal landscape and what possible significance they will have for the GDPR and its application. See, eg, G de Gregorio and P Dunn, 'The European Risk-based Approaches: Connecting Constitutional Dots in the Digital Age' (2022) 59 *CML Rev* 473–500.

as important as personal data. After all, as long as there is law, there will be difficult cases where values collide. My argument is that these collisions of values should be considered from a wider perspective than the current individualistic one.

Admittedly, focusing on data can only solve some problems, while others will doubtless remain. Nevertheless, it could promote new ways of thinking that place greater emphasis on communal values. There is indeed an urgent need to regulate data in ways that make our digital lives safe, equal and just. Still, an approach based on individuals' rights is not the only means of achieving this goal.

This chapter has discussed a mere fraction of the difficulties pertaining to digital societies. The different manifestations of individualism are a problem evident in the everyday practice of the law and inherent in its fundamental ideology. This issue is linked to how liberal capitalist societies work more generally. We need to be aware of the ways in which data processing is entangled with the political economy of digital societies if we want to rethink EU data protection law at a more fundamental level. I do not argue that data protection law would be useless. It serves several purposes of which many are undoubtedly good. Still, it is important to notice also the shortcomings of the law.

10

A Philosophy of Domination and Emancipation

Reimagining EU Foreign Policy through Critical Theory

LUIGI LONARDO

I. Introduction

In this chapter, a contextual analysis of the European Union's (EU's) history reveals security to be the overarching purpose of its foreign policy. However, this chapter reimagines security not as traditional state power or military might, but as a precondition for emancipation. Drawing on critical theory,[1] and in particular on the Welsh School of Critical Security Studies, security is presented as the freedom of individuals and groups from systemic threats like war, poverty, and oppression. This reimagined purpose offers a theoretically-grounded normative guide for prioritising the EU's diverse foreign policy objectives. More analytically, this chapter aims to show two things. In the first place, a contextual approach to law, which is informed by Critical Security Studies, can illuminate the *purpose* of EU foreign policy, and relatedly, its *genesis*. These characteristics of EU foreign policy are often neglected in legal scholarship insofar as they are considered irrelevant extra-legal questions, even though there is a significant body

[1] When this chapter uses the phrase critical theory it does so in the broader sense, as referred to in the Introduction to this volume, as a source of inspiration for the themes of this chapter, without any claims to philological accuracy. In its contemporary expression, critical theory draws from a set of diverse theorists that operate within the traditions painted with thick brushes by A Allen, *The End of Progress: Decolonizing the Normative Foundations of Critical Theory* (Columbia University Press, 2016), since they share similar preoccupations. Not broadly, but *very broadly* speaking, what they all have in common is an interest in the social as a sphere of power relations (domination/emancipation), and a normative programme of critiquing those power relations. (This characterisation is loosely inspired by M Horkheimer, *Critical Theory: Selected Essays* (translated by MJ O'Connell, Continuum, 1972) 188 and following.) These traditions include three broad areas. First, a philosophical school, 'the German tradition of interdisciplinary social theory, inaugurated in Frankfurt in the 1930s, and carried forward today in Germany by such thinkers as Jürgen Habermas, Axel Honneth, and Rainer Forst and in the United States by theorists such as Thomas McCarthy, Nancy Fraser, and Seyla Benhabib' (Allen, ibid, xi.). Second, several fields of studies, 'done under the banner of feminist theory, queer theory, critical race theory, and post-and decolonial theory' (ibid). Third, the French version of it, 'a body of French theory spanning from poststructuralism to psycho-analysis, and including such thinkers as Michel Foucault, Jacques Derrida, Gilles Deleuze, and Jacques Lacan'.

of work on EU foreign policy objectives, since these are included in EU primary law.[2] Even when focused on objectives, (traditional, doctrinal) legal scholarship accepts these objectives as given, whereas critical theory helps bring them to the centre of attention (the diagnostic element), and helps reimagine alternatives (the reimagination element, developed in the rest of the chapter). The stated objectives contained in the EU Treaties, in other words, are not the full picture. Instead, the diagnostic element of critical theory shows things that remain invisible to a traditional (doctrinal) legal analysis, namely, that there is a need to consider carefully the very *raison d'être* of EU foreign policy. This is done in section II.

Secondly, the chapter proceeds to a reimagination of EU foreign policy inspired by the conceptual frame of a suggestive dichotomy of critical theory, that of domination and emancipation. Even though there is no canonical definition, within critical theory, domination and emancipation can be understood as two opposing poles.[3] Domination refers to the unjust social, political, and economic structures that curtail human freedom, while emancipation is the process of liberation from these constraints. Domination operates through a combination of overt coercion and less visible (structural) constraints that limit human potential and perpetuate suffering. For many critical theorists, these are not merely actions of a single oppressive agent but are embedded in social arrangements that appear natural or inevitable.[4] Such an approach seeks to uncover how prevailing social and political systems produce and sustain inequality, thereby constraining what people 'would do if they could choose freely' (perhaps *the* question of the Marxian theory of a happy life). Emancipation, consequently, is envisioned as the progressive 'abolition of social injustice'.[5] It is the process of freeing individuals and groups from the structural constraints (the various forms of domination) that impede their autonomy and well-being.[6] Emancipation is therefore not a distant utopian ideal but an active political practice aimed at challenging and transforming the conditions that create insecurity.

[2] See, eg, J Larik, *Foreign Policy Objectives in European Constitutional Law* (Oxford University Press, 2016); L Lonardo, 'Common Foreign and Security Policy and the EU's External Action Objectives: An Analysis of Article 21 of the Treaty on the European Union' (2018) 14 *European Constitutional Law Review* 584; E Cannizzaro, 'The Value of the EU International Values' in W Th Douma and others (eds), *The Evolving Nature of EU External Relations Law* (TMC Asser Press, 2021); A Lang, 'Assistenza Finanziaria Dell'Unione ai Paesi Terzi e Obiettivi Ambientali Della UE' [2022] Quaderni AISDUE 19; M Cremona, 'Structural Principles and Their Role in EU External Relations Law' in M Cremona (ed), *Structural principles in EU external relations law* (Hart Publishing, 2018); S Velluti, *The Role of the EU in the Promotion of Human Rights and International Labour Standards in Its External Trade Relations* (Springer International Publishing, 2020); E Kassoti and RA Wessel, 'The Normative Effect of Article 3(5) TEU: Observance and Development of International Law by the European Union' in P Garcia Andrade (ed), *Interacciones entre el Derecho de la Unión Europea y el Derecho Internacional Público* (Tirant lo Blanch, 2023).

[3] The two terms, which I defined in a way that may not be commonly shared, are in a relationship that, following Hegel, is known as the master-slave dialectic. In other words, they need each other. L Boltanski, *On Critique: A Sociology of Emancipation* (Polity, 2013) 2.

[4] Critical theory's purpose is precisely to analyse and critique this 'unjust character of the historical period and the suffering which flows from it'. Horkheimer (n 1) 242. I discuss some methodological objections to explanations relating to collective or abstract agents in L Lonardo, 'Marxism in EU Legal Scholarship' in R Deplano et al (eds), *Interdisciplinary Research Methods in EU Law. A Handbook* (Elgar, 2024).

[5] Horkheimer (n 1) 242.

[6] This vision is grounded in what has been described as a fundamental 'emancipatory interest' inherent to humanity, an 'ineradicable human tendency to revolt against structures of domination'. A Honneth, 'Is There an Emancipatory Interest? An Attempt to Answer Critical Theory's Most Fundamental Question' (2017) 25 *European Journal of Philosophy* 908, 908.

As will be elaborated upon at greater length below in this chapter, security can be defined in relation to this polarity between domination and emancipation: traditionally, security has been understood in terms of state power and military might, a perspective that critical theorists argue often reinforces structures of domination by prioritising the state over the individual. A critical approach, however, posits that 'security and emancipation are two sides of the same coin'.[7] True security is not achieved through the accumulation of power but through emancipation, which aims to free people from systemic threats like 'war, poverty, oppression, and poor education'.[8] This perspective reframes security as a struggle for justice and the removal of the very conditions that make people unsafe. Instead of viewing security as the military security of states, in this chapter I show that security could and maybe should be conceived of as a prerequisite to emancipation (section III) – and I then apply this notion of security to selected characteristics of EU foreign policy (section IV). This analysis will also remind us of why EU foreign policy is a good candidate for 'reimagination' with the themes of critical theory: at crucial junctures, the EU has been unable to stop or prevent wars and other catastrophes (such as massive human rights violations and military aggressions).

Consider some of the defining moments of *European* foreign policy of the twenty-first century,[9] which are outstanding examples of misjudgements, if not downright moral and political failures, as well as of the EU's inability to lead and of its continued dependency on the United States (US) in foreign policy matters. The 2003 US-led invasion of Iraq took place on very dubious legal grounds and followed a major political split among European countries supporting and those opposing the operation. The war and subsequent occupation resulted in hundreds of thousands of deaths, and it arguably had also political consequences such as instability (and further conflict) in the region.[10] The 2011 invasion of Libya by NATO forces is widely considered a failure of EU foreign policy (in no small part, precisely because it took place outside EU frameworks).[11] It also had catastrophic human, economic, and political consequences.[12] The response to the 2022 invasion of Ukraine could only develop within the constraint posed by the US (such as former President Biden's 'red line' that the US would not intervene militarily in Ukraine).[13] French President Macron said that the political objective of Strategic

[7] K Booth, 'Security and Emancipation' (1991) 17 *Review of International Studies* 313, 319.

[8] ibid.

[9] European foreign policy refers to the action of European countries, regardless of whether it is within EU structures (in which case, it is referred to as EU foreign policy).

[10] For example on the consequences for Iran see A Ansari, 'Iran and the Iraq War of 2003: The Real Victor?' (*RUSI*, 24 March 2013), available at www.rusi.org/explore-our-research/publications/commentary/iran-and-iraq-war-2003-real-victor; on the rise of the Islamic State, see B Isakhan (ed), *The Legacy of Iraq: From the 2003 War to the 'Islamic State'* (Edinburgh University Press, 2022).

[11] Atlantic Council, 'Diplomats Mourn "Death" of EU Defence Policy over Libya' (*Atlantic Council*, 24 March 2011), available at www.atlanticcouncil.org/blogs/natosource/diplomats-mourn-death-of-eu-defence-policy-over-libya reporting a diplomat commenting.'The CFSP died in Libya – we just have to pick a sand dune under which we can bury it'. I discuss this in more detail in L Lonardo, *EU Common Foreign and Security Policy after Lisbon: Between Law and Geopolitics* (Springer, 2022).

[12] H Singh Puri, *Perilous Interventions: The Security Council and the Politics of Chaos* (Harpercollins Publishers India, 2016).

[13] B Plett Usher, 'Ukraine Conflict: Why Biden Won't Send Troops to Ukraine' (*BBC News*, 25 February 2022), available at www.bbc.com/news/world-us-canada-60499385; I develop this argument further in L Lonardo, *Russia's 2022 War Against Ukraine and the Foreign Policy Reaction of the EU: Context, Diplomacy, and Law* (Palgrave Macmillan, 2023).

Autonomy is for the EU 'not to suffer someone else's choice'.[14] All of this suggests that we need to rethink the nature and perhaps the purpose of EU foreign policy. It is possible that the reader disagrees with these characterisations, or with the conclusion that EU foreign policy should be reimagined. Even then, there is value in considering the questions that critical theory will arise about EU foreign policy: what should this policy be about, what – and whom – should it be for? This (political) debate has a match in the legal realm: EU law is virtually silent on how to prioritise among EU foreign policy objectives, and as a result this is an open (legal) question.

II. What Is EU Foreign Policy For?

We need to distinguish between the objectives of EU foreign policy – which are a matter of primary law – and the *purpose* of EU foreign policy. Considering the latter allows a critical perspective on the former.

A. EU Foreign Policy Objectives

EU foreign policy is codified, as a matter of law, in various 'competences' of the EU: the Common Foreign and Security Policy (CFSP), the Common Commercial Policy (CCP), Development Cooperation, and so on. Doctrinally, the general objectives of the EU 'in its relations with the wider world' are contained in Article 3(5) TEU,[15] to which we shall return below. These objectives are elaborated upon in Article 21(2) TEU.[16]

Article 21(2) TEU, in particular, commits the Union to safeguarding its own values and interests (as if these two were always necessarily aligned), as well as working to consolidate and support democracy, human rights, and the rule of law worldwide. The article also directs the EU to preserve peace, foster sustainable development, protect the environment, and promote a strong, co-operative international system, including for the progressive liberalisation of trade.

Two general observations may be made on Article 21(2) TEU: first, there is no internal hierarchy among those objectives, so, in case of conflict between objectives, it is for EU institutions to find a balance among conflicting interests.[17] For example, there is no doctrinal way to prioritise between the objectives listed in Article 21(2) TEU. Primary law is simply silent on this, or leaves to the institutions the very identification of the (public and/or private) interests to be balanced.

[14] Emmanuel Macron in his speech to the European Parliament of 19 January 2022

[15] Consolidated Version of the of the Treaty on European Union [2008] OJ C115/13 (herein, TEU).

[16] A specific objective exists for the Union's action in its neighbourhood (Art 8(1) TEU: 'The Union shall develop a special relationship with neighbouring countries, aiming to establish an area of prosperity and good neighbourliness, founded on the values of the Union and characterised by close and peaceful relations based on cooperation.'

[17] Cremona (n 2) 7; M Estrada Cañamares, '"Building Coherent EU Responses": Coherence as a Structural Principle in EU External Relations' in M Cremona (ed), *Structural Principles in EU External Relations Law* (Hart Publishing, 2018) 262.

Second, by and large the *terms* of the balancing, ie the competing interests, are not specified in the Treaties (Article 26(1) TEU, for example, leaves to the European Council the task to identify the Union's strategic interests), and this can be contrasted with the specific interests that internal policies shall pursue.[18] There is *some* indication on how to identify these competing strategic interests: for example, it is possible to read limits to the discretion of EU institutions in the broader, general objectives in Article 3(5) TEU. That provision reads:

> In its relations with the wider world, the Union shall uphold and promote its values and interests and contribute to the protection of its citizens. It shall contribute to peace, security, the sustainable development of the Earth, solidarity and mutual respect among peoples, free and fair trade, eradication of poverty and the protection of human rights, in particular the rights of the child, as well as to the strict observance and the development of international law, including respect for the principles of the United Nations Charter.

The reference to international law, and to the principles of the UN Charter thus circumscribes the interests that the Union's institutions can pursue. It would be manifestly outside the boundaries of their discretion, for example, to even simply take into account an interest (of a third country or of a Member State) in acquiring new territory by using force. Having said this, there are difficulties: there may be contradictions among the various objectives, 'peace' and 'protection of human rights' being, occasionally, on a trajectory of conflict, as the 'peace v justice' debate in post-conflict societies show.[19] In addition, the Court of Justice of the EU tends to leave wide discretion to EU institutions in the pursuit of these objectives. It is settled case law that 'the Council has a broad discretion in areas which involve the making by that institution of political, economic and social choices, and in which it is called upon to undertake complex assessments'.[20] Such is the case, for example, when the Council decides how to pursue the objectives when imposing restrictive measures,[21] and *a fortiori* what objectives to pursue.

B. The Purpose of EU Foreign Policy

In sum, the list of objectives tells us something about the purpose of EU foreign policy, but it is far from being the full story. Aside from very abstract hints, the law alone does not really orient the purpose of EU foreign policy. So let us zoom out to the context,

[18] Cremona (n 2) 6; L Lonardo, 'Challenging EU Sanctions against Russia: The Role of the Court, Judicial Protection, and Common Foreign and Security Policy' (2023) *Cambridge Yearbook of European Legal Studies* 1, 17.

[19] Sometimes, to end a war and achieve peace, it is necessary to make deals with the people who committed terrible crimes, perhaps by forgiving them. However, protecting human rights requires holding those same people accountable for their actions to get justice for the victims. This creates a difficult dilemma where the goal of ending the fighting conflicts with the goal of punishing wrongdoing. For this kind of debate surrounding the Special Tribunal for the Crime of Aggression against Ukraine, see especially K Ambos, 'Ukraine and the Double Standards of the West' (2022) 20 *Journal of International Criminal Justice* 875; P Labuda, 'Countering Imperialism in International Law: Examining the Special Tribunal for Aggression against Ukraine through a Post-Colonial Eastern European Lens' (2024) 49 *Yale Journal of International Law* 271.

[20] Case C-72715 *PJSC Rosneft Oil Company v Her Majesty's Treasury and Others* ECLI:EU:C:2017:236, para 113.

[21] Roman Abramovich, for example, contended that the sanctions targeting him are not suitable to bring about a change in Russia's policy, or that they go beyond what is necessary because they prevent him from acting as a channel of communication in the context of peace negotiations. The General Court used the standard formula that the EU legislature must be allowed a broad discretion when it is called upon to undertake complex assessments. Only manifestly inappropriate measures would be struck down. Case T313/22 *Abramovich I* ECLI:EU:T:2023:830, para 140.

which shows a security rationale. The very initial *raison d'être* of the EU (and its predecessor) and therefore of the process of European integration was a foreign policy necessity, which can be summed up with great approximation in the need to secure Western Europe, with US help, against the Soviet threat (later in the 1950s the problem became how to square that need for American security guarantee[22] with the need to ensure 'the independence of the European vis-à-vis the US as the leading power'[23]). The reason why there was no foreign security policy powers attributed to the EU since day one is a matter of historiographical debate.[24] But in essence it only proved feasible to co-operate, incrementally, on energy and economic matters, since political (and military security) integration had proved unfeasible. The EU and its predecessor managed the peace process in Western, and later Northern, and Central Europe, through strategic interdependence (a common market, a single legal order).[25] The Court contributed to shaping such a legal order, and so the Union's powers in international affairs,[26] and in later decades the Member States also conferred powers to the EU to act in political aspects of foreign policy (for example, the EU can decide whether to sanction a third country, it has delegations in foreign capitals, and it has its own diplomatic corps, called the European External Action Service).[27] Foreign policy, in sum, was added later to the legal structures and still remains, as far as security and defence is concerned, somewhat special in the EU's legal order (Article 24 TEU).[28]

What this brief account of the *genesis* of the policy shows is that if there was one overarching *purpose* in EU foreign policy it was a certain conception of *security* (notably, security of Western European states against a possible military aggression, as well as political strength, we would now say resilience, of those countries against communism) as a means to achieve self-preservation. The notion of security is still central to the EU's foreign policy. The legal translation of this is that where Article 21(2)(a) TEU explicitly mandates the Union to 'safeguard its values, fundamental interests, security, independence and integrity' in its international actions, this could be interpreted as making security as the overriding objective, that is, it should be prioritised even over other competing strategic interests (such as the pursuit of EU values). To be sure, a textual or systematic analysis does not bear this interpretation. A contextual one does. Historically, the impetus for European integration stemmed from the desire to prevent the recurrence of devastating conflicts, leading to initiatives, which aimed, as the

[22] G Lundestad, *'Empire' by Integration: The United States and European Integration, 1945 - 1997* (Oxford University Press, 1998) 41.

[23] W Loth, *Building Europe: A History of European Unification* (De Gruyter Oldenbourg, 2015) 53.

[24] C Parsons, 'The Triumph of Community Europe' in Desmond Dinan (ed), *Origins and Evolution of the European Union*, vol 1 (Oxford University Press, 2017).

[25] For this conceptualisation, see especially I Govaere, 'Transformative Impact on the European Union of War (in Ukraine): Existential Conundrums' in I Govaere, S Garben, and E Spaventa (eds), *The Impact of War (in Ukraine) on the EU* (Hart Publishing, 2025) 16.

[26] Since the seminal Case 22/70 *Commission v Council (ERTA)* ECLI:EU:C:1971:32 [1971] ECR 263. For the main case law, see generally G Butler and RA Wessel (eds), *EU External Relations Law: The Cases in Context* (Hart Publishing, 2022).

[27] See, respectively, Arts 28–29 TEU; Arts 32 and 35 TEU; Art 27 TEU. Cremona (n 2) 5–6.

[28] In the field of CFSP, decision-making is chiefly intergovernmental, the institutional involvement is distinctive (there is more limited involvement of the Court of Justice of the EU, of the Commission, and of the European Parliament as compared to other areas of EU policy), and the effects and nature of decisions adopted in this area is not necessarily the same as other EU law.

Schuman declaration so powerfully had it, to make war between European states 'not merely unthinkable, but materially impossible'.[29] So, security has been a foundational rationale of the European integration project, not merely as a policy objective but as a structural imperative that history embedded in its legal architecture.

III. Reimagining the Purpose of EU Foreign Policy

The previous section showed that critical theory – and a contextual historical approach – suggests that security is an overriding objective of EU foreign policy. This section discusses what security means from a critical perspective; and then considers how it can be operationalised in EU foreign policy.

A. Security as Pre-condition for Emancipation: The View from Critical Security Studies

After Marx said that the point of philosophy is to change the world, Horkheimer gave more precise guidance: the goal of critical theory is 'man's emancipation from slavery'.[30] To understand what this means, we can get even closer to us in time, as Geuss writes that '[c]ritical theories aim at emancipation and enlightenment, at making agents aware of hidden coercion, thereby freeing them from that coercion and putting them in a position to determine where their true interests lie'.[31] Leaving aside the 'hidden coercion' part (what is the hidden coercion? Who hid it? The notion of hidden coercion is elaborated upon later in this chapter), this statement can be fruitfully applied to the aims of EU foreign policy: if security is indeed the overarching objective, what does a foreign policy whose purpose is security-as-enabler of-emancipation and enlightenment, putting people in a position to determine where their true interests lie, look like?

Some insights come from the school of Critical Security Studies, also known as the Welsh School, which, by drawing on the teachings of the Frankfurt school (in particular on the goal of emancipatory politics[32]), helps in re-imagining the notion of security. This approach transforms security studies by moving beyond the traditional focus on military threats and state protection to include a wider range of dangers and actors, especially individuals. Among these theorists, the work of Wyn Jones is particularly relevant for our purposes because it connects the notion of security to the normative goal of achieving human emancipation from oppression.[33] The same notion of security

[29] *The Schuman Declaration of 9 May 1950*, Publications Office, 2015, available at https://data.europa.eu/doi/10.2775/065.

[30] Horkheimer (n 1) 246.

[31] R Geuss, *The Idea of a Critical Theory: Habermas and the Frankfurt School* (Cambridge University Press, 1999) 55.

[32] R Wyn Jones, *Security, Strategy, and Critical Theory* (Lynne Rienner Publishers, 1999) chs 1 and 2.

[33] ibid 166; C Peoples and N Vaughan-Williams, 'Inroduction: Mapping Critical Security Studies and Traveling Withou Maps' in C Peoples and N Vaughan-Williams, *Critical Security Studies: An Introduction*, 3rd edn (Routledge, 2021) 31.

as inspired by the telos of emancipation appears in another theorist of the same school, Ken Booth:

> 'Security' means the absence of threats. Emancipation is the freeing of people (as individuals and groups) from those physical and human constraints which stop them carrying out what they would freely choose to do. War and the threat of war is one of those constraints, together with poverty, poor education, political oppression and so on. Security and emancipation are two sides of the same coin. Emancipation, not power or order, produces true security. Emancipation, theoretically, is security.[34]

Security thus assumes almost an existential, ethical (or, to use a terminology closer to that of Booth, psychological[35]) dimension:[36] security thus defined is valuable, and should be achieved. This entails that the state[37] is there to guarantee the security of the individual, not *vice versa*: states are means to achieve the goal of security (for individuals and for groups). This is a very important point because it is where CSS departs from many traditional security thinkers: the critical notion of security relates not so much to protection of the state from military threats (as traditional security has it), but rather to, first, the acknowledgments of, and then emancipation from, forms of coercions against individuals. 'Individual humans – writes Booth – are the ultimate referent' of security.[38] So, security means freedom from domination, and it means the freedom of individuals and of groups. Groups are also important, because they shape identity. Wyn Jones, stated it clearly:

> Identity never occurs in the singular [. . .] The human condition is one of overlapping identities; that is, each person has a number of different identities, all (potentially) in flux, and all of which come into play at different times and in different situations. Thus, a focus on individuals strongly discourages any tendency to reify human identity; it points instead to the complex, multifaceted, and even fluid nature of identity.[39]

B. Retheorising Security through the Polarities of Emancipation and Domination

Rethinking security through the critical lens of emancipation and domination requires a fundamental shift away from traditional, state-centric models. In this view, security is not an end in itself, synonymous with military strength or the preservation of state power, but rather an essential pre-condition for emancipation. This retheorisation posits that security and emancipation are inextricably linked, as the work of the Welsh School of Critical Security Studies recalled above shows. The ultimate goal is to create the conditions in which individuals and groups are free to determine their own

[34] Booth (n 7).
[35] ibid 316.
[36] ibid 321. It ought to be noted nonetheless that some of the 'orthodox' security thinkers, such as Barry Buzan, would also agree on this point.
[37] Or whatever form a polity takes.
[38] Booth (n 7) 319.
[39] Wyn Jones (n 32) 116.

interests and pursue a life of their choosing. This requires a conception of security that is people-centric, focusing on the lived experiences of human beings as logical precursors of the interests of the state. Security, in this sense, becomes the foundational basis upon which the project of emancipation is built.

A critical theorising of security necessitates a conception of freedom. Follow a classic distinction found in Isaiah Berlin, we can consider negative freedom, or 'freedom from', as foundational: it corresponds to the idea of security as the absence of threats. It is freedom from coercion, from war, from poverty, and from the various forms of political and structural violence that constitute domination. (Here, critical theorists differ, and are sometimes a bit vague, as to what exactly constitutes such domination. I try to give some concrete examples below and in the next section.) This is the essential starting point, as individuals cannot begin to shape their own lives if they are constantly under threat. However, this conception alone is insufficient. The theory must also embrace positive freedom, the 'freedom to'. Freedom to do what, exactly? This is also a matter of contention among theorists. We can encounter notions such as 'growth, development, and healthy maintenance of the body',[40] 'self-realisation'[41] or 'flourishing',[42] the theorisation of which goes well beyond the scope of this chapter (and of my abilities). Broadly speaking, positive freedom refers to the capacity of individuals and groups to dedicate themselves to the pursuits they choose, and to participate in shaping their own collective destiny (it has therefore some affinity to the collective right to self-determination). Security thus theorised enables positive freedom by removing the constraints that inhibit agency and providing the stable environment necessary for individuals and communities to pursue their self-defined goals and realise their potential.

This approach to security has universalistic aspirations, yet it must directly confront a core ethical and political problem: the reality that the security of one group has often been achieved at the expense of the insecurity of another. Traditional security paradigms frequently operate on a zero-sum logic, where national security is prioritised even if it means exporting insecurity elsewhere through military intervention, economic exploitation, or political domination. A critical security framework challenges this premise head-on. Because its ultimate referent is the individual human being, it cannot accept a formulation where the emancipation of some is built on the oppression of others. Addressing this issue requires acknowledging that threats are often interconnected and that structures of domination are global in scope. The goal is therefore to identify and dismantle those very systems that produce these security dilemmas, and strive for a universal emancipation where security is indivisible. The next section of this chapter suggests some ways in which critical theory helps identify such systemic constraints and threats.

Let me give two examples, of colonialism and of self-determination, which are applied in more detail to EU foreign policy in the next section. Colonialism arguably represents one of the most explicit and brutal forms of domination in modern history, systematically denying entire peoples their security and freedom for the benefit of the colonising

[40] K Marx, *Capital, Volume 1* (London, Penguin, 1986) 375.

[41] eg A Honneth, 'Organized Self-Realization: Some Paradoxes of Individualization' (2004) 7 *European Journal of Social Theory* 463.

[42] eg M Nussbaum, 'Beyond "Compassion and Humanity"' in C Sunstein and Ma Nussbaum (eds), *Animal Rights: Current Debates and New Directions* (Oxford University Press, 2004) 299–320.

power.[43] In a metaphorical sense, it institutionalised insecurity through military conquest, economic exploitation, and cultural suppression, all of which are, under the definition on which this chapter operates, antithetical to emancipation. A security-as-emancipation framework therefore demands a reckoning with colonial legacies. It recognises that many contemporary insecurities in the postcolonial world are direct consequences of the structural injustices established during the colonial era. Furthermore, it critiques neo-colonial practices where powerful states continue to exert domination through economic and political means, perpetuating cycles of dependency and insecurity. Acknowledging this history is not merely a matter of historical record but a necessary step towards correcting ongoing structural injustices and building a more equitable global order.

Finally, this understanding of security is deeply intertwined with the right of self-determination of peoples under international law. The principle of self-determination is, in essence, the legal and political expression of emancipation at a collective level. It is the right of a people to freely determine their political status and pursue their economic, social, and cultural development without external interference. Bonds of domination, colonial oppression, or foreign occupation are direct impediments to both self-determination and security-as-emancipation. By prioritising the freedom of individuals and groups from such constraints, a critical security perspective provides a normative foundation for upholding the right to self-determination. It insists that a people cannot be secure if they are denied the ability to govern themselves and make their own choices. Therefore, supporting struggles for self-determination and opposing forms of occupation and domination becomes a core component of a foreign policy genuinely committed to security as emancipation.

IV. Reimagining EU Foreign Policy

This section considers the consequences that this understanding of security as emancipation and absence of domination has for EU foreign policy. In particular, let us consider in this section what EU foreign policy would look like if it pursued security as an overriding objective. In this case, the objectives listed in Articles 21(2) TEU would not all be of equal value, security ranking hierarchically higher. The balancing would operate only among the other ones (those contained in Article 21(2)(b) to (h) TEU): among these, preference should be given to those that are closer to pursuing security as emancipation.

A. Domination by European Countries Should Be Acknowledged

The dichotomy domination/emancipation helps cast light on some very dark moments of European history, in which European states established and maintained

[43] See, eg, F Cooper, *Colonialism in Question: Theory, Knowledge, History* (University of California Press, 2005). As applied to international law, see generally A Anghie, *Imperialism, Sovereignty and the Making of International Law* (Cambridge University Press, 2005).

domination over other nations. Acknowledging this could result in prioritising the correction of structural injustices as a foreign policy objective, when this interest collides with another one worthy of protection. The correction of structural injustices refers to fixing large-scale problems that are built into the very systems of a society, such as the international society (with its international law and macroeconomics). Due partly also to their genesis, these systems (indeed, do) create unfair advantages for some groups and disadvantages for others. Correcting them means actively changing these foundational rules and institutions to create a more equitable and fair society for everyone.

Let us illustrate this with a reflection on *the EU as coloniser*. Legal scholarship on EU foreign policy can fruitfully be in conversation with critical theory (in its variant of postcolonial theory and Third World Approaches to International Law), because the latter suggests paying more attention to themes that have traditionally been underestimated (but increasingly less so even by lawyers[44]). More concretely: those literatures suggest to question the genesis of EU foreign policy and in particular the legacy of European empires.[45] Empires, colonisation, and de-colonisation still leaves a mark on what the EU does and on how it frames it (maybe, unwittingly but consequentially so).[46] Reflecting on this may have the positive effect of, to use the title of Chakrabaty's book, *Provincialising Europe*,[47] that is, it helps put what Europe does into perspective.

It is a fact that 'the founding Member States of European integration were the metropoles of [. . .] empires'.[48] There are imperial-colonial legacies in the very set-up of the EU and its predecessors.[49] For example, Algeria was not only part of a founding Member State, but it was an essential component indeed of the common market,

[44] S Rehling Larsen, 'European Public Law after Empires' (2022) 1 *European Law Open* 6 and literature cited therein; P Dann, I Feichtner and J von Bernstorff (eds), *(Post)Koloniale Rechtswissenschaft: Geschichte und Gegenwart des Kolonialismus in der deutschen Rechtswissenschaft* (Mohr Siebeck, 2022). H Eklund (ed), *Colonialism and the EU Legal Order* (Oxford University Press, 2025); B Sjåfjell, 'No Peace without Sustainability, no Sustainability without Peace: The Implementation of EU Treaty Goals' in I Govaere, S Garben, E Spaventa (eds), *The impact of War (in Ukraine) on the EU* (Hart Publishing, 2025) 82. I Solanke, 'War, Xenophobia and the EU Social Order' in I Govaere, S Garben, E Spaventa (eds), *The Impact of War (in Ukraine) on the EU* (Hart Publishing, 2025) 73–75.

[45] C Thomas, 'What Does the Emerging International Law of Migration Mean for Sovereignty?' (2013) 14 *Melbourne Journal of International Law* 392; AE Tendayi, 'Empire, Borders, and Refugee Responsibility Sharing' (*UC Berkeley Law*, 2022), available at https://lawcat.berkeley.edu/record/1241416.

[46] The notion of empire is routinely used to describe the EU (J Zielonka, *Europe as Empire: The Nature of the Enlarged European Union* (Oxford University Press, 2010) and it is common in other disciplines (H Behr, 'The European Union in the Legacies of Imperial Rule? EU Accession Politics Viewed from a Historical Comparative Perspective' (2007) 13 *European Journal of International Relations* 239; R Foster, '*Tabula Imperii Europae*: A Cartographic Approach to the Current Debate on the European Union as Empire' (2013) 18 *Geopolitics* 371.) From a lawyer's perspective, it is suggestive but probably inaccurate, at least under a commonly accepted definition of empire as entity relying on (the threat of military) conquest for the acquisition of new territory. The label may nonetheless capture some aspects of the EU, and I will focus here on what matters for foreign policy.

[47] D Chakrabarty, *Provincializing Europe: Postcolonial Thought and Historical Difference* (Princeton University Press, 2007).

[48] S Rehling Larsen, *The Constitutional Theory of the Federation and the European Union* (Oxford University Press, 2021) 63.

[49] G Garavini and RR Nybakken, *After Empires: European Integration, Decolonization, and the Challenge from the Global South 1957-1986* (Oxford University Press, 2012); P Hansen and S Jonsson, *Eurafrica: The Untold History of European Integration and Colonialism* (Bloomsbury, 2014).

until its independence from France. The relationship between the colonies and the economy of the motherland – was fundamental to the shaping of the first common market.[50]

These legacies continue to manifest themselves in EU foreign policy, for example by shaping the geopolitical and diplomatic priorities of Member States in ways that reflect their former imperial domains. France's enduring presence and strategic focus in the Sahel, Spain's and Portugal's emphasis on ties with Latin America, and Belgium's development engagement in Central Africa are all examples of how historical colonial entanglements continue to inform bilateral relations, regional strategies, and EU-level external action. These preferences influence not only national positions in the Council but also the selection of thematic or geographic foci within broader EU foreign policy instruments, including development aid and trade agreements.

The EU's network of trade agreements often mirrors the old colonial maps of its key Member States, illustrating how these historical legacies persist. For instance, the Economic Partnership Agreements are primarily structured around the African, Caribbean, and Pacific group of states, a bloc composed almost entirely of former colonies. These agreements frequently perpetuate historical economic dependencies, prioritising the EU's access to raw materials and agricultural products in exchange for European manufactured goods and services. Similarly, the strong political impetus from Spain and Portugal has been a driving force behind the EU-Mercosur trade deal, leveraging deep historical and linguistic ties with Latin America. This modern framework of preferential trade is a direct successor to post-colonial arrangements like the Lomé Conventions, which institutionalised a special economic relationship from the early days of European integration.

In parallel, the legacy of empire endures in the form of the extensive diplomatic infrastructure that former colonial powers inherited and continue to deploy. Countries like France and the United Kingdom (UK) (though the latter is no longer an EU member) possess embassies and consular services in nearly every corner of the world, which enhances their ability to project influence and shape EU foreign policy from a position of global reach.

The crucial lesson to be learnt is that these developments have made it difficult to see 'from the inside' (maybe because they are Europe's unresolved guilt[51]) what is obvious 'from the outside': that the EU inherited colonial legacies which are predicated on a domination that many consider grossly unjust. This obscured awareness exposes how practices presented as protective or liberating may in fact reproduce hierarchies of control and dependency that are fundamentally opposed to the notion of security as emancipation defended in this chapter.

[50] M-T Bitsch, G Bossuat and European Community Liaison Committee of Historians (eds), *L'Europe unie et l'Afrique: de l'idée d'Eurafrique à la convention de Lomé 1: actes du colloque international de Paris, 1er et 2 avril 2004* (Bruylant, 2005); D Avit, 'La question de l'Eurafrique dans la construction de l'Europe de 1950 à 1957', available at www.persee.fr/doc/mat_0769-3206_2005_num_77_1_1012.

[51] G Gozzi, *Eredità Coloniale e Costruzione Dell'Europa. Una Questione Irrisolta: Il 'Rimosso' Della Coscienza Europea* (Il Mulino, 2021).

B. Structural Injustices Should Be Corrected by Supporting Self-determination

It has been argued above that the correction of structural injustice should be a strategic interest of the Union. It can be added here, more specifically, that the support for self-determination and emancipation (ie the opposite of domination) should be an EU foreign policy objective, reading self-determination into Article 21(2)(b), as one of 'the principles of international law'.

Clearly, bonds of domination, colonial oppression, or other ongoing form of political inequality that *de facto* or *de iure* curtail the right of self-determination of people are also an impediment to security as emancipation. The stance of the EU on disputed territories is worth scrutinising. Three very contentious cases can be mentioned: Western Sahara, the occupied Palestinian territories, and areas of Ukraine. They evince different attitudes in circumstances where there are those struggling for self-determination and those who disagree. The EU sometimes sides with the former, sometimes with the latter. Formally, the EU follows the position established by international law that Western Sahara is a non-self-governing territory awaiting a process of self-determination.[52] So, the EU does not recognise Moroccan sovereignty over that territory. Despite this, in practice, the EU negotiates with Morocco as if Western Sahara was part of that kingdom. Even more: in its agreements with Morocco, the EU has first implicitly, and then explicitly, inserted provisions affecting Western Sahara.[53] The European Court of Justice has ruled that such agreements cannot apply to the territory of Western Sahara, without the consent of the Sahrawi people.[54] This is because the EU must respect the principle of self-determination and of relative effects of Treaties, so it cannot conclude agreements with Morocco that extend to Western Sahara without the Sahrawis' explicit or implicit consent. The Court has also required products originating from Western Sahara to be labelled as such (to the exclusion of any mention of Morocco).[55]

Moving now to the second example, the EU does not recognise Israeli sovereignty over the Occupied Palestinian Territories, either. The EU considers Israeli settlements in these areas illegal under international law.[56] The EU maintains a policy of differentiating between Israel and the territories occupied since 1967. This policy requires, for example, products originating from settlements to be labelled as such (and not as coming from Israel).[57] The EU has criticised Israeli policies such as settlement expansion and

[52] For a detailed analysis of the EU's and international law position, see especially E Kassoti, 'The EU and Western Sahara: An Assessment of Recent Developments' (2018) 43 *European Law Review* 751, 755.

[53] Article 1(h) of the Sustainable Fisheries Partnership Agreement between the European Union and the Kingdom of Morocco [2019] OJ L77/8.

[54] Joined cases C-778/21P and C-798/21 P *European Commission and Council v Front Polisario* ECLI:EU:C:2024:833.

[55] Case C-399/22 *Confédération paysanne* ECLI:EU:C:2024:839.

[56] As established by United Nations resolutions and the International Court of Justice. For a useful overview of the international law controversies, see R Van Steenberghe, 'The Armed Conflict in Gaza, and Its Complexity under International Law: *Jus Ad Bellum* , *Jus in Bello* , and International Justice' (2024) 37 *Leiden Journal of International Law* 983.

[57] Case C-363/18 *Organisation juive européenne and Vignoble Psagot Ltd v Ministre de l'Économie et des Finances* ECLI:EU:C:2019:954.

restrictions on Palestinian movement,[58] but it (and some Member States) continues to maintain strong economic and political relations with Israel. Some Member States sell weapons to Israel. Despite the current Israeli Prime Minister being the subject of an arrest warrant by the International Criminal Court, EU institutions continue political dialogue with, and in fact welcome to Brussels, ministers of that government.[59]

On the opposite end of the spectrum, the EU recognises Ukraine's sovereignty and territorial integrity within its internationally recognised borders, including Crimea and the eastern regions occupied by Russia. Far from negotiating with Russia as if the Ukrainian territories under the Russian army's control were part of the Russian Federation, the EU has imposed heavy sanctions on Russia in response to the annexation of Crimea and its invasion of Ukraine.[60] Following the full-scale invasion of 2022, in addition, the EU significantly increased its support for Ukraine through financial aid, administrative and military assistance. The EU has also granted Ukraine candidate status for EU membership and has committed to supporting its long-term integration into the EU.[61] The EU maintains that any resolution to the conflict must respect Ukraine's territorial integrity and has condemned Russian actions as violations of international law, also in multilateral fora.

These three case studies demonstrate that the EU's commitment to self-determination as a value (stemming from the respect for international law, Article 3(5) TEU) is not absolute but highly selective and contingent on its strategic interests. While the EU acts as a staunch defender of Ukraine's sovereignty against Russian aggression, its policies towards Western Sahara and the occupied Palestinian territories reveal a tension, if not a gap, between its commitment to upholding international law and its practical political and economic actions. This suggests that the principle of self-determination is not applied as a universal legal norm but is instead subordinated to the EU's economic, political and cultural relationships with occupying powers like Morocco and Israel (and their allies). If this entails the denial of agency and freedom (as indeed it often does), and if self-determination exists for some but not for all, it undermines security as theorised in this chapter.

C. Emancipation of the EU Itself?

At this point, it is useful to distinguish between two different, though related, dimensions of domination. The first concerns the cultural and ideological influence exerted

[58] S Aktan, 'EU's Josep Borrell Condemns Israeli Army's Attack on UNIFIL in Lebanon' (*euronews*, 28 October 2024), available at www.euronews.com/2024/10/28/eus-borrell-condemns-israels-unifil-attack-seeks-sanctions-netanyahu-focuses-on-victory.

[59] 'EU-Israel Association Council, 24 February 2025', available at www.consilium.europa.eu/en/meetings/international-ministerial-meetings/2025/02/24/.

[60] These are contained in Council Regulation (EU) No 833/2014 concerning restrictive measures in view of Russia's actions destabilising the situation in Ukraine [2014] OJ L229/1 and in Consolidated text: Council Regulation (EU) No 269/2014 concerning restrictive measures in respect of actions undermining or threatening the territorial integrity, sovereignty and independence of Ukraine [2014] OJ L78/6, both of which have been amended dozens of time since February 2022.

[61] European Council Conclusions of 22 June 2022, available at www.consilium.europa.eu/en/press/press-releases/2022/06/23/european-council-conclusions-on-ukraine-the-membership-applications-of-ukraine-the-republic-of-moldova-and-georgia-western-balkans-and-external-relations-23-june-2022/.

on Europe by external powers (I will consider here the US), while the second concerns the hegemonic position that Europe itself holds within the structures of international law and global governance.

One dimension that critical theory explores is that of cultural domination, something largely overlooked by lawyers.[62] Cultural hegemony refers to the capacity of one power (often dominant in economic or military terms) to shape the worldview, values, and norms of others, not through coercion, but through consent and diffusion. In the context of EU foreign policy, it sharpens the analytical lens on how domination may occur not only through political or military means, but also by framing what is considered desirable, civilised, or modern. Discussions of European colonialism cannot escape this cultural dimension: domination was enforced not only by armies, but also by language, education, religion, and law. To explore emancipation in EU foreign policy without grappling with its cultural legacy would be to miss one of the most enduring – and least questioned – forms of power.

One issue that is not discussed often in legal scholarship, but which is still far-reaching, is the pervasive influence of American culture in Europe. It has long been a subject of scholarly discourse (and of criticism from the left and the right, at various moments and with varying degrees of intensity[63]), with manifestations across various cultural domains,[64] including film,[65] music,[66] sport[67] and, more recently, social media.[68] Although it uses the notion in a political and miliary, rather than cultural, sense, Geir Lundestad's work on the relationship between the EU and Western Europe after World War II is tellingly (sub-)titled *Empire by Invitation*.[69] Granted, even though 'the American dream' holds important cultural influence in Europe, it does not automatically translate into political unity. Some of the most important moments in contemporary international history showed quite a dramatic split between EU countries: for example, the 2003 invasion of Iraq by a 'coalition of the willing', with UK, Spain, Italy, the Netherlands and Belgium joining the US alongside central and Eastern European countries, with strong opposition by France, Germany, and the Nordics. The invasion was deemed necessary by those who did it because it was believed that Saddam Hussein was hiding weapons of mass

[62] But see the exceptions – not concerned with foreign policy specifically – of S Rehling Larsen, 'Imagining Europe' (2023) 24 *German Law Journal* 705; J Komárek, *European Constitutional Imaginaries: Between Ideology and Utopia* (Oxford University Press, 2023).

[63] For examples of the former, see A Guiso, *La colomba e la spada: lotta per la pace e antiamericanismo nella politica del Partito comunista italiano (1949-1954)* (Rubbettino, 2007); R Girard, 'L'Europe tétanisée face à l'hégémonisme américain' (*Revue Des Deux Mondes*, 11 February 2019), available at www.revuedesdeuxmondes.fr/leurope-tetanisee-face-a-lhegemonisme-americain/ and of the latter.

[64] N Tsvetkova, *Failure of American and Soviet Cultural Imperialism in German Universities, 1945-1990* (Brill, 2013).

[65] B Grantham, *Some Big Bourgeois Brothel: Contexts for France's Culture Wars with Hollywood* (University of Luton Press, 2000).

[66] S Church, 'Resistance, Race, and Myth: A Critical Survey of American Popular Music Culture in the 20th Century' (2024) 6 *Dialogue: The Interdisciplinary Journal of Popular Culture and Pedagogy*, available at https://digitalcommons.unl.edu/dialogue/vol6/iss3/7.

[67] GR Gems, *The Athletic Crusade: Sport and American Cultural Imperialism* (University of Nebraska Press, 2006).

[68] Aside from TikTok, all the tech giants are US companies (Mets, Alphabet, Apple, and so on).

[69] G Lundestad, 'Empire by Invitation? The United States and Western Europe, 1945-1952' (1986) 23 *Journal of Peace Research* 263; G Lundestad, *The United States and Western Europe since 1945: From 'Empire' by Invitation to Transatlantic Drift* (Oxford University Press, 2003).

destruction to attack the US. Another example is the 2011 NATO-led intervention in Libya, with a force that comprised of most countries in Western Europe and the US but not, crucially, Germany or many central and European countries. This time, the invasion was authorised by the UN Security Council to 'take all measures to protect civilians',[70] in what has been considered an application of the political doctrine of responsibility to protect.[71] These examples show that cultural alignment between the EU and US does not guarantee political convergence: hegemony may shape preferences, but it does not go as far as to coerce whoever is under the hegemony. Yet precisely because it works through consent and affinity, cultural hegemony can obscure the persistence of unequal power relations, making domination more difficult to detect and challenge. Critical theory helps draw attention to it, because of its suspicion against 'hidden' forms of domination.

The second strand of analysis concerns not the EU as an object of external domination, but as a potential agent of it itself. From this perspective, the focus shifts from American cultural influence to the ways in which European norms, laws, and institutions perpetuate asymmetries of power on a global scale. The EU and the body of law it champions internationally can be conceived as expressions of cultural hegemony. This view does not rest solely on material disparities in wealth or military capacity, but on the more deeply embedded asymmetries in representation, norm-generation, and institutional design that has the consequence of reproducing historical power hierarchies.[72] As Tully has argued, the international order founded on the Westphalian conception of sovereignty and public international law privileges a particular understanding of statehood and legal personality, one that emerges from European intellectual and political traditions and has the effect of marginalising alternative epistemologies, legal orders, and historical experiences.[73] In this view, international institutions do not simply mirror global inequality: they help to manufacture its legitimacy by embedding it in apparently neutral procedures and rules. They function, in other words, as cultural vehicles of domination.

This line of critique resonates with earlier reflections on the nature of cultural hegemony and its relationship to EU foreign policy. If cultural hegemony operates by framing certain norms, values, and ways of organising society as universal, then the international legal and institutional order may be one of its most enduring artefacts. Just as colonial powers projected their authority not only through military conquest but also through law, religion, and education, the postcolonial international system may continue to reflect the normative assumptions of those same powers, albeit in new institutional forms. From this perspective, the very syntax of international politics remains shaped by the legacies of domination.

Nevertheless, to recognise these asymmetries is not to reject international institutions or international law wholesale (with theorists diverging on this point). For EU foreign policy, this raises an important question. If the Union claims, as it does in Articles

[70] Point 3 of S/Res/1973 (2011). T Achiume and A Bâli, 'Race and Empire: Legal Theory Within, Through, and Across National Borders' (2021) 67 *UCLA Law Review* 1368, 1396.

[71] S Adams, 'Responsibility to Protect' (2012) 3 *Global Centre for the Responsibility to Protect.*

[72] The classic 'critical' history of international law is M Koskenniemi, *The Gentle Civilizer of Nations: The Rise and Fall of International Law 1870–1960* (Cambridge University Press, 2001).

[73] J Tully, 'On Law, Democracy and Imperialism' in S Tierney and E Christodoulidis (eds), *Public Law and Politics: The Scope and Limits of Constitutionalism* (Routledge, 2008).

3(5) and 21(1) TEU, to be guided by the principles of the United Nations Charter and international law, then it must reflect critically on the political and historical context in which these frameworks have evolved. Upholding international law cannot be uncritical compliance with inherited structures; it must involve a commitment to their continual transformation in the direction of greater fairness and inclusivity – in the direction of rebalancing structural injustices as discussed in the previous section.

Practically, this may mean that the EU should adopt a more reflexive and pluralistic approach in multilateral fora, supporting reforms that give greater voice to Global South actors, questioning the legitimacy of procedures that have the consequence of marginalising weaker states, and engaging with non-Western legal and normative traditions as legitimate contributions to the international legal order. It also entails using the EU's considerable diplomatic and economic weight not merely to defend a rule-based international order as it currently stands, but to shape it toward a more emancipatory direction as outlined in the previous sections. In short, acknowledging international institutions as potential instruments of cultural hegemony does not negate their utility; it highlights the need to engage with them critically. For a foreign policy that aspires to support emancipation, the EU must not only participate in multilateralism but do so with the awareness that the very structures it inhabits may require transformation. Clarifying the interplay between these two dimensions (America's cultural hegemony over Europe and Europe's own hegemonic role in global governance) allows the notion of emancipation to be understood in a relational way: the EU must both emancipate itself from external ideological dominance and act responsibly to avoid reproducing similar patterns of domination abroad.

V. Conclusion

This chapter has interrogated the relevance of critical theory for EU *foreign* policy, as a complement to the other chapters of this volume, which analyse chiefly EU *internal* policies.

The inquiry began by highlighting a gap in mainstream legal scholarship: a failure to question the genesis and ultimate purpose of the EU's foreign policy, instead accepting its legal objectives as given. By applying the conceptual lens of domination and emancipation, this chapter moved beyond a doctrinal reading of legal texts to examine the deep-seated structures that shape the EU's actions on the world stage. The central argument is that military security of states, the historical *raison d'être* of European integration, should be reimagined as a precondition for emancipation. Drawing on Critical Security Studies, this reframes security not as the preservation of state power, but as the liberation of people from systemic threats like war, poverty, oppression. This reinterpretation has direct implications for applying EU law. It offers a principled way to navigate the competing objectives listed in Article 21(2) TEU, providing a meta-principle that prioritises actions promoting emancipation over those that reinforce domination.

Even if one rejects the need for reimagination, the diagnostic value of this critical approach remains. Critical theory's insistence on context reveals the structural and cultural forces that shape EU policy in ways a purely formalistic view of law cannot.

It brings to light uncomfortable truths, such as the EU's own colonial legacies and its inconsistent application of the principle of self-determination, which continue to influence its external relations. Domination, in this frame, is shown to be a structural and cultural phenomenon. This chapter also serves as a call for a more imaginative legal scholarship, also outside the context of foreign policy. In contrast to traditional doctrine, which has been accused of merely justifying existing (and sometimes colonial) power structures, this approach embraces a transformative purpose.

11

Critical Theory and EU Migration Law

Navigating the Field and Mapping New Territory

ALEZINI LOXA

I. Introduction to a Familiar Theme

Unlike many other areas of European Union (EU) law, the field of migration and asylum law is no stranger to critique. This field is fraught with legal categories that shape belonging and rights for one category of people while at the same time legitimising the exclusion – more often than not violent – of other people. This is a traditional function of migration law which is based on constructed legal categories such as citizen and alien, sovereignty, state discretion over migration, as well as the conceptualisation of borders as actual or imaginary lines that affect the attribution of rights.[1]

This traditional function of migration law has inspired a wealth of critique from within and outside the legal discipline.[2] The same is true for EU migration law. Great works of critique of EU migration and asylum law and of its legal categories as another iteration of state power have been written in the fields of political science, sociology, economic history and critical social theory.[3] By focusing on works produced by legal scholars, the purpose of this chapter is threefold. First it aspires to provide a systematic overview of the diverse ways in which critique has been used as a method to investigate EU migration and asylum law. Second, it argues for the value of racial capitalism critiques to complement existing critical approaches and to offer a novel and integrated

[1] J Torpey, *The Invention of the Passport: Surveillance, Citizenship and the State* (Cambridge University Press, 1999); M-B Dembour, *When Humans Become Migrants: Study of the European Court of Human Rights with an Inter-American Counterpoint* (Oxford University Press, 2015).

[2] See on international migration law in general, BS Chimni, 'The Geopolitics of Refugee Studies: A View from the South' (1998) 11 *Journal of Refugee Studies* 350; N El-Enany, *Bordering Britain: Law, Race and Empire*, 1st edn (Manchester University Press, 2020); See on international migration from outside the discipline, L Mayblin, *Asylum after Empire: Colonial Legacies in the Politics of Asylum Seeking* (Roman & Littlefield International, 2017); H Cross, *Migration beyond Capitalism* (Polity, 2021).

[3] It would be impossible to even attempt a representative presentation. See D Bigo and others, 'Borders and Security: The Different Logics of Surveillance in Europe' in S Bonjour and A Rea (eds), *The Others in Europe* (Institut d'Études Europeennes : Editions de l'Université de Bruxelles, 2011); N De Genova, *The Borders of Europe: Autonomy of Migration, Tactics of Bordering* (Duke University Press, 2017); E Balibar, 'Europe as Borderland' (2009) 27 *Environment and Planning D: Society and Space* 190.

way of critically studying the phenomenon of migration in EU law. Third it reflects on the value of critique for the study of EU migration and asylum law.

To do so the chapter begins by recounting the history of Europeanisation of this field. Following, I draw a distinction between the different kinds of critical interventions we find in this field (section III), before mapping various ways in which critical social theory has been used in EU migration and asylum law (section IV). Section V advocates for the importance of critiques that connect EU migration and asylum law to the political economy of the EU, and it suggests that racial capitalism can offer a useful analytical tool to move the field forward. The chapter concludes with a reflection on the contribution of critique to this field of study (section VI).

II. The Main Characteristics of EU Migration and Asylum Law

The area of migration and asylum law made a later entry into EU competences.[4] Initially part of the intergovernmental pillar of Justice and Home Affairs, the Area of Freedom, Security and Justice, under which migration and asylum are regulated today, became part of the EU structure with the Treaty of Amsterdam. A full set of constitutional safeguards such as full judicial review by the Court of Justice of the EU came about with the Lisbon Treaty.[5] Even after the Lisbon Treaty, though, this area is affected by the 'institutional idiosyncrasy' of opt outs which allow specific Member States to not be bound by instruments adopted in this area.[6]

The history of how migration and asylum entered the field of EU law is narrated as simple and straightforward. As EU integration progressed towards closer forms of co-operation with the abolition of internal border controls and the realisation of free movement for people (and not just for workers), it became necessary to have common external borders but also to regulate the categories of Third Country Nationals who would to have access to this common borderless space. The main presumption on the regulation of migration and asylum is that it was introduced to ensure that a true Area of Freedom, Security and Justice would be available to EU citizens on the move.[7]

[4] N Walker, 'In Search of the Area of Freedom, Security and Justice: A Constitutional Odyssey' in N Walker (ed), *Europe's Area of Freedom, Security, and Justice* (Oxford University Press, 2004).

[5] In the Amsterdam Treaty, judicial review by the Court of Justice of the EU was limited substantively and procedurally pursuant to Articles 62(1) 68(3) EC for the transitional period prescribed in Article 67 EC. In contrast with the other transitional arrangements of Amsterdam, the limitation to the Court's jurisdiction was only abolished with the Treaty of Lisbon. See S Peers, 'The Jurisdiction of the Court of Justice Over EC Immigration and Asylum Law: Time For a Change?' in A Baldaccini, E Guild and H Toner (eds), *Whose Freedom, Security and Justice?: EU Immigration and Asylum Law and Policy* (Hart Publishing, 2007).

[6] D Thym, *European Migration Law* (Oxford University Press, 2023) 63 See Arts 1 and 2, Protocol (No 21) on the position of the United Kingdom and Ireland in respect of the Area of Freedom, Security and Justice, Consolidated Version of the Treaty on the Functioning of the European Union [2016] OJ C202/295; Arts 1 and 2, Protocol (No 22) on the position of Denmark, Consolidated Version of the Treaty on the Functioning of the European Union [2016] OJ C202/298 on the possibility for Denmark, Ireland (and before Brexit, also the United Kingdom) not to participate in and be bound by instruments adopted in this area.

[7] This is also reflected in Art 3(2). K Hailbronner, *Immigration and Asylum Law and Policy of the European Union* (Kluwer Law International, 2000); Thym (n 6).

This simple story offers an internal explanation of the Europeanisation of EU migration and asylum law that is siloed from broader geopolitical developments within and outside the EU. For example, the fall of the Soviet Union, the anticipated migration flows from the East, the political instability in the Mediterranean region and the continued unemployment in Member States which were relevant for the development of the field are left out of the picture.[8] At the same time, even this simple explanation has offered a fruitful starting point for problematising the drivers and the legal implications of creating a hierarchy of rights between Europeans and non-Europeans and has led to a constant flow of critical scholarship in the field.[9] This critical scholarship however has taken very diverse forms as will be discussed in the next section.

III. Criticism or Critique?

In an area that has been, is being or perhaps has always been in a state of 'crisis', being critical of EU law could be said to be the standard approach in the discipline.[10] Being critical, however, does not always imply the use of critique or, as Neuvonen would put it, there is a difference between substantive criticism and critique as a methodological commitment.[11] The diverse forms of critical literature in the field necessitate a better understanding of what is visible and what becomes concealed or sidelined by different types of critical work. It allows us to understand the limitations and potentials of critical approaches in general and of critical social thought specifically for the reimagination of EU migration and asylum law.

To understand the difference between criticism and critique, let us imagine a critical scholar and a scholar doing critique or using critical social theories.[12] These scholars would possibly share a critical attitude, that is, an approach to the legal text that interrogates its meaning. After all, if legal consequences could be immediately and determinatively drawn from legal text, there would be little value in interpretation. However, these two scholars would have different approaches and methods on how to go about research beyond an immediate reading and description of the legal text. To make this point clear, let us imagine how each of these scholars would engage with the

[8] A Loxa, *Sustainability and EU Migration Law: Tracing the History of a Contemporary Concept* (Cambridge University Press, 2025) 79ff.

[9] See already in the 1990s, D O'Keeffe, 'Recasting the Third Pillar' (1995) 32 *CML Rev* 893; JDM Steenbergen, 'All the King's Horses...: Probabilities and Possibilities for the Implementation of the New Title IV EC Treaty' (1999) 1 *European Journal of Migration and Law* 29.

[10] A Loxa and V Stoyanova, 'Migration as a Constitutional Crisis for the European Union' in S Smet and V Stoyanova (eds), *Migrants' Rights, Populism and Legal Resilience in Europe* (Cambridge University Press, 2022); M den Heijer, J Riijpma and T Spijkerboer, 'Coercion, Prohibition, and Great Expectations: The Continuing Failure of the Common European Asylum System' (2016) 53 *CML Rev* 607; M Scipioni, 'Failing Forward in EU Migration Policy? EU Integration after the 2015 Asylum and Migration Crisis' (2018) 25 *Journal of European Public Policy* 1357; D Thym, 'European Migration Law Between "Rescuing" and "Taming" the Nation State: A History of Half-Hearted Commitment to Human Rights and Refugee Protection' (2024) 2023 8 *European Papers* 1663.

[11] PJ Neuvonen, 'A Way of Critique: What Can EU Law Scholars Learn from Critical Theory?' (2022) 1 *European Law Open* 60, 86.

[12] It is possible that a person can be both a critical scholar and a scholar doing critique, that they express criticism and critique in one and the same output or that they have works where they offer criticism and works where they use critique.

distinction between EU citizens and Third Country Nationals, which is considered to be fundamental for the purposes of EU migration and asylum law.

The critical scholar would normally take a view internal to the system and would not question the distinction between these two legal statuses. Rather, understanding these categories as legitimate for the purposes of shaping the attribution of rights under EU law, the critical scholar would turn their attention to specific problems within EU law. By this, I do not mean that the critical scholar necessarily agrees with the effects of these categories for the social reality or with the politics behind them. Rather, I suggest that for the purposes of critical work, the formal categories that EU law creates cannot be rejected, but rather are understood as an integral part of the legal system.[13] With this in mind, the critical scholar would turn their attention to issues understood as problems for a liberal legal system, an approach typical of a more positivist understanding of legal studies. Potential issues to be examined could be the identification of inconsistencies in the application or interpretation of the law;[14] the fragmentation of the legislation in the field;[15] the use of soft law which is criticised precisely for escaping the legal guarantees that would come with the adoption of hard-law instruments;[16] the interplay of the external and internal dimension of EU migration law and its effects for democracy and the rule of law;[17] and finally respect for or effectiveness of the protection of human rights of migrants.[18] Another example of critical work commonly met in the discipline is

[13] On the options of critical lawyers who stay within the system, see also T Spijkerboer, 'Analysing European Case-Law on Migration: Options for Critical Lawyers' in L Azoulai and K de Vries (eds), *EU Migration Law: Legal Complexities and Political Rationales* (Oxford University Press, 2014).

[14] E Muir, 'Enhancing the Protection of Third-Country Nationals against Discrimination: Putting EU Anti-Discrimination Law to the Test' (2011) 18 *Maastricht Journal of European and Comparative Law* 136; D Kostakopoulou, S Carrera and M Jesse, 'Doing and Deserving: Competing Frames of Intergration in the EU' in E Guild, K Groenendijk and S Carrera (eds), *Illiberal Liberal States : Immigration, Citizenship, and Integration in the EU* (Ashgate, 2009); E Bratanova von Harten, 'The Road Not Taken: Applying the EU Charter of Fundamental Rights to Migration and Asylum Cases' in A Loxa and L Lonardo (eds), *The Reasoning of the Court of Justice of the EU: A Normative Assessment* (Oxford University Press, 2026).

[15] Usually expressed in relation to the regulation of labour migration, see, eg, K Groenendijk, 'Recent Developments in Eu Law on Migration: The Legislative Patchwork and the Court's Approach' (2014) 16 *European Journal of Migration and Law* 313; H Verschueren, 'Employment and Social Security Rights of Third-Country Labour Migrants under EU Law: An Incomplete Patchwork of Legal Protection' (2016) 18 *European Journal of Migration and Law* 373; E Guild, 'The EU's Internal Market and the Fragmentary Nature of EU Labour Migration' in C Costello and M Freedland (eds), *Migrants at Work: Immigration and Vulnerability in Labour Law* (Oxford University Press, 2014); A Beduschi, 'An Empty Shell? The Protection of Social Rights of Third-Country Workers in the Eu after the Single Permit Directive' (2015) 17 *European Journal of Migration and Law* 210.

[16] E Kassoti and N Idriz (eds), *The Informalisation of the EU's External Action in the Field of Migration and Asylum*, vol 1 (TMC Asser Press, 2022); V Moreno-Lax, 'The Informalisation of the External Dimension of EU Asylum Policy: The Hard Implications of Soft Law' in E Tsourdi and P De Buycker (eds), *Research Handbook on EU Migration and Asylum Law* (Edward Elgar Publishing, 2022).

[17] See the contributions in J Santos Vara, P García Andrade and T Molnár, 'The Externalisation of EU Migration Policies in Light of EU Constitutional Principles and Values: Reconciling the Irreconcilable? An Introduction to the Special Section' (2023) 2023 8 *European Papers* 901; And all the chapters in S Carrera, J Santos Vara and T Strik (eds), *Constitutionalising the External Dimensions of EU Migration Policies in Times of Crisis: Legality, Rule of Law and Fundamental Rights Reconsidered* (Edward Elgar Publishing, 2019).

[18] E Guild and K Groenendijk, *Illiberal Liberal States : Immigration, Citizenship and Integration in the EU* (Routledge, 2009); C Costello, *The Human Rights of Migrants and Refugees in European Law* (Oxford University Press, 2016); V Moreno-Lax, *Accessing Asylum in Europe: Extraterritorial Border Controls and Refugee Rights under EU Law* (Oxford University Press, 2017); J De Coninck, *The EU's Human Rights Responsibility Gap: Deconstructing Human Rights Impunity of International Organisations* (Hart Publishing, 2024); S Peers, 'The New Asylum Pact: Brave New World or Dystopian Hellscape?' (2024) 26 *European Journal of Migration and Law* 381 but also implicitly or explicitly in the works cited in the references above.

literature that traces the conflicting objectives of security and population control in the regulation of migration.[19] According to this scholarship, the historical overlap of these objectives has led to the adoption of law that prioritises the protection of the EU from internal and external threats.[20] With every type of external shock, the story goes, the EU continues to focus on security rather than on what should be the normative objective of migration law, the regulation of mobility and the protection of fundamental rights.[21]

Unlike the types of works mentioned above, the scholar doing critique or using critical social theories would not be bound by EU law's formal categories in the same way. Rather, such a scholar would question the assumptions and power relations that lie behind, or, perhaps, are concealed by, seemingly neutral legal categories such as those of EU citizens and Third Country Nationals. The scholar would interrogate how such categories are constructed, and they would investigate what kind of exclusions they produce. In so doing, this scholar would usually draw on a conceptual apparatus borrowed from the social sciences and critical social theory which provides more developed theoretical frameworks to be used in critique. This type of work would allow this scholar to not only problematise the function of legal categories and their effect, but also to potentially propose radical ways of rethinking our current system. While the same scholar can be critical with or without drawing on critical social theories in different kinds of scholarly works, it is the later approach that will be the focus of the next section. [22]

IV. The Many Faces of Critique in EU Migration and Asylum Law

As alluded to in the Introduction, EU migration law has a tradition of critical engagement. This is so not only in relation to the relentless production of criticisms already since the foundation of the field, but most importantly for our purposes, in relation to critique. In the overview that follows I offer a systematisation of various critiques of EU migration and asylum law. Some of the works presented below draw on a conceptual apparatus from the social sciences in order to make sense of EU law and the background

[19] See also chapter 10 by Luigi Lonardo in this book discussing the objective of security in relation to the Common Foreign and Security Policy.

[20] D Kostakopoulou, 'The Area of Freedom, Security and Justice and the Political Morality of Migration and Integration' in H Lindahl (ed), *A Right to Inclusion and Exclusion? : Normative Fault Lines of the EU's Area of Freedom, Security and Justice* (Hart Publishing, 2009); T Kostakopoulou, 'The "Protective Union"; Change and Continuity in Migration Law and Policy in Post-Amsterdam Europe' (2000) 38 *Journal of Common Market Studies* 497; A Gomez Arana, 'The EU and the Migration Crisis: Reinforcing a Security-Based Approach to Migration?' in S Carrera, J Santos Vara and T Strik, *Constitutionalising the External Dimensions of EU Migration Policies in Times of Crisis* (Edward Elgar Publishing, 2019); R Cholewinski, 'The EU Acquis on Irregular Migration: Reinforcing Security at the Expense of Rights' (2000) 2 *European Journal of Migration and Law* 361.

[21] Such concerns are even more pronounced in the area of asylum law where humanitarian considerations should normatively prevail, see V Mitsilegas, V Moreno-Lax and N Vavoula (eds), *Securitising Asylum Flows* (Brill, 2020).

[22] An example from my work would be A Loxa, 'Insiders, Outsiders and the Constructed Limited to Social Rights in EU Law' (2025) 10 *European Papers – A Journal on Law and Integration* for a criticism 163; A Loxa, 'EU Law, Migration and Racial Capitalism: Encounters at the Neoliberal EU (b)Order' (2024) 4 *Retfærd: Nordisk Juridisk Tidsskrift* 11 for a critique.

conditions that shape it. There are also works that explicitly foreground in their analysis the use of critical social theory, understood as a tradition of thought that theorises how law, economy and society are shaped by structures of domination (along racial, material, gendered lines) and that offers theoretical frameworks to analyse the role of law and its function in broader systems of power.[23]

In a field that has lent itself to a wealth of critical engagement, any systematisation will have blind spots and fall victim to the author's own positionality in the field. Still, the mapping presented below hopes to offer an extensive, if not exhaustive, picture of the diversity of critical engagement with EU migration and asylum law. The systematisation offered is based on the critical theoretical thought that has guided various scholars.[24] Depending on the theoretical framework each scholar draws on, the legal categories of EU law would be understood as expressions of different types of domination constituted by the law, more often than not interconnected, and based on race, coloniality and Eurocentrism. What critical scholarship has not done yet is to connect these types of domination to the political economy of the EU, as will be discussed in section V.

A. Europeanisation and the Reproduction of Racial Exclusion

Any presentation of critical engagement with EU migration law would have to begin with works that locate the reproduction of power hierarchies in the very process of Europeanising migration law. As mentioned in the Introduction, migration law has always been a fertile ground for critique due to the dividing line it draws between nationals and aliens as the ground for differentiated access to rights.[25] EU law has been thought of as both upsetting and reproducing this division. To begin with, the creation of European citizenship upset the categories of nationals and aliens by forcing the Member States to treat foreigners who originate in other Member States as nationals. For a while, European citizenship was viewed as having the potential of emancipating citizens from nation-states and as carrying the seeds of a true post-national form of citizenship that could also include non-Europeans.[26] Soon enough it became clear that the status of European citizenship as a status of all the nationals of the Member States was to be contrasted with the status of Third Country Nationals, that is, all those not having the nationality of an EU Member State. The Europeanisation of migration law indeed upset national borders and forced the inclusion of EU nationals, but at the same time it reproduced the division between national and alien at a European level.

[23] See Preface in this book.

[24] Most of them are explicit on this matter. For those that are not, I trace their arguments, methodologies and suggestions in what appears to be the critical theoretical framework guiding them. This means that any misrepresentation would be entirely my own fault.

[25] D Thym, 'Deciphering the Role of (Migration) Law in the Social Construction of "Otherness"' in M Jesse (ed), *European Societies, Migration, and the Law: The 'Others' amongst 'Us'* (Cambridge University Press, 2020).

[26] Y Nuhoğlu Soysal, *Limits of Citizenship: Migrants and Postnational Membership in Europe* (University of Chicago, 1994); D Kostakopoulou, 'Ideas, Norms and European Citizenship: Explaining Institutional Change' (2005) 68 *MLR* 233.

Some scholars have tried to explain the reproduction of such divisions through the lens of 'othering'. Othering would be understood as the result of a discursive process by which 'us' is constructed as a dominant group and differentiated from 'others'.[27] In EU migration law, scholars have looked at the ways in which law has been used as a technique of othering not only between EU citizens and Third Country Nationals, but also in relation to different groups of EU citizens.[28] Others have sought to identify the reason why this 'othering' has been reproduced with race as the main explanation.[29] Scholars like Spijkerboer have traced how the bifurcation produced by the Europeanisation of migration law between two types of human movement, a liberal version under free movement and a restricted version under migration, is also reproduced in a bifurcation of law, which includes Europeans but excludes migrants from the scope of EU law, with reference to case law on the EU-Turkey agreement and humanitarian visas.[30] Others, like Kochenov and Ganty, have mapped the legal techniques used to enforce a European apartheid and have used the term lawlessness law to describe them.[31] The works included in this category draw on concepts from the social sciences to show the constructed nature of the basic legal categories of EU law or to explain the effects produced by EU law. Not all the works however necessarily connect these effects with broader structures of racialised domination connected to Europe's colonial past as is the case for the works included in the next section.

B. Racialised Borders and Colonial Legacies

Closely connected to racialised hierarchies embedded in and reproduced by EU migration law is a strand of critique that emphasises the relation of EU integration to a broader global history of western imperial domination in the Global South.[32] Such works draw implicitly or explicitly on a tradition of post-colonial studies.[33] While authors might have different perspectives on whether the EU is continuing where colonial empires left off or on whether it repeats techniques of governance which existed in past times, they

[27] See, eg, M Jesse, 'The Immigrant As the "Other"' in M Jesse (ed), *European Societies, Migration, and the Law: The 'Others' amongst 'Us'* (Cambridge University Press, 2020).

[28] See S Bonjour, A Rea and D Jacobs (eds), *The Others in Europe* (Institut d'Études Europeennes : Editions de l'Université de Bruxelles, 2011) for an interdisciplinary perspective with political scientiests also drawing on othering as a technique of Foucauldian governmentality; See the contributions in M Jesse (ed), *European Societies, Migration, and the Law: The 'Others' amongst 'Us'* (Cambridge University Press, 2020); See also D Acosta Arcarazo and J Martire, 'Trapped in the Lobby: Europe's Revolving Doors and the Other as Xenos' (2014) 39 *European Law Review* 362 for a theorisation of how the 'other' is understood in EU migration law.

[29] See É Balibar, *Nous, citoyens d'Europe ?* (La Découverte, 2001) who suggested that the process of Europeanisation led to the creation of a European apartheid drawing divisions along racial lines.

[30] T Spijkerboer, 'Bifurcation of People, Bifurcation of Law: Externalization of Migration Policy before the EU Court of Justice' (2018) 31 *Journal of Refugee Studies* 216.

[31] D Kochenov and S Ganty, 'EU Lawlessness Law: Europe's Passport Apartheid From Indifference To Torture and Killing', Jean Monnet Working Paper No 2/2022 (NYU Law School).

[32] See P Hansen and S Jonsson, *Eurafrica: The Untold History of European Integration and Colonialism* (Bloomsbury Academic, 2015); H Kundnani, *Eurowhiteness: Culture, Empire and Race in the European Project* (Hurst & Company, 2023).

[33] F Fanon, *The Wretched of the Earth* (Grove Press, 2004); AD Morris and others (eds), *The Oxford Handbook of W. E. B. Du Bois* (Oxford University Press, 2024).

all understand that migration law plays a key role in the reproduction of racial hierarchies which date back to colonialism and imperialism.[34]

In this category of critique, we find works that suggest that the legal categories and concepts of EU migration law are not neutral. Rather, they are constructed in a continuum of western domination and extraction from the Global South. Important in this field is the work of Achiume who has showed how the construction of the legal category of sovereignty has been key for political subordination in colonial times and relatedly how this should make us rethink how we understand both the act of migration from the Global South and its regulation.[35] Spijkerboer has revisited emergency as a governance technique developed in European colonies and absorbed in international and European law in the regulation of migration.[36] Xanthopoulou has adopted a similar theoretical lens, that is, an understanding of emergency as a technique of power perfected in colonial times and exercised in the present, when examining the shifting state responsibility for asylum seekers and migrants both in the context of the Dublin Regulation and in relation to partnerships with third countries on border controls.[37]

Other scholars have focused on specific policies and have showed how their underlying logics can be traced back to colonial times. By examining EU visa policy as a technology of exploitation dating back to European colonialism and continuing to this day, Achiume has shown how European borders facilitate and sustain neocolonial inequality.[38] Silga has done valuable work in the field of EU development policy.[39] She has shown that the migration-development nexus in the EU exposes an understanding of a civilisation gap between the EU and African countries where migrants are supposed to be migrating exclusively due to underdevelopment (root causes) and where keeping them at home is key for preserving a North-South divide.[40] Similarly, Hocquet has re-read co-operation agreements concluded by the EU with third countries after 2015 by adopting a TWAIL approach, that is an approach that recentres the voices and interests of the Global South and that uncovers the histories and power domination behind law's

[34] E Tendayi Achiume, 'Empire, Borders, and Refugee Responsibility Sharing' (2022) 110 *California Law Review* 1011; E Tendayi Achiume, 'Racial Borders' (2021) 110 *Georgetown Law Journal* 445.

[35] E Tendayi Achiume, 'Migration as Decolonization' (2019) 71 *Stanford Law Review* 1509; See also K de Vries and T Spijkerboer, 'Race and the Regulation of International Migration. The Ongoing Impact of Colonialism in the Case Law of The European Court of Human Rights' (2021) 39 *Netherlands Quarterly of Human Rights* 291, 291 with a focus on the European Court of Human Rights and the relation of migration control to the prohibition of race discrimination.

[36] T Spijkerboer, 'Coloniality and Recent European Migration Case Law' in S Smet and V Stoyanova (eds), *Migrants' Rights, Populism and Legal Resilience in Europe* (Cambridge University Press, 2022) 118.

[37] E Xanthopoulou, 'Mapping EU Externalisation Devices through a Critical Eye' (2024) 26 *European Journal of Migration and Law* 108. Regulation (EU) No 604/2013 of the European Parliament and of the Council of 26 June 2013 establishing the criteria and mechanisms for determining the Member State responsible for examining an application for international protection lodged in one of the Member States by a third-country national or a stateless person (recast) [2013] OJ L180/ 31.

[38] Achiume, 'Racial Borders' (n 34).

[39] J Silga, 'From Political to Migration-Based Conditionality in EU Development Policy: "Plus Ça Change, plus c'Est La Même Chose"' in Eklund (ed), *Colonialism and the EU Legal Order* (Cambridge University Press, 2025); J Silga, 'The Ambiguity of the Migration and Development Nexus Policy Discourse: Perpetuating the Colonial Legacy?' (2020) 24 *UCLA Journal of International Law and Foreign Affairs* 163.

[40] Silga, 'The Ambiguity of the Migration and Development Nexus Policy Discourse' (n 39) 174 ff.

universality.[41] She has suggested that a civilising mission narrative is reproduced at EU level to legitimise stricter migration controls and transfer of responsibility to third countries.[42]

A final example of critical work grounded in post-colonial theory is work that uncovers the history behind the adoption of specific instruments or the creation of legal categories in migration and asylum law.[43] The work of Eklund stands out in the field of EU law. Eklund traced how Member States negotiated the categories of peoples, workers and inhabitants in the Treaty of Rome so as to exclude colonial subjects from the free movement regime set up by the Treaty.[44] While Eklund is not drawing on critical social theory, her critical move lies in how she contextualises archival material in the colonial politics of the Member States at the time of negotiation of the Treaty of Rome.

Overall, in the post-colonial critiques of the EU, scholars have shown how various legal arrangements, doctrines or categories (sovereignty, borders, states of emergency, workers, co-operation with third countries) have been constructed in a specific historical context with the purpose of excluding certain people and imposing power hierarchies on the basis of race. Such works are informed by the centrality of history and genealogical critique in critical theory and they bring colonial histories of oppression to bear in the study of EU law.[45] By exposing the historical context of various EU policies either directly by archival work or indirectly by bringing its context to bear on the development and current iteration of law, they show how EU migration and asylum law actively contributes to the perpetuation of racial injustice.

C. Crisis and Biopolitical Borders

Borders legitimate the distinction between the national and the foreigner, and they express sovereignty as a power to govern a specific population through its differentiation from foreigners.[46] Literature offering a critique to European borders and produced by legal scholars has been focusing on the social reality of violence exercised at the borders of what is commonly called 'Fortress Europe', and it has theorised that reality in view of the way in which it subdues migrants to power.[47] While works mentioned in the previous sections also take the function of borders into account, especially when

[41] C Hocquet, 'Tracking the Civilising Mission's Continuities in Externalised Migration Controls: A Critical Analysis of EU Cooperation with Third Countries' (2024) 12 *London Review of International Law* 181; A Anghie, 'Rethinking International Law: A TWAIL Retrospective' (2023) 34 *European Journal of International Law* 7.

[42] Hocquet, ibid, seen in the benevolent aspects of the co-operation on the part of the EU to help in the development of these countries and in their responsibility for causing migration and destabilising the EU.

[43] See, eg, on the Refugee Convention negotiations, U Krause, 'Colonial Roots of the 1951 Refugee Convention and Its Effects on the Global Refugee Regime' (2021) 24 *Journal of International Relations and Development* 599.

[44] H Eklund, 'Peoples, Inhabitants and Workers: Colonialism in the Treaty of Rome' (2023) 34 *European Journal of International Law 831.*

[45] See also chapter 2 by Kaius Tuori in this book on the centrality of history for genealogical work.

[46] Balibar (n 3) 192.

[47] The delimitation to works produced by legal scholars, while to some extent artificial, is made with the purpose of showing how critique has been used as a method to investigate EU law. It is necessary because borders in general, and EU borders specifically, have been subjected to critique from very diverse disciplinary perspectives whose purpose was not to necessarily offer critical engagement with law.

discussing the racial exclusion they facilitate, the research I present in this section is focused on borders as a technique of governance and iteration of state power.

Especially after the so-called migration 'crisis', scholarly work has critically examined the violence exercised at the common external borders as well as the role of law in the perpetuation of such violence. Moreno Lax has theorised crisis itself as a technique of governance that has allowed the legalised expansion of power at the European borders and the contraction of pre-existing legal frameworks.[48] Others have drawn on Foucaults' biopolitics, on Agamben's state of exception, as well as on Mbembes' necropolitics.[49] These frameworks explain how sovereign power manages human life, how it excludes certain lives from protection and how it produces death by subjecting certain lives to absolute disposability. An example of this type of critical engagement is the work of Nordentoft Mose and Wriedt, who examined the informal agreements of the EU with third countries in the context of the European Neighbourhood Policy, as well as surveillance mechanisms used by Frontex and EUROSUR. The authors theorised these mechanisms as techniques which construct bio/necropolitical borderspaces as zones of exception which extend beyond the territorial EU borders and which are moving with the racialised and gendered bodies of migrant and refugees exposed to such violence.[50] Similarly, Davitti has theorised the emergency framing of 2015–2016 and the EU policy response through Agamben's state of exception.[51] She has traced the legal iteration of this state of exception in the exploitation of the concept of 'safe third country', the reliance on informal readmission agreements, the creation of 'hotspots' in EU external borders but also in the increasing militarisation, privatisation and externalisation of EU borders.[52]

Closely connected to this stream of critical engagement is the work of Corcodel and Fragou.[53] In their work, they build on the conception of biopolitical borders and they trace how risk had been understood and managed in 2015–2016 and in the 2022 'crisis' which led to the activation of the Temporary Protection Directive for Ukrainians fleeing the war with Russia.[54] They suggested that while risk management is a technology integral to the biopolitical power exercised under EU migration and asylum law, such technology produces racialised hierarchies which lead to differential schemes for dealing with 'crisis' in EU law.[55]

[48] V Moreno-Lax, 'The "Crisification" of Migration Law: Insights from the EU External Border"' in S Burch Elias, K Cope and J Goldenziel (eds), *Oxford Handbook of Comparative Immigration Law* (Oxford University Press, forthcoming).

[49] A Mbembe, *Necropolitics* (Duke University Press, 2019); M Foucault, *The Birth of Biopolitics: Lectures at the Collège de France, 1978-79* (Paperback edn, Palgrave Macmillan 2010); G Agamben, *State of Exception* (University of Chicago Press, 2005).

[50] K Nordentoft Mose and V Wriedt, 'Mapping the Construction of EU Borderspaces as Necropolitical Zones of Exception' (2015) 3 *Birkbeck Law Review* 278, 295.

[51] D Davitti, 'Biopolitical Borders and the State of Exception in the European Migration "Crisis"' (2018) 29 *European Journal of International Law* 1173.

[52] ibid, particularly 1186 ff.

[53] V Corcodel and D Fragkou, 'Europe's Refugee "Crises" and the Biopolitics of Risk' (2024) 15 *European Journal of Risk Regulation* 416.

[54] Council Directive 2001/55/EC of 20 July 2001 on minimum standards for giving temporary protection in the event of a mass influx of displaced persons and on measures promoting a balance of efforts between Member States in receiving such persons and bearing the consequences thereof [2001] OJ L 212/12.

[55] These differential schemes were later theorised as closely connected to colonial legacies: V Corcodel, 'Europe's Refugee "Crises" and the Colonial Legacies in EU Migration and Asylum Law' in H Eklund (ed), *Colonialism and the EU Legal Order* (Cambridge University Press, 2025).

More recent work has explored the asymmetry between where EU border control takes place and where the obligation to protect fundamental rights applies under international law and EU law through the lens of critical theoretical work on spatiality. With a focus on particular spatio-legal sites of border control, Wejstål has suggested that the interaction of law and space invisibilises fundamental rights and corresponding state obligations.[56]

D. Queer Critiques and the Politics of Inclusion

A final strand of critique, which has escaped attention in the mainstream analysis of EU migration law, can be found in works which critically reflect on the dark sides of inclusion in EU asylum law.[57] Refugee law had been criticised from a feminist perspective for the absence of gender, sexual identity and sexual orientation from the text of the Refugee Convention.[58] Since the 1990s, state practice and court decisions at European and international levels paved the way for an understanding of sexual identity and sexual orientation as protected grounds for the purposes of asylum recognition through the concept of 'particular social group'.[59] This is the case also under EU law, where sexual orientation and gender identity are explicitly mentioned in Article 10(1)(d) of the Qualification Directive.[60] It is this kind of inclusion that has been examined through a critical lens drawing explicitly or implicitly on the work of queer theorists.[61]

For example, Spijkerboer has examined the inclusion of such types of asylum seekers in EU asylum protection as having the potential to destabilise the exclusionary effects of EU law.[62] He started from the dichotomy of asylum law between an idealised Europe that needs to be protected versus an outside world as a site of oppression. He has suggested that queer asylum seekers risk destabilising this dichotomy by invoking human rights to justify their inclusion despite their outsider (barbarian) status. The claims to protection draw on an understanding of Europe (and the West) as a space of sexual freedom and a symbol of queer rights closely connected to democratic statehood, in short on a

[56] K Wejstål, *At the Border – EU Law, Asylum and the Spatialities of Fundamental Rights* (PhD Dissertation, Gothenburg University, 2024); DB Massey, *For Space* (SAGE Publications, 2005); A Philippopoulos-Mihalopoulos, *Spatial Justice: Body, Lawscape, Atmosphere* (Routledge, 2015).

[57] *cf* D Kennedy, *The Dark Sides of Virtue: Reassessing International Humanitarianism* (Princeton University Press, 2011).

[58] DE Anker, 'Refugee Law, Gender, and the Human Rights Paradigm' (2002) 15 *Harvard Human Rights Journal* 133; J Greatbatch, 'The Gender Difference: Feminist Critiques of Refugee Discourse' (1989) 1 *International Journal of Refugee Law* 518. UN General Assembly, 1951 Convention Relating to the Status of Refugees, United Nations, Treaty Series, vol 189, 137, 28 July 1951.

[59] See N Ferreira and C Danisi, 'Queering International Refugee Law' in C Costello, M Foster and J McAdam (eds), *The Oxford Handbook of International Refugee Law* (Oxford University Press, 2021).

[60] Directive 2011/95/EU of the European Parliament and of the Council of 13 December 2011 on standards for the qualification of third-country nationals or stateless persons as beneficiaries of international protection, for a uniform status for refugees or for persons eligible for subsidiary protection, and for the content of the protection granted (recast) [2011] OJ L337/9.

[61] C Danisi and others, *Queering Asylum in Europe: Legal and Social Experiences of Seeking International Protection on Grounds of Sexual Orientation and Gender Identity* (Springer International Publishing, 2021) 75 ff.

[62] T Spijkerboer, 'Gender, Sexuality, Asylum and European Human Rights' (2018) 29 *Law and Critique* 221.

homonationalist imaginary.[63] Still, they exploit the ambiguities inherent in asylum law to claim protection.[64]

More recent work has been produced on sexual orientation and gender identity, or expression asylum claims. There is a body of work developed by the SOGICA project whose purpose has been to document the social and legal experience of queer asylum seekers.[65] Others have examined how states' discretion and credibility assessments are exercised in granting these claims.[66] In this and other kinds of sociolegal work, the focus is not so much on the potential of inclusion for queer asylum seekers, but rather on interrogating how the subject of the 'real' asylum seeker is discursively produced by reference to specific western tropes of sexual orientation and identity to which asylum seekers must abide by if they are to have a successful claim to inclusion. [67]

It is important to reposition this kind of critical work as part of a broader spectrum of critical approaches to EU migration law as well as to continue to interrogate new types of inclusion.[68] For example, in recent judgments the Court of Justice of the EU (CJEU) has found that women in general and women who have suffered domestic violence should be understood as a particular group for the purposes of refugee protection.[69] The case law has also established that protection should be granted to women who have adopted 'western values' such as those on equality between men and women.[70] While such judgments expand the room for inclusion, and have positive effects for a group of women, those that are lucky enough to have reached EU territory, they do not undo the gendered aspects of asylum law in general and EU asylum law in particular as discussed by Steininger.[71] It is thus crucial to question, how such claims to inclusion which affect the law in a transformative manner can also be 'reabsorbed in a constrictive

[63] See JK Puar, *Terrorist Assemblages: Homonationalism in Queer Times* (Duke University Press, 2017) on theorising homonationalism.

[64] See also T Spijkerboer (ed), *Fleeing Homophobia: Sexual Orientation, Gender Identity and Asylum* (First issued in paperback, Routledge, 2015).

[65] See, eg, Danisi and others (n 61); Special Issue, 'Protezione Internazionale e SOGI' [2018] GenIUS – Rivista di studi giuridici sull'orientamento sessuale e sull'identita' di genere.

[66] J Wessels, *The Concealment Controversy: Sexual Orientation, Discretion Reasoning and the Scope of Refugee Protection* (Cambridge University Press, 2021).

[67] S Zisakou, 'Proving Gender and Sexuality in the (Homo)Nationalist Greek Asylum System: Credibility, Sexual Citizenship and the "Bogus" Sexual Other' (2025) 28 *Sexualities* 1746; S Zisakou, 'Feeling Queer, Feeling Real: Affective Economies of Truth in Queer Asylum Politics' [2024] Ethnic and Racial Studies 1; C Giametta, 'New Asylum Protection Categories and Elusive Filtering Devices: The Case of "Queer Asylum" in France and the UK' (2020) 46 *Journal of Ethnic and Migration Studies* 142; C Giametta, *The Sexual Politics of Asylum: Sexual Orientation and Gender Identity in the UK Asylum System* (Routledge, 2019); K Åberg, 'A Requirement of Shame: On the Evolution of the Protection of LGB Refugees' (2023) 35 *International Journal of Refugee Law* 37; N Ferreira, 'Better Late Than Never? SOGI Asylum Claims and "Late Disclosure" Through a Foucauldian Lens' (2023) 27 *UCLA Journal of International Law and Foreign Affairs* 17; D Akin, 'Discursive Construction of Genuine LGBT Refugees' (2018) 23 *lambda nordica* 21.

[68] With a focus on humanitarianism in general and not on queer asylum seekers specifically, Åberg has proceeded in a similar tactical way. Taking absurdity as an analytical lens, Åberg has traced how EU legal measures adopted with the purpose of promoting a humanitarian vision of the EU have given rise to consequences that harm the people they were supposed to protect. K Åberg, *The Benevolent Border - Humanitarianism and Absurdity in European Migration Law* (PhD Dissertation, Gothenburg University, 2025).

[69] A Loxa, 'International Human Rights Commitments to Protect Victims of Domestic Violence: Refugee Recognition as the First Step for an Integrated Approach under EU Law in Case C-621/21, Intervyuirasht Organ Na DAB Pri MS (Women Victims of Domestic Violence)' (2024) 31 *Maastricht Journal of European and Comparative Law* 535.

[70] Case C-646/21 *K and L v Staatssecretaris van Justitie en Veiligheid* ECLI:EU:C:2024:487.

[71] S Steininger, 'The CJEU's Feminist Turn? Gender-based Persecution as a Ground for Protection' (*VerfBlog*, 20 February 2024), available at https://verfassungsblog.de/the-cjeus-feminist-turn/.

lexicon' and draw new dividing lines between the 'westernised' women and the 'backward' religious, supressed ones that are unassimilable.[72]

V. Introducing Racial Capitalism to EU Migration and Asylum Law

The works discussed in the previous sections have been extremely valuable not least because they have questioned the legitimacy of EU migration and asylum law's legal categories and concepts, and they have connected the field to a longer history of domination that predates and impacts the creation and function of the EU. Nevertheless, what such works have not offered is a lens of analysis that allows us to connect EU migration and asylum law to questions of political economy. So far, analyses that connect this field to the political economy of the EU are marginal, but as I explain in this section, there are a series of reasons why they deserve more attention.

But first, let us discuss what such types of analysis could look like. A first example would be the work of Annete Schrauwen who has investigated the way in which low-skilled EU and non-EU migrants were treated in the Netherlands during the COVID-19 pandemic as a case study in order to suggest that technical categories of EU law accommodate and legitimise discrimination based on class, gender, race and centre-periphery dynamics.[73] In her work she laid bare the contradiction between the EU applauding the contribution of low-skilled workers and the differential impacts of law on those covered by free movement and migration. Schrauwen drew on the framing of neoliberal citizenship as a framework that challenges the dichotomies between insider/outsider in the EU and which shows how rationalities of value play out to exclude, dispose and sacrifice those with low economic and emotional value.[74] In a similar way, that is, in an attempt to challenge dichotomies introduced by EU legal categories, I have found it productive to draw on racial capitalism as an explanatory framework that gives me a language that captures how EU law structures, facilitates and naturalises the injustices caused not only by race, but also by capitalism in the context of migration.[75]

Racial capitalism has no singular iteration.[76] The concept captures the relation between racial inequality and capitalism but there is no uniform set of causal relations or connections between the two as it appears in the relevant scholarship.[77] Táíwò has

[72] See M Croce, 'Queer in the Law: Critique and Postcritique' in E Christodoulidis, R Dukes and M Goldoni, *Research Handbook on Critical Legal Theory* (Edward Elgar Publishing, 2019) who talks about queer critique and law in relation to the regulation of family; *cf* G Chakravorty Spivak (eds), 'Can the Sublatern Speak', in C Nelson and L Grossberg (eds) *Marxism and the Interpretation of Culture* (Univ of Illinois Press, 2007); C Talpade Mohanty, 'Under Western Eyes: Feminist Scholarship and Colonial Discourses' (1988) *Feminist Review* 61; By analogy W Brown, *States of Injury: Power and Freedom in Late Modernity* (Princeton University Press, 1995) with a focus on the risks of identity claims. See also chapter 7 by Raphaële Xenidis in this book on the dynamics of assimilation in EU anti-discrimination law.

[73] A Schrauwen, 'Essential, Invisible, Discriminated and Exchangeable: Labour Migrants in the EU' (2024) 15 *Transnational Legal Theory* 572.

[74] Drawing on L Mavelli, *Neoliberal Citizenship: Sacred Markets, Sacrificial Lives* (Oxford University Press, 2022).

[75] Loxa, 'EU Law, Migration and Racial Capitalism' (n 22).

[76] See J Go, 'Three Tensions in the Theory of Racial Capitalism' (2021) 39 *Sociological Theory* 38, 38.

[77] ibid.

suggested that it is productive to understand racial capitalism as a set of questions on how racism and capitalism work rather than a separate social theory.[78] One does not have to take a position on the necessity or contingency that exists between race and capitalism to be able to use the concept productively in a critique of EU migration and asylum law. The value of racial capitalism for the critical study of EU migration and asylum law becomes clear if we look at the main takeaways of each of its variants.

A first variant of racial capitalism can be traced in the work of Cedric Robinson.[79] He has suggested that ordering based on race has not been restricted to the relations of European and non-European people. Rather, European capitalism has historically initiated 'myths of egalitarianism' while at the same time turning regional, cultural and dialectical differences into racial ones in order to rationalise the domination over and exploitation of other Europeans.[80] This variant allows us to see how difference based on race is constructed both within and beyond Europe to the benefit of capitalist exploitation. In this variant, race is understood as a social construction rather than a biological signifier. And this allows us to trace the implicit appearance of race in references to culture, nationality, integration and occasionally even to poverty. At the same time, it prompts us to investigate the many references to economic considerations, which abound throughout EU migration law, and which have so far escaped the attention of the critical approaches discussed earlier in this chapter, and to trace the relation between migration and class.

A second variant could be found in literature which centres on the relation between capitalist development and North-Atlantic slavery.[81] Despite the context-specific critique of this variant,[82] it remains important because it forces us to confront the relation between slavery and the creation of the European welfare state.[83] It also allows us to see how racialisation and exclusion is not necessarily only experienced by migrants but also by citizens. This forces us to become aware of the reality of racial differentiation not just between Europeans and non-Europeans, but also among these two groups. By seeing this connection, we can bridge distributive analyses that have historically been conducted in the field of EU free movement law to the racial and post-colonial critiques analysed in the previous section in relation to EU migration law, and to expose the shared racial and capitalist exclusions in both frameworks.[84] What is more, this variant of racial capitalism forces us to unsettle the legal categories of EU law and to flip our starting point of

[78] O Táíwò, 'A Framework to Help Us Understand the World' (*Hammer & Hope*, 2023), available at https://hammerandhope.org/article/issue-1-article-8.

[79] CJ Robinson, *Black Marxism: The Making of the Black Radical Tradition* (University of North Carolina Press, 2000).

[80] ibid 26 with reference, among others, to the English Poor Laws, and the construction of Herrenvolk, that is the idea of a superior German race entitled to rule over others.

[81] W Johnson, 'To Remake the World: Slavery, Racial Capitalism, and Justice' *Boston Review* (21 February 2018), available at www.bostonreview.net/forum/walter-johnson-to-remake-the-world/walter-johnson-racial-capitalism-and-human/ .

[82] J Go, 'Theorizing Racial Capitalism: Critique, Contingency & Context' (2024) 3 *Marronnages: les questions raciales au crible des sciences sociales* A1, A3.

[83] See D Ashiagbor, 'Rethinking EU Social and Labour Law through Racial Capitalism' in H Eklund (ed), *Colonialism and the EU Legal Order* (Cambridge University Press, 2025) 146.

[84] See C O'Brien, 'Civis Capitalist Sum: Class as the New Guiding Principle of EU Free Movement Rights' (2016) 53 *CML Rev* 937; A Somek, 'From Workers to Migrants, from Distributive Justice to Inclusion: Exploring the Changing Social Democratic Imagination' (2012) 18 *European Law Journal* 711; See also D Rita Myslinska, *Law, Migration, and the Construction of Whiteness: Mobility within the European Union* (Routledge, 2024) on a racial critique of EU free movement law.

analysis. Instead of problematising the injustices and exclusions produced by the binary of European Citizens and Third Country Nationals introduced in law, the starting point becomes the social reality of migration which is shared by people falling under both these legal categories and which is simultaneously regulated and experienced in very diverse ways depending on their race, gender and class. An example of this diversity is the very different conditions of legal regulation for Swiss finance specialists, Afghan asylum seekers, American software developers, Turkish engineers and Pakistani farm workers, all of whom fall under the notion of 'Third Country Nationals' yet are subject to very different legal frameworks with vastly different rights.[85]

A third variant stems from a South African tradition of social struggle whose purpose was to show that the racial structures of apartheid and capitalism were not mutually exclusive.[86] The resonance of this variant is that it sees the concept of racial capitalism as strategic for political struggles. Even if race and capitalism can be separated analytically, this variant suggests that they cannot be separated empirically, and to contest either system of oppression the struggle has to be common.[87] This variant is important because it forces us to reflect on the dimensions of what an emancipatory project for EU migration and asylum law could look like and how it could be connected to an emancipatory project for free movement law.

At this stage it should also be mentioned that racial capitalism has been criticised for giving primacy to race as the key difference produced and exploited by capitalism.[88] However, such criticism can be addressed and gender can be incorporated in the analysis by drawing on the work of Marxist feminist scholars who identify gender as another category of difference produced by capitalism in order to divide, dominate and exploit populations.[89] In this way racial capitalism critiques of EU migration and asylum law could be useful to expose the intersecting exclusions produced by EU migration law.[90]

[85] Swiss nationals enjoy the same rights to free movement as EU citizens under the Bilateral Agreement concluded between the EU and Switzerland in 2023; Afghans would fall under EU asylum law; American software developers would fall under Directive (EU) 2021/1883 of the European Parliament and of the Council of 20 October 2021 on the conditions of entry and residence of third-country nationals for the purpose of highly qualified employment, and repealing Council Directive 2009/50/EC [2021] OJ L382/1 (EU Blue Card Directive); Turkish engineers could also form under the Blue Card Directive but they could also claim rights under the EEC-Turkey Association Agreement signed in 1963 and Pakistani farm workers would fall under Directive 2014/36/EU of the European Parliament and of the Council of 26 February 2014 on the conditions of entry and stay of third-country nationals for the purpose of employment as seasonal workers [2014] OJ L 94/375 (Seasonal Workers Directive).

[86] Z Levenson and M Paret, 'The South African Tradition of Racial Capitalism' (2023) 46 *Ethnic and Racial Studies 3403.*

[87] G Johnson, M Woker and L Zevounou, 'Capitalisme racial !? Une introduction' (2024) 3 *Marronnages: les questions raciales au crible des sciences sociales 8, 12.*

[88] Go (n 80) A4.

[89] S Federici, *Caliban and the Witch: Women, the Body and Primitive Accumulation* (Autonomedia, 2004) 63–64 on primitive accumulation as accumulation of differences within the working class based on gender and race and which became constitutive of class rule; Starhawk, *Dreaming the Dark: Magic, Sex, and Politics* (15th anniversary edn, Beacon Press, 1997) 218–19 on the connections between the witchhunt, attacks against the idle poor and colonisation.

[90] See, eg, residence rights for victims of domestic violence under Directive 2004/38 who need to prove economic self-sufficiency to establish an autonomous right to reside. Directive 2004/38/EC on the right of citizens of the Union and their family members to move and reside freely within the territory of the Member States [2004] OJ L/77.

At the same time, racial capitalism allows us to reproduce the critical move of queer approaches described earlier. That is, to problematise the inclusion which EU migration and asylum law furnishes to the economically active, the highly skilled, the deserving migrants, the homonormative queer families and the female refugees embracing western values.

Finally, using racial capitalism allows us to connect EU migration and asylum law to law and political economy critiques more broadly.[91] In the field of EU law, scholars have historically shown the constitutive function of law for economic ordering as well as the effects that such ordering has had for the EU political sphere.[92] EU migration law however is never examined through such a lens. It supposedly conforms to a different logic and is subsumed, as discussed in section II, under security considerations. Once we expose and are exposed to the economic orderings produced by EU migration law, we can no longer avoid understanding EU migration law as another area that is closely related to the EU's neoliberal constitution.[93] The presumed exceptionalism of the area falls apart and, in its place, we find a more nuanced and simultaneously a more complete picture of the variable inclusions and exclusions constituted by EU law, as well as the relation of such inclusions and exclusions to the European project of economic growth.

VI. Conclusion: On the Ways and Values of Critique

By this point, it should be clear that critique has a rich tradition in EU migration and asylum law, or at least a tradition that is richer than in other areas of EU law. I tried to capture this tradition not by looking at the ways of doing critique, but rather by thematically grouping the relevant works based on the critical theoretical frameworks lying behind different types of critique and by advocating for mainstreaming racial capitalism critiques. Hoping that I have done no grave injustice to the field and acknowledging the limits of any scholarly exercise to provide an exhaustive picture of reality, I will conclude by reflecting on the various ways of doing critique and their value for EU migration and asylum law specifically, and for critical EU legal studies in general.

A typical approach in the study and research of law is the strive for coherence. Going against this current, critical approaches to EU migration law lay bare the contradictions inherent in the way in which EU law regulates migration and asylum. Some scholars have theorised law as a mechanism of social reality contributing to specific injustices. Others have challenged the legitimacy of EU legal categories as neutral, ahistorical and apolitical expressions of a liberal legal order. This has been done both by exposing the

[91] See I Kampourakis, 'Bound by the Economic Constitution: Notes for "Law and Political Economy" in Europe' (2021) 1 *Journal of Law and Political Economy* 301.

[92] C Joerges, 'What Is Left of the European Economic Constitution?' (European University Institute 2004) Working Paper; FW Scharpf, 'The Asymmetry of European Integration, or Why the EU Cannot Be a "Social Market Economy"' (2010) 8 *Socio-Economic Review* 211; A Somek, 'Alienation, Despair and Social Freedom' in L Azoulai, S Barbou des Places and E Pataut (eds), *Constructing the Person in EU Law: Rights, Roles, Identities* (Hart Publishing, 2016); G Peebles, '"A Very Eden of the Innate Rights of Man"? A Marxist Look at the European Union Treaties and Case Law' (1997) 22 *Law & Social Inquiry* 581.

[93] Loxa, 'EU Law, Migration and Racial Capitalism' (n 22) 27–29.

forgotten histories lying at the origins of various legal concepts and by revealing the power relations they conceal, as well as the inequalities or injustices they perpetuate. Moreover, critical theory is used by some authors to better understand the power asymmetries that EU law constitutes and perpetuates and to present them in a language that is liberated from the limits of the technical categories used in law and that is better aligned with social reality. This diversity in using and doing critique in EU migration and asylum law could guide and inspire the work of critical EU law scholars in general.

At the same time such work, and the use of critical theory in the study of EU law is important for many reasons. As any type of law, EU law and its rules are about *ordering power relations* – deciding whose mobility counts, whose rights are secured, and whose lives should be protected. Without critique, those distributions of power go unnoticed and unchallenged. Moreover, the use of critical theory could be thought of as a scholarly practice that challenges Eurocentrism.[94] Critical theory creates space for bringing into EU law traditions that are often marginalised such as post-colonial theory, critical race theory and queer critiques.[95] It also challenges the assumption that EU law should be studied in isolation from global histories of colonialism, capitalism, and racial ordering.[96]

In addition to this, critical approaches to EU migration and asylum law expand the fields' understanding and challenge its deterministic narratives. By engaging with racial capitalism, or post-colonial critiques, we are pushed to confront the idea that EU law is not just an integration-building project, but also a part of global capitalist and racial hierarchies. This unsettles the prevalent narrative of the EU as a unique progressive legal order 'immaculately' conceived at the ashes of a war that tore European states apart.[97] Historical studies have recentred the role of empires and colonies in the study of European integration.[98] Some of the works discussed in this chapter have brought similar considerations into EU migration law and are tied to a recent turn to the study of the EU in relation to its colonial and imperial past.[99]

Critical research has a central role to play, challenging the determinist history of European integration and the role of migration therein. EU migration and asylum law have a clearly defined place in this history as entering the field of EU competences in the complicated period of the 1990s to make up for a project of closer political integration between the people of Europe. Critique reveals the constructedness of EU law

[94] See I Solanke, 'Decolonizing Research and Teaching in EU Law: Purpose, Principles and Practice' in H Eklund (ed), *Colonialism and the EU Legal Order* (Cambridge University Press, 2025).

[95] Of course, this depends on the kinds of critical theoretical traditions used and the risk of Eurocentrism persists if we think of critique exclusively through the lens of European white male voices critiquing western modernity.

[96] See I Isailović, 'Introduction: Critical Legal Approaches in EU Law—Reflections on New Research Directions' (2024) 15 *Transnational Legal Theory* 493 who identifies the self-referential and self-contained approach that has characterised EU legal scholarship until recently.

[97] C Kinnvall, 'The Postcolonial Has Moved into Europe: Bordering, Security and Ethno-Cultural Belonging' (2016) 54 *Journal of Common Market Studies* 152, 152–53; P Hansen and S Jonsson, 'Eurafrica Incognita: The Colonial Origins of the European Union' (2017) 7 *History of the Present* 1. See also chapter 2 by Kaius Tuori in this book.

[98] M Brown, *The Seventh Member State: Algeria, France, and the European Community* (Harvard University Press, 2022); Hansen and Jonsson (n 32).

[99] See, eg, S Rehling Larsen, 'European Public Law after Empires' (2022) 1 *European Law Open* 6.

and reframes what we understand as the limits of a half-hearted commitment of the Member States to Europeanisation. It unsettles and nuances this narrative. It shows both how EU law was constructed to exclude colonial subjects from its scope, but also how the Europeanisation of migration law is part of a longer history of legal mechanisms that has allowed extraction of labour from the Global South. In this longer history, law has had and continues to have a constitutive role in the perpetuation of injustices. Understanding this role is the first crucial step for the reimagination of a different future drawing on the emancipatory potential of critical social thought.

12

A Post-National Bearing

Europe's Legal Form and the Hope of Constitutional Critique

PAUL LINDEN-RETEK*

I. Introduction

What might it mean to give the work of European constitutional theory – or accounts of the constitutional theory of the European Union (EU) – a post-national bearing? The answer I develop here is that such a bearing – a 'cognitive, normative, and aesthetic-affective orientation to public life' – requires within constitutional law a posture of critique.

If this is so, post-national constitutional theory might propitiously begin from a place where critical theory offers its initial account of law: a critique of *legal form*, that is, the kinds of relations instantiated and legitimated by law. Addressing legal form helps us to see why the problem to which post-national law aims to provide a solution is a problem familiar to modernity and to modernist renderings of legality expressed by the nation-state: *reification*, a process by which constitutional law founds a political project by systematically misattributing social and historical relationships, in essential respects, as timeless relations among things.[1] The feature of reification most important for our purposes is the guiding public orientation of freedom as the pursuit of mastery or control; in reifying and atomising the relations before it, law projects a highly partial rendering of a free life, a rendering that is ill-suited for the post-national project of European integration.

Alongside post-Marxist critiques of legal form and of the commodification of public life through reification, this chapter turns to conceptions of freedom inherited from the Arenditan tradition, most elegantly formulated by Patchen Markell, whose work reminds us of the resilience of sovereigntist thinking in often unexpected places and

* This chapter develops and applies themes drawn from P Linden-Retek, *Postnational Constitutionalism: Europe and the Time of Law* (Oxford University Press, 2023). The chapter's title – and some of its content, as well – are inspired by SK White, *A Democratic Bearing: Admirable Citizens, Uneven Justice, and Critical Theory* (Cambridge University Press, 2017), which thoughtfully advances a 'coherent cognitive, normative, and aesthetic-affective orientation to public life' (xvi).

[1] See M Dimick, 'Race and Reification' (2021) *Historical Materialism*.

thus aspires to more demanding forms of self-criticism as the bases for our freedom.[2] The critique of reification and reified notions of freedom helps draw attention to how the pursuit or desire for mastery can be shifted onto or expressed through many legal statuses, some familiar but others rather surprisingly, statuses in which one might expect precisely to find the mechanisms for resisting the nationalist closure of law.

By scrutinising the manner by which reification and sovereigntism together continue to appear in EU law, I argue, we see why Europe's present legal form – and attempts to build out the EU's legitimacy and normative authority through it – poses a distinctly *constitutional* problem. The work of better criticising these distortions reveals itself to be the task of European constitutional law properly understood – and thus recommends rival legal forms (principles and practices) that might yet realise Europe's post-national aspirations. The constitutional aim to resist reification and to ground critique thereby becomes Europe's post-national bearing.

The chapter elaborates this argument in the following sections: Section II further introduces the task of finding post-national constitutional life in Europe and suggests reasons why this task today leads to frustration. Section III sketches what a critical project of examining legal form and diagnosing the problem of reification entails. Section IV argues that the reified legal form, by projecting a highly partial notion of freedom, poses for the EU a constitutional problem. Solidarity is misshapen and emancipation is confused when law's conception of freedom remains wedded, through legal form, to the expectations of national law. Section V then turns to the chapter's main illustrative example, the case of *Commission v Malta*, noting how competing interpretations of the case share the common failing of reifying the questions of freedom before them. Section VI in response offers an emancipatory rendering of post-national freedom and finds critical resources for this rendering in recent work on relational freedom. The essential point is that post-national emancipation is a project aimed to free the human subject from reification. Section VII concludes with brief, though I hope suggestive, reflections on the relationship between freedom from reification and the pursuit of existential freedom and on the notion of constitutional critique as an act of hope.

II. Searching for Europe's Post-National Constitutional Life

Asserting reification to be Europe's constitutional problem alerts us to the distance that, as Damien Chalmers writes, has opened between EU law and the philosophical ambitions that once animated political thinking about Europe's form of life,[3] a form of life that was expected to have learned something from the colonialism, imperialism, totalitarianism, and nationalism that marked and marred its political expression. Chalmer's appeal makes contact, at least in passing, with thinkers as diverse as Kristeva, Gasché,[4]

[2] See P Markell, *Bound by Recognition* (Princeton University Press, 2003).

[3] D Chalmers, 'The Unconfined Power of European Union Law' (2016) 1(2) European Papers 405–37.

[4] See R Gasché, *Europe, or the Infinite Task: A Study of a Philosophical Concept* (Stanford University Press, 2008), a work to which I have long been indebted, notably for its clear and moving rendering of Jacques Derrida's invocation of European responsibility as a double command of being committed to 'an idea of

Husserl, Habermas, and Oakeshott, seeking resonance in the European project with far-reaching redefinitions of civic identity, affirmations of the excluded, a questioning of the basis of material interests, and the reformulation of political community itself.[5] 'None of these associations correspond with how EU citizens experience the significance of EU law', however; what reigns, Chalmers concludes, is simply 'obscurity about what the EU is about'.[6] European law, amidst such obscurity, has failed to displace the enduring political frame of nationality that continues, despite pretences otherwise, to characterise its political thinking.

Questions concerning the relationship between self and other, the manner by which one mediates subjectivity, and the role of public life in securing an ethical bearing for such mediation are intertwined deeply with the European project and its public philosophy. They are expressed, too – albeit too rarely as the subject of legal criticism itself – through European public law. In what follows, I argue that the state of affairs which Chalmers laments is the product of – reproduced by – Europe's *legal form*: that is to say, a product of the legal form by which European constitutionalism is organised, and by which it poses political alternatives to the people meant to be its authors. My argument suggests that if we study legal form, we learn to consider new lines of diagnosis, as well as new possibilities for remedy; new explanations for why post-national aspirations have run aground in Europe and new means for setting on that course again.

Constitutional theorists, political scientists, sociologists, historians, and economists have in the past decades contributed to a rich, searching literature appraising the EU's political and legal form. It has examined in detail the varied, imaginative architecture of public power and forms of legitimation that attend the European experiment with trans-national and post-national self-government. Yet, for all this variation and imagination, the constitutional subjects that populate this literature are, in a sense, rather conventional: the national citizen; the market actor; the individual human being. And such conventional subjects also project rather conventional ambitions onto post-national constitutional law: the promise of democratic accountability and the self-legislation of a bounded people; a rule of law that would not discriminate on the basis of nationality, only on one's capacity to conform to the legal rules themselves; and the protection of fundamental human rights to ensure a dignified life. That such demands were not always possible to hold together meant that the European constitutional order's cardinal problem was that of pluralism and its correlative task the creation of a structure in which these competing ambitions could be negotiated. The past decades have accordingly yielded constitutional theories that elaborate the federal form, critique the viability

Europe, [and to] a difference of Europe, [to] a Europe that consist precisely in not closing itself off in its own identity'. J Derrida, *Reflections on Today's Europe* (translated by PA Brault and M Naas, Indiana University Press, 1992) 29 (cited in Gasché, ibid, 265). Gasché's work is exemplary in its erudite elaboration of a call to conceive the consciousness of Europe as nothing less than the possibility of thinking Europe anew, of the exposure of its identity to the 'nonegocentric'. See Gasché, ibid, 303–38. This is the possibility of emancipation that runs through the vision of post-national law I identify here.

[5] See Chalmers (n 3) 411, 416. Päivi Neuvonen also foregrounds the work of Kristeva in her groundbreaking analysis of the salience of alterity for the character of EU citizenship and subjectivity. See P Neuvonen, 'Retrieving the "subject" of European Integration' (2018) *European Law Journal* 6–20, 10, 11, 17.

[6] Chalmers (n 3) 411.

of EU law's administrative or functionalist tendencies, or normatively reconstruct putatively shared principles that would guide constitutional adjudication.[7]

And yet conceiving the problem and task of post-national constitutionalism in this way suffers from two lines of unresolved tensions that have long been subjects of concern within the tradition of critical theory. The first is an inattentiveness to political economy: broadly understood as analysis of the material conditions in which communicative structures of legal process function and the consequences for legal principles and practice alike of inequality in those conditions.[8] Related to a concern with political economy is a diagnosis of the ideological work that liberal law – liberal legalism – performs in obfuscating, mystifying, or legitimating inequalities of material or structural power.[9] The second unresolved tension concerns a misconstrual of the complexity of democratic communication and legitimation: the unexamined, often repressed dynamics of exclusion beneath an act of inclusion within a political community; the creation of 'others' by which to assert one's identity; and the persistence of desires for mastery and control that underlie assertions of legitimacy. This is the problem – as Hannah Arendt posed in a warning to the European project, in particular – of a political community's temptations with false closure, creating an 'other' in a bid to define oneself, thereby losing the emancipatory ethical content that nationalism had extinguished but European integration might yet promise.[10] Felt most prominently and painfully when the nation-state encounters the claims of those seeking entry at its borders, these problems are more generalisable to the predicament of post-national constitutional law in the EU. They together suggest the eclipse or denial of *critique* within the European constitutional imagination.

These are important lessons that have yet to be learned from Europe's crisis decade and the EU's constitutional 'mutation' toward executive and technocratic power,

[7] Consider generally K Nicolaïdis and R Howse (eds), *The Federal Vision: Legitimacy and Levels of Governance in the United States and the European Union* (Oxford University Press, 2001); A Menon and M Schain (eds), *Comparative Federalism: The European Union and the United States in Comparative Perspective* (Oxford University Press, 2006); JE Fossum and M Jachtenfuchs, '*Federal Challenges and Challenges to Federalism: Insights from the EU and Federal States*' (2017) 24 *Journal of European Public Policy* 470; M Burgess, *Federalism and European Union: The Building of Europe, 1950–2000* (Routledge, 2000); P Lindseth, *Power and Legitimacy Reconciling Europe and the Nation-State* (Oxford University Press, 2011); T Isiksel, *Europe's Functional Constitution: A Theory of Constitutionalism Beyond the State* (Oxford University Press, 2016); S Larsen, *The Constitutional Theory of the Federation and the European Union* (Oxford University Press, 2021); T Dumbrovsky, 'Federal Solution to the EU Internal Sovereignty Conundrum: The European Doctrine of the Czech Constitutional Court and the U.S. Compact Theory' in L Tichy and T Dumbrovsky (eds), *Sovereignty and Competences of the European Union* (Charles University, 2010) 80–100; T Dumbrovsky, 'Effet Utile as a Unifying Doctrine in a Constitutionally Pluralist Europe' in L Tichy et al (eds), *Effet Utile* (Charles University, 2014) 93–113; R Bellamy, *A Republican Europe of States: Cosmopolitanism, Intergovernmentalism and Democracy in the EU* (Cambridge University Press, 2019); J Habermas, *The Crisis of the European Union—A Response* (Polity Press, 2012).

[8] See generally M Goldoni and M Wilkinson, 'The Material Constitution' (2018) 81 *MLR* 567.

[9] See L Kalman, *The Strange Career of Legal Liberalism* (Yale University Press, 1996); D Loick, 'Juridification and Politics: From the Dilemma of Juridification to the Paradoxes of Rights' (2014) 40(8) *Philosophy & Social Criticism* 757–78.

[10] See H Arendt, 'The Aftermath of Nazi Rule: Report from Germany' and 'Dream and Nightmare' in *Essays in Understanding, 1930–1954: Formation, Exile, and Totalitarianism* (Jerome Kohn ed, Harcourt, Brace & Co, 1994) 250–52, 416–17; see also IM Young, 'De-centering the Project of Global Democracy' in D Levy and others (eds), *Old Europe, New Europe, Core Europe: Transatlantic Relations after the Iraq War* (Verso, 2005) 156 (cited in P Verovšek, 'Meeting Principles and Lifeworlds Halfway: Jürgen Habermas on the Future of Europe' (2012) 60 *Political Studies* 363, 371ff).

broadly unresponsive in its defence of market discipline to the claims of social rights protection and democratic legitimation.[11] Here, the pluralism among national constitutional orders – not only their internal orderings of sovereign debt but also their relative ability to impose or to resist austerity measures[12] – is less fruitfully conceived as a question of diversity and accommodation than as a site of injustice, asymmetrical relations, depoliticisation, and illegitimate claims to authority. In the latter cast, pluralism is rightly the object of constitutional critique, upon which the realisation of constitutional freedom depends. While crisis has elicited criticism of EU law from the outside, this posture has only begun to suggest itself as a template for reimagining the EU's legal and political form itself[13] – that is, not only as the conclusion of a critical diagnosis but, dialectically, as the basis for an anticipatory, prefigurative,[14] utopian form of post-national constitutional law.

A study of reification promises an intervention of this sort. It suggests the difficulty, if not impossibility, of pursuing a post-national constitutional project – with its transformative ambitions – while relying on the legal form that characterises and reproduces the nation-state. If the legal form orders and relates subjectivity – both elite and popular, institutional and symbolic – a post-national constitutional order must seek to revise its understanding of legal form, lest the subtle retention of the old threatens to limit or undermine, at each step, advances towards the new. In considering what a post-national legal form might look like, I thereby have three cardinal aims: (1) to make us think about legal form as an essential dimension of constitutional theory; (2) to suggest why the post-Marxist concept of reification diagnoses important aspects of the resilience of nationalist thinking in European law and, further, provides correlative notions to overturn it; and, finally, (3) to reclaim a particular vision of legality – legal form – that can play a vital, if fragile role in post-national political life and in the normative development of European integration. In outlining reification's distortions and finding alternative legal forms to counter them, we might yet pursue a post-national bearing for European constitutional order. An emancipatory post-national political life requires its own conception of freedom: freedom from reification.[15]

[11] See M Dawson and F de Witte, 'Constitutional Balance in the EU after the Euro-Crisis' (2013) 76 *MLR* 817; AJ Menéndez, 'Editorial: A European Union in Constitutional Mutation?' (2014) 20 *European Law Journal* 127; AJ Menéndez, 'The Crisis of Law and the European Crises: From the Social and Democratic Rechtsstaat to the Consolidating State of (Pseudo)Technocratic Governance' (2017) 44 *Journal of Law & Society* 56; M Salomon, 'Of Austerity, Human Rights and International Institutions' (2015) 21(4) *European Law Journal* 521–45; A Poulou, 'Austerity and European Social Rights: How Can Courts Protect Europe's Lost Generation?' (2014) 15(6) *German Law Journal* 1145–76; Larsen (n 7) ch 5.

[12] See, eg, M Wilkinson, 'Constitutional Pluralism: Chronicle of a Death Foretold?' 22 (ARENA Working Paper 7/2017, 2017); F Mayer, 'Rebels without a Cause? A Critical Analysis of the German Constitutional Court's OMT Reference' (2014) 15 *German Law Journal* 111.

[13] See M Dawson and F de Witte, 'From Balance to Conflict: A New Constitution for the EU' (2016) 22(2) *European Law Journal* 204–24.

[14] See, eg, Martijn Hesselink's project of prefigurative law, available at www.eui.eu/research-hub?id=prefigurative-law-1. This vision of law as critique affirms the 'indirect' effect of politics on a society's system of cultural reproduction and collective self-identification. See generally C Calhoun, 'Imagining Solidarity: Cosmopolitanism, Constitutional Patriotism, and the Public Sphere' (2002) 14(1) *Public Culture* 152–53; J Přibáň, *Legal Symbolism: On Law, Time and European Identity* (Ashgate, 2007) 42ff.

[15] See M Hagglund, *This Life: Secular Faith and Spiritual Freedom* (Pantheon, 2019).

III. The Critique of Legal Form and the Reification of Law

If, as Roberto Unger once diagnosed, the problem with conventional legal analysis lies in its rationalism, by which normative legal rules deny their complicity with force and violence;[16] the analogous problem we see in EU law is its ignorance of sovereignty's transmutations and endurance through European legal form. Scrutiny of legal form, philosophically, is indebted to the Marxist jurist Evgeny Pashukanis and his articulation of the legal form as that which pertains to legal rules but also to the legal subjects presupposed and created by those rules, to how those subjects are related to one another by law and its doctrines over time.[17] Pashukanis considered legal form, in the first instance, as the interpellation of subjects in the fetishistic character and commodity form of the capitalist political economy. The capitalist commodity form is characterised by abstractness and equivalence and, by turn, the law asserts the existence of a legal subject characterised by the same: a projection of the laws of contract that made exchange among putative social equals possible.[18]

In considering the legal form of European constitutionalism, I aim to translate Pashukanis's insights, as the feminist scholar Ruth Fletcher does, from the particular context of commodity exchange to allow them to speak to law as a world-creating force, in which a certain cast of subjects, relations, conceptions of public power and of public freedom selectively take hold.[19] Methodologically, Fletcher aims to 'recuperate legal form analysis as a relational activity which investigates legal form's representation of the social relations it captures',[20] attending to questions of subjectivity and to the dialectical entanglement of content and form in legal subjectification.[21]

It is important to note, as Darryl Li does in his ethnographically-inflected legal work, that the invocation of legal form in Pashukanis is distinct from other strands of Marxist thinking about law as an expression of the ideology of the ruling class, as the Gramscian-inspired theorists of hegemony nevertheless rightly suggest.[22] The persistence and articulation of ideology through law is significant – and, as I shall argue, the conception of freedom as mastery and control are indeed ideologically grounded, in one sense, as paradigmatic expressions of national thinking. But attention to legal form scrutinises something more granular (and farther-reaching) about the mechanisms by which such ideology is propagated and, as a result, allows us to see how such ideology

[16] See R Unger, *What Should Legal Analysis Become?* (Verso, 1996); see also R Cover, 'The Supreme Court, 1982 Term—Foreword: *Nomos* and Narrative' (1983) 97 *Harvard Law Review* 4; R Cover, 'Violence and the Word' (1986) 95 *Yale Law Journal* 1601.

[17] E Pashukanis, *The General Theory of Law and Marxism* (translated by B Einhorn, Transaction Publishers, 2003 [1927]); see D Li, 'How to Read a Case: Ethnographic Lawyering, Conspiracy, and the Origins of Al Qaeda' (2013) 125 *American Anthropologist* 559–69, 569.

[18] See Pashukanis, ibid, 109–20; see also R Mańko, 'Legal Form, Ideology and the Political' in A Sulikowski, R Mańko and J Łakomy (eds), *Legal Scholarship and the Political: In Search of a New Paradigm* (CH Beck, 2020) 17–40, 25.

[19] See R Fletcher, 'Legal Form, Commodities and Reproduction: Reading Pashukanis' in M Drakopoulou (ed), *Feminist Encounters with Legal Philosophy* (Routledge, 2013) 138–57.

[20] ibid 143 (cited in Li (n 17) 562–63).

[21] See Li (n 17) 562.

[22] See ibid 563.

can readily occupy spaces in law that are ostensibly oriented against – and at an ideological level expressly resists – the nationalist rendering of freedom. For this reason, an analysis of legal form, while illuminating ideological capture within law, also critiques a wider array of legal phenomena, some more surprising or unexpected than others.

The level of analysis for a critique of legal form is the manner by which law gathers its subjects, interpolating and thereby creating them as ready to reassemble into particular relations with others. The worry, which again arises in Marxist thought from the legal form's emergence in capitalist relations, is that law's subjectification works and must work only through *reification*. Reification, familiar to Marxist critiques of modernity, was understood by Georg Lukács as a process in which social and historical relationships are misattributed as timeless relations among things. In previous work I have drawn on reification, and the critique of it, to suggest the ways that European law presently fails the project of post-national emancipation; and how a post-national law with emancipatory possibility must, in its legal form, counteract tendencies to reify the relationships that appear before and through it. Drawing on the theories of reification advanced by György Lukács, Theodor Adorno, and Walter Benjamin – and more recent elaborations of them by Axel Honneth, Andrew Arato, Thijs Lijster, and Mathew Dimick – my aim has been to suggest why countering reification demands greater attentiveness to the concreteness, contingency, and utopianism of the world as it is given human interpretation by legal reasoning.[23]

Briefly summarised: from Lukács we derive the essential point of departure that reification is a diagnosis of the tendency, emanating from the relations of capitalism, to see objects in the world, other people, even one's own commitments and principles as 'thing-like objects' and regarded only in light of the utility they potentially bear in exchange.[24] We might point to examples from the law of contract or criminal law, by which price or desert or moral blameworthiness are properties ascribed to an individual person, shorn off from analysis of the social relations and activities of human labour by which these qualities have come to be understood or assigned.[25] Viewing objects as disembedded from this process by which meaning and value are created, the risk to the individual who perceives or is asked to judge is that they a 'detached observer', ceasing to be engaged empathetically or moved existentially by the world: Lukács describes

[23] See Linden-Retek (n *) ch 2. Reification, certainly in its original guise, concerned the social effects of commodification and atomisation under relations of capitalism. Although there is a more complex argument to be made for the entanglement of capitalism itself in Europe's constitutional malaise, my focus here is on the social effects by which reification through European law, relatively autonomously from the material-economic system, confounds Europe's post-national bearing. Compare generally the 'Symposium on Marxist Approaches to EU Law' (2025) 4 *European Law Open* 286 (edited by R Knox, E Nanopoulos and A Woodhouse); see also Michael Wilkinson and Marco Goldoni, in chapters 3 and 4 of this volume respectively.

[24] Lukács developed the concept from the works of Karl Marx, Max Weber, and Georg Simmel and coined the term in a collection of essays published in 1925 entitled *History and Class Consciousness*. G Lukács, *History and Class Consciousness* (translated by R Livingstone, MIT Press, 1971 [1923]). See A Honneth, *Reification: A Recognition-Theoretical View*. The Tanner Lectures on Human Values (University at California, Berkeley, 14–16 March 2005) 91–92. Following Marx, Lukács understood reification to emerge from the fetishism of commodity exchange under capitalism, in which an agent assumes the role of a partner in the exchange of goods that are perceived to be abstracted from their surroundings, their context, their history, and their possible value apart from the exchange itself. See ibid 98ff.

[25] See T Lijster, '"All Reification Is a Forgetting": Benjamin, Adorno and the Dialectic of Reification' in S Gandesha and J Hartle (eds), *The Spell of Capital: Reification and Spectacle* (Amsterdam University Press, 2016) 55–66, 55.

reification as a habit of mere 'contemplation', by which he means, as Honneth writes, that the self retreats into passivity, alienated from the space of shared agency with others.[26]

To this insight regarding the mystification of and alienation from social relations, Adorno warns that reification also obscures the 'primacy of the object', in which an object retains the capacity to resist the calculation of economic exchange or the present patterns of meaning a subject might impose upon it.[27] Adorno here holds open the 'surplus' utopian possibility that an object might reveal to the subject as a matter of their ontology – the account of existence, identity, and self. Thijs Lijster renders the implications of this heady notion poignantly, writing that the 'subject, by consequence, loses its chance of encountering something new and different, something alien to itself, something that could alter the structures of its thought'.[28] The result is that resistance to reification at once promises to restore consciousness of the social world and of its utopian edges, the paths by which it might be otherwise. This utopian thinking is carried home by Walter Benjamin, for whom the 'collector' of objects from the curiosity shops of the Parisian arcades, by reclaiming the lost histories and meanings of the objects he finds, 'dreams his way not only into a bygone world but into a better one'.[29]

The critique of reification in these dimensions is an indictment of society's 'presentism', in which society's perception of time is foreshortened. The histories and labours embedded in the objects around us, the traces that an object contains and the ones it leaves on us as we encounter it, are concealed and no longer subject to interpretation; they are given no political meaning and implicate no political future. The concern that emerges is threefold: reification (1) separates the abstract appearance of value from its concrete reality; (2) naturalises that abstraction as external and unchanging; and (3) drains the object of surplus meaning that would otherwise place utopian pressure on the present scheme of natural or social valuation. The result is a flawed 'immediacy': 'presentism' tells us that all that now appears is all there is presumed ever to be.[30]

The critique thereby offers its obverse, as diagnosis yields emancipatory vision. If reification performs abstraction, timelessness, and immediacy; the project of de-reifying law must centre opposed relational dynamics: concreteness, historicity, and utopian imagination. The hope of resisting reification itself becomes a form and defence of freedom, shifting the ground by which we make judgments, understand ourselves, conceive of political praxis. These are the stakes of a struggle over constitutional freedom, to which I now turn.

IV. Reification as a Problem of Constitutional Freedom

Law's reification – the flawed posture law presently assumed in and towards social time and political possibility – has a great deal to do with the chronically 'thin'[31] quality of

[26] See G Lukács, 'Reification and the Consciousness of the Proletariat' in Lukács (n 24) 86–90; Honneth (n 24) 98–99.

[27] See TW Adorno, *Negative Dialectics* (Continuum, 1973) 191ff; Lijster (n 25) 66.

[28] Lijster (n 25) 63; see also Honneth (n 24) 117.

[29] W Benjamin, *The Arcades Project* (Belknap/Harvard University Press, 1999) 9 (cited in Lijster (n 25) 61).

[30] See Linden-Retek (n *) 66.

[31] See, eg, N Walker in M Avbelj and J Komárek (eds), 'Four Visions of Constitutional Pluralism' (2008) 2 *European Journal of Legal Studies* 325.

contemporary European constitutionalism. By permitting sovereign polities to homogenise their understandings of belonging and value, reification and the particular form of freedom it advances pose a *constitutional* problem for the European project.

When its legal form is reified and furthers reification, constitutional thought tends towards the superficial – to treat disagreement permissively as grounds for avoidance or for the assertion of normative principles without admitting their material, ideological, or exclusionary contradictions. Because such superficiality cannot conceive the forms of social learning and transformation that the appearance of pluralism in truth demands, both paths lead to frustration. Scholars have observed such effects, if not always their causes and not always in these terms, astutely. Eleni Frantziou, for example, has identified the tendencies toward superficiality, partiality, and avoidance that attend the application of certain non-discrimination provisions of the EU Charter of Fundamental Rights through appeal to the existing 'degree of "sharedness"' of constitutional values.[32] The phenomenon depoliticises the process by which EU law comes to assess the substantive interpretations of rights it finds within national constitutional orders; and accordingly mystifies the selective extension of horizontal effect for certain rights to the neglect of others (notably, those under the Charter's solidarity chapter).[33] Frantziou's critique draws attention to this problem as a constitutional dilemma and a crisis of freedom, undercutting the constitutional project as one in which subjects can contest with equal standing the symbolic and material terms of their shared life. Reflecting on the state of transnational legal theory, Sergio Dellavalle formalises the issue as one of competing legal rationalities, ranging from communitarian to holistic and communicative, that complicate the manner by which a political community opens itself to the interests of non-citizens; Dellavalle notes the resilience, in particular, of communitarian traces in legal expression, such that ostensibly shared precepts of legal discourse might reflect not a single, unifying language but multiple languages that are tied subtly but consequentially to more insular presuppositions of sovereign communities.[34]

This tendency toward superficiality and avoidance has come to a head most recently in the proposed elevation of the values enshrined in Article 2 Treaty on European Union (TEU) as homogenising foundations for European public law and 'European society'.[35] Some skeptical responses frame the attempt as 'fantastical', appropriately suggesting a

[32] See E Frantziou, A 'Right to have Rights' in the EU Public Sphere? An Arendtian Justification for the Application of the EU Charter of Fundamental Rights (Institute of European Law, Working Paper, September 2016).

[33] Frantziou's scholarship has focused brilliantly, in particular, on the Court's methods of evaluation in matters concerning the horizontal effect of non-discrimination and social rights, which, as she details, have profound implications for the ordering of public and private power in Europe. See generally E Frantziou, 'The Horizontal Effect of the Charter of Fundamental Rights of the EU: Rediscovering the Reasons for Horizontality' (2015) 21 *European Law Journal* 657; Case C-144/04 *Mangold v Helm* EU:C:2005:709; Case C-555/07 *Kücükdeveci v Swedex GmbH & Co KG* EU:C:2010:21.

[34] See generally S Dellavalle, 'On Sovereignty, Legitimacy and Solidarity, Or: How Can a Solidaristic Idea of Legitimate Sovereignty Be Justified?' (2015) 16 *Theoretical Inquiries in Law* 367. Dellavalle's reconstruction of ideal types of legal rationality within transnational law, which has greatly informed my prior work, suggests why legal actors might speak past one another and how this compromises struggles 'for an opening of sovereign powers to solidarity'.

[35] See, eg, A von Bogdandy, *The Emergence of European Society through Public Law: A Hegelian and Anti-Schmittian Approach* (translated by N Shulman, Oxford University Press, 2024); A von Bogdandy and LD Spieker, 'Countering the Judicial Silencing of Critics: Article 2 TEU Values, Reverse *Solange*, and the Responsibilities of National Judges' (2019) 15(3) *European Constitutional Law Review* 391–426.

concern with the mystification of legal form.[36] And the assertions of constitutional identity by Member States, most recently under Article 4(2) TEU, seem to breathe something of the same self-referential and rarefied air.[37]

These proposals, discussed in greater detail below, reveal a highly partial consideration of the nature and gravity of the problems to which post-national constitutional law is addressed – and a willingness to settle on superficial renderings of them in order to achieve a coherent veneer for constitutional adjudication. The result has been failing to ask the essential (critical theoretical) question: from where – from which symbolic, social, material, and political relationships – has such a disagreement come; and how has law helped to present this disagreement to us in this way or that? The concern with this result is analytic and epistemic – an inability to properly know the nature of the 'shared political predicament'[38] in which the EU's constitutional subjects are implicated. But it is, further and I think more consequentially, a conceptual and ontological misunderstanding of the nature of constitutional freedom proper to the post-national polity – and, with it, the EU's aspiration to counteract the resilience of sovereignty as an 'organizing theme of its constitutional politics'.[39] To put the point sharply: in the absence of asking these questions, the EU's constitutional structure can engender only an impoverished conception of freedom, in which freedom no longer entails sensitivity for inquiry into the background conditions in which constitutional subjects are asked to judge and to act. This form of freedom – whether expressed as market choice, or defence of rational principle, or merely a decisionistic exercise of will[40] – reproduces a narrow and solipsistic desire for control, which is none other than a desire for sovereignty. It sheds pretence to the ambitions of critique, which would aim to steadily inquire into the conditions under which choice or principle or decision are made available as a matter of history and society. It is, in short, a *reified* notion of one's place in the world and what it means to be free.[41]

Critical theorists have contributed greatly to seeing this dynamic as a particular construction of subjectivity through legal process, what Päivi Neuvonen has analysed as the subjectification of the EU citizen.[42] Neuvonen's critique is aimed at the creation of an individual and their perceived status and qualities through law; as someone capable

[36] M van den Brink and M Dawson, 'The European Union's Fantastical Constitution: A Response to von Bogdandy and Spieker' (*VerfBlog*, 27 June 2025), available at https://verfassungsblog.de/the-european-unions-fantastical-constitution/. Compare L Azoulai, 'The Law of European Society' (2022) 59 *Common Market Law Review* 203–14; M Loughlin, The Construction of European Society by European Lawyers: A Methodological Critique (2025) *Hague Journal on the Rule of Law*. See also Epilogue, in this volume.

[37] For a wise summation and rejoinder, see J Scholtes, 'Abusing Constitutional Identity' (2021) 22(4) *German Law Journal* 534–56; J Scholtes, *The Abuse of Constitutional Identity in the European Union* (Oxford University Press, 2023).

[38] See J White, *Political Allegiance after European Integration* (Palgrave Macmillan, 2011) 5ff.

[39] See N Walker, 'Surface and Depth: The EU's Resilient Sovereignty Question' in J Neyer and A Wiener (eds), *Political Theory of the European Union* (Oxford University Press, 2011) 91–109.

[40] See Linden-Retek (n *) chs 6, 7.

[41] We have essentially set the critical project aside; if it exists at all in European politics or law, it has no constitutional dimension. The notion that this kind of social and historical inquiry might in fact be the proper and essential task of post-national constitutionalism is not considered. See P Linden-Retek, 'The Postnational Aspirations of European Law' (2024) 72(5) *Buffalo Law Review* 1619.

[42] See Neuvonen (*n* 5); see also L Azoulai, S Barbou des Places, and E Pataut (eds), *Constructing the Person in EU Law: Rights, Roles, Identities* (Hart Publishing, 2016).

of a specific kind of activity or as someone vulnerable in a particular way, or burdened by a particular set of constraints or priorities but incapable of being burdened by others.

As Neuvonen demonstrates, the elevation of an individual above the social fabric as a site of subjectivation poses many difficulties, but here I wish to emphasise how such subjectification loses a post-national bearing insofar it abstracts from the structural conditions in which struggles over individual rights are given meaning and effect. This entails not just selfishness but a particular – and particularly narrow – rendering of post-national freedom. Examples abound, but consider the formation of what Neuvonen has critiqued as an abstracted view by the CJEU of access to free movement, whilst simultaneously undercutting such access in practice for some more expansive readings of limitations on the basis of financial self-sufficiency or degree of integration.[43] The dissonance in European jurisprudence that results in the marginalisation of immobile or economically disadvantaged EU citizens furthers an account of free movement and its purposes that are divorced from certain underlying considerations that might, in fact, make movement as a human activity meaningful, to begin with, notwithstanding the very real situations of litigants that precisely recommend to the Court consideration of concrete rights such as those to family life, protection of the best interests of the child, or of cultural life. From the opposite end, EU law collapses integration conditions into what are, as Floris de Witte has argued, ultimately perceptions of 'fit' with the host Member State as it is, thereby 'mirror[ing] the exclusionary practices of the Member States' and ignoring the many ways that a Member State might itself be tasked with accommodating or supporting the conditions under which an EU citizen is asked to integrate.[44] In short, these renderings of EU citizenship avoid the hard issues in favour of an abstract and timeless set of concerns, concerns which form only a very partial and limited view of post-national political life.

Abstraction yields timeless qualities of relations that pose no questions of commitment or sacrifice but merely considerations of transaction, efficiency, or functionality. There is, further, an erasure of the utopian dimension that Adorno warned of: the citizen no longer confronts the difficult choice of transformation, of the encounter that might. Here, avoidance becomes an ethical failing of what Honneth has called 'reduced attentiveness'. Lukács's 'detached observer' is the archetypical and seemingly desired status for a European citizen. The reification that EU law inflicts on EU citizens in order to then subjectify them yields a constitutional project that has at the same time shed the resources of affect and attentiveness that could sustain a project beyond the confluence of economic interest. It is for this reason that, as Neuvonen writes, the subjectification of EU citizens comes at the price of their *transnational* subjectification (emphasis added).[45]

The stakes of reification and its particular construction of free subjecthood are significant. When judicial and political discourses 'reify' the issues and subjects before them, they suppress their own temporality and portray themselves as 'presentist': Speaking for certain already fully formed ideas, they make the social and historically specific character of legal or political conflict disappear. Reification explains how socially constituted categories

[43] See Neuvonen (*n* 5) at 8, 12–13; see also P Neuvonen, 'EU Citizenship and its "Very Specific" Essence: Rendón Marin and CS' (2017) 54 *Common Market Law Review* 1201.

[44] See F de Witte, 'The Liminal European: Subject to the EU Legal Order' (2021) 40(1) *Yearbook of European Law* 56–81.

[45] Neuvonen (*n* 5).

– nationhood, race, and class among them – come to be misattributed as natural. No time is left for us to see the possibilities in either our past or future, we find no space in which to seek new relationships with others. And thus our legal and political institutions misrepresent their true character as institutions always in the process of contestation and 'becoming', reflecting a polity whose identity, history, purpose, and legacy are still in formation.[46]

Such a notion of freedom positions post-national constitutional theory awkwardly, and ultimately disappointingly, with regard to the project of emancipation. As Alexander Somek has notably argued, the form of freedom imagined by European integration is not emancipation from the unfreedom of the market through the mobilisation of democratic control over the social question, but instead a privatised, bourgeois form of empowerment.[47] Its essential constitutional subject is the 'entrepreneur', who, in Somek's telling, extracts sovereign control even above the routinised rules of 'market calculation'.[48] The entrepreneur is a private sovereign, the apotheosis of the urge for mastery. Marveling at their own capacity to innovate and change, the entrepreneur's freedom is expressed with reference to no social expectation or responsibility, to no common inheritance of the past nor shared commitment to the future. They desire single-mindedly to set the terms of recognition for others – to control into the future the terms by which others act and choose and believe themselves free.[49]

When this kind of freedom is projected onto law's subjects, constitutional values conventionally co-implicated (co-original)[50] with freedom – solidarity, for example – are rendered ambiguously and weakly, often counter-productively, in the EU's legal order. A legal form premised on empowerment entertains solidarity principally as a form of enlightened self-interest tied to EU law's functional effectiveness,[51] rather than a transformative 'constitutional paradigm' that modulates of one's senses of self and other.[52] It preaches accommodation and negotiation, rather than ethical self-transformation or sacrifice. This goes some way to explaining why scholars, notably Violeta Moreno-Lax, have had to do Herculean work to remind European judiciaries of 'solidarity's reach' and of its more radical implications for the legitimacy of democratic decision-making in light of global justice.[53] The activation of the more critical content of solidarity as a legal principle seems to struggle against the constraints of the legal form through which that content must appear.

[46] Compare D Kysar, *Regulating from Nowhere: Environmental Law and the Search for Objectivity* (Yale University Press, 2010). I am grateful to Doug Kysar and Neil Walker for helping me find the language in which to express this notion of contestation, becoming, and an identity understood to be still in formation.

[47] A Somek, 'The Individualisation of Liberty: Europe's Move from Emancipation to Empowerment' (2013) 4(2) *Transnational Legal Theory* 258–82.

[48] ibid 281.

[49] Compare Markell (n 2).

[50] See J Habermas, *Between Facts and Norms: Contributions to a Discourse Theory of Law and Democracy* (MIT Press, 1996 [1992]).

[51] See E Küçük, 'Solidarity in EU Law: An Elusive Political Statement or a Legal Principle with Substance?' (2016) 23 (6) *Maastricht Journal of European and Comparative Law* 965; E Gill-Pedro, 'Solidarity Through the Lens of Functional Constitutionalism' (2023) 6(2) *Nordic Journal of European Law Special Issue* 113–30.

[52] See M Ross, 'Solidarity—A New Constitutional Paradigm for the EU?' in M Ross and Y Borgmann-Prebil (eds), *Promoting Solidarity in the European Union* (Oxford University Press, 2010) 23, 36 (cited in V Moreno-Lax, 'Solidarity's Reach: Meaning, Dimensions and Implications for EU (External) Asylum Policy' (2017) 24(5) *Maastricht Journal of European and Comparative Law* 740–762, 747).

[53] Moreno-Lax, ibid, 740–62; V Moreno-Lax, 'Solidarity Crimes, Legitimacy Limits: Punishing Civil Obedience as an Abuse of Power' (*VerfBlog*, 17 April 2024), available at https://verfassungsblog.de/solidarity-crimes-legitimacy-limits.

The point I wish to make is this – the legal form inherited from the national constitutional state is, in important respects, a juridical form of reification. It must aim to selectively reify the relationships before it in the pursuit of its political and legal coherence: its closure as a polity. This legal coherence is required because it confirms and expresses a particular form of political agency and emancipation. The problem is that this form of political freedom remains a national form of freedom. Law becomes a disciplinary, not a critical, force. It betrays an orientation towards mastery.[54] It suppresses and masks the underlying dilemma that post-nationalism aimed to speak to what Patchen Markell calls the 'experience of vulnerability, . . . the fact that our identities are shaped in part through the unpredictable responses of other people'.[55] The push of legality here demands that 'others recognize us as who we *already* really are' and demands that we tie our freedom to such recognition, as well.[56] But these demands threaten to unravel precisely that capacity to perceive and thus to remain *responsive* to such vulnerability. It narrows our field of vision to an already (presently) constituted range of actors (public authorities, citizens who are considered to properly belong), such that we lose sight of how such subjectivities (such subjective positions) and their comprehensions of harm are themselves created and recreated *through* legal and policy judgments.[57] Reification, read below through the lens of Markell's Arendtian theory, can thereby be rendered as: (1) being and desiring to be recognised merely as one already is; and 2) a blindness to the patterning of structural relations in which the burdens of such effects and desires of such recognition are unevenly distributed. In what follows, I examine a particular instance of why and how reification and the brand of freedom it promises pose a constitutional problem for the European project.

V. Freedom and Critique: *Commission v Malta* and the Political Economy of Belonging

Commission v Malta has quickly become something of a lodestar and testing ground for theories of constitutional defence, of European society, and for the assertion of Article 2 TEU as essential to the identity of the EU and as a tool to be used freely and creatively to bring Member States into line with the European project. It has been met, equally strongly, with skepticism, assertions of hubristic overreach, of machination that attempts to conjure political ties from mere legalistic pronouncements akin to the mistakes of old.[58]

[54] See generally Markell (n 2) 12ff.
[55] ibid 14.
[56] ibid.
[57] See Linden-Retek (n *) 64ff.
[58] See, eg, G Íñiguez, 'On Genuine Links, Burdens of Proof, and Declaration No. 2: Some Musings on the Court's Reasoning in Commission v Malta (C-181/23)' (*EU Law Live*, 5 May 2025), available at https://eulawlive.com/op-ed-on-genuine-links-burdens-of-proof-and-declaration-no-2-some-musings-on-the-courts-reasoning-in-commission-v-malta-c-181-23/; S Peers, 'Pirates of the Mediterranean Meet Judges of the Kirchberg: The CJEU Rules on Malta's Investor Citizenship Law' (*EU Law Analysis*, 30 April 2025), available at https://eulawanalysis.blogspot.com/2025/04/pirates-of-mediterranean-meet-judges-of.html (cited in D Kochenov and G Íñiguez, 'EU Citizenship's New Essentialism' (2025) 50(4) *European Law Review*, available at https://ssrn.com/abstract=5309895. The issue before us here is only marginally the fidelity of one or the

The case concerned an infringement action against Malta's investor citizenship scheme filed by the Commission, which accused the Member State's programme of commodifying citizenship on the basis of commercial investment without a 'genuine connection' to the polity to be in breach of EU citizenship law, mutual trust, and the principle of sincere co-operation. The CJEU ruled in favour of the Commission, reading a requirement of a 'special relationship of solidarity and good faith' into the form of nationality imagined by Article 20(1) Treaty on the Functioning of the European Union and accordingly holding that Article to impose constraints on the conferral of nationality by a Member State in light of 'the very nature of Union citizenship'.[59]

Commission v Malta has been cast prominently as a controversy about solidarity – and the meaning of solidarity imagined through political belonging.[60] Reframing this discussion in light of the concept of reification, I wish to suggest that the case poses difficult questions, perhaps more consequentially, about the meaning of freedom and the possibility of finding a critical view on what it means, within the EU legal order, to be free. In assessing the conceptions of legal form and of freedom that each interpretation projects onto its object of inquiry, I am less interested in adjudicating between rival interpretive accounts than in suggesting a common fault they share – and by virtue of that fault, what they obscure.

Commentators, dividing sharply on the rectitude of the ruling, invoked either republican or liberal conceptions of citizenship to ground their positions. Representative of the first, Luke Dimitrios Spieker ably reconstructed the Court's vision of a 'republican understanding of Union citizenship', which defends 'belonging to European society [as] a central precondition for solidarity between Member States and Union citizens' and emphasising that 'solidarity . . . needs a stable basis'.[61] The absence of a meaningful requirement of actual residence in Malta's investor citizenship scheme,[62] by belying such precondition, undermines the ideal of active citizenship with the rights and duties of participation in the public life of a community. It reduces political belonging to mere transaction, and 'commercializ[ed] citizenship' is no form of citizenship at all.[63]

By contrast, Dimitry Kochenov and Guillermo Íñiguez valorise the formal and transactional qualities of liberal citizenship, lamenting the Court's further 'contributi[on] to its erosion, now at the supranational level'.[64] Like Anja Bossow in her balanced assessment,[65] Kochenov and Íñiguez note the exclusionary potential of the thicker account of citizenship, potentially unsettling the status of many classes of Europeans.[66] They cast

other interpretation to legal precedent, although to be sure that is not an irrelevant consideration given the historicising ambitions of post-national legality. See M van den Brink, 'Why Bother with Legal Reasoning? The CJEU Judgment in Commission v Malta (Citizenship by Investment)' (*Global Citizenship Inventory*, 2 May 2025), available at https://globalcit.eu/why-bother-with-legal-reasoning-the-cjeu-judgment-in-commission-v-malta-citizenship-by-investment/.

[59] C-181/23 *Commission v Malta* ECLI:EU:C:2025:283, paras 96–99, 95.

[60] See LD Spieker, 'It's Solidarity, Stupid!: In Defence of Commission v Malta' (*VerfBlog*, 7 May 2025), available at https://verfassungsblog.de/its-solidarity-stupid/.

[61] ibid.

[62] See *Commission v Malta* (n 59) paras 102ff.

[63] See Spieker (n 60).

[64] Kochenov and Íñiguez (n 58) 4.

[65] See A Bossow, 'What is Citizenship For?' (*VerfBlog*, 6 May 2025), available at https://verfassungsblog.de/what-is-citizenship-for/.

[66] Kochenov and Íñiguez (n 58), 4–5.

the justification for Malta's scheme of investment migration in the moral bankruptcy of any 'essentialist' conceptions of solidarity and in the 'liberal tolerant promise of the EU's values'.[67] Kochenov and Íñiguez consider, notably, that EU citizenship's great contribution is to offer a specific kind of freedom that resists this essentialism: the 'freedom to disregard Member States' identitarian demands'.[68] The result of invoking thicker strands of solidarity, even on putatively republican grounds, will be an unseemly exercise of parsing distinctions between '"real" and "fake" Europeans'.[69]

Whatever the merits of each argument – and they bear taking seriously, I wish to press in a different direction to challenge the adequacy of the framing. Construed as above, *Commission v Malta* is a case, on the one hand, about republican freedom, in which belonging and civic identity control, which might always suffer or be deformed by a colonisation of the logics of the market – of being bought or sold with the mindset of contract, not belonging. On the other, freedom as the capacity to choose, to elect by contract to be a member without any prerequisites other than the ability to enter into the agreement. Both forms of freedom can be said to be coherent as independent philosophies; yet when seen in the light of the problem of reification, neither informs a post-national form of freedom.

Patchen Markell, in his Arendtian critique of recognition as a political ideal, argues that republican and liberal thought contain a common element that yields, in both, a tendency to resurface aspirations to sovereignty.[70] Ambitions to defend belonging or contract to defend thicker communal bonds or the rights of commercial transaction project an image of freedom in which identity – whether citizen or consumer – governs action. Cast in the figure of the national citizen, identity serves as an antecedent fact about people on whose basis they can either act freely or endure constraint.[71] The image of a membership as a transaction, too, projects an individual – perhaps 'the entrepreneur' – who can introduce at their pleasure their own sense of political life onto others. Each account, however disparate their forms of sovereign imposition might at first appear, presumes that freedom is an application of an identity we have previously secured and known and now work to enact without obstruction: an 'uncompromising self-sufficiency'.[72]

Reification is exactly this presumption about the world and our place within it. The assertion of freedom as control, in both accounts of EU citizenship and the free political life it promises, reproduces that reified presumption. What it obscures, in Markell's language, is the 'patterning and arranging' of sovereign relations, in which some states and peoples enjoy the prerogatives of sovereignty at the expense of others.[73] The inability to perceive such patterning – not the binary debate between thick and thin identities – is the cause of frustrations scholars identify with each approach.[74] This common failing – this alienating form of freedom – is what a post-national subject, in part through post-national law, needs freeing from.

[67] ibid 7.
[68] ibid 21.
[69] ibid 22.
[70] See Markell (n 2).
[71] See ibid 12–13.
[72] H Arendt, *The Human Condition* (University of Chicago Press, 1958) 234 (cited in Markell (n 2) 11); see generally Markell (n 2) Introduction and 58ff.
[73] See Markell (n 2) 5.
[74] See generally Linden-Retek (n *) chs 1–3.

The concrete issue with the holding in *Commission v Malta*, then, is that its reified conception of freedom prevents us from seeing a distinct exclusion in the turn to republican citizenship – not of others who wish to contract into one's society, but of the political economy within which such choices can be made and assessed, to begin with. In short, we fail to ask about the social, historical, and economic consequences of citizenship as a political practice and fail to consider what such consequences might teach us about the possible future of citizenship as a free ideal.

Viktor Kazai, in a wonderfully illuminating analysis of the turn to rule of law conditionality in EU law, makes the case that – however much we might appreciate the liberal values associated with the rule of law, as he of course does – one must remain aware of how rule of law values carry with them not only a political but an economic project. I have relied on Kazai's intervention in previous work, noting his reminder that the EU is an economic union, and that economic interests of relevant institutional actors – both European and national – are integral to the relational context in which the rule of law is either defended or challenged.[75] Kazai in effect critiques the legal form of Article 2 TEU discourses as incapable of giving voice to this relational context, however; and thereby intimates that the invocation of Article 2 values encourage a misunderstanding of freedom as much as they purport to defend it.

This observation renders the invocation by the Court in *Commission v Malta* of the discourse of solidarity particularly ill-suited; for this version of solidarity, invoked to preserve the republican tradition of stronger communal ties against encroachments by the market, enforces an underlying deficit of solidarity. To point this out is not, however, to settle on the view by Kochenov and Íñiguez that valorises liberal citizenship in solidarity's place. There is something telling about the authors' characterisation of the freedom promised by EU citizenship as the freedom to 'disregard', to ignore – a mode of disengagement. The image projected by this form of freedom is an abstraction away from the concrete patterns we might otherwise diagnose – mere 'contemplation', not a call to inquiry about their historical genealogy and possible alteration. This is the equivalent of Spieker's passing but undeveloped acknowledgment of the exclusionary possibilities inherent to thicker conceptions of belonging, noting briefly the unfavourable position of third-country nationals in the EU legal order.[76]

The ends of the binary choice offered in *Commission v Malta* are abstract and ahistorical, and therefore ultimately anti-utopian. They have a conservative flair, despite the rhetoric of defending progressive values. This is why the debate might leave us disappointed, with a sense that its sides speak past one another, avoiding the root cause of the dilemma while attempting, each in their own way, to moralise a path to a principled solution. If we see the spectre in *Malta* to be the 'commercialisation of citizenship', which indeed is a problem, then the turn to republicanism is wise. If, however, we see the spectre to be that which causes the commercialisation of citizenship, then republicanism gets us only so far. Similarly, if we see the problem to be an apology for exclusionary forms of citizenship, then an appreciation for the liberal emancipation that EU law promises is wise. If, however, we see the problem to be an inability to think structurally

[75] See V Kazai, 'Economic Interests and the Rule of Law Crisis in the EU' (*VerfBlog*, 2 May 2020), available at https://verfassungsblog.de/ economic-interests-and-the-rule-of-law-crisis-in-the-eu/.

[76] Spieker (n 60).

about the forms exclusion has taken, then the liberal view gets us, similarly, only so far. We are left, after that, merely to contemplate what amounts to a jurisdictional question. Either Article 2 values control through Article 20(1) TEU, or Member States have exclusive competence. It is, at heart, a conflict over values refracted through a claim about control. It continues, ultimately, to trade in a sovereigntist conception of authority and freedom. The critique of reification helps us see this dilemma plainly.

Post-national freedom requires more. But what is missing in *Commission v Malta*, exactly? In short, it is an absence of critique. Missing is an explanation, an acknowledgement of why it is that some Member States, but not others, are inclined to open their citizenship regimes in the way Malta has. Missing is an essential critical question that follows: what might we learn about the 'patterning of sovereignty' among European states and peoples, were we to consider this concern earnestly? The invocation by Kochenov and Íñiguez of the prevalence of citizenship's 'commercialization' – in Ireland, for example, beginning in 1988 – is for this purpose true and helpful but only one aspect of the socio-historical reality I consider germane.[77] It is an absence, at its core of self-understanding, of having learned something true about where we stand. Not just the economic rationales for such policies – these are quite evident – but a sensibility for why those rationales arise, and how they do so in relation to a political economy shared over time with others. 'How have we come to be this way?'

The literature on the phenomenon of investor citizenship clearly invites this broader question, even if it does not always follow its more radical political economic and structural implications. The point, at least in part, is to begin to give an account of how certain readings of values arise because of one's place in the structure of economic and material relations. As one scholar of the global market in residence and citizenship put it, 'Many people I've spoken to in the Global South separate citizenship from nationality quite clearly. For them, it's just a pragmatic insurance option in a difficult world'.[78]

As a matter of method and approach, such implications define for European constitutional law a certain ambition: an acknowledgement that this way of life – if we believe it worthy of value –was bought at a certain price, imposed upon others with some consequence. And so if such a value of the Union is to be defended, it must be defended with eyes open to its conditions of possibility and with due responsibility for the 'difficult world' it creates.

This ambition requires resistance to reification, a programme to de-reify the objects of concern before the law and to deny the pull of 'immediacy' and 'presentism' and false familiarity that conventional legal form might otherwise reproduce. If *Commission v Malta* suggests insight into why Member States might wish to retain a degree of national competence over their citizenship regimes, it is not for the sake of control; it is for the sake of learning, for the perspective-taking that it makes possible, and for the articulation of historical sensibility that comes from concrete experience. If we might wish for *Commission v Malta* in the end to turn on an articulation of the principle of solidarity

[77] Kochenov and Íñiguez (n 58) 12.

[78] See 'Golden Passports and Visas: The Global Market in Residence and Citizenship', LSE Research for the World Series (15 March 2022), available at www.lse.ac.uk/research/research-for-the-world/politics/golden-visas-and-passports-the-global-market-in-residence-and-citizenship; K Surak and Y Tsuzuki, 'Are Golden Visas a Golden Opportunity? Assessing the Economic Origins and Outcomes of Residence by Investment Programmes in the EU' (2021) 47(15) *Journal of Ethnic and Migration Studies* 3367–89.

– to demand deference by states to the integrity of a shared view of citizenship within a post-national legal order – we are here after a different sort of solidarity: solidarity not as consolidation of a view of freedom that is recognition of what one already is, but solidarity as acknowledgment of one's limits and a commitment to critique.[79] This shift to see values concretely, historically, and with a view to utopia – in a relational register – is at heart a desire, not for control, but to be free from reification.

VI. The Legal Form of Critique: On Freedom from Reification

The preceding identification of legal form and its effects reveals, too, the contingency of legal form. This contingency opens the door to properly dialectical analysis of law and – perhaps – to a critique of legal form that might yield alternate ways to think about law, legal process, and legal subjecthood, ways more attuned to the post-national constitutional project. Such a project would take seriously that the form of emancipation it seeks is emancipation from the confines of reification and from reified notions of self. In law, this requires seeing the possibility of a legal form of critique, which holds different conceptions of what law's authors expect law to do for them and through them and different expectations of how legal form might change the image that legal subjects have of themselves and project onto others.

Such legal form would be better attuned to the world's concreteness (to embeddedness, emotion, to lives lived), to contingency (to the paths not taken and the reasons they were not), and to utopianism (to finding resources for 'dream[ing our] way' into a better world). To de-reify the world requires resources to again concretise, historise, and reimagine social relations. It is, in the first instance, to conceive of ourselves as subjects who are relationally bound to one another, not just in that we bear the effects of one another's actions but that such actions and their effects speak to the heart of who we believe ourselves to be and what we believe ourselves to want.[80]

Päivi Neuvonen speaks precisely of the relational quality of subjecthood, and my invocation of relational freedom aims to continue to think about what it means for a subject to be, in Neuvonen's memorable phrase, a 'subject-in-process'.[81] It requires a conception of freedom in which one perceives the identity one has to always be the product, not just the predicate, of one's unpredictable action with others. Such an Arendtian view, tying freedom to agency's constitutive *limits*, offers subjects a dialectical freedom, which is, in turn, the foundation of a constitutional subject, which means nothing other than the foundation of a structure of legitimation of a constitutional order.

Such an account builds into the desire for freedom a quality of attunement to the mutual effects and dependencies one shares with others, reflections about which can never be made in advance of shared action, nor by those who act alone. In an important

[79] See P Linden-Retek, 'The Refugees We Are: Solidarity, Asylum, and Critique in the European Constitutional Imagination' (2021) 22(4) *German Law Journal* 506–33.

[80] Compare Markell (n 2) 12.

[81] Neuvonen (*n* 5) 10 (drawing on the work of Julia Kristeva and her reading and reappropriation of Jacques Lacan).

sense, one's meaning of action – the potential of a free act – is always deferred, placed into the hands of the other with whom one acts and who will inevitably offer an interpretation of the action's meaning. Tied to the other this way, a constitutional subject begins to find the habit of mind that is distinct from the assertion of sovereignty that had characterised the national constitutional subject, ever in search of the assertion of self-sufficiency and control over their own subjecthood. For a post-national subject, one's law is never merely one's own, for the simple reason that one can never act intelligibly alone.

Put another way, resisting reification and the contemplative disposition is, in the first instance, beginning to entertain something rather elementary – although something we have forgotten: simply asking about the conditions under which particular things or relationships appear valuable, and others are taken to hold less value, or no value at all. Given that we know and suspect that the national, reified consciousness has grasped hold of the categories by which we think such things, part of this resistance requires that we reflect on who – which actors, institutions, structures – have decided that such present conditions of valuation ought to be held. Law, we know, typically applies or merely enforces the effects of this reification; it repeats this valuation to us relentlessly. But, if we make the legal form of national law more contingent and see its effects for what they are, we might remain hopeful for a legal form that, while inevitably offering choices about valuation, also illuminates that very act of selection and, in so choosing, always points to the possibility that such result could have been otherwise.[82]

On this account, the legal form would aim to loosen hold of the presumptions of value and in this sense would locate its own post-national bearing, which entails its own form of post-national emancipation. Here, emancipation, understood to emancipate individuals from the false closure of national constitutional freedom, is emancipation from reification and the rejection of the contemplative disposition in Lukács's and Honneth's sense. If legal form, on this view, is what makes the transmission of ideology possible, then a shift in legal form might yet interrupt the ideological closure of national law, to resist the tenets within constitutional theory that inhibit the development of post-national thought and practice. The work to be done is to consider how, *in what form*, law can aid in such shift of consciousness. Connecting with further articulations of reification by Honneth, let me sketch the kinds of judgments we might seek from this form of post-national law, drawing by way of example from recent work by Floris de Witte and his critique of the 'liminal' European subject.

In that work, de Witte diagnoses a shift in free movement law to the creation of liminal subjecthood: 'highly stratified' and 'commodified', 'precarious and conditional',[83] this subjecthood reflects not an unpredictable responsiveness to the other, as Neuvonen might put it, but instead dooms the subject to the discipline of the pre-ordained.[84] 'Work as such', de Witte writes, 'is no longer enough. Instead, for EU law to offer the migrant worker its protection, such work must be durable, stable, productive, and "sufficiently significant"'.[85] One lesson here seems to be that, in order to sustain the unpredictability

[82] Compare Cover, '*Nomos* and Narrative' (n 16).
[83] de Witte (*n* 44), 74.
[84] ibid 66.
[85] ibid 68.

of an unreified freedom, one must not simply embrace anarchic tendencies or abstract away, in neoliberal fashion, from the ties that bind a citizen to the nation-state. One cannot simply broaden subjecthood out in such a way. Because the ties of nationhood – sovereignty – are enduringly and resiliently binding, what is needed is more faithful and more creative engagement with them. Instead of an appeal to self-actualisation alone, we must seek more attentive appeals to a revised sense of what self-actualisation means in relation with others. As Douglas Kysar in his luminous work on environmental law writes, '[W]e do not enter into the world as self-possessed liberal subjects, already equipped with capacities of reason and discourse' that enable us to judge the worth of others as, effectively, beings entirely separate from ourselves.[86] We must begin from a different place entirely in our judgments.[87] De Witte's reflections suggest the dangers of a legal order or a system of rights that would, too quickly, presume otherwise. Instead of self-sufficiency, we must seek a responsive, affected life among others relieved not of dependency but of mere 'contemplation', which is to say, of reification.

Here, *Dano* is illustrative. In the case and in de Witte's telling of it, the freedom that EU law aims to protect and to value is quite explicitly a freedom tied to self-sufficiency, to the elision of complex questions of dependency or possibility, to questions of history and entanglement, to questions of past and future. As de Witte critiques the jurisprudential approach, his line of approach is precisely to recover these elided questions – first to show that the existing framework is unbearably narrow and then to suggest other questions, broader questions, the Court might have posed and explored as part of its interpretive work. De Witte here restores, in other words, the complex relational field against which a particular claim for freedom and rights is made and, so the argument goes, without which that claim cannot be understood. 'The picture that is painted', he writes, 'is one of a Union citizen migrant who cannot possibly integrate in the host state society for lack of productive qualities and a type of attitude'.[88] Such a vision is narrow substantively, in terms of the bias and presumptions it builds into the forms of work and identity it recognises, but also temporally, in terms of the embedded histories and future developments it perceives in the ongoing, unpredictable relationships among Europeans. Why, he asks, do we not learn that 'Ms Dano's ethnicity (not mentioned anywhere in the case file) likely has caused discrimination in her access (and

[86] Kysar (n 46) 195.

[87] Kysar here turns to the philosophy of Emmanuel Levinas. See ibid. Indeed, the turn to concreteness bears important parallels with critical phenomenological theory, notably that of Levinas, which centres the suffering of the concrete other as a counterpoint to tendencies within liberal argumentation to abstract too quickly from one's embodied and affective experience. Consider, notably, S Hendley, *From Communicative Action to the Face of the Other: Levinas and Habermas on Language, Obligation, and Community* (Lexington Books, 2000). I cannot do justice to this important dialogue between Habermasian and Levinasian theory here, but it deserves further attention within this area of legal study and speaks, in particular, to aspects of the approaches in Paul Kahn's cultural study of law and the work of Robert Cover. See P Kahn, *The Cultural Study of Law: Reconstructing Legal Scholarship* (University of Chicago Press, 1999); J Etxabe, 'The Legal Universe After Robert Cover' (2010) 4(1) *Law and Humanities* 122; M Goldoni, 'Robert Cover's Narrative Approach to Constitutionalism (2010) *Italian Society for Law and Literature* 1–21; D Klusmeyer, 'Law, Narrative and Politics in a Jewish Key: Hannah Arendt and Robert Cover in Comparative Perspective' (2014) 8(2) *Law and Humanities* 217–46; D Cornell, 'Time, Deconstruction, and the Challenge to Legal Positivism' (1990) 2(2) *Yale Journal of Law & the Humanities* 267–97.

[88] de Witte *(n* 44) 70.

completion) to education and the labour market'?[89] Why should the 'caring duties for her nieces (or reproductive work, for that matter) [] not constitute sufficient evidence of work or engagement with the host society to warrant access to the welfare benefits'?[90] *Dano*, de Witte concludes, simply 'throws up more questions about the scope of application of EU law than it answers'.[91]

What de Witte is diagnosing here, without mentioning the technical term, is precisely the reification of life and subjecthood that attends EU law's failure to trace and bear fidelity to relational dynamics. The elements of anti-reification as a post-national bearing and its import for post-national law are all here: concreteness (the rejection of abstraction); contingency (the rejection of present social structure and the reconstruction of orderings and histories); utopia (the hope of finding order again). De Witte effectively asks the law to assume a radically different, radically responsible and imaginative posture to the individuals and societies before it. How is it that this particular confrontation came to be? What must have occurred such that this claim was made at this time and at this place? The work of imagination is not mere abstraction or fantasy; it is directed to the concrete work of historical reconstruction, the study of social structure and social development, and, finally, the appeal to what might have been otherwise – not as an abstract question but as a chain of possibility that emanates from the concrete. Treating legal norms in light of their relationality rejects the notion, as Kysar has put it, that a polity's regulations can simply advance existing national interests or obligations without also endogenously affecting them: the failings of such a cabined vision become evident when powerful systemic crises, such as Europe's sovereign debt and refugee crises, reveal that policy-making cannot hinge exclusively on existing preferences, given that those preferences will be altered significantly by the very outcome of this policy-making.[92] Anti-reification's temporal arc restores the dialectical relationship between subject and object. It reminds us that the norms we author are in fact a product, not just a settled frame or stable basis, of our unpredictable, evolving engagement with others.[93]

VII. Conclusion: The Hope of Critique and Critique as Hope

Nikolas Kompridis speaks beautifully of critical theory – engaged as a critical practice – to depend on 'its ability to disclose alternative possibilities, possibilities that suppose … openness and responsiveness to the world'.[94] This disclosure, for Kompridis, is a form of hope, borne, he writes, 'as one bears a child, to bear it so as it to make a new beginning possible'.[95] In how I have described a post-national bearing and the expectations

[89] ibid; see generally J Guth and S Elfving, *Gender and the Court of Justice of the European Union* (Routledge, 2018) (cited in de Witte (*n* 44) 70).
[90] de Witte (*n* 44) 70.
[91] ibid.
[92] See Kysar (n 46) 17–18.
[93] See Markell (n 2) 14.
[94] N Kompridis, *Critique and Disclosure: Critical Theory Between Past and Future* (Massachusetts Institute of Technology Press, 2006) 258.
[95] ibid.

of freedom in light of it, I have tended toward language that nears the existential. In closing, I wish to defend the use of this language and to emphasise the connections, fragile as they are, between hope, critique, and law. If critique imagines disclosure, what does one hope to disclose? I have tried above to suggest that the practical knowledge one hopes to glean from post-national law is of our relational and historical qualities as human beings.

In that call, I acknowledge that its flirtations with the existential qualities of law and politics has been notably troublesome for and criticised by theorists of European integration. In a generative, soulful article more than a decade old, Jan Komárek wrote about the malaise of the EU, facing deep democratic deficits and problems, asked to wait for a revolution in values. Komárek saw in such appeal the residue of Václav Havel's call for an existential revolution', which Komárek describes and critiques as non-political, tied to conceptions of 'constrained democracy', skeptical of 'technologies of power' and ultimately useless in the face of those who have no misgivings taking the reins of government and, corruptly, advancing their partial interests as they see fit.[96] The existential call, on Komárek's reading, is a turn away from concrete political life and political economy towards abstract 'perfectionism' and moralising appeals to virtues and values, a critique Komárek directed then at a range of theorists from Kumm to Halberstam to Weiler, now germane to von Bogdandy, as well. This critique applies perhaps most of all to the communicative turn in Habermasian critical theory and to the discourse theory of law and the vision of democratic constitutionalism that Habermas carries through to this diagnosis of the EU and his vision of its future. Michael Wilkinson has criticised this approach as one in which post-national democracy remains perpetually counterfactual.[97] Utopia is the politics of the future – and always will be.

These critiques are well-taken; and they are generally a significant part of the turn precisely to political economy, the 'material constitution', and greater attentiveness to the faultlines between core and peripheral Member States, especially concerning the future of the post-socialist states and their experience with planned economies. Too often, the existential call for an emancipatory politics empties, by contrast, into abstraction. But this is not the only way to read either Havel's existential revolution or its imbrication with the future. And it is important that my account of reification and the project of emancipation from reification escapes such a logic.

The hope and utopia I imagine to comprise a post-national bearing are products not of deferral or waiting, but of critique, which amounts to an immanent transformation grounded in social and historical reflection. If we take time to perceive its less psychological and individualistic dimensions, Havel's existential bearing restores its connection with the diagnosis of social crisis – and thus with a critical theory of society. Some readings of Havel and the dissident movement speak to this dimension quite profoundly. In the mid-1990s, political theorist Jeffrey Isaac, in a number of essays that very much merit rereading today, wrote powerfully about the rejuvenating vision of democratic politics to be found in the revolutions of 1989, even as predominant contemporary philosophers

[96] J Komárek, 'Waiting for the Existential Revolution in Europe' (January 2014) 12(1) *International Journal of Constitutional Law* 190–212, 207–209.

[97] See Michael Wilkinson, in chapter 3 of this volume.

(Habermas, Ackerman) suggested otherwise.[98] Isaac focused on the distinctive social critique posed by the Charter 77 dissident movement in Czechoslovakia: its focus, in particular, on the social crisis of moral and political responsibility caused by bureaucratic and economic alienation; the need for popular participation to address it; and the global qualities of this crisis that afflicts both capitalist and socialist societies.[99] The dissidents' formation of a 'parallel polis' held promise, Isaac believed, both theoretically and practically, to revive democratic life away from mere Schumpeterian bargaining among interests, fully formed, and towards the participatory values articulated by John Dewey, C Wright Mills, and Hannah Arendt, among others.[100] If we centre this as Havel's ambition, we see utopia not in a negative, deferred, and disempowering sense, but far closer to a manner reminiscent of Adorno, Lukács, and Benjamin, imagining a rearrangement in concrete institutions and practices. Such rearrangement comes, if never fully, all the time.

And in this social and historical embedding there is a form of ontology, which underpins the project of resisting reification. As Steger and Replogle have argued, the political project prefigured by Havel's existentialism might be said to reflect what Stephen K White speaks of as a 'felicitous weak ontology'.[101] Such ontologies embrace contingency and uncertainty and use them to give 'ethical strength in the practice of one's own life'.[102] Because they provide groundworks that are not foundational in the conventional sense, weak ontologies must reconstruct any foundations in the same gesture as they recognise their inherent contestability.[103] They prefigure, but do not dictate, the shape of our world; they guide, but do not reify, our freedom. The meaning of futurity lies in this gesture – not in abstraction or in deferral but in an immanent contestation, from within, of one's practices and self-perception. Futurity becomes a political idea, as Jonathan White might say, that acts upon the present.[104] The hope that comes from such a bearing discloses to us a certain form of knowledge, specifically, of our relational qualities as free beings.

A post-national bearing would invest legal form with the burdens and hopes of such an ontology and such an aspiration to marry concrete social analysis, democratic mobilisation, and ethical transformation. By freeing European constitutional law of the partiality of its national rendering of freedom, it would open new possibilities for constitutional contestation and settlement. As Kompridis puts it, 'Successful critique depends on the practical ability to see more in things than they are, and on the ability to articulate that "more" in some new way'.[105] We would do well to remember the possible ethical shifts that need attend a critical theory of post-national society and its law.

[98] See J Isaac, 'The Meanings of 1989' (Summer 1996) 63(2) *Social Research* 291–344, 301–305.

[99] ibid 307–308.

[100] See J Isaac, 'Oases in the Desert: Hannah Arendt on Democratic Politics' (March 1994) 88(1) *American Political Science Review* 156–68, 159.

[101] M Steger and S Replogle, 'Václav Havel's Postmodernism' (2005) 4 *Contemporary Political Theory* 253–74.

[102] SK White, *Sustaining Affirmation: The Strengths of Weak Ontology in Political Theory* (Princeton University Press, 2000) 14–15 (cited in Steger and Replogle (n 101) 257).

[103] Steger and Replogle (n 101) 257.

[104] See J White, 'The Future as a Democratic Resource' (2025) *Perspectives on Politics* 1–13; J White, *In the Long Run: The Future as a Political Idea* (Profile Books, 2024).

[105] Kompridis (n 94) 258.

Epilogue

Inside Out: On the Possibilities of Immanent Critique in EU Law

SARAH GLASER, LUCA TENREIRA, AND JACOB VAN DE BEETEN*

I. Introduction

Critical thinkers have long shown how to reveal the *unseen*: Foucault's mad and incarcerated, Spivak's subaltern, Haraway's modest witnesses, Ginzburg's tortured Miller, Geertz's shepherds, Descola's Achuar[1] – each of them provides a new description of the world by unsettling the 'normal', 'natural' or 'expert' point of view. Our ambition is much humbler but in kindred spirit: to ask how European Union (EU) law, too, might be rendered visible in different ways through the use of critical moves, methods and inquiries. Taken seriously, critical theory's potential lies in its commitment to both *describe* and *transform*. To describe is to insist that the way we account for social realities matters; to transform is to refuse to take what exists for granted. In the interplay between these commitments lies critique: restless, situated, and committed to making visible what habit and power keep unseen. In this spirit, we intend to close and open *Critical Theory and European Union Law* with a dialogue about methodological tools and moves able to bring hidden aspects of legal normativity to light.

In what follows we will re-enact past conversations between us, the three authors, with use of fictious personas whose interplay excludes the consolidation of a single authoritative point of view, might it even call itself critical. The Deconstructionist – allergic to self-evidence – delights in breaking open the doctrinal façade of neutrality. The Genealogist, attuned to history's sedimented layers, traces the contingent encounters through

* We are grateful to the Max Weber Programme for providing the funding to organise a workshop on Immanent Critique in EU law at the European University Institute in June 2024. We thank Ivana Isailović, Paul Linden-Retek, Päivi Neuvonen, Vittoria Becci, Davide Tomasselli and Marthe-Hélène De Dinechin for their participation and encouragement.

[1] M Foucault, *Discipline and Punish: The Birth of the Prison* (Pantheon Books, 1977); G Spivak, 'Can the Subaltern Speak? revised edition' in RC Morris (ed), *Can the Subaltern Speak? Reflections on the History of an Idea* (Columbia University Press, 2010); D Haraway, *Feminism and Technoscience* (Routledge, 1997); C Ginzburg, *The Cheese and the Worms: The Cosmos of a Sixteenth-Century Miller* (Johns Hopkins University Press, 2013); C Geertz, *Thick Description: Toward an Interpretive Theory of Culture* (Basic Books, 1973); P Descola, *In the Society of Nature: A Native Ecology in Amazonia* (Oxford University Press, 1996).

which the EU's legal order came to speak in the name of necessity. The Anthropologist, restless among institutions and their rituals, listens for the human and material traces that escape the law's official language. Through enacting a conversation between these fictitious characters we offer different ways of apprehending the law from the *inside out*: in the sense that we 'know the law inside out' and resist the temptation of 'internal' closure by looking at the law from 'the outside'. All three of us have been trained to speak EU law's own language – apprehending doctrines, judicial reasonings, procedures and principles as *our own practice*, while simultaneously we aim to unsettle the internal point of view by calling on law's externalities. We will now let our protagonists introduce themselves:

***The Deconstructionist*:** There is no single definition of 'deconstruction'. I find my aesthetic programme reflected in Picasso's *Demoiselles d'Avignon* – a cubist rendering of five women bathing. On this canvas, mimetic nature-building cedes its obviousness to bodies and things, (mis-)shaped by their social, economic and psychological conditions. Likewise, deconstruction as critical legal method lays bare the material conditions of power at play within a given normative order, whose authority presents itself as natural and depoliticised. In other words, I denaturalise doctrinal authority.

***The Genealogist*:** We work hand in hand. I too engage in a kind of deconstruction, albeit one that unfolds according to a historical logic. The image of a family tree, which immediately springs to mind, is misleading. Rather than figuring organic evolutions, the junctions of a genealogy articulate the meticulous grit of the historian with the critical freedom to place epistemic shifts. Unrooted, free and driven by a desire to know, building a genealogy of European legal integration is an act of defiance addressed to institutional representations of integration aimed at consolidating the legal system's authority.

***The Anthropologist*:** I pick the both of you up at the point where legal authority is being denaturalised and carry the critique further. I address 'the human question' to legal institutions themselves: what is the cultural meaning of legal techniques?[2] Tapping into my own rich critical history, I expand the critical ground on which to seize EU law. Replaced in a wider world, the European legal order is entangled in a web of ecological, social, cultural, political alterities that defy the withdrawal of EU law in its own world of abstractions and concepts.

The conversation unfolds as follows. The need for critique starts the dialogue (section II). Its productive unsettlement of authoritative point of view leads the interlocutors to clarify what they mean by an 'immanent' vantage point (section III). Next, the interlocutors discuss how immanent critique properly understood seeks to understand social reality and tries to translate it back into the law. In this way, they try to reconnect EU law with society, understood not as an attempt to grasp law empirically but to theorise social relationships (section IV). Particularly crucial, in this regard, is moving beyond an institutional vision of EU law through acts of 'scaling' that allows the interlocutors to adopt different perspectives (section V). In doing so, they make a first step in unlocking EU law's transformative potential (section VI).

[2] See, eg, A Riles, 'A New Agenda for the Cultural Study of Law: Taking on the Technicalities' (2005) 53 *Buffalo Law Review* 973; A Pottage, 'Law after Anthropology: Object and Technique in Roman Law' (2014) 31 *Culture & Society* 147.

II. The Need for Critique

***The Anthropologist*:** Where to start?

***The Genealogist (excited)*:** Let's start with the origins! In the beginning was a transfer of sovereignty calling an original legal order to life. It would grow beyond any type of functionalist organisation into emancipating the individual, integrating society, guaranteeing peace between countries and fulfilling pan-European values. All through law.[3]

***The Anthropologist*:** Oh dear...

***The Deconstructionist*:** That's how quick we move from the *Demoiselles d'Avignon* to *Impression, Setting Sun*.[4]

***The Genealogist*:** I was joking, of course. The quest for origins provides the impulse for a teleological narrative about the building of a fated community.[5] Let's leave the *origins* in their mythic waters and turn to the muddy *beginnings* instead, historic beginnings that is. The lack of such beginnings in EU law finds its symptomatic expression in the depiction of the EU as a 'sui generis' legal and political system that has no historical predecessors or contemporary equivalents. Such a 'politics of avoiding history' helped to ensure the legitimacy of the Court and its jurisprudence by obscuring past parallels, but precisely for that reason critical genealogies of EU law are important and even necessary.[6]

This shift alone – from *origins* to *beginnings* – opens the field of European legal studies to critique. Michel Foucault offers a definition of genealogy building in its study of Nietzsche's use of the words '*Ursprung*' (metaphysical origins) and '*Herkunft*' (historic beginnings): the description-bound construction of a genealogy resists the temptation to speculate about origins as ever set to capture 'the exact essence of things, their purest possibilities, and their carefully protected identities, because this search assumes the existence of immobile forms that precede the external world of accident and succession'.[7] Bound to the description of lived experiences, genealogies operate with a non-doctrinal notion of normativity. Europe as a 'lived community' is to be found in the study of material

[3] For one of the most recent re-enactments of this narrative, see European Commission Legal Service (ed), *70 Years of EU Law: A Union for Its Citizens*, 2nd edn (Publications Office of the European Union, 2023).

[4] That is from Picasso's unsettling Cubism to a wordplay on Monet's masterpiece *Impression, Sunrise*, sometimes associated with the announcement of modernity.

[5] See also chapter 2 by Kaius Tuori in this book. Also see M Dani and AJ Menéndez, 'European Constitutional Imagination: A Whig Interpretation of the Process of European Integration?' in J Komárek (ed), *European Constitutional Imaginaries: Between Ideology and Utopia* (Oxford University Press, 2023); CE De Vries, 'How Foundational Narratives Shape European Union Politics' (2023) 61 *Journal of Common Market Studies* 867.

[6] M Erpelding, 'International Law and the European Court of Justice: The Politics of Avoiding History' (2020) 22 *Journal of the History of International Law* 446; M Erpelding, 'Juristes internationalistes, juristes mixtes, Euro-Lawyers : l'apport de l'expérience semi-coloniale à l'émergence d'un droit supranational' [2022] *Clio@Themis: Revue électronique d'histoire du droit* 1; C Joerges and N Singh Ghaleigh, *Darker Legacies of Law in Europe: The Shadow of National Socialism and Fascism over Europe and Its Legal Traditions* (Hart Publishing, 2003).

[7] M Foucault, 'Nietzsche, Genealogy, History' in *Language, Counter-Memory, Practice: Selected Essays and Interviews by Michel Foucault* (Cornell University Press, 1977) 142.

networks, territorial infrastructures, virtual networks, in short, histories of building actual (common) ground rather than in grand institutional narratives on integration.[8]

***The Deconstructionist*:** I would second your point. The lack of historical awareness is also visible in the legal doctrine of the Court of Justice and its refusal to consider how historical injustices perpetuated against minority groups continue to affect individuals today.[9] The liberal paradigm that dominates the Court's case law in discrimination cases illustrates this. The Court foregrounds the individual in certain capacities – as worker, student, or someone who is economically inactive – and assumes that someone is discriminated against in one of those capacities. The Court appears blind to the fact that the discrimination encountered by an individual can also occur because that individual is part of a group that has historically been marginalised, excluded or oppressed.[10]

***The Anthropologist*:** At the start was the beginning, granted. Let me add that this is a move towards history as well as towards grounding our studies in territory. That brings me to the EU's colonial legacies. We all know the EU's origin story is about bringing peace and prosperity to a continent ravaged by war. But that story is incomplete at best. The emergence of European integration was also the product of the decolonisation process, to mention but one other relevant dimension, which helps to explain why it has perpetuated colonial structures in its legal frameworks. Recently legal scholarship has begun to address these questions – hopefully the institutions will soon follow.[11]

***The Deconstructionist (elaborating)*:** Indeed, if we turn from the past to the present, the starting point is a disconcerting avoidance of the historic, sociological, ecological, political anchorage of European scholarship. Partly, this has to do with how EU law has developed as a scholarly field. Due to those who unearthed the institutional archives, we know how the production of EU legal knowledge and the evolution of the EU's legal-political framework developed in parallel.[12] The proximity between the academia and the institutions that has traditionally characterised the discipline gave scholars power but left little, if any, critical distance between them and their object of study. How much distance there exists today, I will let you decide for yourself, but let me note recent warnings against the 'instrumentalisation' of legal scholarship and the 'enchantment' with the European project.[13] I see critical theory as a means to create

[8] T Misa and J Schot 'Inventing Europe: Technology and the Hidden Integration of Europe' (2005) 21 *History and Technology* 1–19.

[9] See also chapter 7 by Raphaële Xenidis in this book.

[10] Hence, the need for a more historically attuned and contextualised approach. See, eg, N Dube, 'A Typology of Comparators and Comparisons in EU Equality Law' (2025) 62 *CML Rev* 63–65.

[11] S Rehling Larsen, 'European Public Law after Empires' (2022) 1 *European Law Open* 6; H Eklund, 'Peoples, Inhabitants and Workers: Colonialism in the Treaty of Rome' (2023) 34 *European Journal of International Law* 831. H Eklund (ed), *Colonialism and the EU Legal Order* (Cambridge University Press, 2025).

[12] See, eg, R Byberg, 'The History of the Integration Through Law Project: Creating the Academic Expression of a Constitutional Legal Vision for Europe' (2017) 18 *German Law Journal* 1531; J Bailleux, 'How Europe Became Law: The First International Academic Congress on the ECSC (Milan-Stresa 1957)' (2010) 60 *Revue française de science politique* (English) 67; M Rasmussen, 'Revolutionizing European Law: A History of the Van Gend En Loos Judgment' (2014) 12 *International Journal of Constitutional Law* 136; A Vauchez, *Brokering Europe: Euro-Lawyers and the Making of a Transnational Polity* (Cambridge University Press, 2015).

[13] R van Gestel and H W Micklitz, 'Why Methods Matter in European Legal Scholarship' (2014) 20 *European Law Journal* 292; P Leino-Sandberg, 'Enchantment and Critical Distance in EU Legal Scholarship: What Role for Institutional Lawyers?' (2022) 1 *European Law Open* 231.

distance between the observer and that which is observed, to overcome the institutional representations of EU law and to render visible those previously ignored and excluded. In summary, critique offers a way for the scholarly field to acquire a more robust sense of self-reflexivity.

The Anthropologist: *A propos* of reflexivity, the EU today is more important than it has ever been and increasingly shapes the lives of hundreds of millions of citizens. Whereas in the past the impotence of the European project explained the reverent and constructive attitude of legal scholars, the very power and influence of the EU today should impel scholars to take a different stance towards their object of study: one that takes more distance from the political project. In my understanding, the emergence of the EU as a veritable power has partly been obscured by its framing as a 'soft power' and its self-presentation as a human rights conscious actor on the world stage.[14] Critique is a way to show the limits of such a self-understanding by zooming in not only on what the EU declares about itself but on how its law actually operates in practice.

The Deconstructionist: Have you not recently written an article that discusses the gap between the declamation and operation of EU law?

The Anthropologist (eager to elaborate): Indeed![15] Let's get technical for a moment and talk about the EU's regulation of global value chains through diligence procedures to illustrate the mismatch. On paper, the Corporate Sustainability Due Diligence Directive appears as a progressive tool: companies must identify, prevent, and remedy environmental and human rights harms.[16] Yet in practice, due diligence is often reduced to a set of managerial procedures – risk matrices, dashboards, audits, you know the drill.[17] These instruments translate ecological devastation into technical categories and filter out what cannot be quantified. A river rendered toxic is recoded as 'adverse impact'; displacement of communities becomes a data point in an 'impact significance' chart. Such procedures are not neutral but narrow our understanding of what counts as harm and who counts as a subject of law. And by that very narrowing, law legitimates rather than constrains forms of extraction. In sum, the forms of knowledge due diligence privileges – managerial, technocratic, procedural – are the very ones that sustain the projects it claims to regulate.

The Genealogist: So the 'why now' of EU critique appears to be double. First, because the EU is more powerful than ever and the role of scholars is to speak truth to power. Second, because that very power generates new struggles, new languages of resistance, and thus new occasions for critique by anchoring the fictions of EU law in social realities.

[14] For example, the Legal Service presents the EU as a 'worldwide promoter of the universality and indivisibility of human rights' in European Commission Legal Service (n 3) 76–94; For a discussion of the idea of the EU as a normative power, see RG Whitman (ed), *Normative Power Europe* (Palgrave Macmillan, 2011).

[15] L Tenreira, 'Greenwashing Investigated in the Landscape of Global Value Chains' (2025) 37 *Journal of Environmental Law* 175.

[16] Directive (EU) 2024/1760 of the European Parliament and of the Council of 13 June 2024 on corporate sustainability due diligence and amending Directive (EU) 2019/1937 and Regulation (EU) 2023/2859 [2024] OJ 2024/1760 (EU CSDDD). J Sinnig and DA Zetzsche, 'The EU's Corporate Sustainability Due Diligence Directive: From Disclosure to Mandatory Prevention of Adverse Sustainability Impacts in Supply Chains' (2025) *European Journal of Risk Regulation* 1.

[17] I Landau, 'Human Rights Due Diligence and the Risk of Cosmetic Compliance' (2019) 20 *Melbourne Journal of International Law* 221.

III. On the Productive Unsettlement of Point of View

***The Anthropologist*:** That seems an accurate summary of our reflections so far, but it also raises a new question, namely, why are you drawn to critical theory in the first place? I suspect that we each have a different answer to that question, while sharing a sense of dissatisfaction with the methodologies and vocabularies that we have been exposed to in the past. My answer would be that in our present situation we can no longer take past certainties for granted and that, perhaps, critique offers a tool to gain a better understanding of today's problems and challenges.[18]

***The Deconstructionist*:** My interest in the tradition of critique in general, and that of immanent critique in particular, stems from the conviction that it is necessary to question the EU and its law in their current form. The doctrinal methods that I was taught in law school have left me poorly equipped for such a task. My problem is that the search for coherence, rationality and objective meaning takes place on the legal order's *own terms*. Such an approach inevitably ends up legitimising rather than questioning the *status quo*, because it takes the conceptual starting points and the conventional vocabulary for granted *(turning to the Genealogist)*. Is this not the trap that an immanent strategy of critique is supposed to avoid?

***The Genealogist*:** I agree with the Anthropologist that when we decided to initiate this discussion, what gathered us was a common sense of dissatisfaction with the way critical theory lands in EU law today, and more specifically the lack of critical transformative approaches. But I have some reservations regarding the idea that critique requires stepping away from the law's own language. My fear is that this leads to a poor understanding of the law as a vehicle of ideologies and interests. In my understanding, the law is also a promising analytical field, where critique can find a fertile ground for renewal.

***The Deconstructionist (developing)*:** For me the law's own language is part of the problem. EU law has been developed in an attempt to get an institutional project off the ground. The invention of new concepts – direct effect, primacy, autonomy, etc. – was guided by the desire to assert the authority and independence of EU law vis-à-vis national and international law.[19] The foundations of EU law thus consist of a distinctive set of self-referential concepts that enable the Court of Justice and legal scholars to construct and develop legal doctrine. These foundational concepts play a *constitutive* role, allowing EU law to operate, while also *limiting* the possibilities of what can be said. The discourse these concepts enable is logically self-sustaining, but ultimately justifies the authority of EU law in relation to its own systemic needs.[20]

***The Genealogist*:** So in your view working within the confines of the language of law is always insufficient?

[18] L Azoulai, *The Turn to European Society and Its Problems: Connecting EU Law and Social Theory* (European University Institute, LAW Working Paper, September 2025).

[19] A Vauchez, '"Integration-Through-Law": Contribution to a Socio-History of EU Political Commonsense' (2008) EUI Working Paper No RSCAS 2008/10.

[20] J van de Beeten, 'In the Name of the Law: A Critique of the Systemic Rationality in EU Law' (PhD thesis, London School of Economics and Political Science, 2024), available at https://etheses.lse.ac.uk/4665/.

***The Deconstructionist*:** Definitely! Legal discourses present that which is contingent and particularistic as timeless and universal.[21] This is problematic because it means that authority is taken for granted, even if such authority might not be deserved. Critical theory can help to restore a view on the power dynamics that lurk beneath the law and to reveal the hidden hierarchies within the law. The point is therefore not to discover the law's essential meaning, but rather to examine the functions of legal discourse in creating and sustaining power. This means that one ought to resist to view the EU legal order as a coherent, autonomous and harmonious whole, but rather to see it as incoherent, dependent on external factors, and rife with tension between, say, centre and periphery, the rich and the poor, and men and women.[22] In other words, it is about showing how law reproduces hierarchies through apparently neutral legal categories. The promise of critical theory is that it exposes such injustices and reveals how material resources are distributed unevenly or how law reproduces societal inequities.[23]

***The Anthropologist (adding nuance)*:** To be critical is to make visible our own reliance on a language that is structurally incapable of reflecting the plurality of concerns it seeks to regulate. This incapacity becomes visible whenever EU law translates situated struggles – say, about precarious work or environmental degradation – into abstract categories like free movement or sustainable growth. Such translations stabilise the system but obscure the heterogeneity of the realities it regulates. Critique, in other words, must challenge rather than perpetuate the perspective of those in power. This is what Shivani Radhakrishnan means when she calls for a decolonial reorientation of immanent critique by bringing into view the epistemologies of the 'exterior'.[24]

***The Genealogist*:** I take it that in your view the language of law is not neutral. By adopting it uncritically, we risk enclosing our findings into the hermeneutical circles that the critical strategy we are looking to implement is supposed to overcome.

***The Anthropologist*:** The shaping and operation of such circles has been documented by socio-legal scholars and historians for some time, as was already hinted at above.[25] But we cannot suffice with pointing out the self-referentiality of these discourses and the way they are produced. For me the problem is that too often EU legal scholarship remains caught in its own abstractions while neglecting how law is actually lived, materialised, and contested. Critique must descend into the *earthly terrains* where law takes effect: the infrastructures it builds, the workplaces it regulates, the border posts it polices, the

[21] A point often made in international legal scholarship, see, eg, J Boyle, 'Ideals and Things: International Legal Scholarship and the Prison-House of Language' (1985) 26 *Harvard International Law Journal* 327; I Venzke and KJ Heller (eds), *Contingency in International Law: On the Possibility of Different Legal Histories* (Oxford University Press, 2021).

[22] D Kukovec, 'Economic Law, Inequality, and Hidden Hierarchies on the EU Internal Market' (2016) 38 *Michigan Journal of International Law* 1; C O'Brien, 'Civis Capitalist Sum: Class as the New Guiding Principle of EU Free Movement Rights' (2016) 53 *CML Rev* 937; S Mantu, '(En)Gendering EU Citizenship' in E Fornalé (ed) *Gender Equality in the Mirror* (Brill Nijhoff, 2022); M Djukovic and DTomasell, 'Manoeuvring EU Law: Queer Feminist Approaches to Sex Work and Social Justice' (*Transformative Private Law Blog*, 14 October 2024).

[23] For examples of such dynamics in EU law, see I Isailović, 'Introduction: Critical Legal Approaches in EU Law—Reflections on New Research Directions' (2024) 15 *Transnational Legal Theory* 493.

[24] S Radhakrishnan, 'Critique as Coloniality: The Decolonial Challenge to Immanent Critique' (2025) 32 *Constellations* 1, 476-83.

[25] H Schepel and R Wesseling, 'The Legal Community: Judges, Lawyers, Officials and Clerks in the Writing of Europe' (1997) 3 *European Law Journal* 165. Also see n 12.

ecological zones it transforms. EU law's immanence cannot be studied solely through its self-referential vocabulary; it must be read in its worldly entanglements. Or, to put it differently, we must 'bring EU law back down to earth'.[26]

***The Genealogist*:** This resonates with me. I find it fascinating to read about how EU law is mobilised by transnational actors, or about how EU law shapes and translates the power struggles between, for example, local authorities and digital platforms.[27] These studies of social practices show how the effects of EU law are mediated, unpredictable and, at times, even counter-productive. They bring EU law's *reality deficit* into view, which we could understand as the contrast 'between the grand discourse of the ever-increasing reach of EU law and the far more complex and modest reality "on the ground"'.[28]

***The Anthropologist (jumps in)*:** Precisely! An exclusive focus on the legal discourse obscures the way in which law frames and distorts social reality. When critique stays within law's own language these moments of disconnection tend to remain unacknowledged; the moments when law's self-description as coherent, complete and harmonious no longer matches the social realities it governs.

***The Deconstructionist*:** I consider such mismatches inherent to law's self-presentation as timeless and socially disembedded; anachronism and decontextualisation are inherent to law's claim to normativity.[29] A large part of the critical effort is to bring the temporal and spatial back into view, as Valverde's focus on legal *chronotopes* illustrates.[30] Consider the emerging legal and political discourse on a 'European Society', which frames the EU's foundational values as homogenous and a-historical entities that can be attributed to a society of Europeans.[31] The notion of 'European Society' is used to explain and justify the legal mobilisation of Article 2 Treaty on European Union (TEU) by the Court of Justice, but in doing so it obscures the contingency and selectivity of the value discourse, while also erasing the profound disagreement about the meaning of these values within European societies and between the Member States of the EU.

***The Anthropologist*:** And yet, immanent critique is not only about diagnosing law's blind spots; it should amplify the practices that prefigure alternatives. Social movements, counter-archives, and the conceptual apparatus they are based on are not simply external to law, they reshape its possibilities. They are, as Papadopoulos might put it, sites of *cosmopraxis*, where legality is reimagined as an instrument of resistance rather

[26] C O'Brien, 'Bringing EU Law Back Down to Earth' (2022) 18 *International Journal of Law in Context* 450.

[27] J Meakin, 'Mobilising Transnational Labour Law in Search of Transformation in Europe' (2025) 54 *Industrial Law Journal* 458; D Kramer, 'Airbnb, the City, and the Drive for European Integration' (2024) 3 *European Law Open* 500.

[28] A Vauchez, 'The Map and the Territory: Re-Assessing EU Law's Embeddedness in European Societies' (2020) 27 *Maastricht Journal of European and Comparative law* 133.

[29] N Wheatley, 'Law and the Time of Angels: International Law's Method Wars and the Affective Life of Disciplines' (2021) 60 *History and Theory* 311; This argument is also made in J Shklar, *Legalism: Law, Morals, and Political Trials* (Harvard University Press, 1986).

[30] M Valverde, *Chronotopes of Law: Jurisdiction, Scale and Governance* (Routledge, 2015).

[31] A von Bogdandy, *The Emergence of European Society through Public Law: A Hegelian and Anti-Schmittian Approach* (Oxford University Press, 2024); F Foret and N Trino, 'The "European Way of Life", a New Narrative for the EU? Institutions' vs Citizens' View' (2023) 24 *European Politics and Society* 336.

than power.[32] In the European context, this means inhabiting EU legality as a field of experimentation: using its principles and procedures to generate new forms of inclusion and justice from within. As Solanke argues, reimagining EU law requires decolonising its institutional imagination – expanding the epistemic and moral horizons of the Union beyond its postcolonial amnesia. This entails recognising how EU law reproduces hierarchies of race, gender, and geography through its doctrines of integration and neutrality, and how it might instead cultivate convivial legality: a mode of law-making attentive to difference, grounded in everyday encounters across Europe's diverse populations.[33] In this sense, decolonisation becomes not only an external critique but an *immanent strategy of renewal*, one that seeks to reorient legality toward – in this case – the coexistence of multiple ways of knowing, belonging, and governing within and beyond the European legal order.

***The Genealogist (consolidating)*:** Now let me put *my own cards* on the table. I agree with both of you that adopting the internal point of view of a doctrinal system can be a way to describe-and-reinforce the system.[34] Yet I also think there is a way to develop a legal language that is capable to describe-and-transform its object of inquiry.[35] The difference lies in how legal critique takes 'the social' into account. To clarify what I mean, let me introduce Rahel Jaeggi's distinction between internal critique and immanent critique.[36] She explains that internal critique is a form of criticism that opposes the intended normative ideals of a social practice with the deficient manner in which such ideals are realised in practice. Internal criticism aims at restoring harmony between the normative and actual by overcoming such deficiencies: it ultimately wants to restore *the status quo ex ante*. In contrast, immanent critique aims to critique an object 'based on standards that are already contained in the object itself' but also 'raises context-transcending claims and has transformative effects.'[37] In other words, it aims to go beyond the *status quo*. The kind of method I am interested in thus transcends the divide between what is internal and external to the law. Such a method investigates the interplay between the language of law and the social practices that sustain its normativity. I would call it 'a productive unsettlement of point of view': looking from the inside out, finding social realities and coming back. This is reflexivity to me.

IV. Finding Reality and Landing Back in the Law

***The Anthropologist*:** Let me try to retrace our conversation up to this point. Based on our discussion, there appear to be two ways in which an immanent critique of EU law can achieve reflexivity: one route consists in a critique of the ideological dimension

[32] D Papadopoulos, *Experimental Practice: Technoscience, Alterontologies, and More-Than-Social Movements* (Duke University Press, 2018).
[33] I Solanke, Re-imagining EU Law and Legal Institutions (EUI Law Working Paper, November 2025).
[34] V Forray and S Pimont, *Décrire le Droit et le Transformer: le Phénomène de la Décriture du Droit* (Dalloz, 2017).
[35] A Orford, 'In Praise of Description' (2012) 25 *Leiden Journal of International Law* 609.
[36] R Jaeggi, *Critique of Forms of Life* (Harvard University Press, 2018) 173–214.
[37] ibid 211. See also chapter 1 by Päivi Neuvonen in this book.

of the European legal order, which shines a light on the actual social effects EU law produces. The other potential object of an immanent critique would be to apprehend how social practices – such as agriculture, travel and work – affect the operation of EU law while also being structured by it.

The second route, on which I myself am walking, is paved with greater uncertainty, because the questions whether social practices are best studied through the law that regulates (or fails to cover) them and what role legal normativity plays in the structuring of a social practice remain ultimately open. Trying to devise an answer is my daily bread and butter. The first route, in contrast, appears to be more grounded in the law.

The Deconstructionist: My objective is the one you mentioned first: a critique of the institutional representations and practices that present themselves as given, non-negotiable and even natural. Vincent Réveillère is spot on when he says that 'lawyers are so immersed in the use of these concepts and technicalities that they often lack a salutary astonishment that could be directed towards their own devices'.[38] The point is, in other words, to defamiliarise and denaturalise legal doctrines, principles and procedures.[39] This can be done by showing that instead of inevitable consequences, or simply the result of the inherent logic of the Treaties, EU legal concepts are contingent and contestable. Or, to use a familiar phrase, the goal is to show that legal doctrine is *made* and not *found*.

The Genealogist: History, in fact, is an excellent tool for such an endeavour. A good description can go a long way. Rather than contradicting a critical engagement with normativity, the quest to make historically situated social realities appear is deeply committed to revealing 'how normative ideas change over time and how these "shifts of meaning" affect different social groups (. . .) how ideas of democracy, equality, or constitution have changed over the course of the integration project'.[40] Building a genealogy is no less normative for being descriptive; it simply empties normativity of any pretence to capture an essential, stable and naturally foundational state by placing it into the social context from which it emerged.

This method puts scholarship on a questioning path: what objects are essentialised in the European legal discourse, either because they are deemed natural or fundamental? These 'ontological' parts of EU law raise the question of the kind of legal authority and system-building they favour. One can, for example, examine how EU law reifies specific understandings of concepts such as 'goods', 'the market' or 'the family'. The Court of Justice's 'metaphysical' language is perhaps the most straightforward example, by which I mean the recurrent references to the 'very identity', 'essential characteristics' and 'original nature' serve to provide a grounding for EU law's foundational doctrines.[41]

[38] V Réveillère, 'Inquiring into Conceptual Practices: Legal Controversy at the Court of Justice of the European Union' in M Rask Madsen, FG Nicola, and A Vauchez (eds), *Researching the European Court of Justice: Methodological Shifts and Law's Embeddedness* (Cambridge University Press, 2022) 136–137.

[39] S Marks, 'Big Brother Is Bleeping Us - with the Message That Ideology Doesn't Matter' (2001) 12 *European Journal of International Law* 109.

[40] PJ Neuvonen, 'A Way of Critique: What Can EU Law Scholars Learn from Critical Theory?' (2022) 1 *European Law Open* 60, 74.

[41] MW Hesselink, 'Knowing EU Law' (2024) 26 *Cambridge Yearbook of European Legal Studies* 155.

***The Deconstructionist (affirming)*:** Yes! This is where the self-referentiality that I mentioned earlier comes in: on the one hand, primacy is both a *consequence* of EU law's *sui generis* nature, but also *constitutive* of that special nature. In other words, the doctrine of primacy operates simultaneously as cause and effect. Such discursive closure sustains the authority of EU law, but also points towards its limits.[42]

***The Genealogist*:** Indeed, genealogy de-naturalises such legal authority by reconnecting it to the negotiation of power, social context and historic circumstances 'at work'. The stabilisation of legal meaning is the result of the judge's work of interpretation; *vice versa*, interpretation is shaped by the workings of legal controversy, shaped in different ways by social, historic and political realities.[43] Critical methods, in other words, apprehend the law as a lived institutional world, shaped by the actors, spaces, and technologies through which it is enacted.[44]

***The Anthropologist (gently pushing back)*:** While I see the value of denaturalising received truths and canons, it seems imperative to me to understand EU law from the perspective of *social practices* rather than *institutional* ones. This is why I raised the question regarding the critique's object in the first place. Collective social realities, even those that are framed, regulated or negated by EU law, necessarily upset legal conceptions of personhood, family ties and work.[45] Rather than taking legal texts as a starting point, the goal is thus to study how social reality and EU law are *co-constituted.* In other words, the legal order both acts within and gives form to the very material, economic, and epistemic conditions through which it operates. I attempt to account for the role EU law plays in relation to the everyday in 'lived communities'.[46]

The Genealogist: Let me ask you a question. The idea of self-reflexivity stands in tension with the idea that there is an 'objective' social reality that can be juxtaposed to the law.[47] For this reason critique requires a theoretical apparatus to make sense of social reality and to identify its inherent contradictions. So my next provocation to your take on social reality as the object of immanent critique in EU law is: how do you prevent falling into the trap of mere empiricism?

***The Anthropologist (taking the challenge)*:** I agree that mere empirical studies fall short of fulfilling the ambition of immanent critique. After all, the purpose of immanent critique

[42] van de Beeten (n 20).

[43] F Nicola and B Davies (eds), *EU Law Stories: Contextual and Critical Histories of European Jurisprudence* (Cambridge University Press, 2017).

[44] Antoine Vauchez's analyses of the professional and epistemic networks that sustain the authority of EU law, Brice Laurent's ethnographies of European regulatory politics, and Lola Avril's studies of legal expertise and everyday bureaucratic practices all reveal how law operates through situated routines, infrastructures, and knowledge practices. See, A Vauchez and B de Witte (eds), *Lawyering Europe: European Law as a Transnational Social Field* (Hart Publishing, 2013); B Laurent, *European Objects: The Troubled Dreams of Harmonization* (MIT Press, 2022); L Avril, '"Civilizing" Professionals? Competition Lawyers in the European Integration Process' (2024) 49 *Historical Social Research* 2, 247.

[45] See, eg, L Azoulai, S Barbou des Places and E Pataut (eds), *Constructing the Person in EU Law: Rights, Roles, Identities* (Hart Publishing, 2016); C Paulesu, 'Consumer Responsibility to Remedy Structural Injustice: European Consumer Law's Capitalistic Strategy' (*Transformative Private Law Blog*, 24 October 2024).

[46] L Azoulai, 'Living with EU Law' (2022) 1 *European Law Open* 140–43.

[47] As Neuvonen (n 40) writes, 'empirical research methods cannot replace the search for a more developed critical method in the study of EU law' because 'the idea of a purely descriptive, non-normative critique is an oxymoron', 69.

is not only to give an account of social reality, but also to transform that reality by identifying certain unfulfilled normative potentials inherent to the object of critique. We need to find methods to speak a language other than the legal one to activate this reflectivity. It has been attempted.[48] Nevertheless, reflecting society's assumptions and rationalities has itself become far more complex than earlier traditions of critique imagined. For me the upshot of these insights is that we need to become polysemic. Taking seriously the 'languages' spoken across society no longer only requires the reconstruction of their rational content,[49] but an inquiry into the sites where practices are lived, contested, and resisted. It demands a capacity for inquiry that is ethnographic as much as normative and that is able to investigate the fields in which forms of life are enacted and resisted.[50]

***The Deconstructionist*:** This sounds very exciting, but I struggle to imagine how such an ethnographic approach would translate to the context of EU law . . .

***The Anthropologist*:** . . . in fact EU legal scholars are increasingly showing an ethnographic sensibility! Sanja Bogojević's work on environmental governance and the Sami reindeer herding communities, for example, situates EU climate and energy law within lived ecological and territorial conflicts, showing how law mediates relations between European regulatory ambitions and Indigenous ways of inhabiting space.[51] Marie Petersmann's research on environmental litigation and the politics of co-existence develops a similar orientation: she traces how EU environmental law materialises in landscapes, infrastructures, and more-than-human assemblages, thereby grounding critique on European soil.[52] Such approaches demonstrate that EU law is not only a system of norms but a socio-material practice enacted through the everyday lives, places, and ecologies it seeks to regulate.

***The Deconstructionist*:** Where are you as part of this list? Are you not also doing fieldwork yourself? And what are the theoretical concepts you work with?

[48] This has been attempted, notably in EU legal theory's engagements with the Frankfurt School – from Christian Joerges's and Michelle Everson's use of Habermas to rethink legitimacy and deliberation in European governance, to Alexander Somek's reconstruction of constitutionalism through Honneth's social freedom, and Damjan Kukovec's deployment of critical theory to expose the structural hierarchies of the EU's internal market. More recently, Poul Kjaer has extended this lineage by drawing on systems and social theory to conceptualise the reflexivity of the EU's legal order within global modernity. See; M Everson and C Joerges, 'Reconfiguring the Politics–Law Relationship in the Integration Project through Conflicts-Law Constitutionalism' (2012) 18 *European Law Journal* 644; A Somek, *The Cosmopolitan Constitution* (Oxford University Press, 2014); D Kukovec, 'Law and the Periphery' (2015) 21 *European Law Journal* 406; PF Kjaer, 'What is Transformative Law?' (2022) 1 *European Law Open* 760.

[49] J Habermas, *The Theory of Communicative Action, Vol. 1, 'Reason and the Rationalization of Society'* (Polity, 1984). Also see D Gaus, 'Rational Reconstruction' in A Allen and E Mendieta (eds.) *The Cambridge Habermas Lexicon* (Cambridge University Press, 2019) 369–78.

[50] On this point, I draw on Rahel Jaeggi's notion of 'forms of life', which treats social practices not as neutral settings for communication but as *normative constellations* – patterns of living whose viability rests on their capacity for learning and self-transformation. Yet, as Titus Stahl reminds us, forms of life may also become oppressive, reproducing hierarchies that render internal critique impossible. See, Jaeggi (n 36) 221–22, 274; T Stahl, 'Oppressive Forms of Life' (2024) 25 *Critical Horizons* 77.

[51] S Bogojević, 'The European Green Deal, the Rush for Critical Raw Materials, and Colonialism' (2024) 15 *Transnational Legal Theory* 600.

[52] M Petersmann, 'Reordering the European Ground – Regrounding the European Legal Order?' (2024) 3 *European Law Open* 180.

***The Anthropologist*:** In my own ethnographic practices I try to get a sense of what Andreas Philippopoulos-Mihalopoulos calls the 'lawscape'.[53] Law is not only a discursive order but a material environment that saturates bodies, infrastructures, and spaces. To investigate EU law critically therefore means to trace its presence in the landscapes – borders, urban spaces, ecological zones – where its normative force is lived and contested.[54] Only by attending to these lawscapes can immanent critique recover the reflectivity that doctrinal language suppresses, and situate EU law back within social realities. The value of this move is twofold. First, it acknowledges that law is never self-contained but always entangled with material environments, infrastructures, and histories. Second, it shifts the purpose of critique from confirming the coherence of law's own concepts to holding open the tensions, frictions, and contradictions that appear when law collides with those environments and histories. In this way, Petersmann reframes critique as an ongoing process of re-composition: one that unsettles law's claims to universality by exposing the plurality of worlds in which EU law intervenes.[55] Such a vision is particularly useful for us, because it shows why an immanent critique of EU law cannot stop at working with its doctrinal language because it – EU law *itself* – is the problem calling for immanence.

V. Thinking of Critique in Terms of Scaling

***The Genealogist*:** This discussion on theorising social relationships leads me to the following thought: in my mind, the question of how to reconnect European legal studies with social reality comes partly down to a question of scaling. Do we apprehend the EU as a whole, meaning its founding doctrines, narratives and myths or the materiality that sustains these? Or do we focus on specific social practices – such as digitalisation, migration, health, agriculture – and look at the way they structure and are structured by EU law? I think that the focus on 'scaling' helps to resist a common pitfall, namely, to naturally adopt an institutional framing of EU law that relies on familiar distinctions such as the basis for exercising legislative competences, the boundary between national and Union law, or the public-private divide. Forcing the legal analysis into such pre-established legal categories risks creating a distorted image of both the law on paper as well as in practice.[56]

***The Anthropologist (somewhat sceptical)*:** How exactly does the idea of scaling help to overcome institutional framings?

***The Genealogist*:** The field of European space law offers a timely example to grasp what is at stake. Recently, the European Commission introduced the EU Space Act as a means

[53] A Philippopoulos-Mihalopoulos, 'To Have to Do with the Law: An Essay' in A Philippopoulos-Mihalopoulos (ed), *Routledge Handbook of Law and Theory* (Routledge, 2018) 475.

[54] V Becci, *Aesthetics and Dynamics in Law and Space: Unpacking Spatial Complexities through Legal Norms and Policies* (PhD thesis, Sciences Po Paris, 2024).

[55] M Petersmann, '"Re/de/composing" International Law' (2024) (*Völkerrechtsblog*, 31 July 2024), available at https://voelkerrechtsblog.org/re-de-composing-international-law/.

[56] A classic example is D Kennedy, 'The Structure of Blackstone's Commentaries' (1979) 28 *Buffalo Law Review* 205.

to create a common framework for space activities, to incentivise the industry and to build a European infrastructure for data collection. The Commission invoked Article 114 of the Treaty on the Functioning of the European Union (TFEU) (on the integration of the common market) as the legal basis for this new instrument rather than Article 189 TFEU that is specifically dedicated to the regulation of space activities. Moreover, the Commission explicitly excluded military and defence space objects from the scope of regulation.[57] In doing so, the Commission frames space law as a purely civilian activity that forms part of its market-building project. But in reality, this is a sector whose technologies typically serve dual commercial and military uses. The starting point of our analysis thus cannot be the legislative text or the way in which the Commission presents the law, because this would lead one to reproduce certain blind spots or political framings. A view primed by such an institutional framing misses a central normative and political dimension of space law.

The Deconstructionist (jumps in): To understand what is happening here, I think we have to look at the EU's 'messianic' legal and political culture.[58] The initial failure of the European Defence Community (EDC) has had a profound effect on the course of European integration, because it inaugurated a more depoliticised project of market-building.[59] The effects we still see today as the EU's political culture still relies on 'dominant ideas of legal neofunctionalism' that enable 'the translation of essentially political questions into legal ones'.[60]

The Genealogist: Exactly. By delving into the 'deep structure' of the EU's legal and political culture, the perspective shifts from the institutional perspective towards the conditions that shape and sustain the EU's institutional ethos in the first place.

The Anthropologist (still sceptical): But turning away from an institutional perspective has to be achieved by resisting its lure from the very beginning of the inquiry. The moment in which we choose an object of study, define our research questions, gather our sources, and select the material we intend to work on is absolutely crucial. In other words, the choices we make in our 'research designs' determine whether we enable ourselves to make forms of EU law visible outside of its consecrated legal concepts and practices. Say, for example, that one's research takes as a starting point the lived experiences of those whose lives are affected by EU law. All three of us have contributed to Loic Azoulai's and Jack Meakin's efforts to conceptualise the 'everyday' in European law.[61] Taking people's personal perceptions of reality as the starting point to reflect on the social effects of EU law is a great way to shift the scales of inquiry. Other approaches are found in the emerging field of 'EU legal geography', which refocuses our attention

[57] Article 2(3) of the Proposal for a Regulation on the safety, resilience and sustainability of space activities in the Union COM(2025) 335 final, accessible via https://eur-lex.europa.eu/legal-content/EN/TXT/?uri=CELEX%3A52025PC0335.

[58] J Weiler, 'The Political and Legal Culture of European Integration: An Exploratory Essay' (2012) 9 *International Journal of Constitutional Law* 678–94.

[59] R Griffiths, *Europe's First Constitution: The European Political Community, 1952-1954* (The Federal Trust, 2001).

[60] P Leino-Sandberg, '"70 Years of EU" – The Politics of a Professional Language' (2026) 86 *Zeitschrift für ausländisches öffentliches Recht und Völkerrecht/Heidelberg Journal of International Law* 59, 63.

[61] L Azoulai and J Meakin, "Is This Europe?" Seminar, European University Institute (EUI), Florence, 14–15 June 2024.

towards the way in which EU law interacts with objects such as soil, cities, differentiated natural environments and transport lanes.[62] The rising attention for infrastructure in European legal studies could also be interpreted as an effort to offer a more permanent methodological tool to 'rescale' our inquiries around material realities that structure collective life.[63]

***The Genealogist*:** That is what 'scaling' is all about! By starting from social practices rather than institutional representations, neglected, exempted, uncovered and destructive aspects of EU law become visible. It helps to see what EU law structures and what *it fails to structure*, the aspects of collective life for which EU law assumes responsibility as well as aspects for which it does not; the principles EU law proclaims and notions of injustice it *doesn't use as corrective* in the formal application of positive law. It helps, in short, to bring *negative* aspects of EU law into focus and reorder how we consider the social significance of the European legal order.

***The Deconstructionist*:** What a great way to deconstruct! *(Turning to the Genealogist)* I have attended several workshops in which historians also engage in 're-scaling' efforts by writing 'histories from below'. Could you tell us more about this?

***The Genealogist*:** Yes, that is another great example of scaling. 'Histories from below' are an attempt to look beyond the institutional archives in Brussels, Luxembourg and Fiesole and explore how (and if) ordinary citizens experienced and engaged with EU law by using other historical sources, such as pamphlets, personal biographies and newspapers.[64] It is all about the 'micro' rather than the 'macro'. In contrast, historians have also begun to question the temporalities that structure institutional histories of EU law. Rather than taking the Schuman Declaration or the Treaty of Rome as the starting point of the European project, such inquiries 'scale up' the perspective. The recent literature on Colonialism and the EU legal order we mentioned earlier is a case in point.[65]

***The Anthropologist (less sceptical)*:** Let me add that such histories do not only aim to change our understanding of the past; they also aim to transform EU law's future trajectories.

VI. Towards the Transformation of EU Law

***The Deconstructionist*:** The idea of EU law's future trajectories inspires me to ask a question that I am least suited to answer. Throughout our conversation, the both of you have intuited that an important dimension of immanent critique is identifying potential for transformation. But what does that mean? And how can one identify such potentials in the law's own principles, premises, and ideals? Although I am sympathetic to

[62] F de Witte, 'Here Be Dragons: Legal Geography and EU Law' (2022) 1 *European Law Open* 1.

[63] L Azoulai, 'Infrastructural Europe: EU Law and Human Life in Times of the COVID-19 Pandemic' (2020) 24 *Revista de Derecho Comunitario Europeo* 343.

[64] B Leucht, M Esmark and M Loth: 'Rethinking European Legal Integration: Legal Text from a Bottom-Up Perspective and the Functioning of European Law, 1957–2000' (2025) *European Law Open* 1–13.

[65] See n 11.

the idea that EU law carries within itself the potential for change, I ultimately remain unconvinced that a critique can do without a utopian vision that lies beyond the current legal-political imagination.

The Anthropologist: I can try to define what transformation is about. Transformation is not simply about reform or adjustment, but about the possibility to alter the normative foundations of the law. This is central to the project of immanent critique: it must reveal how law's own concepts contain the seeds of their transformation. In the context of EU law, this means asking whether the Union's legal vocabulary can be reinterpreted or reconfigured in ways that open new social and normative possibilities, rather than merely reinforcing the existing order.

The Genealogist: To me transformation is critical theory made active. It is a way to understand how a theoretical effort can be made operational in apprehending EU law. The challenge is to develop useful concepts, protocols of questioning, methodological 'moves' susceptible of performing changes in point of view, ways of reframing a legal normativity and making forms of European justice apparent.

The Anthropologist (impelled to say more): Let me add that critique only becomes transformative when it recognises its own standards as provisional and fallible.[66] Without such reflexivity, the danger is that critique ends up reinforcing the very self-sufficiency of EU law's discourse – mistaking doctrinal coherence for critical insight. Azoulai's recent work on the idea of Society as a *method* helps to sharpen this point: for him, reflexivity presupposes reflectivity – the law's ability to absorb and mirror back the matters of concern that animate society.[67] In this way, he resists the attempt to instrumentalise the concept of 'society' to justify the turn towards Article 2 TEU values by turning that concept back on itself. Yet such reflexivity is exactly what EU law's doctrinal idiom resists, since its internal vocabulary is designed to abstract from lived conflicts and to stabilise integration. Reflexivity, then, cannot be performed within EU law's language alone; it depends on bringing into view those social concerns that EU law systematically brackets out.

The Deconstructionist (doubling down): Thank you, this is helpful. But let me give you some more push back. Have you read Rachel Fraser's article on the limits of immanent critique? I oversimplify, but she essentially argues that the idea of immanent critique is an oxymoron . . . it's like having your cake and eating it, too. At best, she suggests, we ought to understand immanent critique as either external critique or a purely evaluative exercise.[68] In other words, there is a trade-off: a fully immanent account of the legal system all too easily risks losing its critical potential, whereas a successful critique requires an external vantage point that is not (fully) immanent to the legal system as such.[69] For our purposes, that would imply that we can either pursue a critique of EU

[66] A Särkelä, 'Immanent Critique as Self-Transformative Practice: Hegel, Dewey, and Contemporary Critical Theory' (2017) 31 *Journal of Speculative Philosophy* 218 .

[67] Azoulai (n 18).

[68] R Fraser, 'IV—The Limits of Immanent Critique' (2023) 123 *Proceedings of the Aristotelian Society* 2, 97–125.

[69] The difficulty to achieve a successful trade-off is discussed in J van de Beeten, 'Unfulfilled Promises: Reconstructing EU Constitutionalism in Times of Crisis and Contestation' (2025) 21 *European Constitutional Law Review* 164.

law that relies on a normative standard that is at least partly external to the law itself, or we can seek to identify contradictions in the EU legal order without hoping to overcome those in our own analysis. It would explain why there are so few – in my view at least – successful examples of immanent critique in EU law.

***The Genealogist*:** What exactly is it that you are thinking about?

***The Deconstructionist*:** Let me first start with an example of immanent critique that appears merely as internal critique. In his book *Protecting Democracy in the EU*, Tom Theuns dedicates a full chapter to an 'Immanent critique of EU tools against Democratic Backsliding'.[70] His method, however, is to assess legal instruments in light of their normative coherence and expressive consistency. Essentially, he identifies evaluative standards from within the legal and political praxis he criticises and, secondly, evaluates the extent to which these practices – in this case the tools against democratic backsliding – live up to their own normative commitment. While I think his arguments are convincing, I would hesitate to call this immanent critique, because I do not see how it is any different from what Rahel Jaeggi describes as internal criticism.[71]

***The Anthropologist*:** Is there a way in which such an approach could meet the more demanding conception of immanent critique that we articulated here? Or at least one of Fraser's alternatives?

***The Deconstructionist*:** That is a good question! This would require identifying contradictions between the ideal of the EU rule of law and the practice of the rule of law that are constitutive of that practice. I think this is something that could be done. In a concise, but piercing article, Toni Marzal has shown how the EU's rule of law is aimed at its own overcoming.[72] In other words, he argues that in the EU's legal and political culture the commitment of legality and legalism are realised through moments of repeated rule-breaking. The EU's institutional understanding of the rule of law therefore appears as 'structurally self-undermining' because rule-breaking is a constitutive part of the EU's rule of law.[73] Identifying such contradictions would be an example of the evaluative approach that Fraser identifies.

***The Genealogist*:** And what about a form of immanent critique that foregrounds external critique?

***The Deconstructionist*:** Here I would mention the work of Paul Linden-Retek on the EU's *Postnational Constitutionalism*.[74] Linden-Retek tries to identify and crystallise the overlooked potential of a post-national sensibility within the texts and materials of EU law with the aim to provide an alternative to current legal-political practices.

[70] T Theuns, *Protecting Democracy in Europe: Pluralism, Autocracy and the Future of the EU* (Oxford University Press, 2025) 65–92.

[71] Jaeggi (n 36).

[72] T Marzal, 'Between Integration and the Rule of Law: EU Law's Culture of Lawful Messianism' (2023) 24 *German Law Journal* 718.

[73] This term is found in Fraser (n 68); For a similar analysis see A Somek, 'Is Legality a Principle of EU Law?' in S Vogenauer and S Weatherill (eds), *General Principles of Law: European and Comparative Perspectives* (Bloomsbury, 2017); Weiler (n 58).

[74] P Linden-Retek, *Postnational Constitutionalism: Europe and the Time of Law* (Oxford University Press, 2023).

Specifically, he presents an approach to legal interpretation and reasoning that resists *reification* by maintaining a sense of the social relations that the law regulates. While Linden-Retek's critique is very convincing, I doubt that the post-national potential that he retrieves from EU law's fragments can be said to be fully immanent. It strikes me as utopian instead! My suspicion comes from the way his argument is constructed, relying heavily on the work of critical theorists, but only tangentially draws on EU legal scholars and the case law of the Court of Justice.[75]

***The Anthropologist (unconvinced)*:** I see, but there are more examples of immanent critique. Take for example the work of Kalypso Nicolaidis on the idea of the EU as a 'demoicracy'.[76] Nicolaidis argues that the 'demoicratic' ideal can be derived from various intrinsic aspects of the EU's legal and political practices, including the practice of mutual recognition, the attempt to balance the national and the supranational and the EU's democratic credentials and commitments. As such, she provides an alternative normative standard to the ideal of 'ever closer union ideal' and its drive towards harmonisation and unification – yet one that remains deeply rooted in the EU's current legal and political praxis.

***The Genealogist (doubling down)*:** Or what about Marija Bartl's *Reimagining Prosperity*? Rather than rejecting prosperity as a normative horizon, she reconstructs how EU law itself invokes prosperity – as growth, efficiency, competitiveness – and then confronts this discourse with the social struggles and solidaristic traditions that it selectively forgets. What looks like a neutral economic objective is revealed as a normative project that sidelines alternative conceptions of prosperity grounded in redistribution, justice, or collective good. Her critique is immanent because it works with prosperity as the Union's own declared aspiration but destabilises its self-sufficiency by showing how that aspiration depends on historical erasures.[77]

***The Deconstructionist*:** These contemporary examples are illuminating, but I want to press the both of you to articulate how you – *in your own work* – identify and realise EU law's transformative potential.

***The Genealogist (jumping on the opportunity)*:** In a way my answer is simple: in order to develop emancipatory visions of justice that are internal to the law but go beyond procedural compliance and formal legality, we need to develop new concepts. Simply put, I aim to forge a legal language that is able to describe obliterated legal practices and invest available legal and sociological notions with new meaning. Let me give you an example that illustrates how I 'go deeper' into the social fundaments of legal *principles*, such as solidarity and equality, in order to renew their meaning. EU law structures bio-innovation as a market in the wake of the industrial production sector. In this activity,

[75] For an elaboration, see van de Beeten (n 69).

[76] For a recent articulation of this idea, see K Nicolaïdis, 'The Third Democratic Transformation: From European to Planetary Politics' (2024) 62 *Journal of Common Market Studies* 845. Also see K Nicolaïdis, 'The New Constitution as European "Demoi-cracy"?' (2004) 7 *Critical Review of International Social and Political Philosophy* 76–93; K Nicolaïdis, 'The Idea of European Demoicracy' in J Dickson and P Eleftheriadis (eds), *Philosophical Foundations of European Union Law* (Oxford University Press, 2012) 247–74; K Nicolaïdis, European Demoicracy and Its Crisis (2013) 51 *Journal of Common Market Studies* 351–69.

[77] M Bartl, *Reimagining Prosperity: Toward a New Imaginary of Law and Political Economy in the EU* (Cambridge University Press, 2024).

human beings supply critical material for the production of knowledge, treatment and devices. Through careful analysis, however, it is possible to identify a powerful counterpull to the market paradigm that runs through regulations and case law alike. Legal scholarship has theorised this protective element as the expression of 'principles', as a European ethical framework, 'subjective rights' for patients, values and 'public health objective'.[78] Taken separately, none of these legal elements fully captures the forms of protection materialised in EU law, but they all express an attachment to human life. We therefore need a concept to bring the structuring ambivalence of the entire European bio-economy to light and to account for the elements in the law that resist the pull of the market. In my work, I conceptualise this element as *care*.[79] Care acts both as a legal concept, which covers a specific set of legal regimes and techniques of interpretation, while also evoking the rich intellectual ground of theories of care.[80] This notion enables me to capture a 'human factor' within the EU's legal practices. That human factor represents, in this example, life incarnated but perhaps we could expand the challenge to a richer notion of life that includes the human and non-human, the individual and the collective, the bodily and the cultural.

The Deconstructionist: It seems to me that you are trying to identify tensions and contradictions within EU law between the economic imperatives of market building and the need to protect non-economic objectives that seek to protect human life. These ethical concerns appear in many different legal forms and different locations which you assemble to construct a new normative standard, a theory of justice as you call it, from within the sphere of EU biomedical law itself. Am I right to suggest that you essentially perform an act of *legal bricolage* by making do with 'whatever is at hand' in an attempt to create something new?[81] Please correct me if I am wrong!

The Genealogist: You are spot on. Let me sum it up: my methodological approach can be framed as follows. Essentially, I ask the question: what concepts and analytical tools, present in the law, are able to apprehend a European attachment to and responsibility for life? The answer to this question can range as far as a European protection of the cultural life emanating from local football clubs against a competitive market the EU itself has liberalised or accounts of local forms of agri-*culture*.[82] In these domains, and many others, one can identify a tension between the pursuit of market-making and

[78] See A-M Farrell, T Hervey and T Murphy, 'A European Law of New Health Technologies?' in M Flear, A-M Farrell, T Hervey and Thérèse Murphy (eds), *European Law and New Health Technologies* (Oxford University Press, 2013) 388–414; S Hennette-Vauchez, 'Of Markets and Principles: The European Perspective' in D Orentlicher and T Hervey (eds), *The Oxford Handbook of Comparative Health Law* (Oxford University Press, 2021) 897–918.

[79] S Glaser, *Clinical Justice* (dissertation defended at Sciences Po Paris, 2025).

[80] For a very partial and incomplete selection, see N Noddings, *Caring A Feminine Approach to Ethics & Moral Education* (University of California Press, 1984); C Gilligan, *In a Different Voice: Psychological Theory and Women's Development* (Harvard University Press, 1993); E Feder Kittay, *Love's Labors: Essays on Women, Equality and Dependency* (Routledge, 2020); V Held, *The Ethics of Care: Personal, Political, and Global* (Oxford University Press, 2006); J Tronto, *Caring Democracy: Markets, Equality, and Justice* (NYU Press, 2013); F Worms, *Soin et politique* (Presses universitaires de France, 2012); M Puig de La Bellacasa, *Matters of Care: Speculative Ethics in More than Human Worlds* (University of Minnesota Press, 2017).

[81] M Tushnet, 'The Bricoleur at the Center' (1993) 60 *University of Chicago Law Review* 1071.

[82] F de Witte, 'You Are What You Ate: Food Heritage and the EU's Internal Market' (2022) 47 *European Law Review* 647–65; F de Witte and J Zglinski, 'The Idea of Europe in Football' (2022) 1 *European Law Open* 286–315.

non-economic objectives. The EU typically protects the latter by placing them outside its regulatory realm, as exceptions to the imperative of the market. Here lies the potential for justice, not as a value judgement but as the result of a critical legal questioning intent to grasp an existential meaning that can be translated into law.

The Deconstructionist (turning to the Anthropologist): And what about the transformative potential of your work?

The Anthropologist: My protocol is what I frame as 'Immanence 2.0'. This is a mode of critique that takes its bearings not from abstract ideals but from the 'grammar of resistance' articulated in concrete social struggles. Such practices of resistance – whether strategic litigation, localised or globalised protests, or everyday forms of refusal – are not mere reactions but productive sites of concept-formation. Across Europe, one can trace a dispersed yet coherent grammar of resistance in which actors do more than contest legal authority – they re-enact it, composing what I previously referred to as a 'cosmopraxis' of legality. These praxes show how legality itself can be reconfigured through contestation.

I will elaborate this point through three illustrations. First, in *Carvalho and Others v Parliament and Council* – the People's Climate Case – families from Portugal, Germany, the Sámi region, and other climate-affected areas engaged in strategic litigation to confront the EU's insufficient 2030 emissions target. Mobilising the Union's own constitutional principles of proportionality and the protection of life and health, they sought to hold EU institutions accountable to the standards they profess. Although the Court dismissed the action for lack of standing, the case redefined the terrain of legal struggle, transforming climate litigation into a form of constitutional critique from below.[83] Secondly, in the Białowieża Forest conflict, it was the sustained mobilisation of environmental activists, local communities, and non-governmental organisations that compelled the Commission to bring infringement proceedings against Poland for unlawful logging in a protected Natura 2000 site. Their documentation, petitions, and alliances with European networks translated ecological defence into legal intervention, enabling the Court to affirm that environmental protection under the Habitats Directive is not a matter of political discretion but a binding legal duty.[84] Thirdly, in the Turów mine dispute, cross-border activists and municipalities, particularly from the Czech Republic and Germany, turned to EU environmental law and litigation to contest Poland's mining extension that endangered shared water resources. Their collective action pushed the Commission and the Court into an unprecedented confrontation over the meaning of shared responsibility and transnational environmental justice, illustrating how localised grievances can scale up into Union-wide normative debates.[85]

These examples should not simply be understood as 'case law', but rather as situated practices of world-making. Each of them is an attempt to translate universalist and

[83] Case T-330/18 *Carvalho and Others v Parliament and Council* EU:T:2019:324; appeal, Case C-565/19 P, Judgment of 25 March 2021, EU:C:2021:252.

[84] Council Directive 92/43/EEC of 21 May 1992 on the conservation of natural habitats and of wild fauna and flora [1992] OJ L206/7) (Habitat Directive). Case C-441/17 *Commission v Poland* (Białowieża Forest Case) ECLI:EU:C:2018:255.

[85] Order of the Vice-president, ECJ, 21 May 2021, Case C-121/21 R *Czech Republic v Republic of Poland* (Turów Mine Case, order to stop mining immediately) ECLI:EU:C:2021:752.

abstract legal vocabularies into embodied, collective experiments of justice. In doing so, they expose the tension at the heart of immanent critique – between inhabiting law's forms and exceeding them – which leads us, inevitably, to the methodological question of how critique can move beyond description toward transformation.

This brings me to a final methodological move inspired from my deep engagement with the work of Marie Petersmann, whose work I have referred to earlier.[86] Contemporary critique faces a structural split between two orientations. On the one hand, *prefigurative critique* seeks to build alternative legal forms here and now – whether in people's tribunals, abolitionist practices, or emergent institutions of environmental justice. It wagers on the possibility of 'law otherwise' through collective experimentation. On the other hand, *para-ontological critique* – articulated most forcefully in Black studies, queer epistemologies, and radical Indigenous thought – resists such normative recuperation, exposing instead the ontological exclusions that make modern law possible: the racialised, gendered, and colonial violences that law cannot contain without erasure. Each approach is indispensable, yet each is also insufficient: prefigurative critique risks being reabsorbed into existing institutions, while para-ontological critique risks nihilism or withdrawal. I see it as my task not to reconcile these positions into a higher synthesis, but to hold them together in productive dissonance.

***The Genealogist (coming to a close)*:** Would you agree that all of this is to say that we think the EU deserves to be critiqued better?[87] With this I do not mean that we critique the EU in an attempt to tear it down, but because we still believe in 'the promise that the European project might inaugurate a radically novel juridical form'.[88] The very appeal of an *immanent* critique lies in such a promise, because it does not give up on European integration, but it offers ways to articulate an emancipatory vision of that project that can inspire future generations.

***The Deconstructionist*:** Yes I like this very much. But let me reiterate that when critique remains too immanent, it risks legitimising the very order it contests. Without some utopian horizon – some external vision of what law could become – we risk being trapped in law's language, even as we try to bend it against itself.

***The Anthropologist*:** The point is that maybe utopia is already present in fragments – in the speculative practices of those who refuse to let EU law have the last word, or in the silent struggles that may only emerge through thick description of social realities shaped by EU law.

[86] M Petersmann, 'Law Otherwise or Otherwise Laws? (Pre)figurative, (Para)ontological, and (De/re) worlding Practices' in *Working with the Negative: Critique at the End of the World* (Edinburgh University Press, 2025).

[87] Neuvonen (n 40) 85.

[88] Linden-Retek (n 74) 11. See also chapter 12 by Paul Linden-Retek in this book.

INDEX

References are to page number.

www.ingramcontent.com/pod-product-compliance
Ingram Content Group UK Ltd.
Pitfield, Milton Keynes, MK11 3LW, UK
UKHW020244290926
15470UKWH00002B/737

9 781509 982028